DEVELOPMENT OF REGIONALISM IN SOUTH ASIA
Some Reflections on SAARC

DEVELOPMENT OF REGIONALISM IN SOUTH ASIA
Some Reflections on SAARC

Shveta Dhaliwal

MD PUBLICATIONS PVT LTD
NEW DELHI
www.mdppl.com

Published by :

MD Publications Pvt Ltd

"MD House", 11, Darya Ganj
New Delhi-110 002
Phone : +91-11-41563325 (Customer Service)
+91-11-41562846 (Editorial)
E-mail (orders): order@mdppl.com
Website : www.mdppl.com

ISBN : 978-81-7533-187-7

Published and Printed by Mr. Pranav Gupta on behalf of **MD Publications Pvt Ltd** at Times Press, New Delhi.

DEDICATED TO MY MOTHER

Late Smt. Savita Kundan

I miss you every second...

ACKNOWLEDGEMENTS

I owe everything to my mother Smt. Savita Kundan. She remains to be my guiding light even after she is physically no more. I thank her for being there for me unconditionally.

The encouragement and direct support behind this effort of mine is my husband Mr. Amol Singh Dhaliwal, literally my better half. I respect him for his honesty, dedication and truthfulness. His selfless support and appreciation for me is my greatest reward. My children Aarza and Seerat are the synthesis of my life. They simply have completed me as a women. I thank them for their lovely and innocent expressions that they care. At the same time I apologise to them for having stolen their share of time for my academic involvements.

I am deeply indebted to my in laws, my father-in-law Sh. Bhajan Partap Singh Dhaliwal and my mother-in-law Smt. Sukarni Dhaliwal for all their encouragement. I thank my sister-in-law Ms. Gazal Dhaliwal for all her affection and support. And ofcourse, my grand father-in-law Sh. Channan Singh Dhaliwal who has successfully completed hundred years of his life and still leads a much more disciplined life than all of us. He is a great inspiration and source of blessings.

I thank my father Sh. Satish K. Kundan, for all his intellectual discussions he has had with me in my childhood. I think his words keep working at my sub-conscious level of mind and do not let me sit idle. I thank my younger sister Ms. Swati Kundan and my brother Mr. Saarang Kundan for considering me the best sister and having faith in me. They are responsible for making me compete with myself.

I am deeply beholden to all my learned teachers who have shaped and directed my approach and have always encouraged me. I have learnt a lot from their teaching as well as their personalities.

I offer my special thanks to Prof. Gurjeet Singh, Vice-Chancellor of Rajiv Gandhi National University of Law, Patiala, Punjab for having guided me as an elder, having taught so much as a teacher. I give him all the credit to have introduced me to a new spectacular world of academics and I will always be thankful to him for this.

I thank Prof. G.I.S. Sandhu, Registrar of Rajiv Gandhi National University of Law, Patiala, Punjab for his kind considerations and wise suggestions at any and every time when I needed them. From him I have learnt a lot of intricacies of teaching profession.

Above all I thank God Almighty for His plans and for keeping me amongst all these loving people of my family who consider my progress synonymous to theirs. And for blessing me with wonderful efficient teachers and administrators, who improved my knowledge, promoted me and appreciated me selflessly.

May God bless each one of those who have been a part of this humble work.

Shveta Dhaliwal

Hemant Batra
Vice President, SAARCLAW
Lead Partner, Kaden Boriss Partners, Lawyers
Chairperson, IICLAM (Singapore)
Advisory Board Member, OIC (USA)

Käden Boriss Building, 495, Udyog Vihar-V,
NH-8, National Capital Region (Delhi),
GURGAON 122016, INDIA
Ph. : +91 124 4040193 (Board Lines)
Fax.: +91 124 4040194
E-mail: hemant.batra@saarclaw.com
E-mail: hemant.batra@kadenboriss.com

SAARC

Käden Boriss

FOREWORD

Irrespective of the particular intellectual legacies, one idea which permeates throughout international regionalism is that, eventually, cooperation leads to integration. Regional integration is more of an ideology than a concept. It can be said that regional cohesiveness is the degree/extent to which a group of people inhabiting an area act and/or represent themselves as a group. Regionalism is a social concept and given the scarce approaches to international regionalism, research on this issue might contribute to a higher infusion of constructive ideas into the international regionalism debates.

This book attempts towards identifying the multi dimensional phenomenon called regionalism in terms of its components such as geographic, historic-cultural, economic, and politico-administrative. In positive terms, regionalism embodies a quest for self-identity and self-fulfillment on the part of the people of an area. In negative terms, it reflects a psyche of relative deprivation on the part of people of an area not always viable in terms of rational economic analysis. It is also believed that deprivation is deliberately inflicted by the people in power which later leads to acuteness of feeling of deprivation on the people of the country. The factor of geographical boundaries to which the people of an area usually relate their quest of a regional identity to also differentiates in degree if not in kind.

Regionalism in South East Asia is celebrated through the South Asian Association for Regional Cooperation (SAARC). It is viewed as a tool to manage the structural dynamics of the region. The purpose of a regional dialogue is to discuss common problems and evolve remedial measures to which all parties can contribute and reap comparable benefits. SAARC is an organization which helps to bridge the barriers between various neighbouring countries. Its objective is to promote the welfare of the people of the region.

During the course of this book, the author has most beautifully tried to capture the essence of SAARC in order to overcome the problems of regionalism by tracing its origin, history, development and the challenges faced by it in today's times. The author also suggests various measures which can be taken to improve the workability of SAARC as an organization and help achieve its objective in a more efficient manner.

SAARC being a unique example of regional cooperation aims to improve the quality of life of the people, accelerate economic growth, social progress, cultural development and to provide all individuals the opportunity to live in dignity and to realize their full potential.

I wish the author Ms. Shveta Dhaliwal all the best in this bold endeavor of hers and pray that through this book, the message of regionalism and SAARC reaches out to more and more people.

HEMANT BATRA
9th April 2009

PREFACE

South Asia is a unique region in several aspects. Historically speaking this region has a variety of colonial legacy to benevolent rule. Politically speaking the region still has a variety of regimes including de-facto military regime, kingdoms, theocracies and established democracies. From the Social aspect the region's societies are divided on almost all social bases including race, gender, religion, class, caste and so on. Economy of this region is also an interesting collage - leaving aside India, no country of this region can claim to be a stable economy. Philosophically, this region is very rich and has been the birth place of many religions like Hinduism, Buddhism, Jainism, Sikhism, etc. These religions have further enriched the culture of South Asia. The region is known for its religious texts. Also Intellectually South Asia has produced many scholars and thinkers. All these features of South Asia justify the uniqueness of this region.

South Asia is represented by South Asian Association for Regional Cooperation (SAARC) since 1985. There were several inhibitions regarding this regional platform. However, this organization has covered a long way learnt its lessons and improved. Recently SAARC has expanded and included Afghanistan as its newest member. There is further a long list of Seekers including China and Japan. SAARC's ties with other leading regional organizations like European Union have also been beneficial.

SAARC is often seen in comparison to ASEAN; another Sub-Asian organization, however, this comparison is unfair due to different economies and financial maturity of the latter. Nevertheless, SAARC and ASEAN have also been collaborating and learning from each other. For Examples Human Rights is one of the aspects of SAARC needs to highlight like ASEAN.

Also SAARC and its growth and development has been analysed from the view point of Europe and Americas. Whereas the regional distinctness needs to be taken into consideration before blaming SAARC for it's so called slow growth. In a highly complex region like South Asia, sustaining and expanding in big enough sign of SAARC's potential to be become stronger in future.

This work is a humble attempt to bring out this fact that every region is different and so are the organizations working within it.

SAARC has a lot of promise to offer and in times of shrinking globe it has even more serious role to play.

This book is a call to all the scholars who work on South Asia and all the people of South Asia to support and participate in the growth of this region.

With the hope that this region gets its due recognition and appreciation in near future.

I am very grateful to Mr. Pranav Gupta, Director of MD Publications Pvt. Ltd., New Delhi for his kind cooperation and support for this book.

Shveta Dhaliwal

CONTENTS

1

EVOLUTION OF REGIONALISM

Individuals and States have one instinct common and that is interdependence and cooperation. In the first case, the result of this instinct is 'The Society' and in the second the result is 'Regional or International Cooperation'. The concept of Inter State cooperation especially in a region is not new to States. In fact the origin of regionalism and regional Organization to materialize it is a contemporary of the origin of State. We have enough facts to prove this.

As societies evolve, expand and multiply, their governing framework's rules and institutions become correspondingly more complex and functionally specific. A necessary consequence of increasingly differentiated structures of governance is the increased space between citizens as self-contained individuals, and the state as a collective abstraction. In contemporary societies, national governments can satisfy only a small and diminishing proportion of the needs of human beings as social animals. Consequently, citizens look more and more to additional actors and layers of governance.

EVOLUTION OF REGIONAL ORGANIZATIONS

- Greeks took (probably) the first step towards regional organization by formally organizing – The Amphietyonic League-in 6th century B.C for regulation relations between city States.
- A little later a confederation; Delos was created between Islands to maintain a common navy.
- Seventy Greek States formed the Achaen League of the Hellenese.
- Vast empire of the Romans (Mediterranean area, most of the west and central Europe) was quite away from the centres of

power such China and India. Therefore, center Romans inter State relations were emphasized.[1]

- Middle ages witnessed several alliances. One such example was of the Hanseatic League formed to promote trade as well as political relations.
- In 1315 a treaty of confederation among 3 Swiss Cantons came into being, which was later joined by 5 other Cantons.
- 17 - 18 Centuries saw some of the best known plans for peaceful international relations. 'Grand Designed' of Henry IV of France, Proposal of 'Parliament of Europe' by William Penn came in 1693. Jeremy Bentham moved a step forward and came up with plea for Universal and Perpetual Peace in 1793.
- As the medieval system disintegrated Machiavelli gave the new idea of Realism to study inter-State relations which proved to be a turning point of international relations and their studies.
- With time Politico-Economic Relations among nations multiplied which resulted in origin of diplomacy, international conferences etc. These international conferences usually resulted in peace treaties one such land mark treaty was concluded in 1648 in the Congress of Westphalia which ended secular authority of the Pope.
- The Peace Treaty of Utrecht 1713 was another step towards the establishment of international organizations.
- The Congress of Vienna met in 1814-15. There was a Quadruple Alliance formed to enforce the Vienna settlement. It consisted of Austria, Great Britain, Prussia and Russia. Later in 1818 it became Quintuple Alliance when France joined it.[2]
- In 1815 at Paris, Holy Alliance was concluded by Tsar Alexander. The Tsar, put forward the ideal of the League of Nations meant to check any threat to the Europe.

---

1 Raja Ram Kalpana, *International Organizations, Conferences and Treaties,* New Delhi, Spectrum Books Pvt. Ltd., 2001, pp. 15-20.

2 Trivedi Sonu, *International Organizations,* New Delhi, Atlantic Publishers and Distributors, 2005, pp.25-30.

- The Hague Peace Conferences of 1899 and 1907 were directly related to international law but contributed a lot in the development of International Organizations as well. "The Hague Conferences were a prelude to the building of the League of Nations" observed Stephen S. Good speed.
- Next came the swing from ad-hoc to standing international institutions. Many institutions came up e.g. the European Commission for the Danube 1856, the Geodetic Union 1864, the International Telegraph Union 1865 (Later renamed International Telecommunication Union) and several others.

However, this indispensable trend of inter-State co-operation and regional bonds reached its peak in modern times. The innovation of present century has been creation of Global-Comprehensive organizations such as the League of Nations and the United Nations.

The League being no more, the United Nations has more relevance when we talk of regionalism. It is so because the U.N. itself recognizes and gives importance to regional preferences e.g. the U.N. has established several regional commissions to know regional problems and to offer needed facilities. Economic Commission for Africa, Europe, Latin America are meant for this purpose.

Chapter VIII of the U.N. Charter envisaged the creation of regional security arrangements, which further strengthen the approach towards regionalism. Today most Universal organizations like U.N. have accepted regional organizations so well that the historical debate or an apprehension that 'Regionalism competes Globalism' seems to be replaced by a new approach in International Politics that 'Regionalism rather compliments Globalism'.[3]

The Congress of Westphalia was undoubtedly the first important event in the development of international organisation, as it was an evolution of the modern State system. Gerard Mangone has aptly described the significance of Congress of Westphalia in the following words:

"No international organisation was established by the Peace of Westphalia in 1648 . . . But the joining of practically every European State in a diplomatic conference, signaled the opening of a new era in international relations. . . . *As* an international assembly, the

---

[3] Karns and Mingst, *International Organizations: The Politics and Processes of Global Governance,* Viva Books Pvt. Ltd., New Delhi, 2005, pp. 97-102.

Congress of Westphalia bore little resemblance to the intricate organisation of twentieth century Peace Conferences ... Of the greatest importance to international organisation, however, were the gathering of hundreds of envoys in a diplomatic conference which represented practically every political interest in Europe and the achievement by negotiation, rather than by dictation, of two great multilateral treaties' which legalished the new order of European international relations."[4]

The second important event in this direction was the Congress of Vienna which met to deal with the European political problems which remained after the defeat of Napoleon. This Congress laid the foundations of a political and international system which for a century shaped the çourse of European and to some extent world affairs. Vienna settlement was enforced by the Quadruple Alliance of Austria, Great Britain, Prussia and Russia. This alliance became quintuple after the addition of France In 1818. Cheever and Haviland have observed in this context that "Thus development was a landmark in the history of international organization for several reasons. First, alliance though forged m war, was continued after hostilities to enforce the peace. Second periodic conferences were instituted when the Great Powers agreed to renew their meetings at fixed intervals. Third, despite the suspicions of the smaller Powers, It generally agreed that the maintenance of peace depended on the sort of Big-power collaboration. These notions were carried over into the League and the U.N."[5]

Out of the experience of the years that followed the Congress of Vienna emerged the informal pattern of conferences and consultations and occasional concerted action which is known as the "Concert of Europe."

Congress of Paris

The third important conference in this context was the Treaty of Paris in 1856 wherein for the first time a non-Christian State, the Ottoman Empire was admitted to participate the conference of

4 Gerard J. Mangone, "A Short History of International Organisation", New York McGraw-Hill Book Co., 1954, pp. 21-22.

5 Daniel S. Cheever and H. Field Haviland Jr., "Organsing for Peace - International Organisation in World Affairs", Houghton Miffins Co., Houston 1954, p. 35.

European States. Later on, Balkan States were admitted to this community of nations. By the close of nineteenth century, other non-Christian States like Japan, Persia, China and Siam were also admitted to this community.

The conference system was the main instrument for international collaboration in that century after Congress of Vienna. Conferences were held with increasing frequency, especially after the middle of the 19th century. Relatively a few of them were political conferences like the Congress of Paris of 1856, and the Congress of Berlin of, 1878. Many more dealt with administrative and technical questions.[6]

Emergence of International Administrative Agencies

One of the most promising developments in the history of international organization after the Congress of Paris was the emergence of a multitude of international administrative agencies or public international unions in the latter half of the nineteenth and the early twentieth centuries. They arose in response to the growing need for co-operation in economic and social problems which could not be handled satisfactorily by States alone or without planned co-ordination. Among the organizations set up were the European Commission for the Danube (1856), the International Geodetic Association (1864), the -International Bureau of Telegraphic Administrations (1868), the Universal Postal Union (1878), the International Bureau of Weights and Measures (1875), the International Copyright Union (1886), the International Office of Public Health (1903) and the International Institute of Agriculture (1905). Some of these are still in existence, others have given over their functions to U.N. Agencies. One of the U.N. Affiliates-the Universal Postal Union, has been described "as one of most significant international organisations in the history of nations."[7]

The First Hague Conference, 1899

The First Hague Conference held in 1899, was however, the fourth important step in this direction, which was attended among

[6] Vide, N.D. Palmer and H.C. Perkins, "International Relations - World Community in Transition", 3rd edition, 2002, p. 301.

[7] Gerard J. Mangone, "A Short History of International Organisation", McGraw-Hill Book Co, New York, 1954, p. 78.

others by five leading European Powers, France, Austria, Great Britain, Prussia and Russia. This conference was indeed a landmark in the history of international relations. In this conference, the appearance of Latin American and Far Eastern States was a negligible factor due to their weak political and economic stability. In this connection Prof. Fenwick has observed, "Throughout the nineteenth century, the Great powers had constituted themselves, as we have seen, a sort of self-appointed executive committee of the family of nations, meeting from time to time, as at the Congress of Vienna in 1815, at the Congress of Paris in 1854-1856[8], and at the Congress of Berlin in 1878[9], to reorganise the political system when collective decisions were called for."

It may, however, be noted that outstanding among the conferences of the years prior to World War I were the Hague Peace Conferences of 1899 and 1907. The story of these conferences relates primarily to the development of International Law, but it is also of great significance in the evolution of International Organisation.

On May 18, 1899, the First Hague Conference met with the primary object of promoting a general limitation of armaments. This conference dismissed summarily the problem of limitation of armaments but sought to promote the general peace by encouraging resort to arbitration for the settlement of international disputes and drew up rules and regulations for the conduct of war. The convention for pacific settlement of international disputes recognised arbitration as the most effective and at the same time the most equitable means for settlement of disputes which diplomacy had failed to settle but imposed no degree of obligation upon the parties to follow the proposed procedure. The convention relating to the laws of war did

---

8 The Congress of Paris took place in 1856 for the purpose of making peace after the almost three year Crimean War. The Congress of Paris was a peace Conference held in Paris, France, between representatives of the great powers in Europe, which at the time were: France, Great Britain, the Ottoman Empire (known today as Turkey), Sardinia, Russia, Austria, and Prussia.

9 Negotiations between the Great Powers in Berlin lasted for an entire month (June 13 to July 13, 1878). The most important issue of the Congress was to decide the fate of the re-established Kingdom of Bulgaria. On the insistence of Russia, however, Bulgarians were excluded from all talks. Also see: Krasner, Stephen D. *Sovereignty: Organized Hypocrisy*, Princeton University Press, New Jersy, 1999, pp. 165.

not encroach upon the sovereign right of the individual State to resort to war as an instrument of national policy. The convention, however, failed to strengthen the political structure of the international community.

The Second Hague Conference, 1907

The Second Hague Conference met on June 15, 1907. This time the conference was attended by forty four States, as against twenty-six in the First Hague Conference. The States included· particularly the entire family of nations. This conference did not differ entirely from the number and scope of the conventions adopted, gave it a greater importance than the First Conference. In this conference the procedure could not be agreed upon the limited obligation of nations for arbitrations. The Final Act of the conference expressed unanimous acceptance of the "principle of compulsory arbitrations" and added to announce that the assembled States succeeded in evolving a lofty conception of the welfare of humanity.

However, the business of the Hague Conferences was clearly the reforms of the rules and methods of the system, rathe. than the solution of the problems arising out of the particular cases of conflict within the system. The major concern of both the Hague conferences was to create devices and agencies which would be permanently at the disposal of States.[10]

The Declaration of London, 1909

The Second Hague Conference, 1907, adopted thirteen conventions of which eleven conventions dealt with the conduct of war, the code of warfare on land adopted in 1899, was revised and it was supplemented by conventions dealing with various aspects of· maritime war, the status of merchant ships at the outbreak of hostilities, the conversion of merchant ships into warship, the laying of submarine contact mines, bombardment by naval forces, the adaptation of the principles of the Geneva Convention to maritime war, and other related matters. Conventions were adopted dealing with rights and duties of neutrals in naval warfare, and provision was made for the establishment of International Prize Courts. The conference, however, failed to agree upon the principles of law to be applied by the Prize Courts.

---

[10] S.J.R. Bilgrami, "International Organisation-A View From Within", Vikas Publishing House Pvt. Ltd., New Delhi, 1977, pp. 5-6.

However, in consequence, the London Naval Conference in 1909. The Declaration of London was signed on February 26, 1909.

The League of Nations

As a result of Treaty of Versailles signed on June 28, 1919, by both Allied and Associated Powers, the Covenant of the League of Nations came into existence. The significance of the Covenant of the League of Nations was in the changes that it effected in the organisation of the community of nations and the amendments made in the substantive and procedural parts of international law. The balance of power system was repudiated in the collective responsibility assumed by all members of the League of Nations for the future peace and security of the world community. [11]

International Labour Organisation was established in 1920 for the betterment of labour conditions in the world at large. Although the International Labour Organisation was regarded as one of the main organs of the League of Nations, it had and still has a large measure of autonomy. In 1940, it moved its headquarter to Montreal, and it continued to function throughout World War II. It becomes an specialized agency of the U.N. in December, 1946.

The United Nations Organisations

During the Second World War, the President of United States and the Prime Minister of Great Britain met on August 14, 1941, and agreed upon a series of common principles on which they hoped that future peace could be established after total destruction of Nazi Government of Germany. Hence, under Atlantic Charter which was proclaimed by the above two leaders, President Roosevelt and Prime Minister Churchill, principles were, laid down for wider and permanent system of general security.[12] In October 1943, the foreign ministers of United States, Great Britain and U.S.S.R. met in Mosco and adopted the declarations, the first of which was that they recognised the necessity of establishing "a general international organisation, based on the principle of the sovereign equality of all peace loving States, and open to membership by such States,

---

[11] For further details see : Julia E. Johnson, Reconstituting the League of Nations, The H.W. Wilson Co., New York, 1943

[12] For further details see : Gilbert Murray, from the league to U.N., Oxford University Press, London, 1948. Also see. The United Nations in the 21st Century, West View Press, Boulder, 2008.

whether large or small, for the maintenance of international peace and security." After a year, a conference of "Big Three Powers" was held at Dumbarton Oaks in Washington in which "proposals for the establishment of a general international organisation" was submitted to the Members of the United Nations for observation. In February 1945, a conference of "Big Three" again met at Yalta in Crimea and it was agreed to have a conference of the United Nations at San Francisco on April 25, 1945 to prepare a Charter of the Organisation along the lines proposed at Dumbarton Oaks.

However, the San Francisco Conference was convened, which adopted on June 26, 1945 the Charter of United Nations after necessary modifications in the original proposals. The Charter was thereupon submitted for formal ratification to the signatory States in accordance with their respective constitutional procedures. The Statute of the International Court of Justice was annexed to, the Charter and it formed an integral part of the U.N. Charter.

Table 1.0

Classifying Types of IGOs	
Geographic Scope	***Examples***
Global	UN WTO WHO
Regional	ASEAN SAARC EU AU
Sub-Regional	Mekong Group Gulf Cooperative Council
Purpose	***Examples***
General	UN OAS
Specialized	WTO WHO UNICEF ILO

Source : Karus and Mingst, International Organisations, The Politics and Processes of global governance, Viva Books, New Delhi, 2005

With the adoption of U.N. Charter, the historical background of the world community came to an end.

In 2003-04, the Year Book of International Organizations identified about 238 International Organizations ranging from 3 members (North American Free Trade Agreement, NAFTA) to more than 190 members (Universal Postal Union, UPU). When these International Organizations are analyzed it becomes clear that most of these are not global but regional in their geographical scope. These International Organizations may serve general or specialized purpose irrespective of their geographical scope. (Table 1.0)

But what is even more important a feature of these organizations is the kind of functions they perform. Primarily the functions of these international organizations are:

(*a*) Informational

(*b*) Providing Forum

(*c*) Normative

(*d*) Rule Making

(*e*) Rule Supervision

(*f*) Operational

According to Joseph Nye a regional organization is based on three conditions namely:

(*i*) Formal arrangement among governments

(*ii*) Possessing diplomatic forms

(*iii*) Assisted by an associated international bureaucracy[13]

Many Regional organizations are formed in international politics based on regional characteristics, conditions and objectives. Many scholars have classified the regional alliances into various categories e.g. cooperative alliances, security or military alliances, functional alliances, regional defense alliances and hybrid alliances. Regional organizations like European Union, ASEAN and SAARC come under the cooperative alliances.[14]

But the question which is most basic in order to understand any regional organization is *What is a Region*?

---

[13] Joseph Nye, *Peace in Parts: Integration and Conflict in Regional Organizations,* Boston, 1971, p. 68.

[14] James and Juliet, *Global Politics,* New York, Houghton Mifflin Co., 2002, pp.40-50.

Table 1.1

IGO Functions	
Informational	Gathering, analyzing, and disseminating data
Forum	Providing place for exchange of views and decision making
Normative	Defining standards of behavior
Rule-Creating	Drafting legally binding treaties
Rule-Supervisory	Monitoring compliance with rules, settling disputes, taking enforcement measures
Operational	Allocating resources, providing technical assistance and relief, deploying forces.

Source : Karus and Mingst, International Organisations, The Politics and Processes of global governance, Viva Books, New Delhi, 2005.

AN EFFORT TO DEFINE A REGION

Trying to define what a 'region' is has been fraught with difficulty. Do regions have to be (heavily) institutionalized? Do they have to be geographically distinct and coherent? Do they have to be at a certain stage of economic development before they qualify for the label? Calleya argues that there is no agreement in the literature on this head, arguing that regions are *de facto* defined by the interactions (social/cultural flows) that they contain.[15] Typologies of regions abound; they can be:

- 'transnational' (network-based, led by cross-border interest groups and informal interaction),
- "intergovernmental' (led by governments) or 'comprehensive' (led by both governments and interests groups),
- 'core' or 'periphery' regions. They can be 'hegemonic' (dominated by one state),
- 'international' (where all component states are roughly equal),

15 Calleya does, however, put forward his own definition of a region, arguing that regions require: regularly inter acting states whose foreign policy has an impact on each other's domestic policy; member states which have geographical proximity to each other; a ruling group of at least two states; and positive external influence from third states.

- Or 'transnational' (of which there are two sub-categories: corporate transnational regions, which seek to promote economic growth, and societal transnational regions, which seek to tackle wealth inequalities).

Moreover, regions, can fluctuate along a continuum comprising five stages of 'region-ness' according *inter alia* to internal flows of senses of regional identity and global level variables.[16] There is thus an emergent view that attempting a narrow definition of the term 'region' is not likely to be productive, and that instead theorists should concentrate on understanding the various processes of regionalization that are unfurling across the globe.

Regionalism is by now a fairly established part of the International Relations, both as a concept, and as an experiment. The terms regionalism and regional organization are used by different scholars in International Relations. The term regionalism is flexible one, which refers to a particular region in world arena. It has been defined on geographical, political, social, or economic basis. The commonsense way of defining region is on the basic of distinct land masses, such as Africa, Asia, Europe North and South America etc. Also Atlantic region, the Baltic region, the Middle Eastern region and South Asian region may be viewed in this sense.

But all such explanations are not enough to grasp the dynamic concept of a region which is getting even more complex in modern times. There is no clear guide to identify the boundaries of a region. Regional Organizations favor memberships to outsiders and many a times different regional organizations working in one region have their members coincided.

Regionalization focuses by definition on process rather than outcome; this helps avoid unnecessary battles over defining the likely or desired end-point, since there may in fact be no such thing. By the same token, no particular end-point for, or institutional configuration of, regionalization is prioritized. In this way,

---

[16] These stages are described by Hettne as: 'regional space' (a geographical unit bound together by trade and settlement links); 'regional complex' (embryonic interdependence); 'regional society' (formal membership organization covering issues of culture, economics, defence/security and politics); 'regional community' (based on shared values and transnational civil society); and 'regional institutionalized polity' (fixed regional political structures with a degree of autonomous power).

teleological assumptions such as those of early neo-functionalists can be avoided. Moreover, the term can be applied to processes of region-construction which have diverse natures and core rationales. Table 1.2 presents a typology of regionalization.

'Regionalization' is a dynamic term, implying fluidity and movement. However, it is not intended to imply that processes of regionalization can, or should only progress/deepen. Moreover, the term connotes a non-monolithic and multi-level focus, because it brings the scholar's attention to transformations of structures, process and agency at the regional level, the level of the component states, and within those states (groups, institutions, individuals): one cannot make or recast a region without altering its component parts and the individual people swept up in, or partly causing, the process. Additionally, 'regionalization' should be understood as a two-way, or multi-way, process in which complex constellations of variables at regional, global, national, local, and even personal/individual levels can combine to produce outcomes at any given time.

Thus, the term is generalizable, by which it could be applied to any instance of cross-border international region-formation in world politics. It expects a link between politics and economics, but does not privilege one over the other. It allows for security issues to be a causal factor, but does not expect this always to be the case, at least if by 'security' we mean military issues. It allows for both normative and more instrumental factors to play a causal role, again without stating which is the more important. Such matters should be explored empirically rather than simply stated at the outset. As a final benefit, it avoids loaded terminology such as 'old regionalism', 'new regionalism', and 'integration' (which NRA scholars, with some justification, see as an irretrievably neo-functionalist term, and thus too closely bound to teleological accounts of regional polity-formation for general use.

Hence, it would not be incorrect to say that to decide as to what constitutes a particular region reflect the perceptions prejudices or desires of those States who constitute a core group for regional activities beginning with 6 members the European members now has 25 members. Application for membership in E.U. of a country like Turkey has created a controversy since not only Turkey lies in West Asia it has undemocratic political systems and has a weak human rights record. Such examples make us think where a region ends and

Table 1.2 : A typology of Regionalization

Type of regionalization	Features	Examples
Structured regionalization	A complex multi-issue entity, using informal politics despite deep institutionalization. No hegemony exists; substantial power is delegated to the new centre in many policy areas, and is costly to 'repatriate'.	European Union (EU); African Union (in aspiration)
Dominance regionalization	An alternative to a global regime, established by regional/global hegemony to counter threats to its power from other regionalization processes or states. Focuses on narrow range of issues, with emphasis on trade.	North American Free Trade Area (NAFTA)
Security regionalization	Focus on security issues, either military or socio-economic. May be geographically contiguous or trans-regional in membership.	Euro-Mediterranean Partnership: North Atlantic Treaty Organization (NATO)
Network regionalization	Regional identity-driven response to globalization. May acquire significant or more limited range of powers, but relies primarily on non-institutionalized or intergovernmental working methods.	Association of Southeast Asian Nations (ASEAN) African Union (in actuality); South American Common Market
Conjoined regionalization	Strategic partnership of one regionalization process with either another such process or with key states outside the region for the sake of economic or foreign policy advantage.	Asia-Pacific Economic Cooperation (APEC); putative Free Trade Area of the Americas

Source : Karus and Mingst, International Organisations, The Politics and Processes of global governance, Viva Books, New Delhi, 2005.

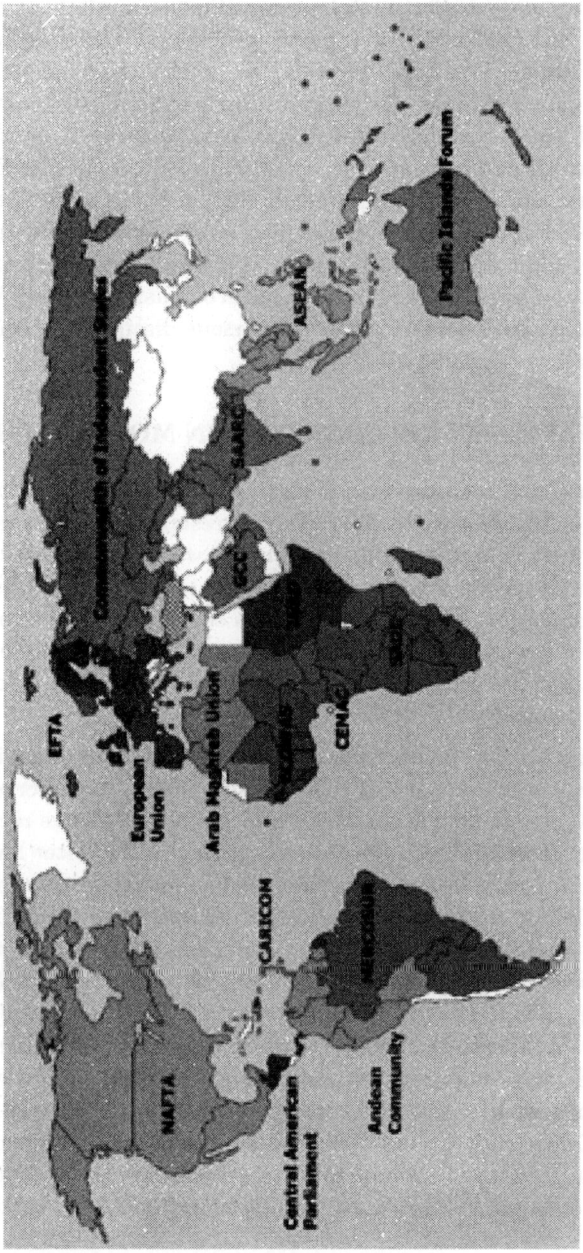

Source : http://images.google.co.in.

another begins?[17] Unfortunately even with such a relatively a simple task as the definition of regions, conceptual controversy creeps in e.g. should Eastern Europe be group with a cluster of nations called Europe? Or these countries should be considered a different cluster called socialist countries? Should Arab speaking Northern Africa be grouped in a region called the Middle East, the Mediterranean, a developing Islamic Region or NATO States? So we have more than one criterion to define a region that's why today the world is densely populated with Regional Organizations. The networks of regional organizations are most dense in Western Europe and least dense in Asia for reasons discussed in succeeding chapters.

TWO WAVES OF REGIONALISM IN MODERN ERA

There have been two waves of regionalism over the last 50 years. The old or the first wave of 1960's was restricted to Europe. It was protectionist in nature and the purpose was mainly few economic gains. In its second wave regionalism in late 80's changed its nature and became more global and made its scope much wider as far as purposes were concerned. Now, the targets were not only economic gains but political harmony, socio-cultural ties, people to people contact, better world order etc. (Table 1.3)

It has become commonplace in the field to distinguish between an older or earlier wave of regionalism (then often referred to as 'regional integration') in the 1950s and 1960s and a more recent new 'wave' or 'generation' of regionalism starting in the latter half of the 1980s and today being a prevalent phenomenon throughout the world. There are, however, both continuities and similarities between so-called 'old' and 'new' regionalism, so that when studying contemporary regionalism one can easily get a feeling of *dèjàvu*. For instance, many regional projects and regional organizations were actually initiated in the 1960s, 1970s or early 1980s, and then simply renewed or re-inaugurated (sometimes with a new name and sometimes with a few different members) in the mid-1980s and 1990s. Under such circumstances it is often difficult to separate the historical from the contemporary. In response to these continuities we have argued elsewhere for identifying 'new' patterns of

---

[17] Karns and Mingst (2005) pp.100-105.

regionalization co-existing with 'older' forms. But after two decades of so-called 'new regionalism', the distinction has lost much of its original meaning (or been too much misused), and we are herewith proposing that it is time to bury the distinction.

Table 1.3 : Two Waves of Regionalism

First Wave: 1950s-1960s	
Europe and Soviet Bloc	*Latin America*
NATO (1949-)	OAS (1948-)
WEU (1955-)	RIO Pact (1947-)
Warsaw Treaty Organization (1955-1991)	Central American Common Market (1961-)
Council of Europe (1948-)	Andean Community (1969-)
ECSC (1952-)	CARICOM (1973-)
Euratom (1958-)	LAFTA (1969-1980)
EEC (1958-)	
Comecon (1948-1991)	Middle East Arab League (1947-)
West and East Asia	
CENTO (1950s)	*Africa*
SEATO (1954-1975)	OAU (1964-2002)
ASEAN (1967-)	AU (2002-)
Second Wave: 1980s-1990s	
Europe	*Latin America*
CSCE (1975-)	Mercosur (1991-)
EEC-EU (1992-)	FTAA (1994-)
CIS (1991-)	NAFTA (1993-)
Asia and Asia-Pacific	*Africa*
APEC (1989-)	ECOWAS (1975-)
ARF (1994-)	SADC (1992-)
SAARC (1985-)	COMESA (1994-)
Middle East	
Gulf Cooperation Council (1981-)	

Source : Karus and Mingst, International Organisations, The Politics and Processes of global governance, Viva Books, New Delhi, 2005.

Having said this, it is still relevant to identify continuities and discontinuities, both in terms empirical practices and theoretical perspectives, and for this purpose we find it more useful to distinguish between the early and the more recent debate. In what follows, we describe the first 'generation' of regionalism studies, focused on regional integration in Europe, and the subsequent 'big leap' from the 'early debate' to the more 'recent debate', which really was the study of regionalisms in the context of globalization.

Even if this distinction between old and new regionalism has been misused and has also lost much of its meaning, it is still consistent to argue for the continued relevance of so-called 'new regionalism' theory, including the new regionalism approach (NRA) which we have both been trying to develop elsewhere. The new regionalism approach or theory is a particular way (or rather ways) of analyzing the phenomenon of regionalism and is not dependent on a tight distinction between old and new regionalism.

The Early Debate

The early theories or approaches to regionalism were all concerned with peace, and tended to see the nation-state as the problem rather than the solution. The most relevant theories were federalism, functionalism and neo-functionalism. Federalism, which inspired the pioneers of European integration, was not really a theory but rather a political programme; it was skeptical of the nation-state, although what was to be created was in fact a new kind of state. There was no obvious theorist associated with federalism. In contrast, functionalism has been much identified with one particular name, that of David Mitrany. This was also an approach to peace - building rather than a theory. The question for functionalist was no which political level various human needs (often defined in a rather technical way) could best be met. Usually, the best way was found to be going beyond the nation-state, but not necessarily going regional. Thus, both federalism and functionalism wanted the nation-state to go, but through different routes and by different means. For the functionalists, international organizations should be established in the promotion of cooperation and transnational activities around basic functional needs, such as transportation, trade, production and welfare. Economics was seen as more important than politics. Functionalism was rather technocratic and therefore unrealistic. Form, in the functionalist view, was supposed to follow function, whereas for federalists it was really form that mattered. Mitrany criticized both federalism and regional integration in general because both were primarily based on territory rather than function. For functional solutions there should be no territorial boundaries.

Territoriality was seen as part of the Westphalian logic and Westphalia implied conflict and war. However, in contrast to the European Community (EC), which was a political community, the European Coal and Steel Community was, according to Mitrany, a functional and therefore acceptable organization (for here the technical question was: how can coal and steel production best be organized?).

Bridging Globalization and Regionalism

Much of the more recent debate on regionalism is strongly focused on conditions related to globalization or world order. In particular, as indicated in the subtitle of this volume, the relationship between globalization and regionalism constitutes one of the main concerns in the research field. This contrasts with many (but not all) earlier regionalism theories, which were heavily concerned with the endogenous forces of regional integration or intraregional theorizing. Contemporary regionalism is thus strongly related to globalization, but there are, as we shall see below, different views about the nature of this relationship. Our analysis rejects any simplified notions about how globalization and regionalism hang together, instead drawing attention to the diversity or relationships. In fact, in a globalized world, regionalism as such is not the appropriate object for theorizing; the focus should rather be on the regional factor or dimension of global transformation.

From Dichotomy to Diversity

Trade blocs have been a crucial aspect in the discussion of regionalism ever since the 1950s. According to neoclassical economics, regional trading arrangements are often seen as a 'second-best' and therefore judged according to whether they contribute to a more closed or more open multilateral trading system, embodied in the so-called 'stumbling block vs. stepping stone' dichotomy. Many of the regional trading arrangements that existed during the era of regionalism in the 1950s and 1960s were inward-looking and protectionist, and were often regarded by contemporary economists as failures. At the time, however, they were widely considered to be instruments for enhancing industrial production, as in the strand of development thinking associated with the United Nations Economic Commission for Latin America (ECLA) and the even more ambitious strategy of the United Nations Conference on Trade and Development (UNCTAD), both led by Raúl Prebisch. The culmination of this process was the demand for a new international economic order. Regionalism developed into a form of global mobilization against an unequal world order, but lost some of its strength in the process.

When regionalism returned in the mid-1980s the stumbling block vs. stepping stone dichotomy reappeared, sometimes under the banner of 'the new protectionism' vs. 'open regionalism'. The new protectionism was basically an early interpretation of the new wave of regionalism by neo-liberal economists who feared that the sudden interest in regionalism heralded a new protectionism. Thus, for the neo-liberals, regionalism was 'new' mainly in the sense that it represented a revival of protectionism or neo-mercantilism, whereas other economists and liberal observers drew attention to the fact that closure of regions was not on the agenda; rather, the current regionalism was 'open regionalism', which emphasized that the integration project should be market-driven and outward-looking, should avoid high levels of protection and should form part of the ongoing globalization and internationalization process of the world political economy.

Regionalism is a multidimensional phenomenon that explains the richness of concepts, theories and perspectives on the topic. Although this pluralism is desirable in many ways, the research field is plagued by a lack of communication between different theoretical perspectives and standpoints.

WHY DO STATES JOIN INTERNATIONAL ORGANIZATIONS?

An argument says that international organizations, (whether of global or regional nature) curb or curtail the sovereign status of a State because as a member it has to follow principles and protocols and has to be ready to adjust, sacrifice or compromise in order to accommodate or encourage other member States. So, there must be enough strong reasons which drive modern day States to join one or the other or as many as possible International Regional Organizations.[18]

[18] Karns and Mingst (2005), pp.97-102.

1. **Identity:** It is a shared perception of being a part of a region. Sometimes, it can get a nation more respectable or reliable position e.g. East Timor, the youngest country, would join a regional organization to make its existence felt.
2. **Accountability:** By being a member of a regional organization a State increases its stretch of influence and support and may use this platform to make its offenders accountable e.g. India at G-8 meeting raised the issue of Mumbai Blasts and Pakistan's alleged involvement behind them. The condemnations of G-8 members made Pakistan's President General Pervez Musharraf to go on live television broadcast to prove his country's innocence and to promise to help India in investigations.
3. **Support:** Regional organizations give support to its members which may be economic, political, moral or any kind. It is this support base which deters other countries to do anything against it.[19]
4. **Internal-External Threats:** Members of regional organizations are bound better and closer because of common internal-external threats. Till the first wave of regionalism a great threat was 'Communism' to the western world. Hence, regional organizations like NATO came up.
5. **Domestic Politics:** Domestic politics frequently becomes a significant variable affecting regional governance initiatives e.g. International agreements or treaties may affect domestic politics may also change the balance of power between the branches of government. Similarly, if the domestic politics of a State is weak its international or regional activities may face more opposition.[20]
6. **Leadership:** Regionalism being a tool of local governance also needs leadership from key individuals e.g. France and Germany played an important role in bringing about post World War II regionalism, Indonesia played a lead role for ASEAN, Bangladesh did so for SAARC.

---

[19] J.P. Garg, *Regionalism in International Politics,* New Delhi, Research Publications, 1984, pp.1-5.

[20] S.D. Muni, and Anuradha Muni; *Regional Cooperation in South Asia,* Kay Kay Publisher, 1984, p.2.

Table 1.4 : Independent Variables of Regionalization

Genesis	Functionality	Socialization	Impact
Why do states participate?	Who leads, how and why?	Impact on senses of identity (at elite and mass levels)	On global economy
Why do states continue as participants?	Who makes day-today decisions? With which decision rules?	Policy learning (exchange of models/ideas, or convergence to new norm)	On democracy in the component states
What are the stated purpose and objectives of the regionalization process?	What role, if any, is played by non-state actors?	Transaction flows (social, cultural, economic)	On distribution of wealth (state-state, and intrastate)
How is the regionalization process defined (inclusion / exclusion)?	Which policy issues are addressed, and why?	Popular awareness and understanding	On influence of the component states (both on each other and vis-à-vis third countries)
	Is the regionalization process stop-go, liner, reversible, or static?	Popular support (legitimacy)	Are certain policy styles/types imposed or made impossible?
	Do the actors involved also collaborate outside the regionalization process? If so, how and why?	Increase in trust (elite or mass)	Are the structures/ constitutions of the component states changed?
	What mixture of informal and formal mechanisms?		Does the regionalization process deepen? Why?
	Implementation and enforcement mechanisms		Does the regionalization process take on more states over time?
	Performance (output)		

In addition to these factors States are bound by certain peculiar features of the region they are part of. These features decide the nature and scope of the concerned organizations, to a considerable extent.

Non-governmental Organizations Contributing to the Dynamism of International/ Regional Organizations

In modern times both are considered a tool of world governance. But it is noteworthy that the growth of NGO's has been much speedier and gained much more relevance as compared to International Organizations.[21] The year book of International Organizations identifies over 65,00 non-governmental organization features:

1. These NGO's have national as well as international dimensions.
2. NGO's ignore formal/political boundaries of regions.
3. NGO's work both formally and informally.
4. NGO's parallel many function provided by International governmental organizations.

Services provided by governments of IGO's are being contracted out to private NGO's. They deliver disaster relief, run refuge camps administer development programs and so on.

Important examples of NGO's are

- International federation of Red Cross,
- Mĕdecins Sans Frontiĕres (Doctors without Borders)
- Human Rights Watch
- Amnesty International

Certain features of NGO's have been adopted by International Organization's[22] e.g. (1) stress on informal ways to cooperate e.g. people to people contacts (2) ignoring the strict limits of a region; as we discussed earlier. (3) targeting people and their welfare more than political issues.

While discussing this relationship between the IGO's and INGO's it is important to mention that neither enormous number of NGO's, nor their multidimensional approach pose a threat to the status or relevance of International (Governmental) Organizations (IGO's) because:

(*i*) Usually NGO needs a backing of International Organizations

---

21 For further details on NGOs visit : http://www.staff.city.ac.uk/p.willetls/NGOs/NGO-HOME.HTM.

22 Also see : Walter Carlsnaes et.al., Handbook on International Relations, Sage Publications, New Delhi, 2002.

(*ii*) International organizations involve highest institution i.e. the States

(*iii*) NGO's are responsible towards the States as well as International Organizations

(*iv*) NGO's may be scraped by the will of States but not International Organizations.

Therefore, it is a futile doubt that NGO's and their growth, which is quite a contrast as shown in graph 1, is a threat to the States of International Organizations also, by this comparison of I(G)O's and NGO's certain doubts regarding International Organizations, such as how to define their region, etc. have been clarified, since it is the adaptation process of International Organizations. This adaptation has enriched and strengthened the concept of International/Regional Organizations even more (Graph 1).

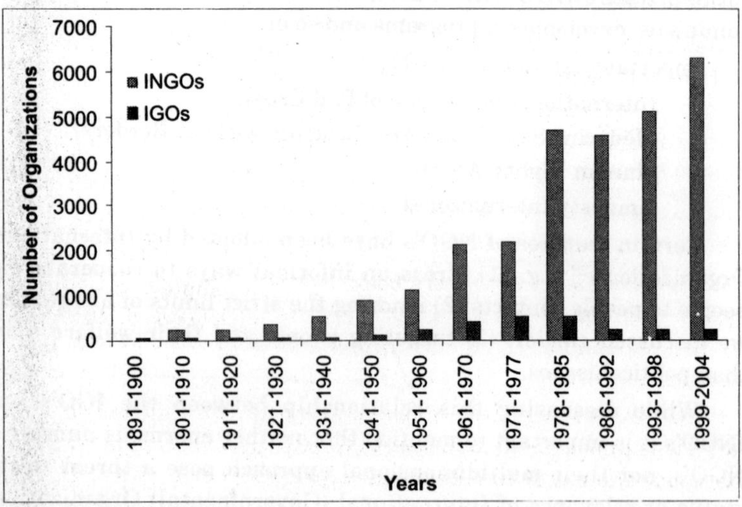

Sources: Yearbook of International Organizations 1985-1986, 1992-1993, 1998-1999, 2003-2004 (Brussels: Union of International Association)

Inspiration Behind this Book

South Asia is very rapidly emerging as a new centre of International Politics and due to that coming up a new focus of study and writings. This book is not the first initiative in the direction of understanding South Asia, rather I would admit that several writings have added to my interest in this region and inspired me for contributing my academic views related to this highly dynamic and vibrant region.

Another reason for analyzing the works which laid foundation for this book is to facilitate comparison and comments to this book by the readers.

The book entitled "SAARC: Challenges before New Millennium" by P.A. Joy, discusses elaborately the regionalism, policy perspective of SAARC, the declarations of the 11th Summit, held in Kathmandu, Nepal during January, 2002. The salient features of the Maldives economy, Nepal's and Pakistan's economy and their trade with SAARC countries and their general and economic scenario have also been discussed. This book also provides information about the trade of SAARC, the various trade agreements, export promotion measures, import substitution and State trading.[23]

Debendra Kumar Das's book 'SAARC: Regional Cooperation and Development", contained the perspectives, problems and policies of SAARC. It studied the regional and economic cooperation among SAARC countries. It is case study of India and Bhutan dealing with problems of trade cooperation among SAARC, South-South cooperation in technology, towards harmonization of trade policies for SAARC.[24]

K. Bhushan and G. Katyal's book, "SAARC: Change Challenges before New Millennium", discusses elaborately the declaration of the 11th SAARC summit, held in Kathmandu, Nepal during January 2002.[25]

Partha S. Ghosh's book "Cooperation and Conflict in South Asia", throws light on some topics like bilateral relations taking India as the common denominator and also discussed regional milieu, the image of India within the region and India's own image of

---

[23] For further details see : P.A. Joy; *SAARC Challenges before New Millennium*, New Delhi, Deep and Deep Publications, 1995.

[24] For further details see : Debendra Kumar Dass; *SAARC: Regional Cooperation and Development*, New Delhi, Deep and Deep Publications, 1995.

[25] For further details see : K. Bhushan and G. Katyal; *SAARC: Challenges before New Millennium*, New Delhi, A.P.H. Publishing Corporation, 2002.

itself as the pre-eminent power therein, and the positive and negative factors that are at work making the SAARC experiment an interesting subject for analysis for both the pessimists and the optimists.[26]

Emanual Nahar's "SAARC: Problems and Prospects" seeks to elaborate and highlight the various problems which have become more acute not only because of the historical and political relations but also due to many other factors. This book also explains India's attitude and perception towards the SAARC.[27]

Shashi Upadhyay's book "Pakistan SAARC", has focused on the working of the SAARC and Pakistan's attitude and policy in the nation-State paradigm. It also discussed the major determinants of Pakistan's policy towards South Asian Regional Cooperation, its political and economic dimensions and its emerging trends (Pakistan and SAARC in 1990's).[28]

S.D. Muni and Anuradha Muni's book "Regional Cooperation in South Asia", deals with South Asian regional cooperation. They have studied the SAARC comprehensively. This book throws light on the prospects and problems in detail and also have given some suggestions to improve cooperation at South-Asian level.[29]

Davinder Kumar Madaan in his book "Indo-Bangladesh Economic Relations and SAARC", has explored the economic relations between India and Bangladesh in the context of SAARC. It also examines the aims and objectives of SAARC and studying bilateral economic relations among the developing countries of the world in general and SAARC in particular.[30]

"SAARC: Origin, Development and Programmes", makes an intensive study on SAARC and its origin and development. It also

---

26 For further details see : Partha S. Ghosh; *Cooperation and Conflict in South Asia*, New Delhi, Manohar Publications, 1995.

27 For further details see : Emanual Nahar; *SAARC Problems and Prospects*, New Delhi, Sehgal Publishers, 1991.

28 For further details see : Shashi Upadhyay's; *Pakistan's SAARC*, Delhi, Kalinga Publications, 2000.

29 For further details see : S.D. Muni and Anuradha Muni; *Regional Cooperation in South Asia*, New Delhi, Vikas, 1984.

30 For further details see : Davinder Kumar Madaan; *Indo-Bangladesh Economic Relations and SAARC*, New Delhi, Deep and Deep Publication, 1998.

throws a light on the SAARC agreements and SAARC summit declarations, which study evolution, essence; various activities of SAARC and declarations of already held nine SAARC summits.[31]

The book authored by L.L. Mehrotra, H.S. Chopra, Gert. W. Kulck, "SAARC: 2000 and Beyond", is a unique study. Its uniqueness lies in its sharp focus on the most critical of the political, economic and social issues relevant to the dynamics of peace and development in the region. It examines SAARC as a framework for regional cooperation, the interplay of adversarial politics that exacerbated conflicts and tensions in the region in the past and now in the post cold war era, how it has become imperative for the member States to cohere for peace and development in the region. It also deals with the economic and social costs of conflicts and benefits of regional cooperation. It also focuses on alleviation of poverty and safeguarding minority communities and human rights. Finally, it considers the relevance of the ASEAN and European Union paradigms to strengthen SAARC and turning it into an instrument of socio-economic transformation for bringing the mainstream of global development.[32]

Mohammed Ayub's contribution "The Primacy of the Political: South Asian Regional Cooperation in Comparative Perspective" and S.D. Muni's "SAARC: Building Regionalism from Below" (Asian Survey, 1985)[33], is a humble attempt no examine the prospects of cooperation in South Asia in an analytical and systematic manner focusing on the intraregional environment. The purpose is to give a comprehensive account of regionalism in South Asia and explain at the same time as to why political issues are of primary concern to the ruling regimes rather than the issues of development and welfare of the masses.

The book "SAARC and Super Powers" by Vandana Mohla, is a study about regionalism, its meaning, and evolution in a conceptual framework. The environmental setting of SAARC, its origin and emergence comprise the evolutionary process of development of

---

31 For further details see : *SAARC : Origin, Development and Programmes*, New Delhi, Deep and Deep Publication, 1997.

32 For further details see : L.L. Mehrotra, H.S. Chopra (eds.); *SAARC 2000 and Beyond*, New Delhi, Omega Scientific Publishers, 1996.

33 For further details see : Mohammad Ayub; *The Primacy of Political SAARC in Comparative Prospective*, Asian Survey, Vol. XXV, No. 4, April 1985.

South Asian Association of Regional Cooperation. An analytical appraisal of the concrete outcome of nine summits held so far reflects the constraints and potential of SAARC. The author also holds that despite serious misgivings and strong differences among the member countries on various issues, the SAARC has taken off. Some of the bilateral disputes have been resolved and the author is also optimistic of the future of SAARC.

The book by Karn and Mingst, 2005 has given as insight of Asian features of regionalism which are very correctly applicable to SAARC. The book offers latest data and a comparative analysis of different tools of global governance, which enables better understanding of regional organization.

S.P. Varma and K.P. Misra's book "Foreign Policies in South Asia", contains some of the most vital problems related to the foreign policies of India, Pakistan, Nepal etc. in regional as well as global contexts, from a really detached and objective point of view. This book also explains about, South Asia as a region and regional development in South-Asia.

K. Bhushan and G. Katyal's work “SAARC: Challenges before New Millennium” emphasizes on the problems of South Asian States and also tells about that South Asian States share the problem of poverty and underdevelopment. Nonetheless in spite of the glaring similarity of their difficulties, it took almost four decades for them to recognize the need to coordinate efforts to tackle their common problems. This book discusses elaborately the declarations of the 11th SAARC summit, held in Kathmandu, Nepal during January 2002.

Besides these books a number of articles published in Journals of repute, by eminent scholars have also been of great help in writing this book.

Aditya Annand; *SAARC The Call for Cooperation and Concept of a South Asian Regime*, South Asia Forum (7), 1984; Ahirro Jitendra, J., *Third Concept*, Vol. 18, No. 205, April 2004; Ahmed Sabina; *SAARC Regional Studies 1 (3) Summ 1983 : 84-10*, South Asia *World Today*, 34 (10) Oct. 1978, 390-400; *A Paper on the Proposal for Regional Cooperation in South Asia*, November, 1980 in From SAARC to SAARC : Milestones in the Evolution of Regional Cooperation in South Asia (1980-88), SAARC Secretariat,

Kathmandu, Vol. I, 1988; Ali, M. Ramjan; *Regional Studies*, Vol. XXII, No. 1, Winter, Islamabad Institute of Regional Studies, 2003-2004; Bahadur Kalim; *The Politics of SAARC,* World Focus, Vol. 25, No. 6, June 2004; Bhatt, Maqbool Ahmad; *The Future of SAARC,* Regional Studies, Vol. 10, No. 1, Winter 1991-92; Brar Bhupinder; *A Region of States or a Region of Regions* in South Asian Survey, Vol. 6, No. 1 (1999) New Delhi, Sage Publications; Chakarvarthy Nikhil; *South Asia as a Concept,* World Focus 4 (11-12) Nov.-Dec., 1983-3-6, Fourth Annual Number, South Asia Today; Chopra, Pran; *Regional Cooperation*, World Focus 4(11-12) Nov.-Dec. 1983, 35-8/Search for South Asia Perspective (8) March 1978, 9-13/3, March 1982, 3-8 Why South Asia and How-World Focus/Commerce (147) 3768 Aug 20, 1983, 2177; Deo, A.R., *Politics of SAARC*, World Focus, Vol. 17, No. 7, July 1996; *SAARC :Making its Mark*, World Focus, Vol. 22, No. 27, July 2001; Dixit Aabha; *SAARC Towards Greater Cooperation*, Strategic Analysis, New Delhi, Vol. XX, No. 4, July 1997; Dixit J.N., *South Asian Regional Cooperation : Problems and Prospects*, South Asian Survey, Vol. 1, No. 2, July-December 1994; *South Asian Survey*, Vol. 6, No. 2, New Delhi, Sage Publication, 1999; Prospects of South Asian Cooperation in the Transformed World, *South Asian Survey*, Vol. 10, No. 1, June-2003, New Delhi, Sage Publication; From SAARC to SAARC : Milestones in the Evolution of Regional Cooperation in South Asia (1980-1988), Secretariat of the South Asian Association for Regional Cooperation, Kathmandu, Vol. 1, December 1988, pp. 135; Gulati Mukesh; *Regional Trading Blocs : Lessons for SAARC*, South Asian Studies, Vol. 30, No. 1, January-June, 1995; Gupta, Subenduda Das; *The Limits of SAARC,* Journal of International Relations, Vol. 5, No. 1-2, July-June 1997-98; Hassan Abdul; *Third SAARC Summit*, SAARC Perspective, Vol. 2, No. 3, May 1988; Hussain Syed Anwar; *Prospects of Peace in South Asia : Politico-strategic Perspective*, South Asia Survey, Vol. 1, No. 2, July-December 1994; Hussain Abid; *Prospects for South Asian Regional Cooperation, Strategic Studies Journal*, Vol. 1, No. 2, July 1988; Iftekharuzzaman; *South Asian Trade Cooperation with SAARC and ASEAN : Potential, Prospects, Realities Biss Journal*, Vol. 10, No. 1, January 1989; India Today, June 9, 1997; Kapur Pratap; *SAARC : Whither Regional Cooperation*, Democratic World, New Delhi, Vol. XII, No. 35, 28 August 1983; Katyal, K.K., *India and SAARC Summit*, World Focus, Vol. 22. No. 7, July 2001; Khanal, Y.N., *South Asian Association for Regional Cooperation : An*

Overview, Kathmandu, April 30, 1991; Khatri, Sridhar K., *A Decade of South Asian Regionalism : Retrospect and Prospect*, Contemporary South Asia, Vol. 1, No. 1, 1992; *South Asian Regional Cooperation : Its Implications for Nepal*, Asian Survey, April 1985; K. Satyamurti; *South Asian Regional Cooperation, Institute of Asian Studies*, Hyderabad, 1982; Kumar, Rupesinghe, Khawar Mumtaz (eds.); *Internal Conflicts in South Asia*, New Delhi, Sage Publications, 1996; Kodirgamar Lakshman; *South Asian Survey*, Vol. 5, No. 1, New Delhi, Sage Publication 1998; Lama, Mohindra P., *SAARC Report : Poverty, Migration and Conflict in South Asia*, World Focus, Vol. 25, No. 6, June 2004; Mehta, Rajesh Bhattacharya Swapank; *SAPTA-I/II, SAPTA and SAFTA : Implications for SAARC*, South Asian Survey, Vol. 2, July-December 1997; Mishra, Pramod Kumar; *Dhaka to New Delhi : One Decade of SAARC*, India Quarterly, Vol. LII, nos. 1-2, January-June 1996; Muni, S.D., *SAARC at Crossroads*, Himal South Asia, Vol. 10, No. 3, May/June 1997; *Strategic Aspects of SAARC*, Strategic Analysis, Vol. IX, No. 1, April 1994; Murthy Padmaja; *Relevance of SAARC, Strategic Analysis*, Vol. XXIII, No. 10, January 2000; Nahar Emanul; *Problems Before SAARC*, Mainstream, Vol. XXVII, No. 5, November 25, 1989; Nayar Kuldip; *Male Summit, Gujral-Sharif Talks and SAARC*, Mainstream, Vol. XXXV, No. 24, May 24, 1997; Niaz A-Naik; *South Asian Survey*, Vol. 6, No. 2, New Delhi, Sage Publications, 1999; Noorani, A.G., *Repression in Kashmir*, Economic and Political Weekly, July 22, 1989; Padmaja Murth; *Role of Smaller Members in SAARC Forum, Strategic Analysis*, XXII (8), November, 1998; Paranjpe Shrikant; *From State Centricism to Translationalism SAARC, SAPTA and SAFTA*, India Quarterly, Vol. LII, No. 18/2, January-June 1996; Pattanaik, Smruti S; *Indo-Pak Relations and the SAARC Summits*, Strategic Analysis, July-September, 2004; Phadnis Shunker; *Progress for Some Visible Gains*, World Focus, Vol. 3, No. 3, March 1983; Phandis Urmila; *Ethnic Tensions in South Asia : Implications for Regional Cooperation*, New Delhi, South Asian Publishers, Vol. II, 1986; Rais, Rasul B., *Politics of Regional Cooperation in South Asia*, Asian Survey, Vol. 30, No. 8, August 1990; Rajni B., *India and South Asianism*, Third Concept Vol. 4, No. 58, December, 1991; Rana A.P.; *New Directions in the Study of SAARC : Evaluating the Basis of Regional Cooperation in South Asia*, South Asian Survey 10:1 (2003) Delhi, Sage Publications; *Regionalism as an Approach to International Order, International Studies*, Vol. 21, JNU, New Delhi,

1979; Reddy, B. Murlidhar; *Sense of Betrayal*, Frontline, Vol. 21, No. 2, January 30, 2004; *SAARC Nations Sign Social Charter*, The Hindu, New Delhi, January 6, 2004; Rizvi Hasan Askar; *Problems and Prospects of South Asian Regional Cooperation*, Regional Studies, Vol. 2, 1983; Sahaha Rishikesh; *Imperatives for Regional Cooperation in South Asia*, South Asia Forum, Vol. I, No. 1,Winter 1982; Sahai, Paramjit S; *Cultural Diplomacy, Mass Media and SAARC : A Case Study of the 12th SAARC Summit*, India Quarterly, Vol. LK, No. 3, New Delhi, July-September, 2004; Sattar Abdus; *Changing Global Scenario* Implications for South Asia, Regional Studies (Islamabad), Vol. VII, No. 1, Winter 1989-90; Sobhan Rehman; *Regional Cooperation in South Asia : A Quest for Identity*, South Asian Survey, Vol. 5, No. 1, January-June 1998; Shrestha, B.P., *Prospects of Economic Cooperation in South Asia*, The Economic Journal of Nepal (Kathmandu), Vol. II, No. 1, January-March 1988; Shukla Vijay; *New Frontiers of SAARC*, India Quarterly, Vol LII, No. 18, 2, January-June 1996; Singh, Hari Govind; *South Asian Cooperation : Problems and Prospect*, New Delhi, Mainstream, Vol. XXVII, No. 14, December 31, 1988; Singh Jagjit; *Transport Linkages in South Asia*, in India Quarterly, Vol. XI, No. 324, July-December 1984; Singh Tarlok; *Special Issue on South Asian Cooperation, Prospects and Potentials*, World Focus, March, 1982; Taneja Nisha; Trade Relations : Opportunities For Growth *Economic and Political Weekly*, Vol. no. XXXIX, No. 4, January 24, 2004; Udaykumar, S.P., *Regional Cooperation in South Asia : The People Factor*, SAARC Perspective, Vol. 3, No. 5, June 1989; Upadhyaya Shashi; *Pakistan's Perception of India's Role in SAARC*, South Asian Studies, Vol. 31, Nos. 1 and 2, January-December 1996; Yatanoor Chandarkant; *Small State in EU,* Third Concept, August, 2003.

After all that has been mentioned above it would be needless to say that lot of work has been done on SAARC from different angles. However, in my opinion this book is a modest attempt to study SAARC from the angle of regional factors, also this book is a humble attempt to assess SAARC by analysing its inbuilt problems and challenges and the threats emerging from intra societal and extra societal environment. My main contribution is to present and analyze the various dimensions of obstacles confronting SAARC and suggest certain mechanisms to strengthen SAARC not only as an Organization but also a Movement.

To begin with I started with the following goals to be achieved through this work:

To trace the evolution of regional organizations in general and to understand their nature and scope. To trace and relate the history of the SAARC and its evolution to the general trends of regionalism in rest of the world. To understand SAARC by studying its various programmes, policies and objectives. And to observe the incorporation of regional features in the working of SAARC. To analyze the obstacles in the way of SAARC by categorizing these. To study the progress of SAARC and to make assessments. To make suggestions for the betterment of SAARC.

However, during this work I realized the magnanimity of the potential of SAARC and its promises amid all odds. (There is suspicion among the members of SAARC. Weak economic structure and challenges of globalization are a hindrance in the way of SAARC. The Summits are not held every year and postponement of summits on flimsy grounds hampers the progress. Unstable and variety of political regimes and difference in ideologies of the members retards the growth of cooperation. The *modus operandi* of SAARC is itself a drawback. SAARC members have not been able to disassociate themselves from the colonial legacies. Globalization is posing a treat to SAARC). This realization has gone further and I am working on other unexplored aspects of SAARC, mainly Human Rights. More I read about SAARC the more convinced I become of its capabilities and prospects.

2

REGIONALISM
Theoretical Perspective

The regional cooperation as a concept and trend toward international regionalism is one of the most interesting developments in recent International Relations. In its present formulation the overwhelming theme is self-reliance through the regional comparative advantageous strategy. Regional cooperation is an out growth of internal and external economics and political pressures which are driving nations together in present era.

Regions recognized by the United Nations:

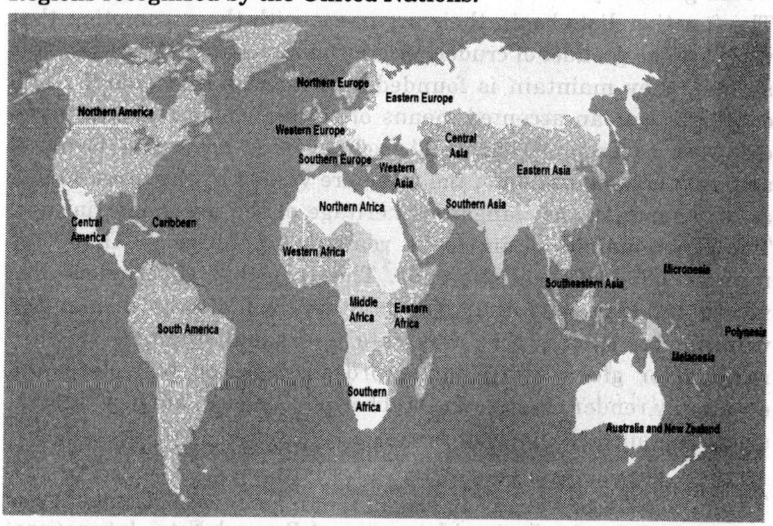

The underlying assumption of the theorists appeared to be that States in a given region would and should eventually attain political unification.[1] A number of variables identified, reformulated and

---

[1] S.D. Muni and Anuradha Muni; *Regional Cooperation in South Asia*, Delhi, Kay Kay Publishers, 1984, p. 2.

explained to chart out the processes and predict the patterns of the said unification. Such variables included background conditions' (like the size of units i.e. States, rate of transactions among them, pluralism and perception of dependence), conditions at the time of union (like the governmental purpose, external pressures and powers of the Union) and 'process condition' (like the decision making styles, rate of transaction in the union, adaptability and power[2] of governments and external pressures). However, neither these variables helped in the proper understanding of phenomenon of regionalism for the predictions made on the basis of the analysis and supported by the real worked situation.[3] Even by the mid seventies, one of the pioneers and strongest exponent of the regional integration theory, Hass, himself confessed to its short-comings and obsolescence.[4]

The most insightful critics of the security conflict conception of international politics have been referred to as functionalists. Functionalism has been presented as an operative philosophy that would gradually lead to a peaceful unified and cooperative world. The functionalists begin their argument with the assumption that wars are the product of crudely organized international system. This system, they maintain is founded on suspicion and anarchy and considers war an accepted means of settling thorny international disputes, sovereignty, national exclusiveness and other forms of arbitrary fragmentation of the globe are viewed by the functionalist as an anarchist and dangerous heritage of the pre-industrial age. The functionalists claim to be realistic in the sense that they recommended of idealistic ends. They say that government has vested interests and that Nation-States will not be dismantled voluntarily. Hence, they advocate a gradual approach toward regional or global unity, an approach designed to isolate and eventually render obsolete the stubborn but inadequate institutional structure called Nation-States.[5]

---

2 Mario Barrera and Ernest B. Hass; "The Organizationalization of Some Variables Related to Regional Integration: A Research Note", *International Organization*, 1969, Vol. 23, No. 1, p. 150.

3 S.D. Muni and Anuradha Muni (1984)

4 Earnst B. Hass; "The Obsolescence of Regional Integration Theory", *International Organisation*, 1976, Vol. 30, p. 1

5 David Mitrany; *A Working Peace System*, Royal Institute of International Affairs, London, 1946, pp. 19-20.

The functionalist's strategy urges the development of piecemeal non-political cooperative organizations which are established most effectively in the economic, technical, scientific, social and cultural sectors. These sectors are referred to collectively as functional sectors. The functionalists assume that it is easier to establish narrow in-scope functional organizations (in sectors such as, energy production, distribution transportations and communications control, health protection and improvement, labor standards and exchanges of customs unions) than to try to develop political institution that jeopardize the national sovereignty of member States. Functionalists, as a matter of strategy tend to emphasize cooperative aspects of international behavior and side steps conflictive aspects. They look at Globe in terms of politics of cooperation and reason rather than the politics of conflict and irrationality. Gradually they hope with the accumulation of large variety of functional organization linking people and their interest across national boundaries, a transformation in both national attitudes and institutions will take place.

Moreover, the functionalists give priority to economy than politics. To put in different words economic expansion will foster greater cooperation among States. It may be partly true in the case of developed world but in the developing world politics will play important role in fostering the international cooperation. Due to lack of modernization in the developing world, the socio-economic pressure groups are dormant. It may be developed or underdeveloped world, the Nation-State has still primary legitimate claims and control over these pressure groups operating within the boundaries of nation. The developing States are hesitant to put any kind of curb on sovereignty.

There are different schools of thought, regarding the preferred methods and approaches to international integration. The federalist school of thought, (solidly positioned in the ranks of idealism) conceives of integration in legal and institutional terms. For federalist scholars integration is an end product rather than a process. It stands for a political union among previously sovereign and independent territories such as war formed in the United States, Switzerland. They recommended the adoption of federalism on both regional-and-global scale, and they consider the anarchic Nation-State system to be primarily responsible for war.

They discount arguments that federalism on a global scale is impractical and utopian. They feel that with reasonable amount of discussion and education, enough people will be convinced that a rational plan for the regulation and governance of humankind should be adopted. Transition to a mutually acceptable model of federalism, according to federalist scholars, should follow a large scale world conference similar to the one that gave birth to U.N.O. Thus, the federalist school of thought emphasizes the institutional approach. But this school talk in terms of 'what ought to be' without analyzing objective conditions.[6] In other words, the institution laws as we have seen in case of League of Nations and U.N.O. will be inoperative though considering the realities of international politics.

A school of thought, which is identified with Karl W. Deutstch and his associates, employ the 'Communication Approach'. This approach (in the scientific tradition) seeks to measure the process of integration by watching the flow of international transaction, such as trade, tourists, letters and immigrants. It expects further, that such transaction will eventually lead to the development of 'security communities' or integrated socio-political system. Duetsch has identified two major sub-categories of 'security community', amalgamated and pluralist. Both are characterized by the absence of intra-community wars. The United States is a good example of an amalgamated security community for it has a single federal government exercising central political control over a continent sized region. For the communication school of thought, then integration can be seen both as a process leading towards political unification and as the end product of that process, amalgamated and pluralist security communities. The communication approach analyses the integration in term of numerous quantifying variables. This failed to give any yardstick to quantify the qualitative communication, putting in different words; qualitative communication may foster greater integration than the mere quantified communication.[7]

---

6 Green Vill Clark and Louis B. Sohn; *World Peace through World Law*, Harvard University Press, Harvard, 1966, pp. 110-111.

7 Karl W. Deutsch et al., *Political Community and the North Atlantic Area*, N.J. Princeton University, Princeton, 1957, pp 1-2. Karl W. Deutsch et al., *France, Germany and the Western Alliance: A Study of Elite Attitude on European Integration and World Politics*, Seribner's, New York, 1967, p. 45.

The fourth school of thought is referred to as neo-functionalists. Neo-functionalist scholars also view integration as both a process and an outcome but they prefer to emphasize cooperative decision making processes and elite attitudes in order to assess the progress towards integration. An able scholar whose work has been identified mainly with this area is, Ernest B. Hass.[8] Neo-functionalists have focused primarily on formal institutions in an attempt to determine the extent to which important functions are carried out by national as opposed to international integrated agencies. Further they have to assess, using systematic survey techniques (Questionnaires and interviews) the degree to which important elites of various countries exhibit nationalist or internationalist orientations.

From our point of view, one should not have to choose among these different approaches to the study of integration. The genesis of 'political actors' whether at the national, regional or global level is too complex a phenomenon to be left to any one method or conceptual approach. The recommendations and findings of federalist, communication analysis, and neo-functionalist should, therefore, be considered as useful steps in the ladder of understanding. Further, we should keep in mind, a very important warning about integration. Whether process or outcome, it should be purely voluntary. History tells that the more prevalent way to political unification has been through the force of arms. But coercive political unification should certainly not be confused with integration. The concept of integration should be reserved only for peaceful political unification. The study of functionalism especially in its applied form has gone hand in hand with the study of regionalism. Given that the functionalist experiment has proceeded most systematically in a West European setting, scholars have assumed that the transition from the State system to a global society must go first through a phase of regional integration.

All these schools of thought are based on European experience. No doubt, these schools contributed a lot regarding international regional cooperation in developing States but conditions prevailing in the developing States are different from the developed States.

---

[8] Ernest B. Hass; *Beyond and National State: Functionalism International Organization*, Standard Callif University Press, New York, 1964, p. 29. Also see: *The Political Dynamics of European Economic Integration*, Prantince Hall, New Jersey, 1970, pp. 11-12.

Therefore, historicity, particularity of developing nations and the regional organization like South Asian Association of Regional Cooperation (SAARC) is necessary for understanding the problems. Moreover, these schools have emphasized uni-dimensional aspect of the problem. The multidimensional approach will be more valid for theoretical understanding of the problem. Even the definition of region itself needs multi-dimensional approach for analysis. After studying all the theories regarding regional cooperation, the foremost problem arises about the definition of region, should we define it on the basis of distant land masses, such as Africa, Asia, Europe, North and South America. Unfortunately even with such a relatively simple task as the definition of regions conceptual controversy creeps in e.g. should Eastern Europe be grouped with a cluster of nation countries called Europe, or with a different cluster called socialist countries? Should Arab speaking northern Africa be grouped in a region called the Middle East, the Mediterranean, a developing Islamic or a NATO State? It soon becomes obvious that different criteria for identifying regions yield altogether different regional configuration.[9]

The following are the most commonly used criteria for grouping Nation-States into regions:

1. **Geographical criteria:** grouping Nation-States on the basis of their location in continents, subcontinents, archipelagoes etc., for instance Europe and Asia.
2. **Military political criteria:** grouping Nation-States on the basis of their participation in alliances, or on the basis of ideological and political orientation, for instance, the Communist Bloc, the Capitalist Bloc, NATO, SEATO, CENTO etc.
3. **Economic criteria:** grouping Nation-States on the basis of selected criteria of economic development, such as gross national product and industrial output (for instance, industrialized-transitional, less-developed States).
4. **Transactional criteria:** grouping Nation-States on the basis of volume and the frequency of exchange of people, goods and services such as immigrants, tourists, trade-

---

[9] See Bruce M. Russet; *International Regions and International System. A Study in Political Ecology*, Rand Mcnally, Chicago, 1967, pp. 5.

messages, for instance, U.S.A., Canada, the Western European Market area, that East Europe Soviet Market area.

Therefore, one can group countries into regions according to a number of other criteria as well, for example, language, culture, population density and climate. It is best not to spend much time in seeking to determine what the 'best' definition on regionalism or which all purpose criteria should be selected for clustering nation States into regions. Instead one should adopt multi-dimensional approach while considering the historicity and particularity of circumstances. If we analyze the history of various regional organizations in the world, we will find that none of the regional organization is based or sustained on one dimension like functionalism, federalism, communication or neo-functionalism. No doubt, the experiences of these organizations will contribute to solidify the SAARC. After reviewing literature on these organizations, we will be able to formulate certain hypothesis.

SAARC is not a new phenomenon, but it has long history of regional organization both on the world and South Asian level. If the study is started about regional arrangements from not very old period even then possible examples of regional arrangement in this century can be found.

Before World War I, regional integration was expressed in multilateral and bilateral treaties. These trends, sometimes, toward economic regionalism resulted in the formation of true regional arrangements, most of them, however, were of a relatively minor and ill-defined character and led no where, because of the frequent succession in regime.

A number of regional arrangements came into being in the interwar period (1918-39). The most obvious example was the little Entente, composed of Czechoslovakia Yugoslavia and Romania, created shortly after the conclusion of the war; it grew out of a series of bilateral mutual assistance treatise among the three countries. It gradually developed into a political organization and, after 1933, came approximate a close diplomatic consideration with definite organizational structure.

Then there were many other attempts through regional arrangements to form groupings of States in Eastern Europe and the Balkan areas, but with the possible exception of the Balkan Entente of 1934 these attempts did not lead to any regional arrangements.

The five power treaty signed by the Belgium, England, France, Germany and Italy in 1925 regarding the Western Frontiers of Germany, the most important of the seven Locarno pacts-seemed to lay the foundation of regional collaboration for a specific purpose, but it was not implemented to the extent necessary to bring a regional arrangement into effective operation. Between the two world wars the regional cooperation was in the context of security and Balance of power system.

ASIAN COOPERATION WITHOUT REGIONALISM 1947-55

The Asian relations conference of March, 1947, described as the 'first outward expression of the new awakening in Asia, was attended by representatives of most of the Asian States. The Asian relation conference was primarily intended for cultural, economic cooperation among the Asian States. A resolution adopted unanimously by the nineteen States represented at the Asian Conference on Indonesia, held in New Delhi in January, 1949, recommended the participating nations to explore the possibilities of regional arrangements within these areas. But the meaning of 'regional arrangements within these areas' was not too clear.

Bandung conference in 1955 was one of the most remarkable international gatherings in history, and seemed to mark the new role of Asia and Africa in World affairs. Its final communiqué expressed a desire for cooperation in economic, cultural and other fields, agreement to establish liaison officers in the participating countries, and hope for prior consultation of participating countries in international forums. But also affirmed specifically it is not intended to form a regional bloc. Prior to Bandung conference there was an effort by Western power to boast Asian regional economic power known as 'Colombo Plan.' The Colombo plan for cooperative economic development in South and Southeast Asia was not an integrated plant at all. It was not a true regional arrangement. Its main agency of cooperation was the consultative committee which was set up at meetings of the commonwealth foreign ministers in Colombo in January 1950, it had 22 members out of which 15 are within the region. They were Bhutan, Burma, Cambodia, Ceylon, India, Indonesia, Laos, Malaysia, Maldives, Island, Nepal, Pakistan, Philippines, South Vietnam, and Thailand. The remaining seven were out of the region, i.e. Australia, Canada, Japan, New Zealand, South Korea, U.K., U.S.A. Colombo plan helped to channel billion of dollars in economic aid to the South East Asian nations. Under the plan approximately 28,500 persons from the region have been sent to the member States of the region. The plan is also involved in three large joint regional schemes, namely the Indus river basin and the Mekong River Development programmes, and the Asian highway scheme for a 30,000 miles network of all weather roads running from Saigon to Istanbul.[10]

SEATO

Flag of SEATO

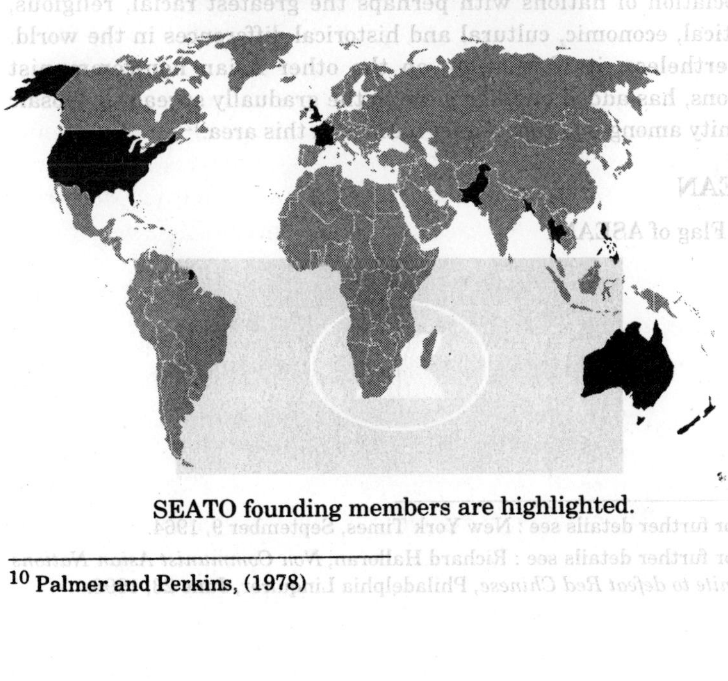

SEATO founding members are highlighted.

---

10 Palmer and Perkins, (1978)

After the Geneva Truce agreements regarding Indo-China in 1954, the USA, U.K., France, Australia, New Zealand, the Philippines, Thailand, and Pakistan agreed to meet in Manila in early September to consider measures for concerted resistance to possible aggression or subversion in South East Asia. Out of this conference emerged the so called pacific charter and the South East Asia collective defense Treaty. Each member agreed that if an armed attack occurred it would act to meet danger in accordance with its constitutional process. SEATO was weak regional defense system but some efforts were made through conferences, exchange of views and information, training programmes, joint military exercise and other means to make it a useful instrument of collective planning.[11]

ASPAC in June, 1966 a significant new regional organization, known as the Asian and Pacific Council, was organized at a conference at the Walker Hill Resort, outside Seoul, of representatives of nine area States-Australia, Japan, Malaysia, Nationalist China, New Zealand, Philippines, South Korea, South Vietnam and Thailand. In a Joint Communiqué these representative announced their determination to preserve their integrity and sovereignty in the face of external threats. ASPAC has a long and difficult way to go to achieve a permanent life because it is an association of nations with perhaps the greatest racial, religious, political, economic, cultural and historical differences in the world. Nevertheless, its formation, on the other Asian non-communist nations, has added another piece to the gradually spreading mosaic of unity among non communist nations in this area.[12]

ASEAN

Flag of ASEAN

[11] For further details see : New York Times, September 9, 1964.

[12] For further details see : Richard Halloran; *Non Communist Asian Nations Unite to defeat Red Chinese*, Philadelphia Linquirer, June 23, 1996.

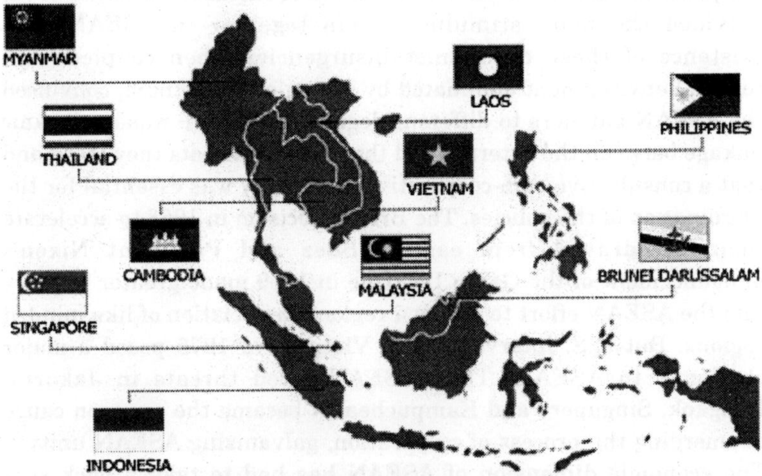

MEMBER COUNTRIES OF ASEAN

In August, 1967, Indonesia, Malaysia, the Philippine, Singapore, and Thailand met in Bangkok, adopted a declaration announcing the establishment of the new organization, which was in fact an enlarged version of ASA - the member countries prefer to accelerate economic growth, social progress and cultural development in the region, "To promote active collaboration and mutual assistance...in the economic, social, cultural, scientific, administrative fields and to promote regional peace and stability". The machinery provided for in the ASEAN declaration consisted of an annual meeting of foreign ministers, a standing committee, ad-hoc committees and permanent committees of specialists and officials on specific subjects, and a National Secretariat in each member country. ASEAN is essentially a new economic grouping in South East Asia. Presumably membership opens to other countries in the area, and even in South Asia as well. It may become an agency to promote regional security. For ASEAN it has been very clear from the beginning that it was conceived as a multipurpose organization whose activities are social and economic cooperation but whose underlying *raison dtre* lay in political co-ordination to cope with a still threatening in environment.[13] Though consideration in economic and social field were no doubt central it was a fact that there was a convergence in

[13] Mohammad Ayub; *The Primacy of Political SAARC in Comparative Prospective*, Asian Survey, Vol. XXV, No. 4, April, 1985, p. 447.

the political outlook of the five perspective member nations...which provided the main stimulus to join together in ASEAN. The existence of these communist insurgencies when coupled with regional environment dominated by struggle for Vietnam, convinced the ASEAN partners to different degrees that there was an organic linkage between the external and the internal threats they faced and that a consultative cum-cooperative machinery was essential for the coordination of the policies. The British decision in 1968 to accelerate their withdrawal from east of Suez and President Nixon's announcement of the Gaum Doctrine in 1969 made greater urgency into the ASEAN effort to evolve a regional association of like minded regions. But U.S. intervention in Vietnam in 1975 posed a major challenge to ASEAN. Then ASEAN faced threats in Jakarta, Bangkok, Singapore and Kampuchea. It became the common cause of emerging the process of cooperation, galvanizing ASEAN unity.[14] The economic dimension of ASEAN has had to take a back seat because in character its core concerns have been political security.

Turning to South Asia we find different situations those prevailing within European community, ASEAN or GCC. The perceived sources of internal and external threats are not only very diverse but quite often emanate from present topic SAARC potential for cooperation is not a new idea but is the product of long history of regional organizations. The trend toward regionalism is now an acknowledged feature of the international science. It has achieved a new meaning and a new significance. While it has not in any real sense breached the barrier of the Sovereign State system, It has provided the impetus and the machinery for much closer cooperation of States on the regional level.

By analyzing all the World Regional Arrangements we can safely conclude that the regional co-operation is a multi dimensional process. Primacy of the variable depends upon the historical condition of that particular time, when the particular regional organization was formulated. For instance, SEATO, CENTO in Asia were by-product of cold war. ASEAN is by-product of detente having ideological orientation.

The present theory of regionalism suffers from a European cultural bias as Western Europe has been the main focus and concern in its formulation. The theory of integration or regionalism

---

[14] Mohammad Ayub (1985) at p. 448

with its functionalist thrust reflects its main occupation with the socio-economic interest and pressure groups as the main agents of regionalism. If it would not have been so, the goal of political unification through regionalism and economic cooperation as envisaged in the integration theory would have been nearly achieved in the case of EEC (European Economic Community).

EEC

Flag of EEC

MAP OF THE MEMBER COUNTRIES OF EEC

COMECON

Flag of COMECON

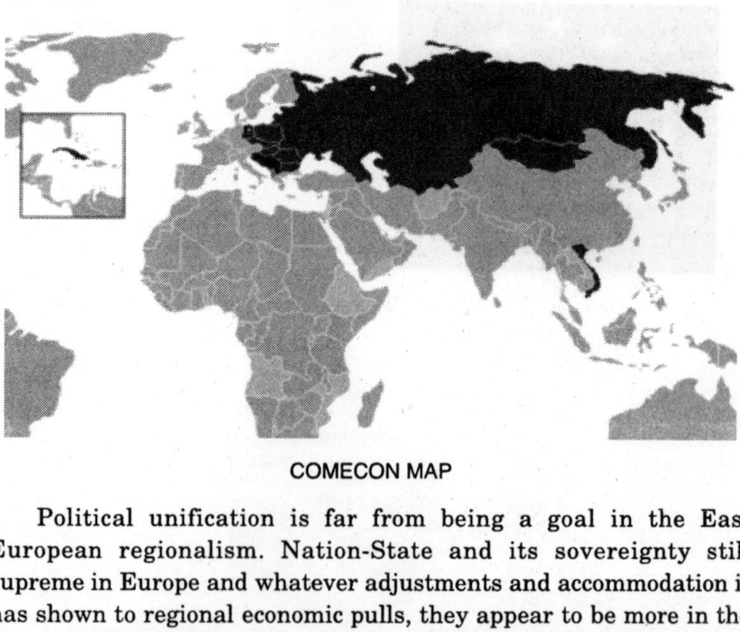

COMECON MAP

Political unification is far from being a goal in the East European regionalism. Nation-State and its sovereignty still supreme in Europe and whatever adjustments and accommodation it has shown to regional economic pulls, they appear to be more in the nature of concessions than erosion. It, therefore, seems that even in European context, political unification is far from being a goal. And theories of integration are becoming obsolescent because three assumptions on which these theories are based have become less relevant to the behavioral pattern actually displayed by government active in regional politics that a definite institutional pattern must mark the outcome of the process of integration. That conflicts of interest involving trade off between ties with regional partners and ties with non members should be resolved in favor of regional partners.

National-State participating in a regional integration organization tends to exhibit strong economic growth rates. Hence, it could be argued, that integration is mutually advantageous for participants. But this finding has been confounded by frequent instances of non participants also experiencing dramatic economic growth rates during the same period e.g. both Japan and Canada experienced dramatic industrial and economic growth in the 1960's without formally integrating themselves with larger political economic communities. These are the two deviations in generalization.

In case of the third world the primacy of politics all the more a dominant characteristic of social reality. The socio-economic interests and agents are highly under developed, very poorly organized and lack considerably in skill and articulation. Their influence in political decision making, therefore, is very seldom decisive. The socio-economic sectors of national life, as also foreign policy postures, including those related to regionalism are conditioned and dictated by political concerns and preoccupations more than anything else. Factors like nationalism and sovereignty are extremely powerful. In the absence of well developed powerful and autonomous socio-economic forces and agents, the State through the governmental sector plays, the most decisive role in all vital decisions. In regional moves incentives of economic gains and the influence of economic agents without their political implications are by and large incidental. This is evident in the functioning of the third world regional groupings in South East Asia, Africa and Latin America: No doubt socio-economic groups and functional differentiation are main catalyst agents of international regional cooperation but the political will and military strategy also played important role in this direction.

In retrospect, it appears that the Western European experience since World War-II has proceeded under sets or rules and assumptions that are quite different from these that apply to other parts of the world, e.g. Middle East, South East Asia, East Asia, Southern Africa, the incidence of internal and international conflicts since World War-II has been higher than the incidence of Western and Eastern European conflict. One could speculate that today's conflict ridden regions are going through the pre-integrated stage that Europe experienced from the 1700's through the 1940's. It is hoped that these regions will not have to experience painful and disillusioning wars and accompanying partition and destruction in order to realize that they must find peaceful feelings for the resolution of territorial and ideological issues. The more the region is cohesive, the more are the chances of success of regional co-operation. The larger the area of a region, the more the chances of penetration of global system.

Common and similar (though not necessarily identical) threats either from internal or external sources, or both, thus provides congruence in security perception. Similar political systems, which provide congruence in ideological/political perception have, common foreign policy orientation regarding major issues, related to the global balance of power and its regional manifestations are surely to have congruence in strategic perceptions. A consensus regarding the role of the pivotal power within the regional grouping, a consensus shared by the pivotal power itself, provides the basis of internal cohesiveness within the grouping and sets the limits beyond which neither the pivotal power not its partners may stray in intra-regional and intra-group relations.

The last but not the least, and effective regional cooperation for the member countries have to prefer one another particularly in trade.

DISTINCT FEATURES OF ASIAN REGIONALISM

In contrast to Latin America, Asian regionalism has been belated and limited several reasons could be attributed to this delayed development these reasons are immensely intricate and interwoven, which is again a peculiar feature of complexity limited to Asia.

1. **Colonialism:** It kept almost all the countries of this continent economically lagging behind, politically less aware and culturally backward. Countries of Asian region have had been involved in getting freedom and then remaining free till as late as second half of twentieth Century. By that time the first phase of regionalism was over in the rest of the world which was completely rather practically missed by Asia.
2. **Cold War Divisions:** Colonial rule retardation of these countries was further added to by cold war era and divisions in the region on ideological basis were introduced.

3. **Absence of Experience and Cooperation:** Slavery and divide and rule legacy in these counties lead to lacked of mutual trust and the idea of a nation. Common concept of development was absent even within the country what to talk of outside the country. Caste system, gap between rich and poor a tussle between 'desi' and 'phirangi' made Asian society even more pathetic.

4. **Absence of the idea of a region:** When the situation was so unfortunate at social or national level how could these countries realize that their State along with its neighbors constitute a closely knit region. In the background of such situations Asian regionalism acquired certain special features which still reflect in the region's international behaviour and approach.

   - The member States are over conscious of their sovereignty and its portrayal.
   - They keep trying to gain or maintain upper hand in the functioning or decision making of the organization.
   - They remain suspicious of external influence of a new form of dependency. It hinders them from taking innovative steps or risk bearing.
   - No country is able to lead because constant leg pulling is exercised e.g. there is China, Japan, India, Pakistan who want to keep themselves one step ahead of each other to prove their leadership potential of Asia.
   - All decisions to be taken by consensus, while taking decisions in regional organizations is another indication that these countries do not trust each other and have inflated image of self assertion which is needless when it comes to regional development.
   - Difference in the nature of political regimes is another Asian feature which has been a big set back to the development of Asian regionalism.[15]

---

[15] Karns and Mingst, *International Organizations: The Politics and Processes of Global Governance*, Viva Books Pvt. Ltd. New Delhi,, 2005, p. 198.

All this has resulted in:

(*i*) Informal Structures (*ii*) Very few rules (*iii*) Loose organization (*iv*) No binding decisions (*v*) Small secretariats (*vi*) Emphasis on consensus decision making, as distinct features of regional organizations working in Asia.

A new trend of Confidence Building Measures is growing in these Asian Countries Such measures are exercised in private capacity of these nations and has shown visible results.

However, Asian countries have covered a long journey, thus, despite the all the above mentioned weaknesses these countries recognize and respect the need for regionalism. Therefore, Asia may have reached the stage of formal regionalism late but has not been alien to inter State cooperation. Among the tangible evidences of Asian and Pacific cooperation or regional awareness are various proposals; notably the first of all was Nehru's 'Asia for Asians' then a number of mutual scrutiny and economic pacts like SEATO, Colombo Plan, The Asian and Pacific Council, ASEAN, ARF, South Pacific Commission, NAM and SAARC.

Scholarly interest in regionalism has been reflected in South Asia, due to the uniqueness of the South Asian features of regionalism. Latest works on this region are far beyond the earlier literature on regionalism, by way of quality as well as quantity. Fields such as religion, history, economics and comparative politics are inescapable in the study of South Asian regionalism.

Regional organizations such as the EEC and the Association of South East Asian Nations (ASEAN) had an implicit function in containing the spread of communism and this common goal provided a context for achieving mutual benefits.[16] They excluded their primary antagonists in favor of uniting with old and newly found allies. These regional organizations were therefore exclusivist in keeping out enemies through the erection of trading and military barriers to rivals outside these alliances. As these rivals also formed their own regional organizations, such as the Council for Mutual Economic Aid (COMECON), the world became divided into mutually exclusive groups which served to reduce tensions among allies but did nothing to reduce tensions among antagonistic regional blocs.

---

[16] S.D. Muni, 'South Asian Regional Cooperation: Evolution and Prospects', *IDSA Journal*, Vol. 19, No. 1, July-September 1986, p. 122.

The East-West and North-South divides remained and may even have been accentuated by regional integration schemes which excluded outside nations.

In this way, virtually the whole world came to be included in assorted regional alliances which formed in antagonism to each other. The one area that remained without a regional alliance was South Asia. This was because its primary antagonists were not external to the region but were within it.

The creation of a regional organization for South Asia in 1985, amid all antagonisms was unique and went against the traditional pattern of regional alliance formation. For this reason there was considerable skepticism about the prospects of SAARC at its formation. From the outset there were assertions that its failure was inevitable due to the lack of a common security perception.[17] Its subsequent track record, while modest, was nevertheless impressive, given the on-going tensions in South Asia and the achievements of other Third World alliances. 'Despite ASEAN being claimed as a relatively successful organization regional cooperation has not done much better in Southeast Asia than in South Asia, and in some respects has lagged much behind".[18]

That enemies rather than allies were brought together in SAARC makes similarities with other regional alliances minimal. The basic contrasts between SAARC and other regions invited comparative analysis, and revealed a number of pre-requisites of a successful integration. However, the 'lack of progress towards development of any coherent theoretical or even descriptive framework' of regional integration means that no comprehensive political theory exists that can adequately explain the South Asian integration phenomenon.[19] If regional organization in South Asia can be an effective forum for the reduction of tensions, this experience

---

[17] William T. Tow, *Subregional Security Cooperation in the Third World*, Boulder, Colorado: Lynne Rienner Publishers, 1990, pp. 7-8.

[18] Pran Chopra, 'SAARC and ASEAN: Comparative Analysis of Structures and Aims', in Bhabani Sen Gupta (ed.), *SAARC-ASEAN: Prospects and Problems of Inter-regional Cooperation*, Delhi: South Asian Publishers, 1988, p. 22.

[19] Barry Buzan, 'Framework for Regional Security Analysis', in Barry Buzan and Gowher Rizvi (eds.), *South Asian Insecurity and the Great Powers*, Macmillan, London, 1986, p. 7.

could provide an example for the incorporation of enemies within regional organizations in other conflict zones.

Out of all these regional ventures for cooperation the SAARC is the youngest it is still growing and is just a toddler in comparison to adult and fully matured regional organizations like ASEAN, EU etc.[20] Therefore, it is expected of SAARC that it might come up with something novel, something very effective, something which might prove to be a turning point for the region. 'SAARC has a long way to go'. But while fixing great expectations we must also keep in mind that before SAARC reaches that maturity level and powerful position, it has to overcome certain 'teething troubles' while an organization is in its process of growth even small obstacles seem huge and insurmountable but as an organization moves on these problems get reduced to their miniature, manageable, surmountable size.

SAARC needs to be studied for it is yet to prove its potential. For a researcher of Political Science it is like an unlimited ocean which has pure untouched pearls in its bosom, waiting for the right time and right approach.

This study is a small attempt to understand **SAARC the youngest organization of the world.**

---

20 L.L. Mehrotra and H.S. Chopra (eds.); *SAARC 2000 and Beyond,* New Delhi, Omega Scientific Publishers, 1996, p. 13.

3

DETERMINANTS OF INTER-STATE RELATIONS IN SOUTH ASIA

As specified by Lama, there are several strategic factors that have determined the cooperation and integration process in other regional blocs. Broadly the economic determinants have been

(*i*) level of economic development in the region and the differences between member countries;

(*ii*) level of existing economic and other interdependence of member countries;

(*iii*) the optimization of the newly formed economic area (zone), with particular reference to the;

(*iv*) complementarity of resources and factors of production as well as to the development potential as a whole;

(*v*) the nature of economic relation with third countries and the position of foreign economic subjects in the national economy of a given groups (like transnational corporations) and,

(*vi*) the suitability of the selected model and types of integration policies in view of the actual conditions in a given group.

Similarly one can roughly identify the political determinants as:

(*i*) the degree of political homogeneity in the region,

(*ii*) level and stability of political will favoring integration,

(*iii*) the pattern of foreign political relations of the groups, especially with super power and former metropolitan powers and

(*iv*) efficiency of common institutes and the possibilities of their creative activity in favor of collective interest within the group[1].

---

1 Oman, Charles, *Globalization and Regionalization: The Challenge for Developing Countries*, Development Centre Studies, OECD, 1994. at p. 15.

Structural characteristics of South Asia are incomparable in the sense that no other region of the world can ever claim that much distinctiveness in geographical, physical and historical terms. The South Asian region which is more or, less equal to sub-continent comprises the main portion of Asia and is larger than Europe, having a total area of two million sq. miles placed between South-west and South-east Asia, stretching from Afghanistan in the west to Burma in the east and from Karakoram to the blue waters of the Indian Ocean. But the concept of South Asia as a distinct regional system is of very recent in origin. Even the concept of South-east Asia evolved only during the Second World War period. Later the Western writers coined the term Southern Asia; to include both what is now termed as South Asia and South-East Asia. In Michael Brecher's concept of five subordinate systems South Asia was defined as consisting of fourteen states extending from Pakistan to Indonesia.[2] But South-East Asia deserves to be viewed as a separate regional system including both China and Japan. Cantori and Speigal in their concept of 'subordinate systems of the world and their subdivisions' identified South Asia as a distinct subordinate system consisting of India (The Core), Ceylon, Nepal, Bhutan, Sikkim, Afghanistan, Maldives Islands, Pakistan (inclusive of Bangladesh) (The periphery).[3]

In most of the definitions Afghanistan[4] is not included in South Asia. Similarly Burma is considered as part of South-east Asia.[5] Some would like to regard Pakistan as a West Asian state. As S.P. Varma puts it "the area possesses geographical continuity, if we

---

2 Cited in Yogesh Atal, "Subordinate State Systems and Nation-States: Tools for the Analysis of External Milieu", in S.P. Verma and K.P. Mishra eds., *Foreign Policies in South Asia,* Sage Publications, New Delhi, 1969, pp. 41-44 and S.U. Kodikara, "Regional Roles and Behaviour in South Asia: A Theoretical Framework for Regional co-operation", in Babani Sen Gupta (ed)., *Regional Co-operation and Development in South Asia*, Vol.1 , Murari lal and Sons , New Delhi, 1986, pp. 31-36.

3 Louis J. Cantori and Steven L. Spiegal, "The International Politics of Regions: A Comparative Approach", *Geographical Review*, Vol. 62, No. 3, July, 1972, pp. 437-439, New Jersey, 1970, p. 9.

4 Pakistan Opposes Kabul's Move to Seek SAARC Membership, Bangladesh also opposed the entry of Afghanistan, *Bangladesh Time,* 28 July 1987.

5 Burma has rejected an Indian suggestion to join the SAARC, *Tribune,* 17 December 1987.

include Afghanistan and Burma, and geographical compactness if we leave them out."[6]

Socio-Political Profile

The successive invasions of external powers like the Turks, Mughals and the Europeans for over a thousand years had its mark on the ethnic configuration and cultural composition of the region.

North-Indians and Pakistanis belong to the Indo-Aryan cultural stock. Monglo-Dravidians constitute a sizable section of the people of Eastern India and Bangladesh. Mongolian races live in Nepal and the adjoining Indian territories. South India as a whole and a part of Sri Lanka are occupied by Dravidians. While the Sinhales are of Aryan origin.[7] Lingustic differences and similarities are more complex and sophisticated than that of ethnic homogeneity and diversity. Urdu is the national language of Pakistan. Punjabi, Puslito, Sindhi are also spoken by the people in different parts of Pakistan. A large chunk of North Indian people also use these languages. Urdu-speaking Pakistanis understand perfectly Hindi-speaking Indians. All these languages are that of the Indo-Aryan language group with an admixture of Turko-Iranian (Baluchi and Pustlm). Similarly, Bengali is the national language of Bangladesh. At the same time, it is the lingua franca in the Indian state of West Bengal. 25 per cent of the Sri Lankan population and the Indian state of Tamil Nadu speak Tamil. Nepali is spoken in the Darjeeling District of West Bengal. "The linguistic dimension of inter-state relation in South Asia is so puzzling and novel that students of international politics including those residents in these countries have failed to grasp the full implications and ramifications of the linguistic affinities cutting across international boundaries... The linguistic boundaries in South Asia do not coincide with, international boundaries."[8]

---

[6] S.P. Verma, *at*, p. 342

[7] S.P. Varma and K.P. Misra (eds) "Foreign Policies in South Asia", Orient Longmans, Bombay, 1969, p. 374. Also see: Ajit Singh Sarhadi, *India's Security in Resurgent Asia* , Vol. 35, No. 2, April-June *Asia,*New Delhi, 1980, p. 138.

[8] P.C. Mathur, Virendra Narian and M.V. Lakhi, "Intra-regional Relations: A Study in Infra-structural Determinants" in S.P. Varma and K.P. Misra eds "South Asia as a Region", Orient Longmans, Bombay, 1969, at p. 97.

Hinduism is the major religion in South Asia. India and Nepal are predominantly Hindu. In secular India, Hindus form 83 per cent of the total population. In Bangladesh, Pakistan and Sri Lanka, they constitute a considerable minority. Islam is the state religion of Pakistan and Bangladesh. Maldives is also a Muslim country. Muslims are minorities in India and Sri Lanka. Buddhism is professed and practiced in Sri Lanka. Buddhism prevails among the people of Nepal, Sikkim, and the Eastern part of the Himalayas. As a result of the British rule, Christianity also has got followers in South Asia, especially in India and Sri Lanka. "In the world state system, there is no comparable example of proximity of states containing adherents of so many different religions. The problem is made more complicated by the fact that substantial religious minorities exist in every state. Religion thus provides a cause of division as well as unison among the South Asian peoples as adherents of one faith have a natural affinity with their co-religionists which they cannot extend towards believers in other faiths. Religion also becomes a factor in the generation of communal feelings."[9] For over a century the South Asian sub-continent was one not only physically but politically also. Western imperialism brought the entire region under the unified control of Great Britain. This resulted in the development of common political, legal and administrative institutions. The basic characteristics of the nationalist movement for freedom in all parts of the region were identical, notwithstanding the growth of separatist tendencies. The educational background, aspirations and world view of the leaders of the freedom movement were more or less the same. All of them were western educated, English-knowing middle class elites of the sub-continent. They imbibed the indispensable qualities of 20th Century English liberalism and hatred towards imperialist subjugation. "The similar socialization of the elites has evolved certain common external national role conceptions in the regional context. For example, the ruling elites of all the states are concerned about the maintenance of *status-quo*."[10] With the withdrawal of the British, the overall control from one centre bid fare-well to the region forever. Four new national entities

---

[9] Ibid., p. 94.

[10] Sivananda Patnaik, "Sri Lanka and the South Asian Sub-system: A Study of Macro International Politics". *India Quarterly*, Vol. 35, No. 2, April-June, 1980, at p. 138.

came into existence in the subcontinent. One among them named Pakistan was carved out of the Muslim majority area of the British India's Western and Eastern flank. Later, in 1971, East Bengal, part of Pakistan but separated by thousands and thousands of miles of Indian soil went away to establish an independent sovereign state of its own. Thus South Asia witnessed the birth of Bangladesh. It may be noted that the region has undergone a reverse historical process. The Indian sub-continent which was one country unto 1947 was partitioned into two in that year. It split further into 'three in 1971. In retrospect, therefore, the region was largely integrated in 1947. But the region was subsequently fragmented into completely independent political entities.[11]

Leo E. Rose has pointed out another aspect of the sub-continent that the sub-continent was never a unified political entity prior to 1947 except under alien rulers with a world view distant from that of Hindu India. In this regard, India contrasts sharply with China, Japan and several South East Asian States.[12]

It is very difficult to distinguish these countries from one another if we consider other spheres of importance. As noted earlier, they have got common religions. Hinduism, Islam, Buddhism, Sikhism and Christianity are shared by all the countries of the region. Ethnically too, there is considerable amount of overlapping. Aryan, Dravidian, and Mangoloid blood are mixed up to blur any sort of ethnic demarcation. Similarly, languages are crossing frontiers. "Geographical compactness and contiguity, added to the British rule of finding expression in political and legal systems and administrative institutions and the overlapping of religions and languages, which make the countries of South Asia so indistinguishable from each other."[13]

The economic policy adopted by various South Asian countries has also got similarities. The approach has been to build up capitalism through centralized planning with a tinge of socialism. The emphasis is on the development of a mixed economy giving

---

[11] Satish Kumar, "Trends in Regional Developments in South Asia", in M.S. Rajan and Shivaji Ganguly (eds), *Great Power Relations World Order and Third World*, New Delhi, 1981, pp. 271-72.

[12] Leo E. Rose, "India", in Wayne Wilcox, Leo E. Rose and Gavin Boyd (eds), *Asia and the International System,* Boston, 1961, p. 238.

[13] S.P. Varma and K.P. Misra (1980) at p. 347.

equal importance to public and private sectors. But the remnants of old pattern of economic structure make its presence felt everywhere. "The economies were characterized by the simultaneous existence of dominant feudal and pre feudal sorts of modes of production along with a marginal land, in some cases, a dependent modern sector."[14] This is because of the economic policy of the colonial master. During the colonial period, South Asian economies were mere appendages of the British Economy. The net result was deindustrialization of South Asian economics.

Geography, religion, ethnically and language arc discussed as the unifying factors. At the very same time, they are operating divisive factors. Even though the British colonial administration was a unifying factor it also laid the seeds of conflict. Their divide and rule policy sowed the seed of differences between Hindus and Muslims. Hindus and Muslims had been living in India as brothers and sister for centuries. The brotherly affection and harmonious relationship existed among these two religious groups were destroyed by the British policy of instigating communal feelings of the fanatics on both the sides. The British succeeded in implanting a sense of insecurity in the Muslim psyche that the Muslims could not live in independent India as co-citizens with the Hindus. This led to the two-nation theory and the bloody partition. As a result, "an unnatural and absurd state system was brought into being by means of partition of the sub-continent and the creation of a disjointed Pakistan. The British rulers, no doubt played the most significant role in this partition, which, as is well known, led to a series of conflicts and hampered co-operative ventures in the region."[15] Partition failed to patch up the once deteriorated relation between the Hindus and Muslims. The flow of refugees further worsened the whole situation. There remained considerable amount of Hindus in Pakistan and Muslims in India. Pakistan Muslims still continue to worry about the fate of their Muslim brothers in India. Similarly, the Hindus of India happened to be worrying about the fate of their co-religionists in Pakistan. "In the history of the world, there are numerous examples of sovereign states projecting a religious identity

---

[14] S.D. Muni, "India and Regionalism in South Asia: A Political Perspective", in Bimal Prasad ed., *India's Foreign Policy in Continuity and Change,* New Delhi, 1979, p. 110.

[15] Ibid., p. 109.

on the external stage and acting in concert with states with a similar religious complexion. With the decline of the role of religion in moulding the behavior of individuals and society, the type of international behavior, has however, been superseded by the emerging pattern of international politics based on politico-economic calculus. The leaders of South Asian states are, by and large, still universal in this calculus of economic rationality and national strategy. They put their faith in the simple rule of the thumb which tells them that only their co-religionists are their best friends."[16]

The presence of religious and linguistic minority groups across national boundaries acted as irritant factor in the past. The future is also clouded by these factors to a great extent. There exists a clear emphasis on particularistic religions, ethnic and linguistic components of social fabric rather than on universalistic goals and tendencies in the nation building processes. The emphasis is on Islam and Urdu in Pakistan, Islam and Bengali in Bangladesh, Buddhism and Sinhalese in Sri Lanka, Hinduism in Nepal and Buddhism of different sects and varieties in Bhutan. All this resulted in the emergence of dominant ethnic groups in the countries of South Asia. Consequently, the politics of nation building in each of these countries gave rise to many complex problems with. Repercussions extending across national boundaries particularly in Pakistan, India and Bangladesh; directly impinge upon the mutual state-to-state relations. Communal relations in South Asia necessarily possess a minority-majority dimension cutting across national boundaries[17].

Political instability is a marked characteristic of South Asia. India stands as an exception. India has not undergone too frequent political changes as is seen in other parts of the region. Moreover, India is adhered to the political philosophy of democracy and social philosophy of secularism, even though there are pitfalls in her secularist orientation. But this is not the state of affairs in other South Asian States. In Sri Lanka Governmental power has alternated, between the United National Party (UNP) and the Sri Lanka Freedom Party (SLFP). After the 1977 election there occurred a change in the political system also. Parliamentary form of Government gave way to French model of Presidential type of

---

[16] P.C. Mathur et. al in S.P. Varma and K.P. Misra (1969) at pp. 92-93.

[17] S.D. Muni (1979) at p. 111.

Government. While in Pakistan military bureaucratic establishment is well entrenched, in Nepal monarchy is well rooted but they are in search of viability in their political system. Bangladesh also witnessed massive political change in 1975. These differences in political system and constitutional instability have got its own share in maintaining intraregional differences.

There are differences with respect to the foreign policy preferences too. Anti-Indian feelings are prevalent in the foreign policy preferences of these states. They feel that any sort of co-operation with India would block development of separate identity which they desire very much. They fear the proverbial big-brother attitude of India. Moreover, the above-said frequent changes in the political system and Government always stand in the way of nation building. Poverty and unemployment have been taking a new turn day after day. The credibility of the Government may be questioned by powerful divisive forces at any time. To check such an eventuality leaders of these countries used to instigate anti-Indian feelings purposefully.

But any standard India is the dominant power in this region. It is not an exaggeration when one scholar called this region Indo-centric and India-dominated. No doubt India has got a pre-eminent position in the region economically, militarily and technically. Ideologically too, India has got a sound footing. Moreover, India is the only state having common frontier with all these states. No other state in the region shares common border with the others.

There have been several attempts by scholars to study the impact of domestic and external milieus in the foreign policy behavior of states in different regions of the world. In this context, the most searching and exploratory points have been raised by the Rosenau School,[18] while developing a scientific basis of the foreign policy behavior of modern states. However, their attempts to explore the infrastructural linkages in international relations have not sorted out all the problems relating to the external behavior of states. Nevertheless, it is not intended here to under-estimate their multi-dimensional emphasis that political analysis would be greatly

---

[18] See James N. Rosenau, "Political Science in a Shrinking World", and for a particular reference to the developing world, Michael O'Leary, "Linkages between Domestic and International Politics in Under-developed Nations" in Rosenau (ed) *Linkage Politics*, New York, 1969, pp. 2-7.

facilitated if propositions that link the stability, functioning of institutions and goals of national political systems to variables in their external environments could be systematically developed.

In this chapter, an attempt will be made to delineate the impact of domestic and external factors in the shaping of foreign policies of the South Asian nations in general and on the emerging trends of intra-regional relations in particular. The domestic factors which otherwise can be termed as the "push factors,"[19] will be analyzed under the following subheadings, viz. colonial legacy, the problem of immigrants, religion and language. Under the external factors, which are otherwise known as the "pull factors,"[20] an attempt will be made to look at the basic goals and interests of major global Powers in the South Asian region. Particularly, it will investigate the points of convergence and divergence in the South Asian policies of Great Powers like the United States, Soviet Union and China.

Colonial Legacy

Almost all the South Asian nations like India, Pakistan, Bangladesh and Sri Lanka had to experience the rigors of British colonialism. In their search for alternate markets for their industrial products, the British not only brought the entire Indian sub-continent under their political and administrative control, but also in that process, had a complete monopoly on its economy. More or less the economy of South Asia became an appendage of the British economy. Even the peripheral land-locked states like Afghanistan and Nepal, which apparently enjoyed a certain amount of political autonomy, were heavily dependent on the British Imperial Power for their economic survival, because their lifeline was controlled by the latter.

Moreover, because of common historical and geographical considerations, certain exportable commodities were produced in one particular country of the region and the economies of the respective nations of South Asia were basically complementary in nature. To cite a single instance, in the pre-colonial era, jute was produced in abundance in the-then East Bengal (now Bangladesh) while most of

---

[19] The "push" factors are those forces which ultimately draw the nations of a region together.

[20] The "pull" factors are those which alienate the regional actors from one another.

the jute mills were located in West Bengal (India). Similarly, the area which now constitutes Pakistan was the major producer of raw cotton, but most of the cotton mills were located in areas which are at present part of India, But with the liquidation of the British Empire and the ensuing bitterness between the ruling elites of the two major states of South Asia, the process of complementarily was reversed. Pakistan, with no substantial resources of coal and iron, in place of exporting from India at a cheaper rate and lesser freight charges, decided to procure them from distant countries at a higher cost, similarly, because of Pakistan's complacency in providing transit facilities, the age-old Indo-Afghan trade in dry fruits, fresh fruits, rice and other items, has naturally suffered a setback.

A major offshoot of British imperialism in South Asia was the growing bitterness and distrust between the core-nation India and other peripheral nations, especially Pakistan, Bangladesh and Nepal. Therefore, with independence most of these nations planned their economies and trade patterns are isolation from one another. Because of such an unnatural diversion of the intra-regional trade in South Asia, the external economic relations of the regional states have become more or less competitive at the global level and quite negligible at the regional level. While looking at the statistics of intra-regional trade in South Asia, which comes down to less than one per cent of the entire foreign trade of the region, one cannot resist the temptation of suggesting that the negative role played by British imperialism has retarded the intra-regional trade in this region.[21]

However, even if one admits the negative impact of British imperialism on the new patterns of regional co-operation in the economic field, on a realistic analysis, this cannot and need not remain a trend for the future. By virtue of the fact that many of the

21 Dev Dutt paints a rather gloomy picture of the prospects of regional cooperation in South Asia because of the legacy of British imperialism. He poses a question as follows: "With different states political, ideological and struggling at different levels of growth and with several external forces, economic . . . pulling them apart in different directions, what kind of stability or equilibrium can be realized?" He emphasizes several built in defects, mostly those relating to the structure of the economy of the respective countries which have stood in the way of a regional economic co-operation. See Dev Dutt, (ed). *The Himalayan Subcontinent,* New Delhi, 1972, at pp. xx-xxi.

South Asian states are common producers of certain exportable items like tea, jute, and cotton, there is no reason why there should not be increasing co-operation at the international level while marketing their products. Moreover, the complementary nature of certain trade items, as it used to exist in the colonial era, still holds good today to a considerable extent. It will certainly be cheaper for Pakistan to import coal and iron ores from India. In return, that country can export a sizable quantity of cotton and natural gas to India, but of course such intra-regional co-operation depends to a great extent upon the political sagacity and broad-mindedness of the ruling elites of the respective countries.

The Problem of Immigrants

The other socio-economic factor which has proved to be a major variable in the intra-regional relations in South Asia, is the process of immigration by the people of one country to another during the heyday of British rule in search of better living conditions. Moreover, with the departure of the British, when the sub-continent was partitioned, millions of people belonging to the Hindu and Muslim communities, were uprooted from their hearths and had to be rehabilitated either in Indian or Pakistan. The Herculean task of resettling such a vast multitude of human beings and the recovery of claims made by refugees from both countries resulted in a lot of misunderstanding and mutual discord between India and Pakistan. Primarily speaking, the intra-regional relations in South Asia are largely determined by the attitude of both India and Pakistan towards each other and their stand on major regional and international issues.

In addition to the mounting intra-regional tension caused by problems of refugees, was the issue of Indian plantation workers. During the colonial era, a large number of Indian workers moved to the colonial era, a large number of Indian workers moved to the neighboring countries, Burma and Sri Lanka, to serve in British owned industries and plantations. They did not face many difficulties during that time by virtue of the fact that almost all the countries of the region were British colonies and there were hardly any restrictions on free movement within the British Empire. These immigrant Indians having improved their lot by hard work did not like to return to their homeland even after the withdrawal of the

British colonial power and the granting of formal independence to its colonies. But they soon became eyesores to the new indigenous leaders in both Sri Lanka and Burma. They called for the repatriation of these peoples of Indian origin on the plea that their national economies could not afford to absorb so many aliens. On the other hand, India, with its mounting pressure of population and poor state of economy, could not afford to take back all these people. The argument put forward by the Government of India was that almost all these Indians had emigrated during the British rule and had settled abroad for several generations. Naturally this problem became a major bottleneck between the major South Asian nations and other peripheral ones like Sri Lanka and Burma. Therefore it would not be an exaggeration to suggest that the problems connected with the refugees and immigrants, became a negative factor in any major attempt for regional integration in South Asia.

Role of Religion

Along with the socio-economic factors, as already mentioned earlier, the socio-cultural factors like religion and language, play no less an important role in the shaping of intra-regional relations in South Asia. South Asia is a unique region in the sense that it provides a platform for a wide variety of religions and languages. Several religions and languages in the region invariably cut across the territorial boundaries of the nation-states. They have therefore, naturally become important factors in the shaping of foreign policies of the respective states and especially in projecting their outlook towards their South Asian neighbors[22]. Let us then look at the relevance of religion and language in the intra-regional relations in South Asia.

It is common knowledge that the people in the Indian sub-continent and its adjacent areas are basically religious by temperament. Religion plays a prominent role in their political life also. Even if its impact is felt much more at the domestic level; the

---

[22] It has been rightly emphasized by some observers that sovereignty in the international political system certainly overrides socio-cultural loyalties, but in case of the constituent states of South Asia, the socio-cultural forces affect their behavior as sovereign Powers to a very large extent, especially in the intra-regional sphere. See Mathur, *et al.* in S.P. Verma and K.P. Mishra, Ed., *Foreign Policies in South Asia* , at pp. 90-105.

foreign policy formulations by the ruling elites is also heavily loaded with religious sentiments. There is no denying the fact that the "strikingly different social values, institutions and patterns of behavior" of different nations in South Asia are rooted in their diverse religious traditions.[23] Besides, what is equally striking is that one can trace religious pluralism both at the regional as well as at the national level. The net result is that the religious majority in one nation becomes a religious minority in the neighboring one. So, logically, the ruling elites in one nation feel concerned for the socio-political status of their fellow-religionists across the border.

While analyzing the relevance of religion in the intra-regional relations in South Asia, its three aspects have been focused[24], these are as follows:

(*i*) religion as a great ideal;

(*ii*) religion as a national identity and

(*iii*) religion as a communal irritant. Broadly speaking, one cannot dispute such an analysis. As a matter of fact a great amount of tension in the intra-regional affairs of South Asia has occurred because of the lack of realization on the part of the ruling elites, especially in Pakistan and Bangladesh, that religion is a great ideal.

So far as the second aspect, i.e. religion as a national symbol is concerned, it is clear that Pakistan and Bangladesh have taken it to the extreme. Islam serves as a sort of national identity for the ruling elites of both these states. The Pakistanis in their overzealous interpretation of the two-nation theory and Pan-Islamism have gone out of the way to cultivate the friendship of the Islamic countries in West Asia and South East Asia. But as a matter of contrast, so far as Pakistan's relations with other nations of South Asia with the exception of India, is concerned, Islamic ideology hardly plays any role. On the other hand, the ruling elites in Islamabad have left no stone unturned to realign as many peripheral nations in South Asia as possible against India. In that respect, they are guided by utilitarian considerations.

---

23 For details see Denald Eugene Smith Ed., *South Asian Politics and Religion,* Princeton, 1966.

24 Mathur *et al.* in Verma and Misra Ed., at p. 95-6.

The third aspect, i.e. religion as a communal irritant, is perhaps more relevant while looking at the neighborhood diplomacy of the major South Asian nation (India) with its peripheral neighbors and vice versa. Whenever a communal riot occurs in one of these nations, its impact is felt beyond the international boundaries. The Pakistanis or Bangladeshis feel greatly concerned whenever there is any large-scale killing of Muslims in a communal riot in India. Similarly the ruling elites in India project a sort of moral responsibility to protect the interest-of-the Hindu minority in both Pakistan and Bangladesh. Even at times some stray cases of anti-Hindu agitation in Sri Lanka have had their simultaneous reaction in India.

In a nutshell, while summing up the relevance of religion in the intra-regional relations in South Asia, the following scenario emerges. Instead of playing a unifying role in this region, its role has been primarily destructive; instead of drawing the people of neighboring nations together, it has taken them apart by fomenting tension and antagonism. But that is mainly due to the narrow and chauvinistic interpretation of religion by most of the leaders of the region. Even India with its cherished ideal of secularism, has not been up to the mark, especially when one looks at the frequent helplessness of the government to give protection to the religious minorities.

Role of Language

The relevance of language in the intra-regional relations in South Asia lies in the fact that two major states (India and Pakistan) are essentially multilingual. Besides, a number of languages are either spoken or understood in more than one country in the region. For instance, Urdu is spoken by a large number of North Indians and by a considerable number of people in South India especially in the areas of the old princely state of Hyderabad. In Pakistan it is recognized as the official language. Bengali is the official language of Bangladesh and is one of the regional languages in India. Nepali, the official language of Nepal, is largely spoken in the Darjeeling district of West Bengal in India. Tamil, one of the regional languages in India, has been recognized also in Sri Lanka as a second language. So, on the whole, one notices a unique feature in this region, where international boundaries do not necessarily coincide with the linguistic boundaries. Moreover, one hardly notices the co-relation of any religion to a particular linguistic group.[25]

Because of the colonial legacy, the elites in South Asia speak or understand English. Of course English has been replaced by a native language for all official purposes in a number of states in the region. However, a few of them have retained English as an alternate official language.

Because of the overlapping of' some languages in the South Asian states, one often notices concern of the leaders of one nation for the recognition and upliftment of a particular language in the Pakistan, because of the fact that Urdu has been recognized as its official language, its ruling elites have always supported any move for its upliftment in India. Again, mainly because Bengali is spoken by a large segment of the Indian population, its leaders used to support the people of East Bengal, in undivided Pakistan, in their movement for the official recognition of Bengali as a national language.

Although the Government of India has not expressed any overt sympathy on the status and grievances of the Tamil minority in Sri Lanka, by and large, the people of Tamil Nadu have been largely concerned at the discrimination and unfair treatment meted out to the Indian Tamils in Sri Lanka. The process of granting Sri Lankan citizenship to some of them and repatriating the rest to India, has been unfortunately very slow and has remained a major bottleneck in Indo-Sri Lanka relations.

Another instance of language playing a negative role in the intraregional relations in South Asia can be noted in Nepal's special concern for the protection of Nepali language in the Darjeeling district of West Bengal, even though it falls within the exclusive domestic jurisdiction of India.

All the above mentioned examples are likely to intervene indirectly in the internal affairs of a neighbor. And obviously it has left a negative impact in the intra-regional relations in South Asia. However, such a negative pull can be converted into a positive force, provided the leaders of the region, while looking back to a common linguistic culture, can join hands in certain co-operative ventures.

---

[25] Ibid., p. 97.

One can trace similar interaction between some of the Latin American countries with some of the nations of Western Europe based on identity of language. Such a cultural affinity based on language cannot of course be treated as a universal principle.

External Factors Shaping Foreign Policy

National interest has different connotations in different nations of the world. However, without entering into that controversy, for the present analysis "the protection of territorial integrity and political independence,"[26] would be taken as the criteria.

Keeping such a broad perspective in mind, when one looks at the application of the concept of national interest by the leaders of South Asia, one often comes across some local variations. To the Indians, it means the provision of "an economic and secular base to their infant democracy." As far as the Pakistanis are concerned, the Islamic ideology has got to be emphasized for the defense of its national interest. For the land-locked buffer state of Nepal, it is not only linked with unrestricted transit facility for its economic development but also to the defense of its political sovereignty by maintaining the so-called equidistance between India and China. For the small island republic of Sri Lanka, it is in its national interest to assert its identity in the periphery of a big neighbor with whom it has centuries-old ties.

Keeping such diverse national interpretations on national interest in mind, it becomes easier for an analyst to look at the mutual behavior of South Asian states towards one another. A broader analysis can be possible in their common outlook on the region and the world at large. Any divergence in their regional and international outlook can also be easily focused.

As has been emphasized earlier, while looking at the mutual behavior of South Asian states towards one another, the influence of

---

26 The late Jawaharlal Nehru gave two interpretations to the concept of national interest. The first one relates to a rather narrow national interest, and most people see it that way. The second one being a long term view of national interest, may lead to the conclusion that a country's national interest is served by extending the hand of friendship to other nations, and by World Peace. See Michael Brecher, *New States of Asia* (London, 1961), p. 204. See also for a wider assessment of national interest, a Appadorai in Varma and Mishra, at p. 18.

the so-called "intrusive system"[27] cannot be ignored. In fact its role is more or less complementary to those of the socio-economic and sociocultural linkages.

A study of the role of the major global Powers, which are otherwise treated as intrusive Powers, is necessary to understand the four pattern variables, as identified by Cantori. These are cohesion, communication, level of power and structure of relations.[28]

In reference to the first variable, it has been suggested that it is rather difficult on the part of the external Powers to create social cohesion. As a matter of fact, such a situation is generally dependent on three major factors, i.e., timing, local conditions and the degree of primacy of the concerned global Power. A comparative analysis of five loosely identified subordinate systems indicates that the Spanish and the Portuguese, as colonizers, were quite successful in stimulating social cohesion in the Latin American region. On the other hand, in Southeast Asia, especially in the mainland, the major global Powers have used the existing atomism and have failed to promote cohesive elements.

Now, while keeping such an observation in mind, if one looks at the South Asian region, even though it was almost entirely colonized by Britain, because of a keen competition amongst major global Powers to increase their spheres of influence, cohesion in a literal sense hardly exists. On the other hand, the region continues to remain tense and volatile. Therefore, one more or less tends to agree

---

[27] The "intrusive system" normally indicated the politically significant involvement of major external Powers in the international relations of a subordinate system. Politically significant involvement primarily denotes the following. (i) participation of external Powers in the regional balance of power by virtue of their Possession of a colony; (ii) transfer of economic and military aid which in place of being confined to commercial objectives is often attached with a 'political string' and (iii) military alliance, troop commitment or any agreement which cause the external Power to undertake military intervention. See for details, Louis J. Cantori and Steven L. Spiegel, "International Regions: A Comparative Approach to Five Subordinate Systems", *International Studies Quarterly* Detroit, Michigan (Special issue on International Subsystems), Vol. 13, no. 14, December 1969, pp. 376-8.

[28] ibid., pp. 376-8.

with Cantori's proposition that where a single Power is dominant within a region, cohesion can be encouraged; where the Super Powers are competing for their spheres of influence in a particular region, their effect upon cohesion is largely negative.

While looking at the second variable, communication, one is again confronted with contrasting scenarios among different regions. For instance, almost all aspects of communication in Western Europe is controlled by the United States as an intrusive Power. On the other hand, as Cantroi rightly perceives, in the West Asian and Southeast Asian regions, because of keen rivalries amongst the major global Powers and partly because of a retarded economic growth, there is hardly any region-wide communication network. South Asia more or less falls into the latter category.

As regards the third variable, the level of power, it is again proposed that it is easier for the "intrusive Powers" to raise the level of military and motivational elements, than to raise the material elements of power.[29] However, it must be emphasized that over-zealous participation of an external global Power in raising the military capability of a weak and volatile region, can be counter-productive in the long-run. To cite a single instance from the South Asian region, Pakistan has received substantial support in terms of strategic weapons from the United States and China. But as a consequence of that, rather than introduce a healthy political climate in South Asia, it has brought about a lot of tension and instability.

Structure of relations, as the last variable, is more or less analogous to level of power, It has been observed that in case of the Southeast Asian and West Asian regions, the primary effect of the intrusive Powers has been to exacerbate conflict, whereas in the case of. Western Europe and Latin America, the dominant influence by

---

[29] Citing the case of Western Europe as one extreme, Cantori rightly suggests that under the impact of American assistance by such means as the Marshall Plan and NATO, the intrusive Power participation is almost complete during the post-war period. On the other hand, as he adds, in all other identified region of the world, the effects of intrusive Power participation have been less consistent and the objectives have been more complex. See ibid. If one looks at the South Asian region, Cantnori's later generalization becomes more or less applicable.

United States has so far proliferated the means of co-operation. South Asia generally fits into the second scenario, as the involvement of major global Powers has further accentuated conflicts in the region.

Although Cantori's theorization on the impact of "intrusive Powers" on several regions of the world may not always be accepted in entirety, it certainly deserves the attention of scholars working on international relations. One of his propositions suggests that the "intrusive Powers" are relatively weak in their ability to alter social cohesion and only slightly stronger with respect to economic cohesion.[30] Their major efforts are usually most effective in building political and organizational cohesion. While looking at the South Asian region, there is hardly any problem as regards the applicability of the earlier part of the above proposition. But so far as the effect of major global Powers on the organizational and political cohesion of the above-mentioned region is concerned, one finds an altogether different scenario. It is hereby suggested that global Powers by their meddling and muddling in the affairs of South Asia, have rather stalled any move for organizational and political cohesion.

His second proposition is that when nation-states in a subordinate system distinctively lack internal communication, intrusive Powers tend to concentrate on the domestic arena and support a few regional projects. However, it sounds inappropriate in case of South Asia, as in this region, with a very poor state of internal communication. The major Powers have extensively participated in either the internal communication process or in any worth-while regional venture. Although China has got involved in both Pakistan and Nepal in building highways in some of the sensitive areas, it has been generally motivated by its desire to browbeat India, a regional Power.

In the next proposition, it is suggested that in terms of level of power, when "intrusive Powers" are in competition, military aid and motivational influence tend to have more political relevance. Although such a scenario can be envisaged in several regions of the

30 Ibid.

world, in the South Asian subcontinent, there is hardly any possibility of one external Powers dominating. So, naturally, military aid by the external Powers instead of solving any political crises within the region, has a tendency to accentuate them.

In his final proposition, Cantori rightly believes that intrusive Powers are often as important in limiting conflict and even, on occasion, encouraging co-operation as they are in intensifying strife.[31] However, he fails to identify the different responses in the developed and the developing regions towards the involvement of major global Powers in their affairs. Moreover he does not take into account such a situation, when the major global Powers have a tacit understanding not to go beyond a particular point while interfering in a regional dispute.

Although one comes across a few attempts by scholars and journalists on the role of major global Powers in the affairs of the South Asian region, these do not present an all-comprehensive and balanced picture.[32] Their generalizations are at best value-loaded and inconclusive. While taking into account the domestic milieu in South Asia and the interplay of global Powers in different regions, the following broad generalizations emerge. These could be tested in the light of the present socio-economic and political climate in South Asia. The major global Powers, for the purpose of our enquiry, are the United States, Soviet Union and the People's Republic of China.

Until the liquidation of British imperialism in the sub-continent, this region was largely under the sphere of influence of one major

---

31 Ibid.

32 Zafar Imam in his attempt the interplay of global Powers in the affairs of South and Southeast Asia has confused a number of issue areas and has wrongly assumed that China is mainly responsible for brining of tri-polarity in this region. But one is in agreement with his presentation that the states of the region being motivated by a sense of intense nationalism, try to promote their national interest and this process generally comes into conflict with the institutionalization of major outside Powers. For details see Zafar Imam, *World Power in South and South East Asia* (New Delhi, 1975) pp. 217-8. See also Devi Dutt Ed., *The Himalayan Sub-continent*, New Delhi, 1972 at p. xxvi and M.L. Chopra, "South Asia and its Strategic Environment" in *U.S.I. Journal,* New Delhi, July-September 1977, pp. 205-06.

global Power. But soon after Britain's loss of major Power status and its formal declaration of granting Independence to the region, the rivalries of the United States, Soviet Union and Communist China to make their presence in the region became evident. In other words, there was a competition to increase their spheres of influence in South Asia.

As a corollary to the first, the factors responsible for the involvement of major global Powers in South Asia are mainly as follows: narrow and intense nationalism, urgent need for economic development, domestic instability in the South Asian periphery, and common suspicions of the peripheral nations against any hegemony by the core nation-India.

Another basic objective of the major global Powers has been to perpetuate their national interests, which is largely determined by their security perceptions. Their commitment to a particular ideology has receded to the background while trying to increase their sphere of influence in this region.

Fourth, the major interests of outside global Powers in South Asia converge at certain point and diverge at others. These interests, as aptly described by an analyst[33] are "crisis-management by which any conflagration in the region would be prevented from escalation, low-profile presence and assurance that none of them [global powers] assumed a hegemonistic stature in South Asia and no regional Power becomes dominant."

Finally, as a result of major involvement of global powers in the intra-regional relations in South Asia, the regional actors have very limited options at the regional and international levels. In fact, their degree of maneuverability and freedom of choice are limited to the extent they are dependent on the external Powers, both economically and politically.

The following table shows the political trends in the countries of the region which help us to understand the effectiveness and nature of the political regimes in this region.

---

[33] S.D. Muni (1979), p. 205-6.

Table 3.0 : Bangladesh: Regimes, Policies, and Outcomes

	Major events	Policy Regime Characterization	Policy Regime	Outcomes
1971	Independence	(1971-82) Recovery and Reconstruction Amidst Political Turmoil	State Controlled Economy (ISI)	FFW and VGF started Priority for population
1974	Change of Regime Famines Military Coup d'état		-	DFKs set up NPAs Privatization
		Partial deregulation in second half of 1970s Liberalization Private Sector led development		
1980		(1980-2 to 1988-9) Authoritarian; slow growth with growing macroeconomic instability	Continued inward orientation Authoritarian, illegitimate govt. Crony capitalism Massive debt deficit	First wave of privatization Emergence of NGOs as conduits of developments services
1988	Flood			
1989		(1989-90 to 1992-3) Crisis driven economic reforms and formation of favourable initial condition	SAF ESAF Rapid liberalization Unified exchange rate	Creeping devaluation
1993	Continued political instability	(1993-4 to 1999-2000) Higher growth and faster social development	Liberalization and outward orientation Emphasis on agriculture and rural development Strong emphasis on NGOs.	
1998	Severe flood			
2000				

Note: FFW (Food for Works); VGF (Vulnerable Group Feeding); DFI (Development Financial Institution); NPA (Non-Performing Assets); SAF (Structural Adjustment Facility); ESAF (Extended Structural Adustment Facility); 1983-4; *1981-91; **1991-2000.

Source : Kirit S. Parekh (ed.), *Explaining Growth in South Asia,* Oxford University Press, Oxford, 2002.

Table 3.1 : India: Regimes, Policies, and Outcomes

	Major events	Policy Regime Characterization	Policy Regime	Prime Ministers
1947	Independence, partition and large scale riots and migrations			
1950	Constitution	Purposive central planning initiated	Congress Party Government	Jawaharlal
1957	Foreign exchange			
1960		Heavy industry first strategy Public Sector to dominate		
1962	Border conflicts with China			
1964	Nehru's death			Lal Bahadur Shastri
1965	Conflict v. Pakistan			
1966	Shastri's death			Indira Gandhi
1970	War with Pakistan First Oil Shock	Strengthening of ISI Strategy Nationalization of Banks		
1975	Emergency declared	MRTP		
1977	Election		Janata Dal	Morarji Desai/ Charan Singh
1980	Second Oil Shock Election	Some industry and trade liberalization	Congress	Indira Gandhi
1984	Indira Gandhi assassinated			Rajiv Gandhi
1989	Election	Janata Dal	V.P. Singh / Chandrasekhar	
1991	Election	Deregulation, Liberalization	Congress	Narashimha Rao
1996	Election		Janata Dal	Deva Gawda / I.K. Gujaral
1998			BJP	A.B. Vajpayee

Note: FERA (Foreign Exchange Regulation Act); MRTP (Monopolies and Restrictive Trade Practices Commission).

Source : Kirit S. Parekh (ed.), *Explaining Growth in South Asia,* Oxford University Press, Oxford, 2002.

Table 3.2 : Nepal: Regimes, Policies, and Outcomes

	Political system	Policies
1966-80	Autocratic panchayat systems with absolute monarchy	Vigorous development planning Expansion of public sector ISI Centralization No transparency or accountability No participation of citizens No right to information scope Scope to misuse funds
1981-90	Liberal panchayat system	Liberal trade, industrial, and financial policies Initiation of outward oriented economic policy Basic involvement of private sector Forex control eased Sixth plan (1981-5) focused on basic needs Economic Stabilization programme 1985 SAP in 1987
1991-2000	Multi-party democracy	Economic liberalization, privatization ESAP in 1992 Liberalization of trade, industry, and transport sector Deregulation Current account convertibility Market determined exchange rate Financial deregulation Administered prices withdrawn Agri-input subsidies eliminated Food subsidy declined to 0.2% of GDP in 2000 from 2% in 1990

Note: (1) SAP (Structural Adjustment Policy);
(2) ESAP (extended Structural Adjustment Policy).

Source : Kirit S. Parekh (ed.), *Explaining Growth in South Asia,* Oxford University Press, Oxford, 2002.

Table 3.3 : Pakistan: Regimes, Policies and Outcomes

	Events	Policy Regime	Government
1947	Independence		
1948	Jinnah's death		
1951	Assassination of Liaquat Ali Khan	1950-8 Industries protected Agri. neglected Rupee devalued in 1955 Many controls	
1956	First Constitution		6 PMs 3 Governor Generals
1958	Military coup, Martial law, Constitution abrogated	1958-70 Strict controls on price, profit Price control dismantled Sound macro management Promote industries Incentives Tax benefits, etc. Protection	President Ayub Khan Basic democracy
1970	First Election with adult franchise		Gen. Yahya Khan
1971	Bangladesh created	1970-9	Z. Bhutto as (Martial Law) administrator of civilian govt. of PPP till 1973
1973	New Constitution oil shock	Nationalization of Banks, insurance and many industries controls on trade unions protected	
1980	Election, Military takeover, suspended Constitution	1980-9 Decentralization Deregulation Liberalization of industry and agriculture Widening deficit funded by borrowing New HYV cotton introduced	Gen. Zia ul Haq
1990	Party based election	1990-9 Liberalization Tariff reduction Exports promotion EPZs	Democracy Benazir Dismissal of 4 elected governments $8\frac{1}{2}$ years
2000	Military coup		Gen. Musharraf removes Nawaz Sharif in 1999, takes over

Note: EPZ (Export Promotion Zone)

Source : Kirit S. Parekh (ed.), *Explaining Growth in South Asia,* Oxford University Press, Oxford, 2002.

Table 3.4 : Sri Lanka: Regimes, Policies, and Outcomes

	Events	Policy Regime	Government
1947	Independence		UNP Govt.
1952	Election	1947-56 Colonial Free Market Economy (CFME) Continued with FME	UPP Govt.
1956	Election	1956-77	SLFP led Coalition
1959	Bandaranaike assassinated		
1960 March	Major turning point caretaker government	Regulated Economy ISI Strategy (1956-65)	UNP led Coalition
1960 July	Election		SLEF
1965	Election	Partial and gradual liberalization (1965-70)	UNP led Coalition
1970	Election	Intensification of ISI and state intervention (1970-7)	SLFP left wing coalition (UF)
1977	Election Political Reforms	Post 1977	UNP
1980	Major turning point	Liberalization export oriented strategy From control to liberalism in economic sphere From liberalism to control in political sphere Private sector given a major role and encouraged	Democracy Benazir
1989	Election		UNP
1990	Political reform		
1993	Premadasa assassinated		
1994	Election	Continued with liberalization export oriented policies	SLFP led people's alliance (PA)
2000	Election		SLFP led people's alliance (PA)
2001	Election	UNP led coalition (UNF)	

Note: UNP (United National Party); SLFP (Sri Lanka Freedom Party); MEP (Mahajana Eksath Peramuana); UF (United Front); PA (People's Alliance), UNF (United National Front).

The percentages refer to growth rate over the period

Source : Kirit S. Parekh (ed.), *Explaining Growth in South Asia,* Oxford University Press, Oxford, 2002.

4

SAARC
Historical Background

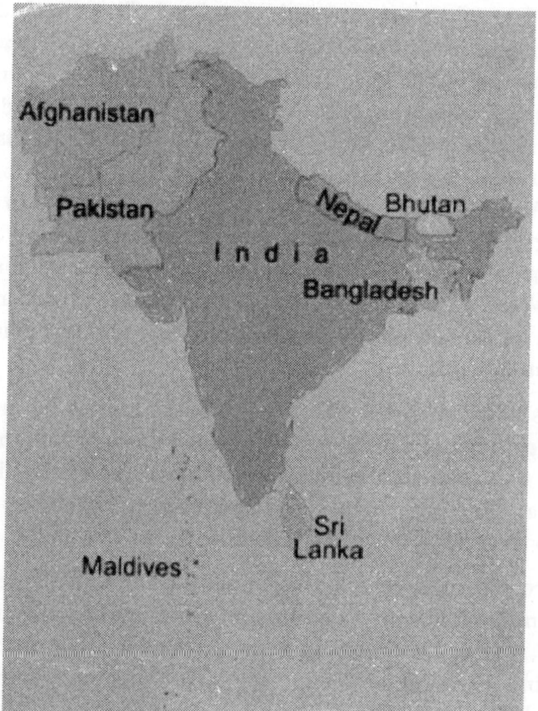

Map of Members Of SAARC

Flag of SAARC

Scholarly interest in regionalism has been reflected in South Asia, due to the uniqueness of the South Asian features of regionalism. Latest works on this region are far beyond the earlier literature on regionalism, by way of quality as well as quantity. Fields such as religion, history, economics and comparative politics are inescapable in the study of South Asian regionalism.

Regional organizations such as the EEC and the Association of South East Asian Nations (ASEAN) had an implicit function in containing the spread of communism and this common goal provided a context for achieving mutual benefits.[1] They excluded their primary antagonists in favor of uniting with old and newly found allies. These regional organizations were therefore exclusivist in keeping out enemies through the erection of trading and military barriers to rivals outside these alliances. As these rivals also formed their own regional organizations, such as the Council for Mutual Economic Aid (COMECON), the world became divided into mutually exclusive groups which served to reduce tensions among allies but did nothing to reduce tensions among antagonistic regional blocs. The East-West and North-South divides remained and may even have been accentuated by regional integration schemes which excluded outside nations.

In this way, virtually the whole world came to be included in assorted regional alliances which formed in antagonism to each other. The one area that remained without a regional alliance was South Asia. This was because its primary antagonists were not external to the region but were within it.

The creation of a regional organization for South Asia in 1985, amid all antagonisms was unique and went against the traditional pattern of regional alliance formation. For this reason there was considerable skepticism about the prospects of SAARC at its formation. From the outset there were assertions that its failure was inevitable due to the lack of a common security perception.[2] Its subsequent track record, while modest, was nevertheless impressive, given the on-going tensions in South Asia and the achievements of

---

[1] S.D. Muni, 'South Asian Regional Cooperation: Evolution and Prospects', *IDSA Journal,* Vol. 19, No. 1, July-September 1986, p. 122.

[2] William T. Tow, "Subregional Security Cooperation in the Third World", Lynne Rienner Publishers, Boulder, 1990, pp. 7-8.

other Third World alliances. 'Despite ASEAN being claimed as a relatively successful organization regional cooperation has not done much better in Southeast Asia than in South Asia, and in some respects has lagged much behind".[3]

That enemies rather than allies were brought together in SAARC makes similarities with other regional alliances minimal. The basic contrasts between SAARC and other regions invited comparative analysis, and revealed a number of pre-requisites of a successful integration. However, the 'lack of progress towards development of any coherent theoretical or even descriptive framework' of regional integration means that no comprehensive political theory exists that can adequately explain the South Asian integration phenomenon.[4] If regional organization in South Asia can be an effective forum for the reduction of tensions, this experience could provide an example for the incorporation of enemies within regional organizations in other conflict zones.

THE BIRTH OF THE SAARC

The idea of regional cooperation among South Asian countries is not new. Such cooperation has been taking place both bilaterally, as well as multilaterally, under the umbrella of various fora, such as the ESCAP, Non-Aligned Movement and the Common-wealth. These are, however, broad groupings, which do not touch specifically on the needs and potentialities of cooperation in the South Asian region. Only a regional forum or association comprising the member countries of the region can be expected to meet this objective. While sub-regional associations have proliferated in practically all the regions of the world, this had so far been conspicuous by its absence in South Asia.[5]

---

[3] Pran Chopra, "SAARC and ASEAN: Comparative Analysis of Structures and Aims", in Bhabani Sen Gupta (ed.), *"SAARC-ASEAN: Prospects and Problems of Inter-regional Cooperation"*, South Asian Publishers, Delhi, 1988, p. 22.

[4] Barry Buzan, 'Framework for Regional Security Analysis', in Barry Buzan and Gowher Rizvi (eds.), *South Asian Insecurity and the Great Powers*, London: Macmillan, London, 1986, p. 7.

[5] M.S. Aggwani and Ashwini K. Ray (eds.); *"South Asia, Stability and Regional Cooperation"*, Man and Development Publications, Chandigarh, p. 17.

Following the initiative of the late Gen. Zia-Ur-Rahman of Bangladesh, certain arrangements have been hammered out for regional cooperation in South Asia in a number of sectors. The details of these sectors for an integrated programme of action have been worked out after a series of meetings of South Asian Regional Cooperation (SAARC) at various levels culminating in the two foreign minister's meetings at New Delhi and at Villigili (Male) in August 1983 and July 1984, respectively. In these meetings significant decisions regarding institutional aspects of SAARC were also taken up, the most important of which was the holding of the first SAARC summit meeting in Dhaka in the last quarter of 1985 so that the regional arrangements would have sanction at the highest level.[6]

Being defined the need for regional cooperation with adequate safeguards; the working paper identified eleven possible areas of cooperation. These were

(1) Telecommunication
(2) Meteorology
(3) Transport
(4) Shipping
(5) Tourism
(6) Agricultural/Rural sector
(7) Joint ventures
(8) Market promotion in selected commodities
(9) Scientific and technological cooperation
(10) Education and technical cooperation and
(11) Cultural cooperation. A short explanation on each of these subjects was given in the working paper.

The origin Secretaries of South Asian States had met three times. At the invitation of Sri Lanka the Foreign Secretaries of seven South Asian countries namely Bangladesh, Bhutan, India, Maldives, Nepal, Pakistan and Sri-Lanka met in Colombo for the first time from April 21 to 23, 1981, to consider the Bangladeshi proposal as outlined in the working paper. The second meeting was held in

---

6 Bhabai Sen Gupta; *Regional Cooperation and Development in South Asia*, South Asian Publishers, New Delhi, p. 1.

Kathmandu on November 2-4, 1981 and the third one in Islamabad on August 7-9, 1982.

The choice of areas of co-operation in the Bangladeshi paper was based on the premise that a beginning should be made in the economic field. It also stipulated that co-operation should aim at maximum overlapping of function. The Bangladesh's Foreign Secretary expressed the hope in the first meeting that from the beginnings already made one could progressively enlarge cooperation to wider areas and the process could become self-generating.

In marked contrast to this, the Foreign Minister of Sri-Lanka, in his inaugural speech at the first meeting of foreign secretaries, commanded a more comprehensive approach to cooperation, encompassing political as well as economic matters.

Pakistan proposed that in the beginning, regional cooperation should be limited to only four out of the eleven areas identified in the Bangladeshi working paper.

India's stand on the scope for regional cooperation appears to be nearer to that of Bangladesh. While refraining from making any reference to political or security objectives. It laid stress on expanding cooperation in cultural, infrastructural, scientific and technological fields as also in relation to global negotiations with the developed countries. India's role had been significant in determining new areas of cooperation. As most of these had been earlier indicated in the Bangladesh working paper, a convergence of views between the two countries was indicated.

India's position on institutionalization of regional co-operation converged with that of Pakistan. The Indian representative sounded notes of caution and warned that the selecting up of an institutional framework of association among South Asian nations was premature. He suggested that priority should be given to exploration of the areas of co-operation.[7]

In the third meeting of Foreign Secretaries, the Bangladesh representative emphasized that a positive basis for co-operation within a viable operational framework had emerged in South Asia. "What was needed now", he stated, "is an affirmation for launching this comprehensive programme of action at the political level". He

[7] Pran Chopra (1988) at pp. 18, 22, 25.

was strongly in favor of convening a ministerial level meeting at an early date. As he put it, "only a meeting at a high political level could spark the imagination of the people of South Asia and generate sustained support to make the concept a reality. The commitment made at Kathmandu, to hold the ministerial level meeting in 1982 needed to be honored, he emphasized".[8]

Maldives and Nepal felt that second meeting of foreign secretaries could be held before the proposed one at the level meeting would be a source of great encouragement and strength of the programme of regional cooperation. It could provide political guidelines to expedite the process. Though favoring an early meeting of foreign minister, Nepal took a flexible stand in regard to its timing. The Bhutanese representative also endorsed the line that a meeting of the foreign ministers might expedite progress in regional cooperation.

It thus appears that, while two of the smaller South-Asian States, namely Bangladesh and Sri-Lanka had been anxious to hasten the pace of SAARC, India, and to some extent, Pakistan had been urging restraint and caution against hasty decisions. Nepal, Bhutan and Maldives, while generally toeing the lines set by Bangladesh and Sri-Lanka, had been less vocal. Pakistan's rigid attitude with respect to the areas of cooperation at the first meeting appears to have become somewhat flexible by the end of the second and third meetings.[9]

ISSUES BARRED FROM THE SCOPE OF SAARC

In order to avoid involving SAARC in the bilateral and political issues of the regions the charter provides that bilateral and contentious issues should be excluded from SAARC activities. To compound the issue further a rather complicated clause, relating to unanimous decision making being mandatory is added in the charter. The above clause was motioned in the charter keeping in view the unequal size and potential of the member countries. That the big might not dominate the small in the decision making was the reason behind the acceptance of the principle of unanimity. As S.D. Muni, has observed, "the principle of decision on the basis of

---

[8] For further details see : Indra Nath Mukerji; *Attitude and Perceptions*, p. 26.

[9] William T. Tow (1990) at pp. 26, 28.

unanimity gives a near veto to any member to refuse that aspect or area it considers incompatible with its vital national interests".[10]

PHASES IN THE EVOLUTION OF SAARC

Looking at SAARC in retrospect, the group felt that the association had passed through two distinct phases. The first phase was the preparatory phase, based on a gradual and step by step approach to initiating regional cooperation, mostly in non-controversial and peripheral areas such as Confidence-Building Measures. The Integrated Programme of Action (IPA) is an example of such an approach. It was during this phase that the minimum necessary institutional mechanisms were put in place for the operationalization of a limited number of activities under the SAARC framework.

In second half of its evolution, SAARC moved into the expansionary phase, when regional cooperation was expanded both in the social and core economic sectors. Many major commitments with far reaching implications for the region, were undertaken, including the coming into force of the South Asian Preferential Trading Agreement (SAPTA). However, the member States did not nest in out these commitments to ensure the expected level of effectiveness. As a consequence, a disjunction developed between the decisions taken by the association and their implementation.[11]

The objectives of the SAARC is embedded in its charter which outlines the welfare of the peoples of South Asia and to improve their quality of life, the respect for the principles of sovereign equality, territorial integrity, political independence, non-interference in internal affairs to each other countries and to cooperate with international and regional organizations with similar aims and purposes. The Charter also directs the heads of the member-nations to meet once a year or more, if considered deemed necessary by the members.

---

[10] S.D. Muni; *SAARC: Building regionalism from Below*, Asian Survey, 1985, Vol. 25, No. 4, p. 399.

[11] Mahendra P. Lama; South Asian Survey, Sage Publications, Jan.-June, 2001, Vol. 8, No. 1, New Delhi, pp. 137-138.

AN OUTLINE OF SAARC'S CHARTER

The SAARC was established in 1985 at the first SAARC summit held in Dhaka, Bangladesh, even though the idea for a regional grouping of South Asian nations had been mooted in 1980. Currently, SAARC is made up of Bangladesh, Bhutan, India, Maldives, Nepal, Pakistan and Sri Lanka. The countries of this region are afflicted with poverty, underdevelopment, low levels of production, unemployment and pressure of population, which call for a common outlook on socio-economic development for the whole region. Further twelve elements have been identified for the intertwined crisis of South Asia :

(*a*) Deep seated poverty;

(*b*) Rapid population growth;

(*c*) Low-per capital income;

(*d*) High unemployment;

(*e*) Unsatisfactory human development;

(*f*) Inadequate supply of human resources;

(*g*) Environmental degradation;

(*h*) Sluggish private sector;

(*i*) Inefficient public sector;

(*j*) Slow growth of non-agricultural economy;

(*k*) Energy crisis; and

(*l*) Terrorism.

SAARC's main goal is to accelerate economic and social development in member States through joint action in certain agreed areas of cooperation. The potential of countries in the SAARC region is vast and yet much of it is untapped. There are some identifiable reasons for this:

- Conflicts within and between member States.
- Rigid and inflexible economic policies.
- Unnecessary bureaucracy and rampant corruption.

However, many improvements are now taking place as a pragmatic approach towards solving economic and social troubles gains acceptance among the member States. After all, there are many more good reasons for promoting regional cooperation.

- Reducing danger of external intervention.
- Reducing political, military and economic tensions within the region.
- Expanding trade and other economic ties within a much larger market formed by the reduction and elimination of trade barriers.
- Coordinating measures for mutual benefit in diverse areas ranging from poverty eradication to environment protection, and
- Improving the already close cultural links that exist among the South Asian States.

To date, South Asia remains a symbol of eastern promise-golden opportunities yet to be realized fully. SAARC may be the catalyst that helps to promote fulfillment of the dream.

CONSTITUTION OF THE SOUTH ASIAN ASSOCIATION FOR REGIONAL COOPERATION

Preamble

We, the Heads of State or Government of Bangladesh, Bhutan, India, Maldives, Nepal, Pakistan and Sri Lanka;

Desirous of promoting peace, stability, amity and progress in the region through strict adherence to the principles of the UNITED NATIONS CHARTER and NON-ALIGNMENT, particularly respect for the principles of sovereign equality, territorial integrity, national independence, non-use of force and non-interference in the internal affairs of other States and peaceful settlement of all disputes;

Conscious that in an increasingly interdependent world, the objectives of peace, freedom, social justice and economic prosperity are best achieved in the SOUTH ASIAN region by fostering mutual understanding, good neighborly relations and meaningful cooperation among Member States which are bound by history and culture;

Aware of the common problems, interests and aspirations of the peoples of SOUTH ASIA and the need for joint action and enhanced cooperation within their political and economic systems and traditions;

Convinced that regional cooperation among the countries of SOUTH ASIA is mutually beneficial, desirable and necessary for promoting the welfare and improve quality of life of the peoples of the region;

Convinced further that economic, social and technical cooperation among the countries of the SOUTH ASIA would contribute significantly to national and collective self-reliance;

Recognizing that increased cooperation, contacts and exchanges among the countries of the region will contribute to the promotion of friendship and understanding among their peoples;

Recalling the DECLARATION signed by their Foreign Ministers in NEW DELHI on August 2, 1983 and noting the progress achieved in regional cooperation;

Reaffirming their determination to promote such cooperation within an institutional framework:

DO HEREBY AGREE to establish an organization to be known as South Asian Association for Regional Cooperation hereinafter referred to as the Association, with the following objectives, principles, institutional and financial arrangements:

Objectives

The objectives of the Association shall be:

- to promote the welfare of the peoples of South Asia and to improve their quality of life;
- to accelerate economic growth, social progress and cultural development in the region and to provide all individuals the opportunity to live in dignity and to realize their full potentials;
- to promote and strengthen collective self reliance among the countries of South Asia;
- to contribute to mutual trust, understanding and appreciation of one another's problems;
- to promote active collaboration and mutual assistance in the economic, social, cultural, technical and scientific fields;

- to strengthen cooperation with other developing countries;
- to strengthen cooperation among themselves in international forums on matters of common interests; and
- to cooperate with international and regional organizations with similar aims and purposes.

Principles

- Cooperation within the framework of the Association shall be based on respect for the principles of sovereign equality, territorial integrity, political independence, non-interference in the internal affairs of other States and mutual benefit.
- Such cooperation shall not be a substitute for bilateral and multilateral cooperation but shall complement them.
- Such cooperation shall not be inconsistent with bilateral and multilateral obligations.

So far 15 Summits of SAARC have been held.

1st Summit

THE DHAKA DECLARATION

The Dhaka Declaration of the Heads of State or Government of the Member Countries of South Asian Association for Regional Cooperation issued on 8th December 1985.

INTRODUCTION

The President of Bangladesh, the King of Bhutan, the Prime Minister of India, the President of Maldives, the King of Nepal, the President of Pakistan and the President of Sri Lanka met in Dhaka on 7 and 8 December 1985.

The Heads of State or Government underscored the historic significance of their first ever South Asian Summit meeting. They considered it to be a tangible manifestation of their determination to cooperate regionally, to work together towards finding solutions towards their common problems in a spirit of friendship, trust and mutual understanding and to the creation of an order based on mutual respect, equity and shared benefits.

They recognized that periodic meetings at their level were central to the promotion of mutual trust, confidence and cooperation among their countries.

The Heads of State or Government reaffirmed that their fundamental goal was to accelerate the process of economic and social development in their respective countries through the optimum utilization of their human and material resources, so as to promote the welfare and prosperity of their peoples and to improve their quality of life. They were conscious that peace and security was an essential prerequisite for the realization of this objective.

The leaders of the South Asian countries reaffirmed their commitment to the UN Charter and the principles governing sovereign equality of States, peaceful settlement of disputes, non-interference in internal affairs and non-use or threat of use of force against the territorial integrity and political independence of other States. They reiterated that the United Nations constituted the most important forum for the resolution of all issues affecting international peace and security.

They also reaffirmed their deep conviction in the continuing validity and relevance of the objectives of the Non-aligned movement as an important force in international relations.

The Heads of State or Government acknowledged that the countries of South Asia, who constituted one-fifth of humanity, were faced with the formidable challenges posed by poverty, underdevelopment, low levels of production, unemployment and pressure of population compounded by exploitation of the past and other adverse legacies. They felt that, bound as their countries were by many common values rooted in their social, ethnic, cultural and historical traditions, regional cooperation provided a logical response to these problems. They were conscious of their individual and regional strengths, their potential as a huge market, their substantial human and natural resources and the complementarities of their economies. They were confident that with effective regional cooperation, they could make optimum use of these capacities for the benefit of their peoples, accelerate the pace of their economic development and enhance their national and collective self-reliance. They were convinced that their countries, which had made important contributions to the enrichment of human civilization, could together play their due role in international relations and influence decisions which affected them.

The Heads of State or Government emphasised that strengthening of regional cooperation in South Asia required greater involvement of their peoples. They agreed to increase interaction and further promote people-to-people contacts at various levels among their countries. To this end, they decided to take steps to create awareness and public opinion in the region.

The Heads of State or Government welcomed the progress already made in the implementation of the Integrated Programme of Action in the nine mutually agreed areas. They expressed their desire to consolidate and further expand cooperative efforts within an appropriate institutional frame work in a spirit of partnership and equality.

The leaders were convinced that they could effectively pursue their individual and collective objectives and improve the quality of life of their peoples only in an atmosphere of peace and security. In this context, they expressed concern at the deteriorating international political situation. They were alarmed at the unprecedented escalation of arms race particularly in its nuclear aspect. They recognized that mankind today was confronted with the threat of self extinction arising from a massive accumulation of the most destructive weapons ever produced. The arms race intensified international tension and violated the principles of the UN Charter. The leaders called upon the nuclear weapons-states for urgent negotiations for a comprehensive Test Ban Treaty leading to the complete cessation of testing, production and deployment of nuclear weapons. In this connection, they welcomed the recent meeting between President Reagan and General Secretary Gorbachev in Geneva and expressed the hope that the meeting would have a positive effect on international peace and security.

The Heads of State or Government expressed deep concern at the continuing crises in the global economy. They underscored that deteriorating economic and social conditions had seriously retarded developing countries. Sharply falling commodity prices, deterioration in the terms of trade, intensification of protectionist measures, spiralling debt burden and a decline in the flow of external resources, especially concessional assistance, had caused a serious setback to the economic development of the developing countries. These had been compounded by natural disasters and precarious world food security situation affecting developing countries. They also expressed concern over the diminishing capacity of international financial and technical institutions to respond effectively to the needs of the disadvantaged and poorer countries and regretted that the spirit of multilateral cooperation had begun to falter and weaken. This was particularly disturbing in the face of increased interdependence of developed and developing countries and the fact that economic revival of North was closely linked to economic progress in South. They believed that developments during the past decades had clearly demonstrated the structural imbalances and inequities inherent in the existing international economic system and its inadequacy to deal with problems of development.

They strongly urged that determined efforts should be made by the international community towards realization of the goals and targets of the International Development Strategy as well as the Substantial New Programme of Action for the Least Developed Countries. They called for urgent resumption of the North-South dialogue and early convening of an International Conference on Money and Finance for Development with universal participation.

The Heads of State or Government were conscious of the historic importance of the Dhaka Summit and reiterated their conviction that the launching of the South Asian Association for Regional Cooperation (SAARC), which they had established at this meeting, would place regional cooperation on a firm foundation, play an important role in accelerating the pace of economic and social development of their countries, promote the objectives of individual and collective self reliance and further the cause of peace, progress and stability in their region and the world.

The Heads of State or Government of Bhutan, India, Maldives, Nepal, Pakistan and Sri Lanka were deeply appreciative of the exemplary Chairmanship of their Meeting by the President of Bangladesh. They expressed their profound gratitude for the warm and gracious hospitality extended to them by the Government and the people of Bangladesh and for the excellent arrangements made for the meeting.

2nd Summit

THE BANGALORE DECLARATION

The Bangalore Declaration of the Heads of State or Government of the member countries of the South Asian Association for Regional Cooperation issued on November 17, 1986.

INTRODUCTION

The President of Bangladesh, the King of Bhutan, the Prime Minister of India, the President of Maldives, the King of Nepal, the Prime Minister of Pakistan and the President of Sri Lanka assembled at the second SAARC Summit in Bangalore on 16 and 17 November, 1986.

The Heads of State or Government reiterated their desire of promoting peace, stability, amity and progress in the region through strict adherence to the principles of the United Nations Charter and Non-alignment, particularly respect for the principles of sovereign equality, territorial integrity, national independence, non-use of force and non-interference in the internal affairs of other States and peaceful settlement of disputes.

The Heads of State or Government reaffirmed the will of their peoples and Governments to work together in accordance with the SAARC Charter to devise common policies and approaches for finding common solutions to the shared problems that all of them face. They stressed that mutual trust, goodwill and understanding must animate their cooperative effort under SAARC. Progress and prosperity in each country would redound to the benefit of others. This was what constituted the SAARC spirit.

The leaders reaffirmed that the principal goal of SAARC was to promote the welfare of the peoples of South Asia, to improve their quality of life, to accelerate economic growth, social programmes and cultural development in the region and to provide all individuals the opportunity to live in dignity and to realize their full potential.

The Heads of State or Government recalled that the countries of South Asia had been linked by age-old cultural, social and historical traditions. These had led to enriching interaction of ideas, values, culture and philosophies. These commonalities constituted solid foundations for regional cooperation for addressing more effectively the economic and social problems.

The Heads of State or Government recalled that the South Asian Association for Regional Cooperation was the most populous regional grouping in the world. The countries of the region had large, rich and varied human and natural resources. They expressed their determination to achieve the optimum utilization of these resources by intensifying their cooperation, bearing in mind the immense present and potential complementarities among their economies. They recognized that this would require increasing exchange among their countries, on the basis of mutual benefit, of ideas, experience and technology as well as goods and services, which utilize and enhance the productive capacity of each of their countries and build their collective self reliance. They were convinced that the countries of South Asia which had been the cradle of human civilization and culture could, acting together co-operatively and cohesively, once again play their due role in the comity of nations.

The Heads of State or Government reiterated the great importance of the increasing involvement of the people for ensuring the success of regional co-operation. They emphasized the need for promoting greater contacts among the peoples of the region through such action as regular and frequent interchange of scholars, academics, artists, authors, professionals and businessmen as well as facilitation of tourism.

The Heads of State or Government noted with satisfaction that considerable progress had been achieved in the implementation of SAARC Integrated Programme of Action. They expressed their firm commitment to consolidate and streamline further the implementation of the IPA. They agreed that a progressive movement towards more concrete and action-oriented projects and programmes was essential to ensure more tangible benefits from SAARC to the peoples of the region. The Heads of State or Government emphasized the importance of expanding cooperative endeavors under SAARC. They welcomed the establishment of the Technical Committees on Women in Development, and on the Prevention of Drug Trafficking and Drug Abuse.

The Heads of State or Government welcomed the signing of the Memorandum of Understanding on the establishment of the SAARC Secretariat by the Council of Ministers and their decision to locate the Secretariat in Kathmandu and appoint Ambassador Abul Ahsan of Bangladesh as the first Secretary-General of SAARC. They were convinced that the establishment of the Secretariat would assist in the coordination of SAARC activities and more fruitful implementation of its programmes and projects.

The Heads of State or Government recognized that meeting the needs of all children was the principal means of human resources development. Children should, therefore, be given the highest priority in national development planning. The Heads of State or Government underlined the importance of enhancing public consciousness and building a national political consensus on the rights of the children. In this context they called for an early conclusion and adoption of the UN Convention on the Rights of the Child. They subscribed to the goals of universal immunization by 1990, universal primary education, maternal and child nutrition, provision of safe drinking water and adequate shelter before 2000 A.D. They also believed that it should be possible to ensure at the end of the century, that no child need die or be denied development, for reasons of material poverty in the family. They directed the Standing Committee to undertake annual reviews of the situation of children in the SAARC countries, monitoring of programmes and exchange of experience.

The Heads of State or Government agreed that co-operation among SAARC States was vital if terrorism was to be prevented and eliminated from the region. They unequivocally condemned all acts, methods and practices of terrorism as criminal and deplored their impact on life and property, social economic development, political stability, regional and international peace and co-operation. They recognized the importance of the principles laid down in UN Resolution 2625 which among others required that each State should refrain from organizing, instigating, assisting or participating in acts of civil strife or terrorist acts in another State or acquiescing in organized activities within its territory directed towards the commission of such acts.

The Heads of State or Government expressed their concern at the crisis facing the United Nations system. They reiterated their deep commitment to the purposes and principles of the United Nations Charter and their support for and faith in the United Nations as the most important international forum for addressing issues of peace, disarmament and development and an essential instrument for bringing about justice and equity in international political and economic relations. They resolved to concert their efforts in all multilateral fora within the United Nations system to preserve and strengthen the Organization and to prevent erosion of its role, functions and principles.

The Heads of State or Government reiterated their deep commitment to the principles and objectives of the Non-aligned Movement and underlined the historic role the Movement had been playing in strengthening international peace, promoting development, establishing equitable and just economic relations and strengthening international co-operation in all fields. The success of the Harare Summit of the Non-aligned countries was yet another demonstration of the strength and unity of the Movement and the increasing respect that it had come to command in the international community. They affirmed full support for the decisions adopted at the Summit and called for their early implementation.

The leaders of the South Asian countries were convinced that an environment of peace, security and respect for international law was essential for their growth and stability. Unfortunately, this environment had become increasingly adverse for the pursuit of their cherished goals. The international political scene was marred by strife and tension due to Great Power policies and practices of domination and intervention as well as the increased resort to the treat or use of force, aggression, occupation, pressure, economic coercion and interference in flagrant violation of the principles and purposes of the Charter of the United Nations. The arms race, particularly the nuclear arms race, had escalated to a point where it jeopardizes the most fundamental of all human rights - the right to live.

The Heads of State or Government noted with deep disappointment that the promise held out by the Reykjavik Summit could not be realized. They, however, noted with satisfaction that the proposals made at the Summit were still on the table. They expressed the earnest hope that the negotiations would be resumed without delay so that a decisive step could be taken towards realizing the ultimate goal of eliminating nuclear weapons altogether. The Heads of State or government called for the early conclusion of a Comprehensive Test Ban Treaty.

The Heads of State or Government were deeply concerned that the world economy continued to be in the throes of crisis, with particularly harsh and severe consequences for the economies and development prospects and aspirations of the developing countries. They endorsed the Declaration of the SAARC Ministerial Meeting on International Economic Issues held in Islamabad and its analysis of the exceptionally adverse external economic environment which retards the development of the South Asian and other developing countries. These negative factors include depressed commodity prices, rising protectionism, global recession, lower export earnings, net outflow of financial resources from developing countries and an aggravated debt crisis.

The Heads of State or Government noted that the rates of growth in the developed countries had turned out to be much lower than what was earlier projected and that the projection for future growth in these countries was not at all encouraging. They expressed their concern at the implications of these trends for the development prospects of the developing countries. They welcomed the recent recognition by the developed countries that the chronic problems of massive payment imbalances, high interest rates, unstable exchange rates and high unemployment are structural in nature. In view of global interdependence, the co-ordination of macro-economic policies, contemplated at the Tokyo Summit of the seven major industrialized countries, cannot be effective in achieving sustained global economic growth unless it encompasses the developing countries.

The leaders urged that the recent retreat from multilateralism should be urgently reversed through a revival of the North-South dialogue which is responsive to the changed circumstances in the world economy. This must include a process of reform of monetary and financial system, through an International Conference on Money and Finance for Development, and urgent measures for preserving and strengthening the multilateral trading system. In the search for revival of global growth, priority must be accorded to exploiting the vast potential for expanded production, consumption and trade which exists in the developing countries. In all these endeavors, high priority should be accorded to supporting the development of the least developed countries, in particular, through the full and effective implementation of the Substantial New Programme of Action for the Least Developed Countries for the 1980s.

The Heads of State or Government noted with satisfaction that at the SAARC Ministerial Meeting on International Economic Issues a number of priority objectives of the SAARC countries have been identified. These include: enlarged concessional assistance, the doubling in three years of the financial flows for the development of developing countries, amelioration of official debts, trade liberalization, especially in textiles and agriculture, commodity price stabilization, transfer of technology and special treatment for least developed SAARC countries. The Heads of State or Government agreed that the SAARC members should closely and regularly consult and co-operate in relevant international economic conferences and institutions in order to promote the above mentioned objectives. They recognized that an important opportunity in this context would be provided by UNCTAD VII.

The Heads of State or Government were of the view that the forthcoming New Round of Multilateral Trade Negotiations posed a challenge for their countries as well as an opportunity to accelerate their development through the expansion of their exports. They underlined the importance of the effective implementation with immediate effect and continuance until the formal completion of the negotiations, of the commitment to observe a standstill on protectionist measures and to roll these back under multilateral surveillance. They also expected that the principles of transparency and differential and more favorable treatment for the developing countries would be applied systematically and in concrete terms in the negotiations. They decided to concert their positions in these negotiations with a view to deriving maximum benefits from them in accordance with their national objectives and priorities.

The Heads of State or Government expressed their conviction that the Bangalore Summit had helped in consolidating the gains of regional co-operation activities so far undertaken by SAARC while, at the same time, exploring new avenues and possibilities for such co-operation. The Bangalore Summit had made a significant contribution to strengthening and streamlining the institutional basis for such co-operation.

The Heads of State or Government reiterated their determination and will to expand and strengthen their co-operation under SAARC. They underlined their belief that SAARC reflected a resurgence of the South Asian consciousness which had inspired the peoples of this region over several millenia. The leaders expressed their deep conviction that South Asian regional co-operation would not only have a salutary effect on bilateral relations between the countries of the region, but also impart strength and stability to these relations.

The Heads of State or Government of Bangladesh, Bhutan, Maldives, Nepal, Pakistan and Sri Lanka were deeply appreciative of the exemplary manner in which the Prime Minister of India discharged his responsibilities as Chairman of the Meeting. They expressed their profound gratitude for the warm and gracious hospitality extended to them by the Government and people of India and for the excellent arrangements made for the Meeting.

3rd Summit

THE KATHMANDU DECLARATION

The Kathmandu Declaration of the Heads of State or Government of the member countries of the South Asian Association for Regional Cooperation issued on November 4, 1987.

INTRODUCTION

The President of Bangladesh, the King of Bhutan, the Prime Minister of India, the President of Maldives, the King of Nepal, the Prime Minister of Pakistan and the President of Sri Lanka assembled for the Third Summit of the South Asian Association for Regional Cooperation (SAARC) in Kathmandu on 2-4 November, 1987.

The Heads of State or Government recalled with pleasure the launching of SAARC which marked the beginning of a new era of regional cooperation for the promotion of peace and progress, mutual trust and goodwill in South Asia and underlined the importance of annual meetings at their level, as a prime mover, in consolidating and accelerating the pace and process of overall social, economic and cultural development in the region. They renewed their commitment to the SAARC Charter. They reiterated their desire of promoting peace, stability, amity and progress in the region through strict adherence to the principles of the United Nations Charter and Nonalignment, particularly respect for the principles of sovereign equality, territorial integrity, national independence, non-use of force and non-interference in the internal affairs of other States and peaceful settlement of disputes.

The Heads of State or Government emphasized that a fundamental goal of SAARC was to promote the welfare of the peoples of South Asia and to provide them with the opportunity to live in dignity and realize their full potential. They were conscious of the formidable tasks ahead of eradicating poverty, hunger, disease, illiteracy and unemployment and alleviation of environmental degradation facing South Asia today. They were convinced that the peoples and governments of South Asia could, acting in unison, surmount these challenges.

The Heads of State or Government expressed their faith in and commitment to the principles and purposes enshrined in the United Nation Charter. They further believed that the United Nations has an important role to play in promoting universal trust, understanding and concerted actions for the attainment of lasting peace, global development and general disarmament. They reiterated their concern at the crisis facing the United Nations. They expressed their commitment to the multilateral negotiating process and called upon all states to help strengthen the UN system. They reaffirmed their belief that SAARC will reinforce this process by promoting South Asian cooperation.

The Heads of State or Government also reaffirmed their deep commitment to the principles and objectives of the Non-Aligned Movement. They underscored the validity of its philosophy and the historic role the Movement has been playing and continues to play in strengthening world peace and harmony as well as in promoting development with justice and equity. They also noted that institutionalization and strengthening of regional cooperation in South Asia had further nurtured the spirit of South-South cooperation on the basis of mutual respect, equity and common benefit. They expressed satisfaction over the result of the Ministerial Conference on Nonaligned Countries held in Pyongyang in June 1987 and urged the Non-aligned and other developing countries to take action to implement effectively the Pyongyang Declaration and Plan of Action on South-South Cooperation.

The Heads of State or Government recognized that the external environment had a critical bearing on the development of the economies of the South Asian Region. They noted with deep concern that growth in the world economy had again slowed down with adverse consequences for South Asia and other developing countries, especially for the least developed and landlocked countries. They observed that equitable participation of the developing countries in international trading and economic systems and in arrangements for the coordination of global macro economic policies was essential for enhancing prospects and performance of the world economy.

The South Asian leaders noted that the world economy had long suffered from a structural disequilibrium. The pace of global economic expansion had further slowed down. The downward trend in commodity prices had continued. The net export earnings had fallen aggravating payment imbalances in developing countries. The terms of trade had further deteriorated with enormous losses to developing countries. At the same time, the diminishing financial flows to developing countries remained unchanged with contraction in new lendings and growing burden of debt servicing. In fact there had been a reverse flow of resources from developing to developed countries. The trade conflicts had also sharpened with the rise of protectionism thus further weakening the international trading system and eroding the principle of special and differential treatment in favor of developing countries.

The Heads of State or Government reiterated the urgent need for resumption of North-South Dialogue with a view to promoting coordinated actions by developed and developing countries to channel trade surpluses for development, revive growth in flagging economies, overcome debt difficulties, expand export access to the developing countries and stabilize commodity prices, regulate capital flows and exchange rates more closely, and provide emergency relief and assistance to the poorest countries. They called for an early convening of the International Conference on Money and Finance for Development. They also stressed the need for preserving and liberalizing the multilateral trading system with renewed efforts both within and outside the GATT Uruguay Round of Multilateral Trade Negotiations. They also underscored the importance of the developed countries fully respecting the commitments made in Punta del Este on "standstill and rollback" and called for the early and effective implementation of this commitment. The Heads of State or Government also reviewed the outcome of UNCTAD VII. They hoped that UNCTAD would play an increasingly effective role in promoting harmonious and equitable international economic relations.

The Heads of State or Government reaffirmed the need for special measures in favor of the least developed countries in order to strengthen their resource capabilities and structural transformation and urged the international community, in the light of recent decisions at UNCTAD VII, to speed-up tangible assistance including increased resource flows to these countries within the framework of the Substantial New Program of Action (SNPA) for the Least Developed Countries for 1980s.

The Heads of State or Government expressed concern at the deteriorating international political environment which was due to great power policies and practices of domination and intervention as well as the increased resort to threat or use of force, aggression, occupation, pressure, economic coercion and interference in violation of the principles and purposes of the Charter of the United Nations. These destabilizing measures were creating a climate detrimental to the policies of peace, goodwill, stability, prosperity and respect for each other.

The Heads of State or Government believed that the escalation in military expenditure was a major constraint on world development. In this regard they noted that the UN Conference on Disarmament and Development had clearly established a link between disarmament and development and had provided a valuable frame work for future action in this vital area.

They welcomed the understanding reached between the United States and the Soviet Union on Intermediate Nuclear Forces. This should be a precursor of further accords between them to reduce drastically their strategic nuclear missiles and to refrain from extending the arms race to Outer Space. They called for the early conclusion in the Geneva Conference on Disarmament of a Comprehensive Test Ban Treaty and a Convention to Ban Chemical Weapons. They declared their intention to continue their efforts to contribute to the realization of the objective of halting the nuclear arms race and eliminating nuclear weapons. They declared their resolve to support every effort to conclude a treaty prohibiting vertical and horizontal proliferation of nuclear weapons.

The Heads of State or Government expressed their deep concern at the fast and continuing degradation of the environment, including extensive destruction of forests, in the South Asian region. They also noted that South Asia was afflicted with such natural disasters as floods, droughts, landslides, cyclones, tidal waves which have had a particularly severe impact recently, causing immense human suffering. At the same time they expressed concern over the danger posed by the global sea level rise and its effects on South Asian countries. These natural disasters and the degradation of the environment were severely undermining the development process and prospects of the member countries. They, therefore, decided to intensify regional cooperation with a view to strengthening their disaster management capabilities. They also decided to commission a study for the protection and preservation of the environment and to the causes and consequences of natural disasters in a well-planned comprehensive framework. They entrusted the Secretary-General with this task.

The Heads of State or Government reaffirmed their conviction that the region being most populous in the world and having age-old socio-cultural links, rich and varied human and natural resources, offered immense scope and potential for regional cooperation and that the growing interaction among its people had added stimulus towards this end. They reiterated their determination to pursue their individual and collective efforts for the optimal utilization of the vast human and untapped natural and other material resources.

The Heads of State or Government reviewed with satisfaction the progress made so far in the implementation of the SAARC Integrated Programme of Action and emphasized the need to further consolidate and streamline the process. They were conscious of the need to exercise greater discretion in the selection of activities in different sectors. They took note of the criteria and procedures relating to administrative structuring and financing of regional institutions endorsed by the SAARC Council of Ministers. They directed that the establishment of such regional institutions should proceed only after taking into account their viability and benefits to the member countries with due consideration to economy and efficiency.

The Heads of State or Government expressed satisfaction at the launching of the SAARC Audio Visual Exchange programme coinciding with the opening of the Third SAARC Summit in

Kathmandu. While taking note of the dates for the institution of the SAARC Chairs, Fellowships and Scholarships and the commencement of Organized Tourism among SAARC member countries, they directed that the schemes for the SAARC Documentation Centre and the SAARC Youth Volunteer Programme be implemented at the earliest.

The Heads of State or Government noted with satisfaction the signing of the Agreement establishing a South Asian Food Security Reserve and expressed confidence that this will provide a much-needed cushion against food shortages and scarcity situations in the region.

The Heads of State or Government expressed happiness at the signing of the SAARC Regional Convention on Suppression of Terrorism and considered it a historic step towards the prevention and elimination of terrorism from the region. In this regard, they also reiterated their unequivocal condemnation of all acts, methods and practice of terrorism as criminal and expressed their abhorrence of their impact on life and property, socio-economic development, political stability, regional peace and cooperation.

The Heads of State or Government reaffirmed their agreement to expand SAARC activities in other concrete areas of cooperation in order to ensure more tangible benefits from SAARC to the peoples of the region. They were convinced that regional cooperation could be consolidated and expanded on the basis of growing regional complementarities and interdependence. They believed that the SAARC long-term perspective should, therefore, focus on measures to expand and strengthen such areas of regional complementarities and interdependence not only through formulation and implementation of more concrete and action-oriented programmes but also through coordination of national policies and approaches for finding common solutions to their common problems.

The Heads of State or Government welcomed the first annual review of the Situation of Children in the SAARC member countries. They reiterated their commitment made in the Bangalore Declaration to accord highest priority to the needs of children in national development planning and emphasized that more intensified action should be taken for the welfare and well-being of children. They further reiterated their call for an early conclusion and adoption of a United Nations Convention on the Rights of the Child.

The Heads of State or Government expressed their satisfaction at the establishment of the SAARC Secretariat in Kathmandu, strengthening further the process of regional cooperation in South Asia. They expressed their gratitude to His Majesty King Birendra Bir Bikram Shah Dev for most graciously inaugurating the SAARC Secretariat.

The Heads of State or Government were conscious of the aspirations of the peoples of South Asia to communicate and cooperate with each other at the people-to-people level. They recognized that academics, researchers, non-governmental organizations and others have an important role to play in promoting the SAARC spirit and giving impetus to regional programmes and projects. They further observed that the interest and enthusiasm so far demonstrated by the increased interactions and exchange of information at the inter-governmental level should be capitalized and translated into tangible programmes and projects. They recognized the vast potential for the generation of friendship, goodwill and trust through interactions between the peoples which would foster harmonious relations in South Asia.

The Heads of State or Government expressed their deep conviction that the Kathmandu Summit has further consolidated the gains of SAARC and given a renewed thrust and direction to the future course of regional cooperation. They were also convinced that the Kathmandu Summit has helped to create an atmosphere conducive to strengthening this process, besides generating further goodwill and friendship among the member countries in the larger interest of the region.

The Heads of State or Government were conscious that SAARC should be increasingly oriented to the people's needs and aspirations so that the masses of the region could be drawn to a greater extent into the mainstream of SAARC activities. This, they firmly held, would help bring about a qualitative improvement in the general atmosphere of the region contributing to peace, friendship and cooperation in the areas.

The Heads of State or Government reiterated their firm commitment to the spirit and objectives with which the South Asian Association for Regional Cooperation was launched and reaffirmed their determination to work, individually and collectively, towards the attainment of these objectives.

The Heads of State or Government of Bangladesh, Bhutan, India, Maldives, Pakistan and Sri Lanka were deeply appreciative of the exemplary manner in which His Majesty the King of Nepal discharged his responsibilities as Chairman of the Meeting. They expressed their profound gratitude for the warm and gracious hospitality extended to them by His Majesty's Government and the people of Nepal and for the excellent arrangements made for the Meeting.

4th Summit

THE ISLAMABAD DECLARATION

The Islamabad Declaration of the Heads of State or Government of the Member Countries of South Asian Association for Regional Cooperation issued on 31st December 1988.

INTRODUCTION

The President of Bangladesh, the King of Bhutan, the Prime Minister of India, the President of Maldives, the King of Nepal, the Prime Minister of Pakistan and the President of Sri Lanka met at the Fourth Summit of the South Asian Association for Regional Cooperation at Islamabad from 29-31 December, 1988.

The Heads of State of Government expressed their deep satisfaction at the progress achieved by the Association since the last Summit. They reiterated their commitment to the SAARC Charter and renewed their determination to cooperate in promoting the welfare of the peoples of South Asia and to improving their quality of life by eradicating poverty, hunger, disease, illiteracy, unemployment and environmental degradation.

They recalled that their countries were linked by cultural, social and historical ties and they had at their disposal substantial human and natural resources. They recognized that these provided a sound basis as well as immense opportunities for regional cooperation. They therefore expressed their determination to make optimal use of their resources for the benefit of their people by working jointly to pursue their shared objectives. They were aware that by acting in concert they could realize the full potential for regional progress, taking into account complementarities and growing interdependence.

The leaders endorsed the decision of the Council of Ministers that any country in the region subscribing to the objectives and principles of the SAARC Charter may be admitted as a member of the Association by a unanimous decision of the Heads of State of Government.

The Heads of State of Government expressed satisfaction at the progress so far made in the implementation of the SAARC Integrated Programme of Action. They underlined the need for closer cooperation in the activities undertaken under this programme. They took note of the measures to streamline and re-orient various SAARC activities to make them more action-oriented so as to improve the quality of life of their peoples. They directed that the Secretary General may submit recommendation to the Standing Committee which should in turn decide how to streamline SAARC activities and make them more effective. They welcomed the establishment of the SAARC Agricultural Information Centre (SAIC), as well as the steps being taken for the establishment of other regional institutions.

The Heads of State of Government lauded the smooth functioning of the SAARC Audio Visual Exchange (SAVE) Programme which had proved to be a useful medium for promoting a South Asian consciousness amongst the peoples of the region. They decided that SAVE Programmes should also emphasize social, economic and technical themes. They also noted with satisfaction the successful launching of the Youth Volunteers Programme and the SAARC Chairs, Fellowships and Scholarships Scheme. They decided that Education may be included as an agreed area of cooperation.

The Heads of State of Government expressed satisfaction that the South Asian Food Security Reserve had become operational on 12 August 1988. The Reserve would serve as a cushion against food shortages and was a tangible manifestation of the spirit of cooperation in the region.

The Heads of State of Government noted with satisfaction that the SAARC Convention on Suppression of Terrorism had been ratified and had come into effect on 22 August 1988, thus reflecting the sincere desire on the part of the Member States to enter into meaningful cooperation to eliminate the scourge of terrorism from the South Asian region. They called for the adoption of enabling measures by Member States to implement the Convention at the earliest.

The Heads of State of Government expressed grave concern over the growing magnitude and the serious effects of drug abuse, particularly among young people, and drug trafficking. They recognized the need for urgent and effective measures to eradicate this evil ad decided to declare the year 1989 as the "SAARC Year for Combating Drug Abuse and Drug Trafficking". They agreed to launch a concerted campaign, as suited to the situation in their respective countries, to significantly augment SAARC efforts to eliminate drug abuse and drug trafficking. These included closer cooperation in creating a greater awareness of the hazards of drug abuse, exchange of expertise, sharing of intelligence information, stringent measures to stop trafficking in drugs and introduction of more effective laws. They directed that the Technical Committee concerned should examine the possibility of a Regional Convention on Drug Control.

The Heads of State or Government expressed their deep sense of sorrow and profound sympathy at the loss of valuable lives and extensive damage to property suffered during the year by Bangladesh, India, Nepal and Pakistan as a result of unprecedented floods, cyclones and earthquakes. In this connection, they recalled their earlier decision at Kathmandu in November, 1987 to intensify regional cooperation with a view to strengthening their disaster management capabilities and took note of the recommendations of the meeting of the SAARC Group of Experts on the Study on the Causes and Consequences of Natural Disasters and the Protection and Preservation of the Environment, that met in Kathmandu in July 1988. They expressed the conviction that identification of measures and programmes as envisaged by the Group of Experts would supplement national, bilateral, regional and global efforts to deal with the increasingly serious problems being faced by the region as a result of the recurrence of natural disasters and the continuing degradation of the environment. They urged that the study should be completed in the shortest period of time so that it could provide a basis for the member countries to draw up an action plan for meaningful cooperation amongst the Member States. They decided that a joint study be undertaken on the "Greenhouse Effect" and its impact on the region.

The Heads of State or Government noted with satisfaction that modalities for studies to be carried out for cooperation in the areas of trade, manufactures and services had been worked out by a Group of Experts, which met in Islamabad recently. They emphasized the need for the completion of the studies within the agreed time schedule. They directed that the Fourth Meeting of Planners should examine the possibility of cooperation in agreed areas of trade, manufactures and services, which would promote the objectives of meeting the basic needs of the peoples of the region. The report of the Planners should be considered at the next Council of Ministers meeting, with a view to making specific recommendations to the next Summit.

The Heads of State or Government reviewed the progress on the Situation of Children in SAARC countries. They reiterated their commitment made in the Bangalore Declaration to accord the highest priority to the needs of children in national development planning and stressed that the concept of Human Resource Development should lay particular emphasis on the welfare and well-being of children, especially in the literacy and health spheres. They called for the conclusion and adoption of the UN Convention on the Rights of the Child in 1989. They decided to declare 1990 as the "SAARC Year of the Girl Child".

The Heads of State or Government noted with satisfaction the effective functioning of the SAARC Secretariat and its role in coordinating SAARC activities. They also noted that a Headquarters Agreement had been signed between the Secretariat and the host Government. They thanked His Majesty's Government of Nepal for the assistance and cooperation extended to the Secretariat.

The Heads of State or Government noted that the decision to involve regional NGOs or professional bodies in SAARC activities, taken at the Fifth Session of the Council of Ministers, pursuant to the direction given by the Kathmandu Declaration, was an important step towards the promotion of people-to-people contact which has always been emphasized by the Association.

The Heads of State or Government stressed the need for closer and more frequent contacts among the peoples of SAARC. As a beginning, they decided that Supreme Court Judges and Members of the National Parliaments of each member State would be entitled to a special SAARC travel document which would exempt them from visas. They further directed the Council of Ministers to examine what other categories of persons should be given this facility and to submit their recommendations.

They further noted with satisfaction the mandate given to the Secretary General by the Council of Ministers at its Fifth Session on the question of contacting organizations with similar aims and purposes.

The Heads of State or Government expressed their determination to give concrete shape to the objectives of SAARC. In this context they emphasized the need to progressively carry out SAARC activities within a broad framework of a long-term perspective and to harmonize their efforts to ensure tangible benefits to the peoples of South Asia as a whole. They were conscious of the fact that all South Asian countries faced problems in varying degrees in areas such as food, clothing, shelter, education, primary health care, population planning and environmental protection. Towards this end they were of the view that all Member States should identity areas of core interest in their national perspective plans or prepare such plans and consolidate them into a regional plan to be called "SAARC-2000 : A Basic Needs Perspective", with specific targets to be met by the end of the century.

They recognized that Human Resource Development is one of the means of realizing these objectives. In this context they welcomed the offer of the Government of Pakistan to host a Centre for Human Resource Development and directed the Secretary-General to set up a Group of Experts from Member States to examine the proposal on the basis of a paper to be prepared by the Government of Pakistan and to submit its recommendations to the Standing Committee.

The Heads of State or Government reaffirmed their abiding commitment to the purposes and principles enshrined in the UN Charter, particularly those enjoining respect for the sovereign equality, territorial integrity and national independence, non-use or threat of use of force, non-interference in the internal affairs of other states and peaceful settlement of all disputes. They reiterated their faith in the United Nations as the most important forum for the maintenance of international peace and security and for the promotion of international cooperation aimed at the progress and prosperity of mankind.

The Heads of State or Government noted with satisfaction the relaxation of global tensions through intensified super-power dialogue on a broad range of international issues and welcomed the progress towards the resolution of protracted regional disputes and conflicts. They agreed that these developments had enhanced the prospects for disarmament, security, peace and progress for all peoples of the world. They appreciated the important role played by the United Nations in bringing about these positive changes in the international political environment. They also called upon all States to strengthen the capacity of the UN system in all respects to achieve the purpose of the UN Charter.

The Heads of State or Government reiterated their deep commitment to the principles and objectives of the Non-aligned Movement as an important force for strengthening world peace and harmony as well as for promoting development with justice and equity. In this context they expressed satisfaction over the results of the Ministerial Conference of the Non-aligned Movement held in Cyprus in September 1988 and expressed the hope the decisions of the Conference would contribute to the reduction of tensions and to the promotion of development. They hoped that the current discussions on the improvement in the methodology of the Non-Aligned Movement would result in strengthening the movement and enable it to play its role with greater effectiveness.

The Heads of State or Government believed that the escalation in military expenditure was a major constraint on world development. In this regard they noted that the UN Conference on Disarmament and Development had clearly established a link between disarmament and development and had provided a valuable framework for future action in this vital area. They urged that resources saved through disarmament measures should be diverted in particular to developing countries for development.

They welcomed the agreement between the United States and the Soviet Union on Intermediate Nuclear Force. They hoped this would be a precursor to further accords to reduce strategic nuclear arsenals drastically and to prevent an arms race in Outer Space. They called for the early conclusion in the Geneva Conference on

Disarmament of a Comprehensive Test Ban Treaty and a Convention to Ban Chemical Weapons. They declared their intention to continue their efforts to contribute to the realization of the objective of halting the nuclear arms race and eliminating nuclear weapons. They declared their resolve to support every effort to conclude a treaty prohibiting vertical and horizontal proliferation of nuclear weapons.

The Heads of State or Government noted with deep concern the continued structural disequilibrium from which the world economy had long suffered. This had resulted in slower growth in the developing countries, downward trends in commodity prices, decline in the net export earnings of the developing countries and deterioration in their terms of trade. These developments combined with the overwhelming debt burdens, the reverse financial flows from the developing to the developed countries and the sharp rise of protectionism in the developed world had further aggravated the economic difficulties of the developing countries.

The Heads of State or Government emphasized the interdependent character of the economies of the developed and the developing countries. They called for the resumption of the North-South dialogue with a view to restructuring the international economic system and to establishing the New International Economic Order based on justice and equity. They called for coordinated actions by the developed and the developing counties to increase the net flow of developmental assistance, overcome debt difficulties, expand the access of the developing countries to the markets in developed countries, arrest the deterioration in terms of trade of the developing countries and stabilize commodity prices.

The Heads of State or Government reiterated the need for preserving and liberalizing the multilateral trading system with renewed efforts both within and outside the Uruguay Round of Multilateral Trade Negotiations. They also underscored the importance of the developed countries fully respecting and implementing the commitments made in Punta del Este on "standstill and rollback" arrangements. They expressed concern that on account of differences between major trading entities on the question of agricultural subsidies, the Montreal Meeting on the midterm review of the Uruguay round was inconclusive. They particularly regretted that there was no progress in the negotiations on issues of major interest to developing countries such as trade in textiles and a Safeguard System. They were disappointed that on some of the issues of interest to developing countries on which there was agreement, particularly tropical products, it would not be possible even to implement the decisions taken, from the beginning of 1989 as envisaged. They emphasized that the development dimension must be taken into account in the negotiations on new issues, particularly services and intellectual property rights. They agreed to take concerted action to this end in the forthcoming negotiations.

The Heads of State or Government fully supported the call for the initiation of a comprehensive process for the preparation of an International Development Strategy for the Fourth United Nations Development Decade as well as the proposal of the Group of 77 for convening a Special Session of the General Assembly in 1990 to revive growth and development in the developing countries.

The Heads of State or Government reemphasized the need for increased resource flows and special measures in favor of the least developed countries within the Framework of the Substantial New Programme of Action (SNPA) for these countries. They supported the convening of a high level United Nations Conference on the least developed countries in 1990 to review progress and formulate national and international policies and measures for accelerating the development process in the least developed countries during the 1990s, especially in order to help them achieve their long term socio-economic objectives.

The Heads of State or Government of Bangladesh, Bhutan, India, Maldives, Nepal and Sri Lanka expressed their deep appreciation for the exemplary manner in which Prime Minister of Pakistan chaired the meeting. They expressed their profound gratitude for the excellent arrangements made for the meeting and for the warm and generous hospitality extended to them by the Government and the people of Pakistan.

5th Summit

THE MALE DECLARATION

The MALE Declaration of the Heads of State or Government of the Member Countries of Asian Association for Regional Cooperation issued on 23rd November, 1990.

The President of the People's Republic of Bangladesh, His Excellency Mr. Hussain Muhammad Ershad, the King of Bhutan, His Majesty King Jigme Singye Wangchuck, the Prime Minister of the Republic of India, His Excellency Mr. Chandra Shekhar, the President of the Republic of Maldives, His Excellency Mr. Maumoon Abdul Gayoom, the Prime Minister of Nepal, The Right Honourable Krishna Prasad Bhattarai, the Prime Minister of the Islamic Republic of Pakistan, His Excellency Mr. Mohammad Nawaz Sharif and the Prime Minister of the Democratic Socialist Republic of Sri Lanka, His Excellency Mr. Dingiri Banda Wijetunga met at the Fifth Summit of the South Asian Association for Regional Cooperation at Male' on 21-23 November, 1990.

The Heads of State or Government reiterated that cooperation among the countries of South Asia was necessary for improving the quality of life of the peoples of the region. They recalled their conviction that the objectives of peace and stability in South Asia could be best served by fostering mutual understanding, cooperation and good neighborly relations. They reaffirmed their commitment to the purposes and principles of the South Asian Association for Regional Cooperation and renewed their resolve to intensify cooperation under its aegis in pursuit of their common objectives.

The Heads of State or Government stressed their desire to promote peace, stability, amity and progress in the region through strict adherence to the principles of the United Nations Charter and the Nonaligned Movement, particularly respect for the principles of sovereign equality, territorial integrity, national independence, nonuse of force, noninterference in the internal affairs of other States and peaceful settlement of disputes.

The Heads of State or Government expressed satisfaction that the launching of SAARC in 1985 and the initiatives under the Integrated Programme of Action for strengthening regional cooperation in South Asia had generated much enthusiasm and hope in their peoples, and that the South Asian consciousness necessary for the success of regional cooperation was gradually permeating the region. They reiterated their resolve to make optimal use of the positive forces of goodwill, trust and understanding existing among their peoples and to turn SAARC into a dynamic instrument for achieving its objectives and creating an order based on mutual respect, equity, cooperation and shared benefits.

The Heads of State or Government reviewed the status of children in South Asia and noted that the recent World Summit for Children had imparted a new impetus to the ongoing efforts in this field. They believed that relevant recommendations of the World Summit could be usefully incorporated into a Plan of Action in the South Asian context and its implementation should be reviewed annually. The guidelines for such Plan of Action could be prepared by a panel of experts to be appointed by the Secretary General and examined by the Technical Committee on Health and Population Activities. They also welcomed the adoption of the Convention on the Rights of the Child and its entry into force. They expressed the hope that those Member States, who have not already become party to the Convention, would do so at an early date.

The Heads of State or Government endorsed the recommendations made by the Second SAARC Ministerial Meeting on Women in Development held in Islamabad in June 1990. They noted with satisfaction the enthusiastic response in all Member States to their collective call for the observance of 1990 as the "SAARC Year of the Girl Child". They decided that in order to maintain focus on the problems of the Girl Child, the years 19912000 AD should be observed as the "SAARC Decade of the Girl Child".

The Heads of State or Government noted with satisfaction the growing regional cooperation in combating the problems of drug trafficking and drug abuse. They expressed serious concern over the growing linkages between drug trafficking and international arms trade and terrorist activities. They agreed that observance of 1989 as the "SAARC Year for Combating Drug Abuse and Drug Trafficking" had had a profound impact in drawing attention to the menace and to the need for its elimination. They expressed satisfaction that following the decision of the Fourth SAARC Summit, the SAARC Convention on Narcotic Drugs and Psychotropic Substances had been signed at Male'. They urged the Member States to take early measures to ratify the convention for its entry into force. They were convinced that the Convention would help in making SAARC efforts in this area more effective.

They endorsed the decision of the Council of Ministers in regard to the timeframe for completion of the Regional Study on the Causes and Consequences of Natural Disasters and the Protection and Preservation of the Environment. They noted with satisfaction that the methodology for undertaking the Study on the 'Greenhouse Effect' and its impact on the region was likely to be finalized in the near future and desired that the Study itself be completed for consideration at the Sixth Summit. In this context, they noted that the destruction of rainforests, the world over, was contributing significantly to adverse climatic changes and this aspect should also be covered in the proposed Study. They expressed the hope that these Studies would lead to an action plan for meaningful cooperation in the field of Environment and Disaster Management.

Recognizing that environment had emerged as a major global concern, the Heads of State or Government noted with alarm the unprecedented climatic changes predicted by the Intergovernmental Panel on Climate Change (IPCC). They urged the international community to mobilize additional finances and to make available appropriate technologies to enable the developing countries to face the new challenges arising from climate changes and sea level rise. They agreed that Member Countries should coordinate their positions at international fora on this issue. They also decided to observe 1992 as the "SAARC Year of Environment".

The Heads of State or Government noted with satisfaction that the national studies on Trade, Manufactures and Services had been completed. They underlined the need for expeditious action for completing the Regional Study within the timeframe stipulated by the Council of Ministers. They expressed the hope that it would open new avenues of cooperation for the prosperity of the peoples of the region.

The Heads of State or Government approved the recommendations of the Council of Ministers regarding Special SAARC Travel Document and decided to launch the scheme.

The Heads of State or Government expressed concern that Member States were compelled to divert their scarce resources in combating terrorism. They called for expeditious enactment of enabling measures for the implementation of the SAARC Regional Convention on Suppression of Terrorism. They also urged Member States to continue to cooperate in accordance with the Convention.

The Heads of State or Government noted that as their countries stood on the threshold of the next millennium, the world was undergoing profound transformations characterized by popular upsurge for democracy, liberty and exercise of human rights, lowering of ideological barriers and the relaxation of global tensions and progress towards disarmament and the resolution of a number of regional and global conflicts. There was also a welcome trend towards the opening up of the global economy and integration of national economies into the mainstream of the world economy. They further noted the trend of increasing integration of the pattern of global production, consumption and trade, growing multipolarity of the world economic structure and integration of the markets of the developed countries in order to maintain their technological lead and competitive edge. These changes presented new challenges and opened up new opportunities to the South Asian countries, as to the rest of the developing world. The Heads of State or Government were convinced that their mutual cooperation can be a critical factor in enabling them to pursue these objectives more effectively.

The Heads of State or Government, noting the vital importance of biotechnology for the long term food security of developing countries as well as for medicinal purposes, decided that cooperation should be extended to this field and, in particular, to the exchange of expertise in genetic conservation and maintenance of germplasm banks. In this connection, they welcomed India's offer of training facilities and agreed that cooperation in the cataloguing of genetic resources stored in different SAARC countries would be mutually beneficial. Taking note of the proposal made by the Group of Fifteen Developing Countries (G15) for the establishment of a gene bank for developing countries, they agreed to participate in this venture.

The Heads of State or Government welcomed the idea of setting up of a Fund for regional projects which could make available credit on easy terms for the identification and development of regional projects. They agreed that representatives of the national development banks of the Member Countries should get together to work out the precise modalities for the source of funds and the manner in which these could be related to joint venture projects. They accepted India's offer to host this meeting.

The Heads of State or Government regarded the recent developments in the Gulf as the most unfortunate aberration from the present trend of detente, cooperation and peaceful settlement of disputes. They reaffirmed their adherence to UN Security Council Resolutions on this issue. While emphasizing the need for a peaceful solution of the issue, they called for immediate and unconditional withdrawal of Iraqi forces from Kuwait and the restoration of its legitimate Government. They stated that the Gulf crisis had dealt a severe blow to their economies. They needed massive international assistance to compensate the loss suffered by them due to a sharp decline in remittances, setback to their exports and severe strain on their balance of payments position imposed by increased oil prices. They recognized the potentiality of cooperation among themselves for mitigating the impact of these adverse consequences.

The Heads of State or Government noted with satisfaction that the initiative of the Government of the Maldives for the Protection and Security of Small States at the UN in 1989, which they all supported, had also received overwhelming support of the international community. They agreed that, because of their particular problems, small states merited special measures of support in safeguarding their independence and territorial integrity.

The Heads of State or Government expressed the hope that the talks between the two Super Powers on arms control would culminate in the conclusion of an agreement for substantial reduction in their nuclear arsenals leading to the total elimination of nuclear weapons. While welcoming the measures being considered for arms reduction at the global level, they were convinced that the objective could be best achieved through the promotion of mutual trust and confidence among the Member States. They underlined the inherent relationship between disarmament and development and called upon all countries, especially those possessing the largest nuclear and conventional arsenals, to re-channel additional financial resources, human energy and creativity into development. They expressed their support for the banning of chemical weapons and early conclusion of a Comprehensive Test Ban Treaty. In this context, they welcomed the convening of the UN Conference in January 1991 to consider amendments to the Partial Test Ban Treaty to convert it into a Comprehensive Nuclear Test Ban Treaty.

The Heads of State or Government expressed concern that the international economic environment for the developing countries had been characterized by negative resource flows, high trade barriers, serious external debt problems and high interest rates. The need of SAARC countries for increased concessional resources and technology as well as access to markets for their exports could not, therefore, be under estimated. They called for collective efforts based on mutuality of interest and felt that regular North South consultations were essential for ensuring equitable management of global interdependence.

The Heads of State or Government recalled the usefulness of the First Ministerial Meeting on International Economic Issues held in Islamabad in 1986. They agreed that the second such Ministerial Meeting be held in India in 1991 to review the outcome of the Uruguay Round and to coordinate positions at international conferences including the U.N. Conference on Environment and Development, 1992.

Notwithstanding the continuing efforts on the international economic plane, the Heads of State or Government emphasized the pressing need for the Ministerial Meeting to address itself vigorously to the objective of self-reliance. They directed the Ministers to prepare a strategy for mobilizing regional resources which would encourage and strengthen individual and collective self reliance in the region.

The Heads of State or Government expressed their support for the Paris Declaration (1990) and the Programme of Action adopted by the Second United Nations Conference on the Least Developed Countries. They called upon the international community to contribute to the successful implementation of the Programme of Action which is of special importance for the socioeconomic development of the region.

The Heads of State or Government recognized the imperative need for providing a better habitat to the peoples of South Asia through optimum utilization of indigenous technology, knowhow and material, and decided that 1991 be observed as the "SAARC Year of Shelter".

The Heads of State or Government noted that millions of disabled persons lived in the SAARC region and immediate action was required to reduce their sufferings and to improve their quality of life. They decided to observe 1993 as the "SAARC Year of Disabled Persons".

The Heads of State or Government were particularly happy that the Fifth SAARC Summit coincided with the Twenty Fifth Anniversary of the Independence of the Maldives which provided them with the opportunity to express their solidarity with the people and the Government of the Maldives. They expressed their conviction that the Male' Summit had helped in consolidating the gains of regional cooperation and in strengthening the institutional base of SAARC.

The Heads of State or Government gratefully accepted the offer of the Government of Sri Lanka to host the Sixth SAARC Summit in 1991.

The Heads of State or Government of Bangladesh, Bhutan, India, Nepal, Pakistan and Sri Lanka expressed their deep appreciation for the exemplary manner in which the President of the Maldives had discharged his responsibilities as Chairman of the Meeting. They expressed their profound gratitude for the warm and gracious hospitality extended to them by the Government and the people of the Maldives and for the excellent arrangements made for the Meeting.

6th Summit

THE COLOMBO DECLARATION

The Colombo Declaration of the Heads of State or Government of the Member Countries of South Asian Association for Regional Cooperation issued on 21st December 1991.

INTRODUCTION

The Prime Minister of the People's Republic of Bangladesh, Her Excellency Begum Khaleda Zia; the King of Bhutan, His Majesty King Jigme Singye Wangchuck; the Prime Minister of the Republic of India, His Excellency Shri Narasimha Rao; the President of the Republic of Maldives, His Excellency Mr. Maumoon Abdul Gayoom; the Prime Minister of Nepal, the Rt. Hon. Girija Prasad Koirala; the Prime Minister of the Islamic Republic of Pakistan, His Excellency Mian Mohammed Nawaz Sharif and the President of the Democratic Socialist Republic of Sri Lanka, His Excellency Ranasinghe Premadasa met at the Sixth Summit of the South Asian Association for Regional Cooperation (SAARC) at Colombo, Sri Lanka on 21st December, 1991.

The Heads of State or Government reaffirmed their commitment to the principles and objectives enshrined in the Charter of SAARC. They resolved to promote regional cooperation for the benefit of their people, in a spirit of mutual accommodation, with full respect for the principles of sovereign equality, independence and territorial integrity of all States and in strict adherence to the principles of nonuse of force, the peaceful settlement of disputes and noninterference in each other's internal affairs. They also reiterated their commitment to the principles of the United Nations Charter and the Non-aligned Movement.

The Heads of State or Government emphasized the vital importance of assessing the nature and extent of international economic interdependence and of the need for reviving the North/South dialogue. They noted the recent developments that had radically transformed the international development relationship deeply affecting the prospects for the economies of the seven SAARC countries. The Heads of State or Government emphasized the need for vigorously promoting South-South economic cooperation to offset the negative consequences of international economic developments.

The Heads of State or Government also exchanged views on the priorities of their respective national economies. They identified, for the further development of their economies, the importance of securing less restrictive trading and marketing opportunities for their products, more extensive technology and resource transfers to South Asia, debt relief and access on favorable and on more concessional terms to resources from multilateral financial institutions. They agreed to keep an open dialogue on these aspects through mutual consultations.

The Heads of State or Government assessed current international developments in the political sphere particularly those that affected the lives of the people of South Asia. They noted the changing power structures in international relations and the reduction of confrontations and tensions, particularly among the Super Powers. These have contributed to the receding of the threat of nuclear confrontation and to agreements on disarmament measures. The Heads of State or Government hoped that these developments would restrain the pursuit of military power in all areas of the world. They expressed the hope that the peace dividend would be used for promoting further development of developing countries. They welcomed the trend towards popularly based democratic governments in different parts of the world including in South Asia.

The Heads of State or Government observed however that some political issues in particular the Palestine question, the final elimination of Apartheid as well as other problems remained unresolved despite efforts towards their settlement.

In regard to human rights, the Heads of State or Government observed that civil and political rights on the one hand and economic and social rights on the other are interdependent and of equal importance Human rights issues should not therefore be viewed in narrow and exclusively political terms. In this context they underlined the need to view the efforts of States to guarantee human rights in their full context, through the pursuit of development for all citizens in conditions of stability, which in turn guarantees the enjoyment of human rights of all persons.

The Heads of State or Government while reaffirming their commitment to democracy, human rights and the rule of law, emphasized the need to ensure that development remains at the centre of international attention.

The Heads of State or Government agreed to participate in the ongoing process of revitalizing the United Nations as an effective universal instrument for addressing international issues on an equitable and democratic basis, taking full account of the interests and concerns of all states, including those in South Asia. Issues such as the protection and preservation of the environment and the equitable and sustainable management of global resources, economic development and the alleviation of poverty, the suppression of terrorism, drug trafficking and other international crimes required global responses and solutions calling for action by all states.

In the context of the SAARC Charter objective to strengthen cooperation among Member States in international fora, the Heads of State or Government resolved to encourage consultations among delegations of SAARC countries at all international fora and to promote articulation of joint positions where such action would be in the interests of all. They felt that the development of a collective position in international fora would accord them greater credibility and enhance the international profile of South Asia.

The Heads of State or Government welcomed the Report presented by the Chairman of the Fifth SAARC Summit, the President of Maldives, and the Head of Government of Bangladesh on the adoption of a more businesslike and functional approach in the conduct of SAARC meetings, as well as the Report submitted by the Chairman of the Ninth Session of the Council of Ministers, the Foreign Minister of Maldives, on rationalizing SAARC activities. The Heads of State or Government also considered other proposals submitted by Member States and by the Secretariat to make the Association a more effective instrument for the realization of the aspirations of the people of South Asia.

They decided that the Standing Committee should meet in special session in Colombo in April 1992 in order to collate and study all proposals and comments in this respect and to submit a report with its recommendations to the Eleventh Session of the Council of Ministers.

The Heads of State or Government reemphasized that regional self-reliance should be resolutely promoted through closer cooperation among countries of the Association and that this would help mitigate the adverse consequences of negative international developments operating against them.

The Heads of State or Government requested the Standing Committee at its Special Session to study the question of cooperation between SAARC and appropriate international and regional organizations taking into account the evolution of SAARC activities in the core economic areas and to report to the Eleventh Session of the Council of Ministers.

The Heads of State or Government noted the progress made by the Integrated Programme of Action (IPA) in expanding to cover a number of sectors crucial for the economic and social progress of the peoples of South Asia. They were of the view that the challenge facing the IPA was to achieve its identified targets within specific time periods. The Heads of State or Government welcomed the proposals made and the discussions proceeding in SAARC to heighten the effectiveness of the IPA.

The Heads of State or Government accorded the highest priority to the alleviation of poverty in all South Asian countries. They affirmed that South Asia's poor could constitute a huge and potential resource, provided their basic needs were met, and they were mobilized to create economic growth. This requires that the poor are empowered and are irreversibly linked to the mainstream of development. It was noted that each South Asian country has had significant success cases of this approach to poverty alleviation.

Recognizion that a great majority of these people remain below the poverty line, they evinced keen interest in a "Daal-Bhaat", or assured nutritional standards approach towards the satisfaction of basic needs of the South Asian poor.

Deeply conscious that primary education is the cutting edge in the struggle against poverty and the promotion of development, the Heads of State or Government reaffirmed the importance of attaining the target of providing primary education to all children between the ages of 6-14 years by the year 2000. They agreed to share their respective experiences and technical expertise to achieve this goal.

The Heads of State or Government decided to establish an independent South Asian Commission on Poverty Alleviation consisting of eminent persons from each SAARC Member State to conduct an in depth study of diverse experiences of the seven countries on poverty alleviation, and to report to the Seventh Summit, their recommendations on the alleviation of poverty in South Asia.

The Heads of State or Government were pleased to note the establishment of the Committee for Economic Cooperation as an important outcome of the Regional Study on Trade Manufactures and Services. They declared their commitment to the liberalization of trade in the region through a step by step approach in such a manner that all countries in the region share the benefits of trade expansion equitably.

The Heads of State or Government approved that the Inter Governmental Group (IGG) set up on the recommendation of the Committee on Economic Cooperation should formulate and seek agreement on an institutional framework under which specific measures for trade liberalization among SAARC Member States could be furthered. It should also examine the Sri Lankan proposal to establish a SAARC Preferential Trade Arrangement (SAPTA) by 1997. They directed that the IGG should meet as early as possible and report to the Committee on Economic Cooperation. The Heads of State or Government accepted the offer of the Government of Sri Lanka to host the Second Meeting of the Committee on Economic Cooperation at Colombo in June/July 1992 at which the report of the Inter Governmental Group would be considered.

The Heads of State or Government recognized that the degradation of the environment has emerged as a major global concern. While the protection of the environment is a common imperative for all humankind, the main responsibility in this regard rests on developed countries since most of the emission of pollutants originates in those countries and since they also have greater capacity for taking or facilitating corrective measures.

The Heads of State or Government called on the international community to address the question of unsustainable production and consumption patterns and lifestyles which lead to environmental degradation. They were also of the view that environmental standards applicable to developed countries may have excessive and unwarranted economic or social costs if applied in developing countries.

Adequate new and additional resources are needed for developing countries to pursue an environmentally sensitive process of development that will banish the underlying causes of environmental degradation poverty, malnutrition and unemployment. Such resources should be transferred to developing countries on an assured basis together with environmentally sound technology at preferential and concessional terms.

The Heads of State or Government expressed their conviction that the framework could be laid for an equitable global partnership of all countries with a view to safeguarding the environment.

The Heads of State or Government noted that in preparation for the SAARC Year of the Environment, SAARC countries had taken various national as well as regional measures for the preservation of the environment.

The Heads of State or Government expressed their satisfaction at the completion of Regional Study on the Causes and Consequences of Natural Disasters and the Protection and Preservation of Environment. They urged the member countries to promote cooperation amongst themselves for enhancing their respective disaster management capabilities and for undertaking specific work programmes for protection and preservation of the environment. They endorsed the decision of the Council of Ministers to establish a Committee on Environment to:

- examine the recommendations of the Regional Study
- identify measures for immediate action
- decide on modalities for their implementation and welcomed the offer of Bangladesh to hold the first meeting of the Committee in Dhaka.

The Heads of State or Government noted with satisfaction the decision of the Standing Committee concerning the time frame to finalize the regional study on the " 'Greenhouse Effect' and its Impact on the Region". They urged member countries to consult each other on key issues concerning climate change, Biodiversity and Biotechnology, a global consensus on forestry principles, transfer of environmentally sound technology, management of waste and other issues for discussion at Intergovernmental Negotiating Committee and the UNCED in 1992 so that the concerns of SAARC countries could be effectively articulated and projected, keeping in mind their respective national priorities.

The Government of India renewed its offer to host a Ministerial Meeting to harmonize the views of SAARC countries on these issues before UNCED 1992. The Heads of State or Government welcomed the offer.

The Heads of State or Government noted the useful activities conducted during 1991 which was observed as SAARC Year of Shelter. They decided to continue to work towards the global objective of "Shelter for All by the Year 2000."

The Heads of State or Government were of the view that Governments should play the critical role of facilitator and supporter of the initiatives of the people and non-governmental agencies in the field of shelter. In this role, they should be involved in the provision of affordable sites with secure tenure, making housing finance available on an affordable and sustainable basis, providing infrastructure development such as water supply and sanitation, energy and waste disposal, increasing the supply of building materials at reasonable prices using indigenous resources, removing constraints to building activities, and creating maximum opportunities for public participation in decision making and management of shelter activities in the overall context of poverty alleviation. Such activities would be facilitated by the exchange of experience, personnel, research and information among the SAARC countries.

The Heads of State or Government welcomed the recommendation on the establishment of a shelter information network to be called "SHELTERNET".

The Heads of State or Government accorded the highest priority to the question of child survival, protection and development. They welcomed the adoption of a Plan of Action on Children for South Asia which incorporated relevant recommendations of the World Summit on Children.

The Heads of State or Government noted in this context that some member countries had completed their national Plans of Action and urged other member countries to complete their respective Plans. They also urged Member States to ensure coordinated follow up action on their respective Plans.

The Heads of State or Government welcomed the offer of Sri Lanka to host a Conference on Children in South Asia in 1992 to consider implementation of the regional Plan of Action.

The Heads of State or Government welcomed the adoption of the Plan of Action for 1991-2000 A.D. as the SAARC Decade of the Girl Child. They requested the Council of Ministers to ensure an annual review of the status of implementation of the Plan of Action during the decade.

The Heads of State or Government expressed serious concern on the spread of terrorism in the region affecting the security and stability of all Member States and unequivocally condemned all acts, methods and practices of terrorism as criminal. They deplored all such acts for their impact on life, property, socio-economic development and political stability as well as on regional and international peace and cooperation.

They recognized that cooperation among SAARC States was vital if terrorism was to be prevented and eliminated from the region. In this regard they urged Member States to take all necessary measures to give full effect to their obligations under the SAARC Regional Convention on Suppression of Terrorism. They stressed in particular, the urgent need for the expeditious enactment of enabling legislation by those Member States which had not yet done so, for the implementation of the Convention and the need for a constant dialogue and interaction among the concerned agencies of Member States, including submission of periodic recommendations to the Council of Ministers.

The Heads of State or Government welcomed the initiative of the Government of the Republic of Maldives in drawing the attention of the international community to the protection and security of small states. They noted with satisfaction that the resolution submitted by the Maldives to the United Nations during the 46th Session of the General Assembly and cosponsored by 65 countries including all the members of SAARC was adopted without a vote. They agreed that small states may be particularly vulnerable to external threats and acts of interference in their internal affairs and that they merit special measures of support in safeguarding their sovereign independence, territorial integrity and the welfare of their people.

The Heads of State or Government noted with satisfaction the increasing regional cooperation in combating the problem of drug trafficking and drug abuse. They expressed serious concern over the growing linkages between drug trafficking, international arms trade and terrorist activities. While expressing satisfaction at the signing of the SAARC Convention on Narcotic Drugs and Psychotropic Substances at the Fifth SAARC Summit at Malé, they urged Member States which had not yet done so to ratify the Convention for its entry into force. They also recognised the need for greater cooperation, including the submission of periodic recommendations to the Council of Ministers.

The Heads of State or Government recalled that important initiatives had been taken at the Bangalore and Kathmandu Summits which had subsequently resulted in the increased involvement of the peoples of South Asia in the process of Regional Cooperation. They welcomed the steps being taken by business organizations/ professional bodies, scholars, academics, National Cultural Councils and the media in South Asia to form regional entities/ bodies. They called on the Standing Committee to expedite the formulation of guidelines for extending recognition to such groups and bodies.

The Heads of State or Government welcomed the setting up of a SAARC Fund for Regional Projects (SFRP) for identification and development of regional projects. They noted that the Fund would be managed by a Regional Council of Development Financing Institutions of the SAARC Member States and that the First Meeting of the Council would take place in India.

The Heads of State or Government requested the Secretary-General of SAARC to set up a panel of experts to examine the proposal of His Majesty the King of Bhutan to undertake a pre-feasibility study for the establishment of a South Asian Development Fund, taking into account the views of all Member States.

The Heads of State or Government noted with satisfaction that the Scheme in regard to the entitled categories of Members of Parliament, Judges of the Supreme Court, Heads of national academic institutions and the accompanying spouses and dependent children will become operational from 1st March 1992. They called for expeditious action to implement the scheme as well as to consider other categories eligible for exemption.

The Heads of State or Government were conscious of the vast potential being afforded by current advances in scientific research for the application of science and technology towards the wellbeing of the peoples of South Asia. They agreed that for the South Asian region to derive the maximum benefit, scientific and technological cooperation should transcend national frontiers.

Recalling the decision of the Malé Summit to institutionalize cooperation in the field of biotechnology, they welcomed the proposal for the establishment of a networking arrangement between Research and Development Centres in the Member States as an important step in advancing such cooperation. They also welcomed the emphasis on organized study tours, workshops and seminars proposed in the identified areas of cooperation in the field of science and technology.

The Heads of State or Government gratefully accepted the offer of the Government of Bangladesh to host the Seventh SAARC Summit in 1992.

The Heads of State or Government of Bangladesh, Bhutan, India, Maldives, Nepal and Pakistan expressed their deep appreciation for the exemplary manner in which the President of Sri Lanka had discharged his responsibilities as Chairman of the Meeting. They expressed their profound gratitude for the warm and gracious hospitality extended to them by the Government and the people of Sri Lanka and for the excellent arrangements made for the Meeting.

7th Summit

THE DHAKA DECLARATION

The Declaration of the Seventh SAARC Summit of the Heads of State or Government of Member Countries of the South Asian Association for Regional Cooperation issued on 11th April 1993.

INTRODUCTION

The Prime Minister of the People's Republic of Bangladesh, Her Excellency Begum Khaleda Zia, the King of Bhutan, His Majesty Jigme Singye Wangchuck, the Prime Minister of the Republic of India, His Excellency Mr. P. V. Narasimha Rao, the President of the Republic of Maldives, His Excellency Mr. Maumoon Abdul Gayoom, the Prime Minister of Nepal, the Rt. Hon. Girija Prasad Koirala, the Prime Minister of the Islamic Republic of Pakistan, His Excellency Mr. Mohammed Nawaz Sharif and the President of the Democratic Socialist Republic of Sri Lanka, His Excellency Mr. Ranasinghe Premadasa met at the Seventh Summit of the South Asian Association for Regional Cooperation (SAARC) at Dhaka, Bangladesh on 10 - 11 April, 1993.

Regional Cooperation

The Heads of State or Government reiterated their commitment to the principles and objectives of the South Asian Association for Regional Cooperation (SAARC), to the five principles of peaceful co-existence, the UN Charter and non-alignment. The Heads of State or Government noted the progress achieved in regional cooperation under the aegis of SAARC. They felt that time was now opportune for SAARC to provide a further dynamic impetus to activities in the core areas of economic, social and cultural cooperation in the SAARC region.

Integrated Programme of Action (IPA)

The Heads of State or Government welcomed the recent specific steps taken to consolidate and further streamline IPA-related SAARC activities. They also stressed the need for a progressive movement towards undertaking more well-defined, target-oriented and time-bound projects and programmes to ensure tangible benefits for the peoples of South Asia.

Activities Outside IPA

The Leaders welcomed the recent decisions to institutionalize cooperation in the core areas.

More Business-Like and Functional Approach in the Conduct of SAARC Meetings

The Heads of State or Government approved the recommendations of the Eleventh Session of the Council of Ministers for adopting a more business-like and functional approach in the conduct of Summit meetings. They also noted with satisfaction the guidelines and procedures approved by the Eleventh Session of the Council in this respect relating to other SAARC meetings. They decided to meet informally whenever necessary, between Summits.

Consensus on Eradication of Poverty in South Asia

Conscious that the sheer magnitude and complexity of South Asian poverty constituted a major political and economic challenge, the Heads of State or Government reiterated their commitment to continue to accord a high priority to its eradication from the region in the shortest possible time.

They pledged to overcome this challenge through the implementation of appropriate pro-poor development strategies at macro and micro levels.

In this context, the Heads of State or Government welcomed the Report of the Independent South Asian Commission on Poverty Alleviation established at the Colombo Summit. The Report provided valuable insight and illustrative examples of successful poverty alleviation programmes in individual Member States.

Acknowledging that the abiding human qualities of dignity,

creativity and productive potential are eroded by chronic poverty, the Heads of State or Government reiterated their commitment to empowering the poor for enhanced growth, consistent with human development and equity.

The Heads of State or Government committed their Governments unequivocally to the eradication of poverty in South Asia, preferably by the year 2002 A.D. through an Agenda of Action, which would, inter-alia, embody :

- A strategy of social mobilization involving the building of organizations of the poor and their empowerment through appropriate national support mechanisms, with the assistance of respective Governments;
- A policy of decentralized agricultural development and sharply focussed household level food security through universal provision of `Daal-Bhaat' or basic nutritional needs;
- A policy of decentralized small scale labour intensive industrialization, with the choice of efficient and cost-effective technology;
- A policy of human development, including the enhancement of the social role and status of poor women, the provision of universal primary education, skill development, primary health care, shelter for the poor and protection of children;
- A policy to support the above initiatives with adequate financial resources.

The Heads of State or Government stressed that within the overall conceptual approach of `Daal-Bhaat', the right to work and the right to primary education should receive priority.

The Leaders also underscored the critical link between the success of national efforts aimed at poverty alleviation and the external factors affecting growth and development. They urged all major actors in the world economic scene, particularly the industrialized countries and multilateral and regional financial institutions, and Non-Governmental Organizations to create an enabling international atmosphere that is supportive of poverty alleviation programmes in South Asia. This would require a new dialogue with donors.

The Heads of State or Government agreed to the follow-up action indicated below :

- a national level pro-poor plan to be drawn up by each Member State. This plan is to be harmonized with the open economy and structural adjustment strategies;
- to share during the next Summit, information regarding the progress achieved.

Trade, Manufactures and Services

The Heads of State or Government reaffirmed the need to liberalize trade as early as possible through a step by step approach. They underscored that this should be done in such a manner that all countries in the region could share the benefits of trade expansion equitably.

In this context, the Heads of State or Government welcomed the finalization of the framework Agreement on SAARC Preferential Trading Arrangement (SAPTA). They expressed their deep satisfaction over the signing of the framework Agreement. The Leaders stressed that all necessary steps should be taken to begin the first round of trade negotiations to exchange trade preferences among Member States under the Arrangement.

The Heads of State or Government further underlined the critical importance of urgently promoting intra-regional cooperation, particularly in the area of manufactures in order to enhance the productive capacity of the Member Countries, and to promote sustained growth and development to prevent the marginalization of South Asia's trade interest in the larger global context.

Environment

The Heads of State or Government expressed their deep concern at the unabated degradation of the environment and recurrence of devastating natural disasters. They also underscored the risks and dangers involved in overlooking the challenge posed by these problems. They expressed their commitment to implementing at all levels - national, bilateral, regional and global - programmes for the protection and preservation of the environment and prevention of its degradation. The Heads of State or Government recognized that the completion of the Regional Study on the "`Greenhouse Effect' and its Impact on the Region" was a significant step forward in promoting regional cooperation in this vital area. They also stressed the importance of continuing the ongoing SAARC activities in the field of environment.

The Heads of State or Government welcomed the outcome of the United Nations Conference on Environment and Development held in Rio de Janeiro in 1992 and underscored the imperative need to ensure the flow of resources to successfully implement the wide range of suggested initiatives and actions contained in Agenda 21. The Heads of State or Government noted that all international actions in the area of environment should be based on common but differential responsibilities, collective endeavors and a balanced perspective. Such actions, they stressed, must consider the protection of environment, economic growth and eradication of poverty as mutually reinforcing. All environmental initiatives, they underscored, must preclude the imposition of arbitrary and one-sided pre-conditions and ensure a harmonious blending of environmental and development concerns. They further noted with satisfaction the establishment of the Commission on Sustainable Development. They urged that the Commission approach environmental problems of developed and developing countries in an equitable manner.

The Heads of State or Government expressed their satisfaction over the adoption of a common position by Member States prior to the United Nations Conference on Environment and Development. They expressed their determination to continue in future the practice of intra-SAARC consultations on matters of common concern.

Population

Recognizing the sovereign right of all countries to promote, adopt and implement their population policies and mindful of their cultures, values and traditions, the Heads of State or Government stressed the need to integrate demographic objectives and population strategies in the formulation of the development strategies of Member Countries. In this context, they also noted the importance of adequate investment in the health and education sectors for the success of their population programmes. They agreed that cooperation among Member States should be strengthened, both through sharing experiences and in other practical ways, to enhance their capacity to deal with the population problem. The Leaders urged Governments of developed countries, as well as all concerned international and regional organizations, to strengthen their financial and technical support in the areas of health and education as part of their strategy of assistance to developing countries in their development efforts.

The Heads of State or Government welcomed the offer of Nepal to host a SAARC Ministerial Conference on Women and Family Health in Kathmandu in October/November 1993.

Shelter

The Heads of State or Government reiterated that housing was a basic right for all people and that Governments should act as facilitator and supporter of shelter programmes initiated by the people. They urged Member States to continue to work towards the global objective of "Shelter for All by the Year 2000".

Children

Reaffirming their commitment to accord the highest priority to child survival, protection and development, the Heads of State or Government noted with satisfaction that all Member States had completed their National Plans of Action on Children. They reiterated their call at the Colombo Summit to continue to ensure coordinated follow-up action by Member States on their respective plans.

The Heads of State or Government endorsed the "Colombo Resolution on Children" adopted by the Second SAARC Ministerial Conference on Children held at Colombo in September 1992 and urged Member States to implement programmes as appropriate in their respective national contexts, to achieve the illustrative goals embodied in the Resolution, and the goals of the SAARC Plan of Action on Children.

The Heads of State or Government noted, in particular, the need to take effective measures to protect children against all forms of neglect, cruelty and exploitation and agreed to promote cooperation among Member States in devising such measures.

Youth

Stressing that the youth of South Asia constituted a vital

resource for national development and that mobilization of their latent power was imperative, the Heads of State or Government focussed special attention on the needs of the Youth in South Asia and their development.

The Leaders noted that the youth of South Asia faced a number of serious problems requiring urgent attention and remedial measures. They welcomed the offer of the Maldives to host a Ministerial Conference on Youth in South Asia in 1994 to address the problems of the Youth and focus on the broad theme of youth and development. They also agreed to designate 1994 as the "SAARC Year of the Youth".

Plan of Action for the Disabled Persons

The Heads of State or Government while recalling their decision at the Male' Summit to observe 1993 as the "SAARC Year of Disabled Persons", adopted the Regional Plan of Action for the Disabled Persons. They urged Member States to take concrete steps to implement the Plan.

They welcomed the offer of Pakistan to host a Ministerial Conference on Disabled Persons in September 1993.

Women in Development

While reviewing the situation of women in the region, it was noted with satisfaction that over a period of time, the content of regional cooperation which addresses the issue of development, gender and equality for women has steadily grown in SAARC. The Heads of State or Government hoped that the cooperation thus developed will enable Member States to achieve the ultimate goal of bringing women into the mainstream of development with independence and equality.

The Heads of State or Government recalled that in pursuance of their collective will expressed in the Male' Summit to observe the 1990s as the " SAARC Decade of the Girl Child", Member States had undertaken to formulate National Plans of Action for the improvement of the condition of the Girl Child giving priority to her survival, protection and development. They expressed satisfaction that some Member States had already completed this task and others were expected to do so soon.

Science and Technology

The Heads of State or Government emphasized that cooperation in the field of Science and Technology was of utmost importance in order to accelerate the process of development in South Asia.

They called for further intensification of efforts by Member States in this important area, particularly to facilitate research and exchange of information through networking arrangements in the field of biotechnology, genetic engineering, energy modelling techniques and other identified areas of cooperation.

Terrorism

The Heads of State or Government reiterated their unequivocal condemnation of all acts, methods and practices of terrorism as criminal. They strongly deplored the adverse consequences of terrorism.

They noted with grave concern that the efforts to combat the growing threat of terrorism had resulted in the diversion of valuable scarce resources from urgent development programmes.

The Leaders reiterated the need to give high priority to the enactment of enabling legislation at the national level to give effect to the SAARC Regional Convention on Suppression of Terrorism, while urging the Member States which had not yet done so, to make every effort to finalize this matter before the Eighth SAARC Summit.

While recognizing that some progress had been achieved in the fields of consultation and exchange of information, they stressed the need for further enhancing cooperation in these fields as well as for coordinated action. They called for the expeditious implementation of the recommendations formulated for advancing cooperation in this regard in pursuance of their decision at the Colombo Summit.

Drug Trafficking and Drug Abuse

The Heads of State or Government reiterated their grave concern at the growing menace of drug trafficking in the region and the aggravation of the problem of drug abuse among the South Asian population, particularly the youth.

They recognized the devastating impact of drug abuse on the very fabric of society and the serious threat to security and stability posed by drug trafficking through its growing linkages with organized crime, illicit arms trade and terrorism.

The Heads of State or Government were gratified to note the expanding cooperation among Member States to combat and eliminate the scourge of drug trafficking and drug abuse.

They reiterated the need for further strengthening cooperation in this field and called for the expeditious implementation of the recommendations formulated for this purpose in pursuance of their decision at the Colombo Summit.

Security of Small States

The Heads of State or Government reaffirmed their commitment to pay special attention to the monitoring of the security of small States and underscored the need to consider special measures of support to preserve their sovereign independence, territorial integrity and the well-being of their people. They further noted that real protection of small and weaker States should be firmly rooted in the Rule of Law and strict adherence to universally accepted principles and norms relating to the sovereign rights and territorial integrity of all States - big or small. This, they stressed, should be ensured by all countries either severally or collectively through the pursuit of appropriate actions.

People-to-People Contact

The Heads of State or Government stressed the need to further promote people-to-people contact in order to ensure increased involvement of peoples of South Asia in the process of regional cooperation. In this context, they noted that the formulation of guidelines and procedures for extending recognition to regional apex bodies would facilitate participation of these bodies in promoting regional cooperation at the people-to-people level.

The Leaders expressed the hope that the recent recognition of the SAARC Chamber of Commerce and Industry would contribute positively to enhancing cooperation in the crucial areas of trade and economic relations.

The Heads of State or Government expressed their appreciation to the Government and people of India for hosting the First South Asian Festival of SAARC Countries in 1992. The Festival provided the people of the region the opportunity to share in the rich cultural heritage of South Asia. The Heads of State or Government hoped that the South Asian Festival would become a regular feature.

Association of SAARC Speakers and Parliamentarians

The Heads of State or Government welcomed the initiative of the Speakers of Parliaments of SAARC Countries in forming an "Association of SAARC Speakers and Parliamentarians". They were of the view that the establishment of this Association would add another important dimension to the process of regional cooperation.

South Asian Development Fund

The Heads of State or Government endorsed the recommendation of the Council of Ministers for the establishment of an Inter-Governmental Group (IGG) on South Asian Development Fund (SADF) on an ad-hoc basis. They directed that the IGG define in clear terms the size, structure, resources and operational modalities of the proposed Fund. They also directed the IGG to examine the complementarities between the SAARC Fund for Regional Projects (SFRP) and SADF, and their relationship, including the possibility of their merger. They welcomed the offer of the Maldives to host the meeting of IGG.

International Political Developments

The Heads of State or Government had wide-ranging discussions on the current global political trends and future prospects, particularly those issues that affect South Asia. In this context, they reiterated their deep commitment to the purposes and principles of the UN Charter and reaffirmed their resolve to strengthen the United Nations as the central instrument for peace, security, disarmament, development and cooperation among the nations of the world. To this end, the Leaders supported all constructive initiatives aimed at strengthening the United Nations. They, however, underscored that any move to adapt or reform the United Nations must be undertaken with the sole objective of rendering the United Nations more democratic, efficient and effective and not to limit the focus of its attention to a narrow and isolated range of objectives.

The Heads of State or Government reiterated their firm commitment to the principles and objectives of the Non-aligned

Movement and underlined the continued validity and relevance of these principles and objectives in the contemporary global political and economic context. They recalled the important role the Movement had been playing in strengthening international peace, promoting development and establishing more equitable and just economic relations and enhancing international cooperation in all areas. They expressed their deep conviction that the Movement's innate strength uniquely equipped it to continue to play a most constructive role in laying the foundations and defining the characteristics of a new world order which should be based on the principles of justice, equity and democracy in international relations. In this context, the Heads of State or Government welcomed the success of the Jakarta Summit of the Non-aligned countries and called for the expeditious implementation of its decisions.

The Heads of State or Government noted that the end of the cold war presented new opportunities and challenges. They observed that despite many positive developments and recent successes in resolving some regional conflicts, the international political scene was still marred by strife and tension. They expressed their serious concern over the unfortunate and tragic consequences of ethnic conflict and violence afflicting people and communities in many parts of the world. They stressed that efforts must be intensified to find peaceful and viable solutions to conflicts of long standing nature and new problems through greater respect for international law and universally accepted humanitarian norms and standards.

The Heads of State or Government noted a number of recent positive developments in the area of nuclear, chemical and conventional disarmament including the agreements on bilateral arms reductions between the United States and the Russian Federation. They expressed their hope that the implementation of the far-reaching arms reduction agreed in the Washington Agreement of June 1992 and START II signed in Moscow in January 1993 would be successfully carried out. The Leaders urged all Nuclear-Weapon States to collectively endeavour to attain the ultimate goal of complete elimination of nuclear arsenals in the shortest possible time.

They also underscored the imperative to further broaden and deepen the dimensions to disarmament and to complement bilateral approaches to disarmament with effective multilateral approaches.

While welcoming the recent progress in arms reduction at the global level, the Leaders were convinced that this objective could be best achieved through the promotion of mutual trust and confidence among Member States.

International Economic Issues

The Heads of State or Government noted that while it was important to build peace and create conditions of stability in the world, it was equally important to promote economic and social development. They underscored that international cooperation for development and eradication of poverty were inextricably linked with the preservation of international peace and security and hence needed to be treated on an equal footing and pursued with equal vigour. The Heads of State or Government expressed their grave concern over the continuing deterioration in economic situation in the majority of developing countries. The economies of developing countries, they observed, continued to suffer as a result of limited market access for their exports, dwindling resource flows, absence of adequate foreign investment, mounting external indebtedness, inadequate transfer of technology and the inequities in the global monetary, financial and trading systems. The Heads of State or Government noted that although the developing countries themselves had the primary responsibility for their economic development, the role of developed countries remained central to the revival of the growth of the world economy - in particular the economies of the developing countries.

The Heads of State or Government reiterated the vital importance of economic interdependence among nations and of the need for reviving North-South dialogue. They fully endorsed the view that there should be more equitable economic opportunities for all nations. These should include such important features as the strengthening of a free, open and non-discriminatory multilateral trading system, effective macro-economic coordination and fiscal discipline to ensure stable conditions conducive to development in the global economy. They also reiterated their firm support for the broadening of the coordination of international macro-economic policies to take into account concerns of all countries, specially the developing countries. Referring to the competing demands for capital and investment resources, the Heads of State or Government underscored the need to ensure the adequate flow of investment resources to the developing countries through increasing global savings and a more equitable utilization of the peace dividends. In this context the Heads of State or Government also underscored the need to fulfil the internationally agreed aid targets for the developing countries and the Least Developed Countries. They emphasized on the need for exceptional finance to facilitate implementation of economic reform programmes in SAARC Countries.

The Heads of State or Government also strongly underlined the need to continue efforts to seek a comprehensive, durable and growth-oriented solution to the external indebtedness of the developing countries. This, they stressed, was essential to accelerate the process of growth in these countries. A lasting solution to the debt crisis, the Heads of State or Government noted, must take into account the need to significantly reduce the stock and service of all types of debts of indebted developing countries to augment the concessional aid flows to SAARC Countries and work out anticipatory measures to prevent the recurrence and proliferation of the debt problem.

The Heads of State or Government also underlined the importance of a strengthened and liberalized international trading system. In this context, they noted that the successful conclusion of the Uruguay Round of Multilateral Trade Negotiations was a matter of great importance to the developing countries. Failure of the Round, the Leaders noted, would only further impair economic growth and encourage protectionist policy seriously weakening the multilateral trading system. The Heads of State or Government strongly urged the major partners in the Negotiations to demonstrate their political will and take positive steps to ensure without further delay a satisfactory conclusion of the Uruguay Round. They further stressed that although the main thrust of these negotiations in the recent past had been in respect of new issues, there was an imperative need to ensure that the Uruguay Round fully take into account the concerns and interests of developing countries. This, the Heads of State or Government stressed, was particularly important. The Leaders underscored the need to speedily conclude the current round of negotiations in a transparent, balanced and expeditious manner. They also stressed that before the conclusion of the Uruguay Round of Multilateral Trade Negotiations, an evaluation of results be held from the point of view of developing countries.

The Heads of State or Government expressed their concern over the increasing stock of anti-dumping and countervailing duty investigations against the exports of developing countries and the new threats to a liberal trading order in the form of measures taken in pursuit of the goals relating to workers' rights and the environment.

Projection of Collective Positions

The Heads of State or Government were of the view that greater consultations among the delegations of SAARC Countries in all international fora on the major issues of common concern to them would be in the interest of all their countries. They felt that the development of collective positions on such issues in the international fora would enhance the international profile of South Asia and would enable the countries in the region to articulate their position on them more effectively. They reiterated their common resolve to concert their position in all international fora and negotiations with a view to deriving maximum benefits from them in accordance with their needs and common priorities.

The Heads of State or Government underscored the vital importance attached by their countries to the forthcoming Second World Conference on Human Rights in 1993, the World Population Conference in 1994 and the 1995 World Conference on Women. They also supported the convening of a World Summit for Social Development. The Heads of State or Government stressed the need to develop a common South Asian perspective on the issues to be discussed by these important international conferences. They also underscored the imperative to coordinate the position of SAARC countries in order to ensure a balanced equitable and action oriented outcome of these conferences.

Observer Status

The Heads of State or Government decided that an Expert Group of the Member States will examine the various requests for observer status at SAARC/SAARC meetings in all its aspects on the basis of a working paper to be prepared by the Secretariat and make appropriate recommendations to the Nineteenth Session of the Standing Committee. In this respect, they welcomed the offer of Sri Lanka to host the Expert Group Meeting.

Conclusion

The Heads of State or Government expressed their deep satisfaction over the positive outcome of the Seventh SAARC Summit and expressed their conviction that this Summit would greatly contribute towards strengthening the policies and cooperative actions of the Member States in response to the challenges of the 1990s and beyond in areas where SAARC has a distinct contribution to make. They also reiterated once again their determination to strengthen and enrich SAARC as an instrument - endowing it with a clear set of forward looking goals and objectives as well as all the requisite institutional capacities - so that it can continue to work to enrich not only the lives of its own members but also promote peace, progress and stability in South Asia in a larger context.

Date and Venue of the Eighth Meeting of the SAARC Heads of State or Government

The Heads of State or Government gratefully accepted the offer of India to host the Eighth SAARC Summit in 1994.

The Heads of State or Government of Bhutan, India, the Maldives, Nepal, Pakistan and Sri Lanka expressed their sincere appreciation for the exemplary manner in which the Prime Minister of Bangladesh had conducted the Meeting and guided its proceedings in her capacity as Chairperson. They expressed their deep gratitude for the warm and generous hospitality extended to them by the Government and people of Bangladesh and for the excellent arrangements made for the Meeting.

8th Summit

THE DELHI DECLARATION

The Delhi Declaration of the Heads of State or Government of the Member Countries of South Asian Association for Regional Cooperation issued on 4th May 1995.

INTRODUCTION

The Prime Minister of the People's Republic of Bangladesh, Her Excellency Begum Khaleda Zia, the King of Bhutan, His Majesty Jigme Singye Wangchuck, the Prime Minister of the Republic of India, His Excellency Mr. P.V. Narasimha Rao, the President of the Republic of Maldives, His Excellency Mr. Maumoon Abdul Gayoom, the Prime Minister of Nepal, the Rt. Hon. Manmohan Adhikari, the President of the Islamic Republic of Pakistan, His Excellency Mr. Farooq Ahmad Khan Leghari and the President of the Democratic Socialist Republic of Sri Lanka, Her Excellency Mrs. Chandrika Bandaranaike Kumaratunga met at the Eighth Summit of the South Asian Association for Regional Cooperation (SAARC) at New Delhi, India on 2-4 May 1995.

SAARC Decade

The Heads of State or Government expressed their satisfaction on the achievements of the First Decade of SAARC and resolved to celebrate its completion of the First Decade both in the individual Member States and collectively. They endorsed the proposal of the Council of Ministers to convene a Commemorative Session of the Council on the theme "SAARC - Vision for the Second Decade" to identify the areas on which SAARC should focus in its Second Decade.

Regional Cooperation

The Heads of State or Government reaffirmed their resolve to intensify regional cooperation in order to accelerate the process of promoting the welfare and improving the quality of life of the peoples of South Asia. They reiterated their commitment to the principles and objectives enshrined in the SAARC Charter, particularly, to the principles of sovereign equality, territorial integrity, national independence, non-use of force and non-interference in each other's internal affairs. They recalled their conviction that in an increasingly interdependent world, regional cooperation was a dynamic instrument for promoting economic prosperity, mutual understanding and good neighborly relations to achieve the objectives of peace and stability in South Asia. In this context, a climate of peace and stability would contribute to the economic growth.

Eradication of Poverty in South Asia

The Heads of State or Government reaffirmed their commitment to the eradication of poverty in South Asia, preferably by the year 2002 A.D. through an Agenda of Action.

The Leaders endorsed the recommendations of the Finance/Planning Ministers' Meeting held in Dhaka in July 1994 which recommended that a mechanism should be set up which would act as a forum for exchange of information on poverty eradication programmes, in the context of the policies and strategies adopted, particularly exchange of information on technologies that are relevant to efforts at poverty eradication. They agreed that this process could be strengthened by sharing and exchanging relevant studies carried out by independent research institutions and experts. This mechanism would be in the form of a three-tier institutional structure as recommended in the Report and would meet once a year. They noted that such a mechanism has been set up enabling the procedures of exchange of information to commence and welcomed the offer of India to host the first round of the three-tier mechanism.

The Heads of State or Government directed that the next meeting of Finance/Planning Ministers consider the efficacy of such mechanism towards eradicating poverty in the region and report on the progress achieved to the Ninth SAARC Summit, through the Council of Ministers.

In this context, they decided to declare 1995 as the "SAARC Year of Poverty Eradication".

Acknowledging that the abiding human qualities of dignity, creativity and productive potential are eroded by chronic poverty, the Heads of State or Government reiterated their commitment to empowering the poor for enhanced growth consistent with human development and equity.

Recognizing that poverty is a complex multi-dimensional problem with origins in both national and international domains, country-specific programmes to tackle poverty and international efforts supporting national efforts and the parallel process of creating a supportive international environment conducive to economic growth and social development of developing countries, are crucial for a solution to this problem. The World Summit for Social

Development recognized the need for focusing the attention of the international community on and support the special needs of countries and regions in which there are substantial concentrations of people living in poverty, in particular those in South Asia and which face serious difficulties in achieving social and economic development. The Heads of State or Government reiterated their commitment to eradicate poverty and noted with appreciation the outcome of the World Summit for Social Development.

The Heads of State or Government committed themselves to addressing the fundamental causes of poverty and to provide for the basic needs of all. They reaffirmed their commitment to work for guaranteeing the realization of the rights of all, in particular those of the poor, to food, work, shelter, health, education, resources and information.

The Heads of State or Government reaffirmed their commitment to provide expanded opportunities to the poor to enhance their overall capacities and improve living conditions and to adequate economic and social protection during unemployment, disability and old age. While recognizing the need to improve, expand and deregulate markets to promote sustained economic growth they felt it was essential to mitigate any negative features created by the market forces and make all efforts to make the markets friendly to the poor. The Heads of State or Government reaffirmed the necessity to ensure that financial systems and other public policies are geared towards poverty eradication and warned against increase in socially divisive disparities.

The Heads of State or Government agreed that the Governments of SAARC countries will have to play a lead role in promoting the support structures needed for poverty eradication, including people's institutions and non-governmental organizations in the context of organizing the people and fostering decentralisation and local self-governance and encouraging organisation of the poor, in the context of their social and economic interests.

SAARC Preferential Trading Arrangement (SAPTA)

The Heads of State or Government noted with satisfaction that subsequent to the signing of the Framework Agreement on SAARC Preferential Trading Arrangement (SAPTA) during their Seventh Summit in Dhaka in April 1993, the first round of trade negotiations to exchange trade concessions among Member States has been completed. They directed that all necessary steps should be taken to facilitate ratification by all Member States and operationalise SAPTA by the end of 1995 as mandated.

The Leaders reiterated their firm belief that the operationalisation of SAPTA will herald the beginning of a new and significant process of regional cooperation and would lend strength to SAARC as an institution for promoting the welfare of the peoples of South Asia.

In view of the fast changing international economic environment, creation of major trading and economic groupings, establishment of the World Trade Organization subsequent to the successful conclusion of the Uruguay Round of Multilateral Trade Negotiations and unilateral economic liberalization measures being adopted by Member Countries, the Heads of State or Government emphasized the urgency of broadening and deepening cooperation within a specific and rapid time-frame in the core areas of trade and economic relations in the region. These developments call for added urgency to achieve more progress towards operationalisation of SAPTA and intensification of cooperation to expand regional trade. To that end, they decided that the "Components" and "Additional Measures" identified in Articles 4 and 6 respectively of the SAPTA Agreement should be implemented.

Integrated Programme of Action

The Heads of State or Government noted the progress made through the Integrated Programme of Action covering a number of crucial areas and activities.

Regional Centres

The Leaders welcomed the establishment of the SAARC Documentation Centre (SDC) in New Delhi in May 1994 and the SAARC Meteorological Research Centre (SMRC) at Dhaka in January this year.

Women in Development

Noting that increased political and social consciousness in the region had highlighted the issues of elimination of gender-disparity and empowerment of women which are essential for their socio-economic development, the Heads of State or Government underlined the urgency of addressing these issues through further affirmative action.

The Leaders endorsed the "Kathmandu Resolution on Women and Family Health", adopted by the Ministerial Conference on Women and Family Health in Kathmandu in November 1993, and expressed satisfaction that appropriate programmes were being undertaken to implement the Resolution at the national level by the Member States.

The Leaders noted the progress in the implementation of the Plan of Action to mark 1991-2000 as the 'SAARC Decade of the Girl-Child', and requested the Council of Ministers to conduct a comprehensive mid-decade review for presentation to the Ninth SAARC Summit.

Recognizing the serious threat faced by certain groups of Girl Children in Especially Difficult Circumstances (GCEDC) including those orphaned, disabled and exploited, the Leaders decided that an urgent appraisal of the situation of these children be undertaken by the Council of Ministers and specific recommendations be presented to the Ninth SAARC Summit.

Considering that the exploitation of the Girl Child is a direct reflection of the status of women in society, the Leaders reaffirmed their resolve to take necessary measures to eliminate all forms of discrimination against women and girl-children.

Children

The Heads of State or Government expressed satisfaction that the annual reviews of the situation of children in SAARC countries for the years 1993 and 1994 had been completed which indicated reduction in infant mortality and significant progress in the immunization programme for children in the region.

Recalling the mid-decade goals of the World Summit for Children, the Heads of State or Government resolved to intensify their efforts both at the national and regional levels for attainment of these goals.

The Leaders welcomed that all Member States have become party to the Convention on the Rights of the Child. They felt that the recently held Cairo International Conference on Population and Development (ICPD) in September 1994 and the Copenhagen World Summit on Social Development in March 1995 had imparted fresh impetus to the on-going efforts for the survival, protection and development of children in South Asia.

Youth

The Heads of State or Government endorsed the Malé Resolution on Youth adopted by the Ministerial Conference on Youth in South Asia held in the Maldives in May 1994 and noted that the Conference had, inter-alia, served to focus attention on the status of the youth and the challenges faced by them. The Leaders noted with satisfaction that the Agenda for Action incorporated in the Resolution is being implemented by Member States with a view to integrating the youth into the process of national development. They noted with satisfaction that the SAARC Youth Resolution had been adopted and the SAARC Youth Awards Scheme has been established.

The Leaders expressed satisfaction on the implementation of the Plan of Action to mark 1994 as the SAARC Year of the Youth in Member States and resolved to continue the momentum generated in Member States.

Persons with Disability

The Heads of State or Government noted with satisfaction that the Ministerial Conference on Disabled Persons was held in Islamabad in December 1993. They endorsed the Islamabad Resolution on Disabled Persons and the recommendations of the Conference and noted that the Conference had further increased awareness among the peoples of South Asia regarding the needs and problems of the disabled persons. They welcomed the activities and programmes launched by the Member States in pursuance of the Resolution for the protection and promotion of persons with disability.

Shelter

The Heads of State or Government, recognizing that housing was a basic right for all people and that, in addition to governmental efforts, private initiatives of the people and non-governmental agencies should be supported, reaffirmed their commitment to work towards the global objective of "Shelter for All by the Year 2000."

Literacy

The Heads of State or Government noted that illiteracy is one of the major causes of poverty, backwardness and social injustices and called on the Member States to initiate more concrete programmes aimed at eradicating illiteracy in the region preferably by the year 2000 A.D. They decided to observe 1996 as the "SAARC Year of Literacy".

Environment

Reaffirming the need for a concerted action for the protection and preservation of the environment, the Heads of State or Government expressed their satisfaction over the formulation of a common position by Member States prior to the World Conference on Natural Disaster Reduction and the presentation of the collective position at the Yokohama Conference. They recognized that international cooperation is vital for building up national capabilities, transfer of appropriate technology and promotion of multilateral projects and research efforts in natural disaster reduction.

The Heads of State or Government expressed their deep concern at the unabated degradation of the environment and recurrence of devastating natural disasters. They also underscored the risks and dangers involved in overlooking the challenge posed by these problems. They expressed their commitment to implementing at all levels - national, bilateral, regional and global - programmes for the protection and preservation of the environment and prevention of its degradation. The Heads of State or Government stressed the importance of continuing the on-going SAARC activities in the field of environment.

The Heads of State or Government noted that although some work has been carried out in the area of disseminating information on the problems of environmental degradation and their impact on the region, progress in the implementation of the recommendations of the SAARC Regional Study on the Causes and Consequences of Natural Disasters and the Protection and Preservation of the Environment and the Regional Study on Greenhouse Effect and its

Impact on the Region, which were completed in 1992, had been slow. They stressed the importance of effective and speedy implementation of the recommendations of the two Studies and requested Member States to take all necessary steps without further delay in vital areas such as sharing and developing scientific capabilities to protect and manage the environment. They further directed the Technical Committee on Environment to monitor the progress made in the implementation of the recommendations of the two Studies, and submit a report to the Ninth Summit through the Council of Ministers.

The Heads of State or Government recalled the decisions expressed in the Dhaka Declaration of April, 1993 on the outcome of the United Nations Conference on Environment and Development (UNCED) of June, 1992 and reiterated the urgent need to ensure the flow of new and additional resources that are adequate and predictable to successfully implement the programmes of Agenda 21. They also recalled the United Nations minimum target for developed countries of 0.7 percent of GNP as Official Development Assistance, a target which is yet to be approximated by most developed countries. The Heads of State or Government also noted that international actions in the area of environment protection should be based on partnership and collective endeavors and should reflect the principle enunciated in the UNCED, of common but differentiated responsibilities. Integral to such actions is the promotion of economic growth in developing countries, that is both sustained and sustainable and direct action in eradicating poverty.

The Heads of State or Government also noted that the Commission on Sustainable Development set up to monitor the implementation of the Rio agreements has met thrice since their earlier meeting and expressed the hope that the Commission would be able to facilitate the necessary flow of resources and technology.

The Heads of State or Government also noted that the Convention on Biological Diversity and the United Nations Framework Convention on Climate Change have both come into force and the first meetings of the Conferences of Parties to each Convention have been held. Welcoming these developments they urged that developing countries should be assisted in meeting their commitments under the Conventions. The establishment of the restructured Global Environment Facility (GEF) is a beginning in this direction. However, the Heads of State or Government urged that funds of a much larger order would be necessary if the needs of the Conventions are to be met.

Terrorism

The Heads of State or Government expressed serious concern on the spread of terrorism in and outside the region and reiterated their unequivocal condemnation of all acts, methods and practices of terrorism as criminal. They deplored all such acts for their ruinous impact on life, property, socio-economic development and political stability as well as on regional and international peace and cooperation.

The Heads of State or Government once again emphasized that highest priority should be accorded to the enactment of enabling legislation at the national level to give effect to the SAARC Regional Convention on Suppression of Terrorism. They urged Member States, which had not yet done so, to enact expeditiously enabling legislation at the national level to implement the convention and reiterated the need for a constant dialogue and interaction among the concerned agencies of Member States, including submission of periodic recommendations to the Council of Ministers.

They underlined that cooperation among SAARC Member States was vital if the scourge of terrorism was to be eliminated from the region.

Drug Trafficking

The Heads of State or Government recognised that drug abuse and drug trafficking with its linkages with organised crime, illicit arms trade and terrorism continues to pose a serious threat to the security and stability in the region.

While noting the efforts made by Member States as well as the regional cooperation underway to combat this pernicious trade, the Leaders stressed the urgency of further strengthening the process of cooperation.

The Leaders welcomed the ratification of the SAARC Convention on Narcotic Drugs and Psychotropic Substances by all Member States and entry into force of the Convention in September 1993. They urged all Member States to take necessary follow-up action for effective implementation of the Convention.

Science and Technology

The Heads of State or Government reiterated that cooperation in the area of Science and Technology should be accorded high priority. Noting that some progress had been made towards establishment of networking arrangements, inter-alia, in the fields of Bio-Technology, Genetic Engineering, Energy Modelling Techniques and Low-Cost Housing and Building Technologies, the Leaders called for further acceleration of this process.

People-to-People Contact

Reiterating their earlier resolve to further promote people-to-people contact through increased involvement of the peoples of South Asia in the process of regional cooperation, the Heads of State or Government noted with satisfaction that such interaction has been taking place through various fora both within and outside the SAARC framework and has contributed to the promotion of mutual understanding in the region.

The Leaders noted that SAARCLAW (an association for persons of the legal communities of SAARC countries) had been accorded recognition by SAARC. The Leaders hoped that SAARCLAW would play an effective role in fostering closer cooperation among the legal communities in the region.

The Leaders noted with satisfaction that the SAARC Chamber of Commerce and Industry (SCCI) has been functioning satisfactorily. They expressed hope that the SAARC Chamber and its constituent units in the Member States will do their utmost to promote trade and economic cooperation in the SAARC region. The Leaders commended the SAARC Chamber for disseminating information on the scope, content and potentials of SAARC Preferential Trading Arrangement (SAPTA) among the business community in the region.

The Heads of State or Government expressed satisfaction that the SAARC Visa Exemption Scheme is being implemented smoothly and has enhanced the scope of people-to-people contacts.

South Asian Development Fund (SADF)

The Heads of State or Government endorsed the establishment of a three-window South Asian Development Fund with the merger of SAARC Fund for Regional Projects and the SAARC Regional Fund and a third window for social development and infrastructure development.

Projection of Collective Positions

The Heads of State or Government recalled their decision taken at the Seventh SAARC Summit regarding development of collective positions in international fora on such issues as would enhance the international profile of South Asia and would enable the Member States to articulate their position on them more effectively. They noted that Council of Ministers had formulated a procedure for projection of SAARC collective positions at such international fora.

They noted with satisfaction that pursuant to the decision at the Seventh SAARC Summit, collective positions were formulated by Member States which were presented at the World Conference on Natural Disaster Reduction and the World Summit for Social Development. The Leaders also noted with satisfaction that a SAARC collective position will also be presented at the Fourth World Conference on Women in Beijing in September 1995.

Security of Small States

The Heads of State or Government reaffirming their commitment to universally accepted principles and norms relating to the sovereign rights and territorial integrity of all States, recognized that small States, because of their particular problems, required special measures of support for safeguarding their independence and territorial integrity. They reiterated that real protection of small and weaker States should be firmly rooted in the rule of law. This, they stressed should be ensured by all countries either severally or collectively through the pursuit of appropriate actions.

International Political Developments

The Heads of State or Government noted that the end of the Cold War had resulted in fundamental changes in the political landscape. It was therefore important that a new idiom be found to address new concerns. The disappearance of the confrontation between the two power blocs presented an opportunity towards building a genuine consensus for a new international order.

The Heads of State or Government had wide ranging discussions on the current global political trends and future prospects, particularly those issues that concern South Asia. In this context, they reiterated their deep commitment to the purposes and principles of the UN Charter and reaffirmed their resolve to strengthen the United Nations as the central instrument for peace, security, disarmament, development and cooperation among the nations of the world. While pledging their support to all constructive initiatives aimed at strengthening the United Nations, the Leaders emphasised that such initiatives must be undertaken with the sole objective of rendering the United Nations and all its organs more democratic, efficient and effective and not to limit the focus of its attention to a narrow and isolated range of objectives.

Appreciating the role of some SAARC Member States in the UN Peace Keeping Operations in various parts of the world, the Heads of State or Government felt that such participation had contributed towards maintenance of peace and security in the world.

The Heads of State or Government reiterated their firm commitment to the principles and objectives of the Non-aligned Movement and underlined the continued validity and relevance of these principles and objectives in the contemporary world. They recalled the stabilizing role played by the Movement in global affairs since its inception. They expressed their deep conviction that the Movement's innate strength equipped it to continue to play a most constructive role in laying the foundations of a new world order based on the rule of law, non-discrimination, equity and cooperation.

The Heads of State or Government noted that while the international community had successfully created the norm against chemical and biological weapons, it had, unfortunately, been unable to do the same with regard to nuclear weapons. The Leaders were convinced that more needs to be done and at a far greater pace. Reiterating that the utmost priority was to be given to nuclear disarmament, given the danger posed by nuclear weapons, they urged the Conference on Disarmament to negotiate an international convention prohibiting the use or threat of use of nuclear weapons under any circumstances and undertake negotiations for the complete elimination of all nuclear weapons within a time bound framework.

The Heads of State or Government expressed their strong

commitment to the promotion and protection of human rights. They agreed to take all necessary steps to achieve this objective.

International Economic and Social Issues

The Heads of State or Government welcomed the successful conclusion of the Uruguay Round of multilateral trade negotiations and reaffirmed their commitment to implement fully and as scheduled, the Final Act of the Uruguay Round of multilateral trade negotiations. They also welcomed the coming into existence of the WTO and expressed the hope that it would help to expand international trade, particularly that of the developing countries. They reaffirmed the immediate need to elaborate policies to enable developing countries, to take advantage of expanded international trading opportunities, in the context of the full implementation of the Round. They called on all countries to refrain from any unilateral measure not in accordance with international law, the Charter of the United Nations and enlightened regionalism and globalism that creates obstacles to trade relations among States and thereby impedes the full realization of social and economic development.

Recognizing that the promotion of mutually reinforcing broad-based sustained economic growth on a global scale, as well as a non-discriminatory, and multilateral rule-based international trading system, provided a basis for social development, the Heads of State or Government called for the establishment of an open, equitable, cooperative and mutually beneficial international economic environment. They also called for a reduction of trade barriers and promotion of expanded access to global markets.

The Heads of State or Government reaffirmed their commitment to safeguard the basic interests of workers. They called upon countries to refrain from erecting trade barriers in the guise of promotion and protection of workers' rights. They deplored the tendency to impose any conditionalities on international trade, whether as a "social clause" or as the "environmental clause", while reiterating their commitment to ensuring workers' rights as well as protection of the environment.

Special Measures for the Least Developed and Land-Locked Countries

The Heads of State or Government noted with deep concern that economic growth in the Least Developed Countries and Land-Locked Countries is not satisfactory and emphasized the need to take special measures for accelerating the process of development. They reiterated the need to fulfil the internationally agreed aid targets for the developing countries and the Least Developed Countries. They emphasized on the need for exceptional finance to facilitate implementation of economic reform programmes in SAARC Countries.

Dates and Venue of the Ninth Meeting of the SAARC Heads of State or Government

The Heads of State or Government gratefully accepted the offer of the Government of Maldives to host the Ninth SAARC Summit. The dates would be finalised in consultation with Member States.

The Heads of State or Government of Bangladesh, Bhutan, Maldives, Nepal, Pakistan and Sri Lanka expressed their deep appreciation for the exemplary manner in which the Prime Minister of India had discharged his responsibilities as Chairman of the Meeting. They expressed their profound gratitude for the warm and gracious hospitality extended to them by the Government and the people of the Republic of India and for the excellent arrangements made for the Meeting.

9th Summit

DECLARATION

The Male' Declaration of the Heads of State or Government of the Member Countries of South Asian Association for Regional Cooperation issued on 14th May 1997.

INTRODUCTION

The Prime Minister of the People's Republic of Bangladesh, Her Excellency Sheikh Hasina; the King of Bhutan, His Majesty Jigme Singye Wangchuck; the Prime Minister of the Republic of India, His Excellency Mr. Inder Kumar Gujral; the President of the Republic of Maldives, His Excellency Mr. Maumoon Abdul Gayoom; the Prime Minister of Kingdom of Nepal, Rt. Hon. Mr. Lokendra Bahadur

Chand; the Prime Minister of the Islamic Republic of Pakistan, His Excellency Mr. Mohammad Nawaz Sharif and the President of the Democratic Socialist Republic of Sri Lanka, Her Excellency Mrs. Chandrika Bandaranaike Kumaratunga met at the Ninth Summit of the South Asian Association for Regional Co-operation (SAARC) at Malé, Maldives on 12-14 May 1997.

Regional Cooperation

The Heads of State or Government reiterated their commitment to SAARC and resolved to accelerate regional cooperation in order to realize the aims and objectives of the Association. They reaffirmed their commitment to the principles enshrined in the SAARC Charter, especially to the principles of sovereign equality, territorial integrity, national independence, non-use of force and non-interference in each others' internal affairs. They were convinced that regional cooperation was indispensable in an interdependent world for the realization of the full potential of the South Asian region.

The Heads of State or Government welcomed the holding of the Commemorative Session of the Council of Ministers in New Delhi in December 1995 to mark the First Decade, on the theme "SAARC - Vision for the Second Decade". They observed that over the past decade SAARC has matured as an institution and the scope and volume of cooperative activities have expanded. They expressed satisfaction that in addition to continued cooperation in agreed areas, SAARC has now moved into the core areas of economic cooperation.

The Heads of State or Government noted that, in the twelve years of its existence, SAARC has seen progress in various fields of its Endeavour. They directed that a Group of Eminent Persons (GEP) be constituted, with distinguished backgrounds in activities pertaining to regional cooperation, comprising of one representative from each Member State, with the discretion of each Member State to appoint an additional representative. This Group, to which the SAARC Secretary-General will be invited, will undertake a comprehensive appraisal of SAARC, and identify measures including mechanisms to further vitalise and enhance the effectiveness of the Association in achieving its objectives. They further decided that the Group may develop a long-range vision and formulate a perspective plan of action including a SAARC Agenda for 2000 and Beyond which will spell out the target that can and must be achieved by the year 2020. The Group may report to the Heads of State or Government at the Tenth SAARC Summit.

With a view to enhancing the effectiveness of the role and functioning of the Secretariat, the Heads of State or Government agreed to amend Article V (1) of the Memorandum of Understanding on the Establishment of the Secretariat and decided that the tenure of the Secretary-General, with immediate effect, shall be for a non-renewable term of three years.

The Heads of State or Government reiterated their determination to reinforce the unity and cohesion of SAARC. With the objective of enhancing regional solidarity and promoting overall development within SAARC, the Heads of State or Government encouraged, under the provisions of Articles VII and X of the Charter, the development of specific projects relevant to the special individual needs of three or more Member States.

They agreed that a climate of mutual accommodation and purposeful cooperation was needed to impart further impetus to the SAARC process during the second decade of SAARC in order to address the developmental challenges facing the region.

Enhancing Political Cooperation

The Heads of State or Government recalled their commitment to the promotion of mutual trust and understanding and, recognizing that the aims of promoting peace, stability and amity and accelerated socio-economic cooperation may best be achieved by fostering good neighborly relations, relieving tensions and building confidence, agreed that a process of informal political consultations would prove useful in this regard.

Eradication of Poverty in South Asia

The Heads of State or Government were unequivocal in their commitment to the eradication of poverty in South Asia at the earliest, preferably by the year 2002 A.D. through an Agenda of Action. They noted with satisfaction the establishment of a three-tier mechanism on poverty eradication and endorsed the recommendations of the two rounds of meetings under this mechanism hosted by India and Pakistan, respectively. They desired that the Ministers of Finance/Planning should meet again in the near future to give further impetus to this process.

In considering the Report of the Ministers of Finance/Planning, the Heads of State or Government agreed that effective implementation of poverty eradication programmes required a focus on greater participation of target groups in the formulation and implementation of such programmes through social mobilization. They, therefore, decided to designate 1997 as the "SAARC Year of Participatory Governance".

The Heads of State or Government welcomed the successful holding of the Micro-credit Summit in Washington, D.C. in February 1997 and its Declaration of support to launch a global campaign to reach 100 million of the world's poorest families, especially women, with credit for self-employment and other financial and business services, by the year 2005 A.D.

Recognizing that micro-credit programmes have successfully demonstrated their usefulness toward achieving many goals of socio-economic upliftment, including the eradication of poverty and empowerment of women, the Leaders agreed to intensify endeavors in their respective countries so that the outreach of these programmes becomes widespread.

The Heads of State or Government were convinced that an enabling international environment to support poverty eradication efforts of the SAARC countries is an essential element in attaining success for these efforts. They urged all donor countries, international institutions and other bodies engaged in eradication of poverty to increase their support and assistance to these efforts.

Acceleration of Economic Cooperation

The Heads of State or Government noted with satisfaction the entry into force of the Agreement on SAARC Preferential Trading Arrangement (SAPTA) on 7 December 1995. They recognized the importance of achieving a free trade area by the year 2001 A.D. and reiterated that steps towards trade liberalization must take into account the special needs of the smaller and the Least Developed Countries and that benefits must accrue equitably.

While expressing satisfaction at the conclusion of the two Rounds of Trade Negotiations under SAPTA, the Heads of State or

Government welcomed the decision to launch the Third Round of Trade Negotiations shortly. They agreed that preferential tariff concessions should cover products which are being actively traded amongst Member States. They further agreed that the Third Round should deepen tariff concessions along with the removal of non-tariff barriers and structural impediments in order to move speedily towards the goal of SAFTA.

The Leaders welcomed the holding of the First Meeting of the Commerce Ministers and the First SAARC Trade Fair in New Delhi in 1996 and noted the decision of the Commerce Ministers to meet annually. They further welcomed the offer of Pakistan to host the second SAARC Trade Fair to coincide with the SAARC Commerce Ministers' Meeting.

The Heads of State or Government agreed that the efforts to enhance trade and economic co-operation in the region would be further strengthened by initiating specific steps to promote and protect investment, increase complementarities in economic activities of Member States and other measures supportive of promotion of SAARC joint ventures. They also welcomed the offer of India to host a meeting on promotion and protection of investment and the offer of Pakistan to host a meeting on avoidance of double taxation. They also welcomed measures of cooperation in the areas of customs standardization, arbitration and enhancing industrial economy and management.

The Heads of State or Government agreed that in intensifying economic cooperation the interests of smaller countries, especially the least developed among them, should be taken into account through the implementation of special measures in their favor.

The Heads of State or Government noted that inadequate communications facilities amongst the Member States were a major hindrance to closer economic co-operation. They stressed the importance of developing infrastructure and adequate communication networks among Member States to reinforce the process of economic co-operation. In this regard, they highlighted the need for the simplification of complex documentation procedures and transactional software to facilitate economic interaction across the region. They welcomed the offer of Sri Lanka to host a Meeting of the Communication Ministers of the Member States.

The Heads of State or Government reaffirmed their determination to encourage the private sector in the region to contribute increasingly to the strengthening of intra-SAARC links in key areas of trade, investment and finance. They welcomed the decision by the SCCI to convene annually an Economic Cooperation Conference in conjunction with the annual meeting of SAARC Commerce Ministers and SAARC Trade Fairs.

Integrated Programme of Action (IPA)

The Heads of State or Government emphasised the need to make the Integrated Programme of Action (IPA) more effective through the selection of target-oriented and time-bound activities within an overall framework of enhanced co-operation among Member States. In this context, they noted that the Secretary-General had been authorized by the Council of Ministers to constitute a Group of Experts to review the IPA.

Regional Centres

The Heads of State or Government noted that Regional Centres have an important role to play in harnessing the resources and capabilities within the SAARC region in addressing specific and shared concerns of Member States. They welcomed the decision of the Council of Ministers to establish a Human Resource Development Centre in Pakistan.

They stressed that Regional Centres should implement action and result-oriented programmes and highlighted the importance of rationalizing the functioning of these Centres.

Women in Development

The Heads of State or Government recognized that increased social and political awareness in the region had brought positive contributions to the issues of gender equality and empowerment of women. They further emphasized the need for enhanced cooperation to achieve the desired objective of bringing women into the mainstream of socio-economic development in the region. In this context, they emphasized the urgency to effectively implement the recommendations of the "Dhaka Resolution on Women", issued at the conclusion of the SAARC Ministerial Conference on Women and presented to the Fourth World Conference on Women.

Taking note of the mid-decade review of the SAARC Plan of Action on the Girl-Child, the Heads of State or Government expressed their determination to accelerate efforts at reduction of malnutrition and mortality rates, raising education and literacy rates, reduction of the proportion of early marriage among girls, and the postponement of the age of first pregnancy, thereby contributing to the increased welfare of the girl-child and reduction of population growth rates.

The Heads of State or Government reaffirmed their commitment to take urgent action to alleviate the situation of Girl Children in Especially Difficult Circumstances (GCEDC), including those orphaned, disabled and/or exploited. In this context, they endorsed the recommendations made by the Council of Ministers, aimed at the creation of a socio-economic environment in the SAARC region which would provide equal opportunities to children from all economic sections.

Expressing grave concern at the trafficking of women and children within and between countries, the Heads of State or Government pledged to coordinate their efforts and take effective measures to address this problem. They decided that existing legislation in Member States should be strengthened and strictly enforced. This should include simplification of repatriation procedures for victims of trafficking. They also decided that the feasibility of establishing a Regional Convention on Combating the Crime of Trafficking in Women and Children for Prostitution be examined by the relevant Technical Committee.

Children

The Heads of State or Government expressed satisfaction that the annual reviews of the situation of children in SAARC countries for the years 1995 and 1996 revealed significant progress in reducing infant mortality and in enhancing the coverage of immunization in the region. They stressed that sustained efforts should be made by Member States to consolidate the gains in these areas. In this regard, they welcomed the decision to designate 7th December, 1997 and 18th January, 1998 as "SAARC Polio Immunization Days".

The Heads of State or Government resolved to implement appropriate policies at the national level to achieve the targets and objectives set out in the Rawalpindi Declaration issued at the end of the Third Ministerial Conference on the Children of South Asia held in August 1996, including the call to eliminate the evil of child-labour from the region by the year 2010 A.D. They called for stringent measures to protect children from all forms of exploitation. To this end, the Leaders agreed to set up a Study Group at an appropriate level to examine the social compulsions that create the problem.

They reaffirmed their commitment to improve the status of children in disadvantaged circumstances in the SAARC region. They recognized that the problems of these children are inextricably linked to the prevailing socio-economic conditions and problems of the region, and therefore, called for a holistic approach to address them. They expressed the need to formulate a Convention on Regional Arrangements on the Promotion of Child Welfare in South Asia in launching the SAARC Decade of the Rights of the Child, from the year 2001 A.D. to 2010 A.D.

Nutrition

Noting that malnutrition, often severe, is a serious concern in South Asia, the Heads of State or Government agreed to launch an Initiative on Nutrition aimed at promotion of availability of food of essential nutritional value to individual household and evolving policies for supplementing and fortifying essential micro-nutrients, deficiencies of which have affected the well being of the most vulnerable sections of the population, particularly women and children.

The Heads of State or Government emphasised that the provision of a safe, secure and clean environment was an essential pre-requisite for the welfare of the most vulnerable sections of society in the region, particularly for the proper growth and development of children, and agreed on the need for launching technology missions to develop low-cost, easily replicable technologies appropriate local conditions for sustainable harvesting of water, provision of clean drinking water and sanitation.

Youth

The Heads of State or Government welcomed the operationalization of the SAARC Youth Awards Scheme and noted that the Scheme will be reviewed in the near future with the purpose of expanding it. They also welcomed the initiative to organize Youth Camps in the region on various themes.

Persons with Disability

Conscious of the continuing problems faced by disabled persons, the Heads of State or Government reaffirmed their resolve to continue the implementation of the recommendations of the Ministerial Conference on Disabled Persons held in Islamabad in December 1993.

Shelter

The Heads of State or Government emphasized that housing was a basic right of all people and reiterated their determination to sustain efforts to improve the condition of human settlements in the region, with a view to achieving the global objective of "Shelter for All by the Year 2000".

Literacy

The Heads of State or Government recognized that illiteracy is one of the major causes impeding the development of the vast human resource potential of the region and a major factor contributing to the region's economic backwardness and social imbalance. They noted that the Member States had observed "1996 as the SAARC Year of Literacy" and reiterated their commitment to continue endeavors to eradicate illiteracy from the region.

Recognizing the resource, manpower and infrastructural constraints to the promotion of vocational and higher education in the region, the Leaders agreed that new and innovative methods like Open Learning and Distance Education can play an effective role in meeting regional needs in a cost effective and flexible manner. Accordingly, they agreed that the institutional facilities in such education available in the region should be utilised on a regional scale. The possibility of the creation of a Consortium of Open Universities in the region should also be explored.

Environment

The Heads of State or Government expressed concern about the continuing degradation of the environment in different parts of the world including the SAARC region. While recognizing that collective initiatives were required urgently to address the challenge posed by such degradation, they noted that unsustainable consumption patterns in the developed countries and widespread poverty in the developing countries are major factors contributing to ecological degradation in different parts of the world. In this regard, they noted that although both developed and developing countries were required to undertake specific initiatives to face environmental concerns, stress should also be laid on the acceleration of development in developing countries to enable them to face environmental challenges.

Reviewing the work carried out in the area of disseminating information on the problems of environmental degradation and their impact on the region, the Heads of State or Government expressed the urgent need for the implementation of the recommendations of the SAARC Regional Study on the Greenhouse Effect and its Impact on the Region, and the Regional Study on the Causes and Consequences of Natural Disasters and the Protection and Preservation of the Environment. They welcomed the offer of the Maldives to host a meeting of the SAARC Environment Ministers to focus more directly on the Environment concerns of the region including the formulation of a Plan of Action for immediate implementation of recommendations contained in the two Studies, taking into account the recommendations made by the Meeting of the Environment Ministers in New Delhi in April 1997. The Leaders felt that the meeting may also consider the feasibility of drawing up a Regional Treaty on Environment in the context of existing international Conventions on the subject. They reiterated their view that Member States should take all necessary steps in vital areas such as sharing and developing scientific capabilities to protect and manage the environment.

The Heads of State or Government agreed on the urgent need for cooperation through exchange of information, strategies and technologies for combating pollution of air and water and for evolving common minimum standards which could be applied region-wide in this regard. Recognizing the wealth of bio-diversity in the South Asian region and expressing concern at the threat of its progressive depletion through degradation and fragmentation, they affirmed their commitment to take steps towards the protection and conservation of these genetic resources. They noted that many areas rich in bio-diversity in South Asia lay along shared borders and agreed to cooperate in the creation of contiguous protected areas where identified. They also agreed to cooperate in the prevention of illegal trafficking in flora and fauna and devise an appropriate mechanism for this purpose, including the possibility of concluding a Convention. They decided that the meeting of SAARC Environment Ministers should be institutionalized henceforth as an annual event.

While expressing concern at the slow progress in the implementation of the Agenda 21, the Heads of State or Government called for the urgent implementation of the commitments, recommendations and agreements reached at the United Nations Conference on Environment and Development held in Rio de Janeiro in June 1992. In particular, they also called for the early implementation of the United Nations Framework Convention on Climate Change and the adoption of a Protocol or another legal instrument for reduction of greenhouse gas emissions by developed countries within an early timeframe, but not later than the year 2005 A.D.

The Heads of State or Government underlined the importance of projecting an effective, and coordinated collective position of SAARC at the forthcoming Special Session of the United Nations General Assembly to Review and Appraise the Implementation of Agenda 21. In this regard, they fully endorsed the New Delhi Declaration issued at the end of the SAARC Ministerial Conference on Environment held from 2-3 April 1997, as amended at the Eighteenth Session of the Council of Ministers.

Terrorism and Drug Trafficking

Recognizing that terrorism and drug trafficking pose a serious threat to security and stability of Member States, the Heads of State or Government reiterated their firm commitment to combat these activities in the region. They emphasized the urgent need to complete enabling legislation in order to implement the SAARC Regional Conventions on Suppression of Terrorism and on Narcotic Drugs and Psychotropic Substances.

The Heads of State or Government recalled the adoption of the 1996 UN Declaration on Measures to Eliminate International Terrorism and urged all Member States to work towards its implementation. They called for international action to prevent the abuse of Refugee Conventions and to halt activities which help terrorist groups to collect funds for their activities in South Asia.

The Heads of State or Government noted the establishment of the SAARC Terrorist Offences Monitoring Desk (STOMD) and the SAARC Drug Offences Monitoring Desk (SDOMD) in Colombo. They agreed on the need to maintain regular flow of relevant information to enable the Monitoring Desks to function effectively.

The Heads of State or Government noted with appreciation the convening of the First SAARC Conference on Cooperation in Police Matters in Colombo during July 1996. They endorsed the outcome of the Conference, particularly, the call for sharing of expertise with regard to the different areas of police investigation and investigation of organized crime and drug related crimes. They welcomed the offer of the Maldives to host the second Conference in 1997.

Science and Technology

Noting that cooperation in the field of Science and Technology was imperative in ensuring the acceleration of the process of development in the region and recognizing the progress made in this field, the Heads of State or Government emphasized the need to continue cooperation in this area, especially in facilitating research and exchange of information in the fields of bio-technology, genetic engineering, energy modelling techniques and low-cost housing and building technologies.

Tourism

Emphasizing that tourism plays an important role in promoting people to people contact in the region, the Heads of State or Government stressed the importance of strengthening cooperation with the aim of realising its full potential in the region. They were convinced that greater cooperation in this area would contribute to the enhancement of people-to-people contact within the region as well as to the economic development of Member States.

The Heads of State or Government noted that organized tourism in South Asia has not yet achieved its full potential, and recommended that appropriate measures to promote tourism be given priority, and in this regard, welcomed the offer of Sri Lanka to host the SAARC Ministerial Meeting on Tourism in Colombo in 1997.

People-to-People Contact

The Heads of State or Government reiterated their conviction that enhanced people-to-people contact would contribute to strengthening mutual understanding and goodwill among the people in the region. In this context, they noted the positive contribution made by SAARC Chamber of Commerce and Industry (SCCI) and SAARCLAW.

They observed that SAARC Chairs, Fellowships and Scholarships Scheme should be increasingly used to facilitate greater interaction among students, scholars and academics in the region.

The Heads of State or Government noted with satisfaction the inclusion of new categories of persons from different walks of life in the SAARC Visa Exemption Scheme and believed that this would further promote people-to-people contact.

They noted the offer of Sri Lanka to host the First SAARC Film Festival in Colombo in 1998 to coincide with the 50th anniversary of the Independence of Sri Lanka.

The Heads of State or Government agreed that the SAARC countries possess enormous tourism potential that should be properly utilized for the benefit of the people of the region. In this context, they decided that the civil aviation authorities of Member States should meet in the very near future with a view to establishing direct air services between SAARC capitals which would promote people-to-people contact and encourage tourism. They welcomed the offer of Bangladesh to host the first meeting of the civil aviation authorities.

South Asian Development Fund (SADF)

While expressing satisfaction that the South Asian Development Fund (SADF) had been established in June 1996 initially with its headquarters in Dhaka, Bangladesh, the Heads of State or Government recognized the need to make the Fund operational at the earliest.

Projection of Collective Positions

The Heads of State or Government reiterated their commitment to develop collective SAARC positions in international fora on issues of common concern, in order to enhance the international profile of

South Asia as well as to enable Member States to articulate their position on such issues in a more effective manner. In this regard, they noted with satisfaction the collective SAARC positions finalized and presented prior to the Fourth World Conference on Women held in Beijing in September 1995, HABITAT II held in Istanbul in June 1996, and World Food Summit held in Rome in November 1996. They also expressed satisfaction with the formulation of a SAARC common position before the forthcoming Special Session of the United Nations General Assembly to Review and Appraise the Implementation of Agenda 21.

Security of Small States

The Heads of State or Government recognized that small states, because of their particular vulnerabilities, require special measures of support from the international community for safeguarding their sovereign independence and territorial integrity. They further reaffirmed their view that such support should be firmly rooted in the scrupulous adherence to the UN Charter, the rule of law and strict adherence to universally accepted principles and norms related to sovereign rights and territorial integrity of all States irrespective of size. This, they emphasized, may be ensured by all countries either severally or collectively through the pursuit of appropriate action.

International Political Developments

The Heads of State or Government had wide ranging discussions on current international issues, particularly those that affect South Asia. In this context, reiterating their deep commitment to the purposes and principles of the UN Charter, the Heads of State or Government recalled that the commemoration of the 50th anniversary of the founding of the United Nations in October 1995 had highlighted the need to strengthen, revitalize and reform the Organization. They reiterated their support to the on-going process of restructuring and revitalizing the Organization and reaffirmed their resolve to make it a more effective universal instrument for addressing international issues on an equitable and democratic basis, taking full account of the interests and concerns of all states.

Addressing the question of reform of the United Nations, the Heads of State or Government laid particular emphasis on the principle of sovereign equality of States and on equitable geographical representation in regard to the question of increase in the membership of the Security Council. They recognized the need to make the Security Council more representative, democratic and transparent, so that it is better equipped to uphold its responsibility for the maintenance of international peace and security.

The Heads of State or Government reiterated their firm commitment to the principles and objectives of the Non-Aligned Movement (NAM) and underscored the continued validity and relevance of these principles and objectives in the contemporary world. They expressed their deep conviction that the Movement's innate strength equips it to continue to play a most constructive role in laying the foundations of a new world order based on the rule of law, non-interference, equity and cooperation.

The Heads of State or Government while expressing support to the continuation of the peace process in the Middle East, expressed concern at the setback to the peace process and unleashing of violence against Palestinian people in occupied territories and the resulting threat to the peace process due to policies of the Government of Israel in establishing and enlarging existing Jewish settlements in the occupied Palestinian territories. They were convinced that the peace process should be continued by honoring previous commitments made by all parties involved. They also called for the restoration of the inalienable rights of the Palestinian people, including the right of self determination and the establishment of a sovereign State under the leadership of PLO, their sole legitimate representative, which could co-exist with its neighbors in peace and harmony.

Noting that the end of the Cold War had created unprecedented opportunities in the field of disarmament, the Heads of State or Government recognized the need for the international community to pursue nuclear disarmament as a matter of highest priority. In this regard, they recognized the need to start negotiations through the Conference on Disarmament and to establish a phased programme for the complete elimination of nuclear weapons within a specified framework of time, including a Nuclear Weapons Convention.

While reiterating their commitment to the promotion and protection of human rights, the Heads of State or Government resolved to take all necessary steps to achieve this objective.

International Economic and Social Issues

The Heads of State or Government noted that current trends of globalisation and liberalisation were imposing a heavy burden on developing economies, in particular, the least developed countries (LDCs) which are becoming marginalised from the mainstream of the world economy. They also expressed concern over trends to erect new protectionist barriers by linking imports from developing countries to politically motivated social and environmental values and concerns, such as human rights. They observed that the impact of these trends is compounded by new challenges relating to issues of access to markets, capital and new technologies. They also noted with regret the overall decline in the Official Development Assistance (ODA) over the years which has contributed to the aggravation of the condition of the LDCs.

The Heads of State or Government reaffirmed the promotion of a non-discriminatory and multilateral rule-based global system of economic relations in order to engage the developing countries constructively and on the basis of reciprocal shared benefits in the process of liberalization, as well as to assist them integrate into the global economy.

The Heads of State or Government called on the developed countries to assist the developing countries through the creation of a favorable and supportive global economic environment, in particular, through domestic action in their countries for purposes of accelerating investment flows to developing countries thereby generating a positive impact on the developmental efforts of developing countries as well as assisting their integration into the multilateral trading system. They also called on the developed countries to substantially reduce tariff and non-tariff barriers and desist from restrictive trade practices, which would negatively affect the access of developing countries to global markets.

Special Measures for the Least Developed and Land-Locked Countries

The Heads of State or Government emphasized the need for priority action on various international development commitments, such as the Paris Declaration and the Programme of Action for LDCs for the 1990s.

While noting with deep concern that economic growth in the Least Developed and Land-Locked Countries is not progressing well, the Heads of State or Government stressed the need to take special measures for accelerating the process of development. They emphasized the need to fulfil the internationally agreed aid targets for ensuring accelerated and sustained economic growth in developing countries particularly in the Least Developed Countries. They stressed on the need for adequate resources to facilitate implementation of economic reform programmes in SAARC countries.

The Heads of State or Government emphasized that the review of the criteria for the determination of LDC status for consideration by the United Nations General Assembly this year, must take into account the special significance of the extent and magnitude of incidence of poverty in the poorest countries and the special vulnerabilities of small island states.

Dates and Venue of the Tenth Meeting of the Heads of State or Government

The Heads of State or Government accepted with deep appreciation the offer of the Government of Sri Lanka to host the Tenth SAARC Summit. They further decided that the Eleventh and Twelfth Summits will be held in Nepal and Pakistan, respectively.

The Heads of State or Government of Bangladesh, Bhutan, India, Nepal, Pakistan and Sri Lanka expressed their sincere appreciation for the exemplary manner in which the President of the Republic of the Maldives had conducted the Meeting and guided its proceedings in his capacity as Chairman. They expressed their deep gratitude for the warm and generous hospitality extended to them by the Government and the people of the Maldives and for the excellent arrangements made for the Meeting.

10th Summit

THE COLOMBO DECLARATION

INTRODUCTION

The Prime Minister of the People's Republic of Bangladesh, Her Excellency Sheikh Hasina; Chairman, Council of Ministers and Head of Government of the Royal Government of Bhutan, His Excellency Lyonpo Jigmi Y. Thinley; the Prime Minister of the Republic of India, His Excellency Mr. Atal Behari Vajpayee; the President of the Republic of Maldives, His Excellency Mr. Maumoon Abdul Gayoom; the Prime Minister of the Kingdom of Nepal, Rt. Hon. Mr. Girija Prasad Koirala; the Prime Minister of the Islamic Republic of Pakistan, His Excellency Mr. Muhammad Nawaz Sharif; and the President of the Democratic Socialist Republic of Sri Lanka, Her Excellency Mrs. Chandrika Bandaranaike Kumaratunga met at the Tenth Summit of the South Asian Association for Regional Cooperation (SAARC) at Colombo from July 29 to 31, 1998, in the year of the Golden Jubilee of the Independence of Sri Lanka.

Regional Cooperation

The Heads of State or Government re-affirmed their firm commitment to the objectives, principles and provisions of the Charter of the South Asian Association for Regional Cooperation (SAARC) and to the pursuit of regional cooperation on the basis of their acceptance of the principles of sovereign equality, territorial integrity of States, political independence, non-interference in each others internal affairs, non-use of force, the peaceful settlement of all disputes and mutuality of benefit.

The Heads of State or Government recognized that the rich potential for productive, equitable regional cooperation among the Governments and people of South Asia which accounts for a fifth of humanity should be fully realized.

Cultural Unity

The Heads of State or Government recognized that South Asia, while reflecting a rich, complex and varied plurality of cultural and religious traditions, was heir to a profound common civilizational continuum of great antiquity which constitutes a historical basis for sustaining harmonious relations among the people of the region. They acknowledged that the SAARC process could draw more deeply from the vitality and strength of South Asia's shared cultural heritage as a source influencing and enhancing creative energies in all fields.

The Heads of State or Government welcomed the offer of Sri Lanka to host a meeting of the Ministers of Cultural Affairs of

SAARC to prepare a practical Action Plan to network the national institutes of cultural relations and to establish a South Asian Cultural Center to promote the distinctive arts of South Asia. They requested the Government of Sri Lanka to circulate a concept paper on the issues to be addressed by the meeting including financing arrangements for the proposed institute.

Enhancing Political Cooperation

The Heads of State or Government reiterated their commitment to the promotion of mutual trust and understanding and, recognizing that the aims of promoting peace, stability and amity and accelerated socio-economic cooperation may best be achieved by fostering good neighborly relations, relieving tensions and building confidence, agreed that a process of informal political consultations would prove useful in this regard. The Heads of State or Government further recognized that this process would contribute to the appreciation of each other's problems and perceptions as well as for decisive action in agreed areas of regional cooperation.

Appraisal of SAARC Activities

The Heads of State or Government continued their review of the nature, extent, and effectiveness of the cooperative activities of SAARC. They considered the Report and Recommendations of the Group of Eminent Persons mandated by the Ninth Summit in Male' to undertake a comprehensive appraisal of SAARC and to develop an Agenda for 2000 and beyond. They expressed appreciation for the Chairman of the Ninth Summit, His Excellency Mr. Maumoon Abdul Gayoom, the President of the Maldives for convening the Group of Eminent Persons (GEP) and encouraging them to complete their work within the time frame given to them by the Ninth SAARC Summit.

The Heads of State or Government directed the Council of Ministers to examine the Report of the Group of Eminent Persons in depth at their next Session, taking into consideration the views of Member States with regard to the viability of the recommendations and the method of their implementation.

SAARC in the Changing International Economic Environment

The Heads of State or Government assessed the implications of current global economic developments on the economies of South Asia and other developing countries. They noted the profundity of the widespread changes being effected in the economic, technological, social and information fields and their apparent unpredictability. They expressed serious concern over the severe distortions produced by the process of unrestrained globalization as has been evidenced in the downturn of economies of several Asian States. The challenges and opportunities inherent in these fast evolving developments could best be met and the full potential of South Asia realized through effective practical regional and bilateral cooperation among Member States.

They noted that the benefits of the so described "liberalization" have been disappointingly asymmetrical with the process proceeding at a much slower pace in areas of special interest to developing countries. Increased opportunities in trade and investment have bypassed many developing countries. The Least Developed Countries have in particular been marginalized through a series of developments including the shrinking of ODA, concessional and other financial flows to these countries.

The Heads of State or Government noted the initiation of links between SAARC and economic unions and trading groups that were emerging in the wake of globalization and liberalization and considered how best relationships of mutual benefit could be established.

The Heads of State or Government observed that following the WTO Ministerial Conference in Geneva, a process has been initiated at the WTO where implementation issues, built in agenda issues, issues arising out of the WTO Ministerial Conference and other multi-lateral trade issues will be considered with a view to making recommendations to the next Ministerial Conference of the WTO in 1999. These issues and the decisions arising from this process will have far-reaching consequences for our development strategies and prospects. The Heads of State or Government, therefore, resolved that SAARC countries would Endeavour to coordinate their decisions on these issues in areas of common concern so as to protect and promote the interest of the developing countries. They expressed concern about the erection of protectionist barriers and the tendency to impose arbitrary "norms" relating to labor conditions, environmental regulations, governance and other extraneous issues to regulate trade exchanges, which would amount to additional non-tariff barriers, that would have the effect of restricting market access for developing countries including preferential access by Least Developed Countries (LDCs) into markets of developed countries. They agreed on the need for collective strategies to promote a rule-based, non-discriminatory and equitable international trading system in which the interests and concerns of developing countries would be fully safeguarded and served.

The Heads of State or Government noted that emerging issues relating to copyright, patents and marketing franchises including on foodgrains, plants and herbs indigenous to South Asia require firm collective responses to preserve these bio-resources from unregulated commercial exploitation by extra-regional interests. They emphasized in this regard, the principle of sustainable development of bio-resources and the provisions of the UN Convention on Bio-diversity which provided for regulated access to such resources on terms and conditions to be agreed upon with the State in which such resources are located.

The Heads of State or Government cautioned that potential efforts to formulate a new Multilateral Investment Agreement should not overlook the need to ensure the continued independence of developing countries and Least Developed Countries (LDCs) to formulate specific investment policies appropriate to their stage of development.

While reviewing the beneficial effects of globalization, the Heads of State or Government stressed the fact that systemic crises are becoming unpredictable with increased globalization. They expressed their concern about the shortcomings of the international monetary and financial system, and its tardiness in anticipating impending financial market crises sufficiently in advance, so that pre-emptive remedial action be adopted. They noted that the problem is systemic, and not unique to Asia, nor confined to emerging economies, and that it can have global ramifications, unless more fundamental reforms are put in place.

They recognized the risk that ad-hoc approaches, however prompt, once crises supervene, may lead to excessive social costs in the attempt to restore financial discipline. More effective social safety nets would, therefore, need to be devised for protecting vulnerable groups and a more appropriate balance between financing and adjustment found in a reformed international system or architecture, if both the economic and social aspirations of SAARC countries are to be realized. They acknowledged the need to strengthen the individual financial systems of SAARC countries through enhancing institutional capacity, surveillance mechanisms as well as through closer consultations on, and coordination of macro-economic policies where appropriate.

The Heads of State or Government recognized that notwithstanding all national and regional endeavors for economic development and financial stability, the pervasive global economic environment continued to exert a major, sometimes negative influence on the outcome of these endeavors.

Against this background of the need to address systemic issues, they agreed on the vital imperative for strengthened cooperation among SAARC Members to identify, analyze and effectively contend with the complex multi-faceted challenges inherent in the global economic environment that is changing so radically, particularly in this last decade preceding the new millennium. They acknowledged the need to enhance the collective capacity of SAARC in respect of policy analysis, with a specific emphasis on international financial, monetary, trade and investment issues and their domestic ramifications.

The Heads of State or Government also expressed their abhorrence over the practice of imposition of unilateral coercive economic measures as an instrument of policy against developing countries. They called for their immediate cessation.

They stressed the need for more efficient capacity building to enable informed decision-making in these areas to enable innovative collective intervention to safeguard South Asian interests in international negotiations, as well as to develop some edge for effective leverage in such negotiations. The Heads of State or Government agreed on the urgent need for harnessing the rich intellectual and resource capacity of South Asia for this purpose.

The Heads of State or Government requested Sri Lanka, as Chairperson of the 10th Summit, to conduct consultations with

Member States for the convening of a network of researchers comprising members of the Private Sector, Central Banks, Planning Ministries, Research Institutes and eminent economists nominated by Governments to identify, analyse and help SAARC faced up to current global, financial and economic developments affecting the region. They requested Sri Lanka to co-ordinate on necessary practical measures while keeping Member States informed in the matter. Heads of State or Government welcomed the offer of Sri Lanka to host a meeting in Colombo of representatives of SAARC, nominated by their Governments to study the matter further and report with practical recommendations on the matter in advance of the 21st Session of the Council of Ministers to facilitate early decisions.

Acceleration of Economic Cooperation

The Heads of State or Government assessed progress made in the two rounds of negotiations already undertaken under SAPTA. They decided that the third round should be concluded well before the Twenty-first Session of the Council of Ministers. The Heads of State or Government decided that to accelerate progress in the next round of SAPTA negotiations, deeper preferential tariff concessions should be extended to products which are being actively traded, or are likely to be traded, among Members; that discriminatory practices and non-tariff barriers should be simultaneously removed on items in respect of which tariff concessions are granted or have been granted earlier. Measures to remove structural impediments should also be taken in order to move speedily towards the goal of SAFTA. They also directed that domestic content requirements under SAPTA Rules of Origin should be reduced and that the SAPTA Committee of Participants should meet by mid-October '98 in Colombo to finalize the extent of reduction in keeping with the decision of the Second SAARC Commerce Ministers' Meeting. The Heads of State or Government reaffirmed that measures to enable smaller and Least Developed Countries to benefit equitably from economic liberalization were especially important.

The Heads of State or Government reiterated the importance of achieving SAFTA as mandated by the Ninth SAARC Summit. To this end they decided that a Committee of Experts, in consultation with Member States, be constituted with specific Terms of Reference (TOR) to work on drafting a comprehensive treaty regime for creating a free trade area. The Heads of State or Government expressed the view that such a treaty must incorporate, among other things, binding time-frames for freeing trade, measures to facilitate trade, and provisions to ensure an equitable distribution of benefits of trade to all states, especially for smaller and least developed countries, including mechanisms for compensation of revenue loss. They emphasized the importance of finalizing the text of the regulatory framework by the year 2001.

The Heads of State or Government agreed that the benefits of economic liberalization would be more extensive and better balanced through the promotion of trade- creating joint ventures, investment and trade in services such as tourism.

The Heads of State or Government noted with satisfaction the outcome of the Second Meeting of the SAARC Commerce Ministers in Islamabad and welcomed their decision to coordinate SAARC's position on issues of common concern at the WTO. They welcomed in this connection the Declaration issued by the SAARC Commerce Ministers on the eve of the Second WTO Ministerial Meeting in Geneva, setting out a SAARC approach on these issues. Recognizing that critical issues would be decided at the Third WTO Ministerial Conference in the USA in 1999, the Heads of State or Government urged SAARC Commerce Ministers to work closely with a view to evolving better co-ordinated positions on all issues. They directed the Consultative Group of SAARC Permanent Representatives to the WTO at Geneva to consult closely with like-minded countries to advance the interests of developing countries at all WTO Conferences.

The Heads of State or Government noted the progress made in preparations for the Second SAARC Trade Fair to be held in Sri Lanka from September 8-15, 1998. The Heads of State or Government welcomed the offer of Bangladesh to host the Third Meeting of SAARC Commerce Ministers in 1999 and the offer of Pakistan to stage the Third SAARC Trade Fair in 1999.

People-to-People Contact

The Heads of State or Government noted arrangements being finalized by Sri Lanka to host the First SAARC Film Festival in Colombo in 1998 in commemoration of the 50th Anniversary of the Independence of Sri Lanka.

The Heads of State or Government stressed that more convenient travel connections between SAARC countries were essential to facilitate fruitful interaction among people in the region, in particular, professional groups, creative artists, pilgrims and journalists.

The Heads of State or Government considered means of encouraging more productive co-operation and collaboration between governments and the private sectors, including in the commissioning of studies relating to regional economic interaction.

They welcomed the contribution made by the SAARC Chamber of Commerce and Industry in facilitating the engagement of the private sector in regional economic interaction as well as initiating linkages with other regions for the purpose of promoting SAARC exports. The Heads of State or Government noted that a document entitled "Road Map to SAFTA" was presented by the President of the SAARC Chamber of Commerce and Industry (SCCI) to the Chairperson of the Twentieth Session of the Council of Ministers.

Links with Other International and Regional Organizations

The Heads of State or Government noted links initiated between SAARC and other international and regional organizations. They considered the prospects for the development of SAARC projects and programmes in association with such organizations with which SAARC has cooperative arrangements as well as through other forms of cooperation. The Heads of State or Government were of the view that priority needs to be given in establishing contact with those regional groupings which have experience in economic cooperation and functional regional cooperation.

The Heads of State or Government also noted proposals for developing cooperation between SAARC and individual States outside the region. They requested the Council of Ministers to consider such proposals with a view to developing such contacts on the basis of mutual benefit and for the advancement of SAARC objectives.

Projection of Common Positions

The Heads of State or Government reiterated their resolve to promote the articulation of joint positions at the United Nations and other fora where such action would be in the clear interest of all members of the Association.

Sub-Regional Cooperation

With the objective of enhancing regional solidarity and promoting overall development within SAARC, the Heads of State or Government encouraged the development of specific projects relevant to the individual needs of three or more Member States under the provisions of Articles VII and X of the Charter.

Security of Small States

The Heads of State or Government recognized that due to their particular vulnerability, small States require special measures of support from the international community for the safeguarding of their sovereign independence and territorial integrity. They reiterated that real protection of small States should be firmly rooted in scrupulous adherence to the UN Charter, the rule of law and strict adherence to universally accepted principles and norms related to sovereign rights and territorial integrity of all States irrespective of size. This, they stressed should be ensured by all the countries either severally or collectively through the pursuit of appropriate action.

Special Measures for Least Developed and Land-Locked Countries

The Heads of State or Government emphasized the need for priority action on various international development commitments, such as the Paris Declaration and the Programme of Action for LDCs for the 1990s.

While noting with deep concern that economic growth in the Least Developed and Land-Locked Countries is not progressing well, the Heads of State or Government stressed the need to take special measures for accelerating the process of development. They emphasized the need to fulfil the internationally agreed aid targets for ensuring accelerated and sustained economic growth in developing countries particularly in the Least Developed Countries. They stressed on the need for adequate resources to facilitate implementation of economic reform programmes in SAARC countries.

The Heads of State or Government emphasized that the review of the criteria for the determination of LDC status for consideration by the United Nations General Assembly this year, must take into account the special significance of the extent and magnitude of incidence of poverty in the poorest countries and the special vulnerabilities of small island states.

Education and Literacy

The Heads of State or Government were in agreement that illiteracy was a major impediment to economic development and social emancipation and that the eradication of illiteracy in the Region including through co-operative endeavors within SAARC must continue to be pursued resolutely.

The Heads of State or Government noted that the concepts of Open Learning and Distance Education could help substantially towards equal opportunities and access to knowledge. The Heads of State or Government directed that SAARC should build on the substantial expertise already existing in the Region in the field of open education, by establishing a SAARC Forum of Vice Chancellors of Open Universities. This Forum, consisting of regional leaders in the field, should strengthen cooperation in areas such as the sharing and joint development of programmes, credit transfers for specific programmes and the translation of existing programmes.

The Heads of State or Government urged the Forum, to spearhead the development of distance education outside the Open University System as well, drawing on the advances in Information Technology, to reach out to the remote and under-privileged sections. They welcomed the offer of Sri Lanka to host a meeting of Vice-Chancellors of SAARC Open Universities during the last quarter of 1998 to discuss the modalities for the establishment of the Forum and to draw up a programme to achieve the objectives identified by the Heads of State or Government. The Heads of State or Government requested the Forum to report to the Standing Committee on a continuous basis on its programmes.

Eradication of Poverty in South Asia

The Heads of State or Government reiterated the commitment of SAARC to the eradication of poverty in the Region at the earliest possible, preferably by the year 2002. They emphasised the need to encourage maximum participation by target groups in the formulation and implementation of poverty eradication programmes. The Heads of State or Government were of the view that such participation is essential for success of efforts in this field. They stressed the need for effective utilisation of the SAARC Three-Tier Mechanism on Poverty Eradication and in that context welcomed the offer of the Government of Pakistan to host the next meeting of the SAARC Finance/Planning Ministers under the Mechanism in October 1998.

The Heads of State or Government noted that the South Asian countries have provided leadership in developing and implementing Micro Credit Programmes, which have immense potential to contribute to the eradication of poverty. They were of the view that their respective programmes in this regard have proven to be effective and Member States would benefit by sharing experiences and exchanging information and expertise in this important area.

The Heads of State or Government noted that Human Resource Development is a key element in any poverty eradication programme. The Heads of State or Government, therefore, agreed that once the SAARC Centre for Human Resource Development in Islamabad is established, it could look in to the possibility of its contributing to the strengthening of the human resource development components of the regional poverty eradication programmes.

Social Charter

The Heads of State or Government reviewed the progress made in the social sector by SAARC and determined that, in order to increase effectiveness, it would be necessary to develop, beyond national plans of action, a regional dimension of action including a specific role for SAARC. In this context, they agreed that it would be necessary for SAARC to develop a Social Charter, which would focus on drawing up targets with a broad range to be achieved across the region in the areas of poverty eradication, population stabilization, the empowerment of women, youth mobilization, human resource development, the promotion of health and nutrition and the protection of children. The Heads of State or Government further directed the Council of Ministers to initiate work on drawing up a Social Charter.

Communications

The Heads of State or Government welcomed the results of the First Conference of SAARC Communication Ministers held in Colombo in May, 1998. They noted that technological advances were making telecommunications an important medium for socio-economic development and developing commercial and business relations as well as promotion of people-to-people contact. They called for the speedy implementation of the Plan of Action adopted by the First Meeting of the SAARC Communication Ministers.

Tourism

The Heads of State or Government recognized that further efforts were required for South Asia to effectively tap the economic potential afforded by the global tourist industry as well as to encourage intra-SAARC tourism. They welcomed the convening of the First SAARC Tourism Ministers' Meeting in Colombo as a step towards this end and called for the effective implementation of its decisions, including the encouragement of active private sector participation in the promotion of tourism, both intra-regionally and internationally, simplification of visa-procedures for tourists and pilgrims, more convenient air and other travel links among SAARC countries including special regional fares and the co-ordination of activities of tour operators.

The Heads of State or Government identified the need to strengthen the existing air services between their respective Capitals, with a view to both facilitating tourism as well as people to people contacts. They called in this regard, for an early meeting of the Chairpersons/Chief Executive Officers of the national air lines.

Science and Technology

The Heads of State or Government noted that the development of a regional self-reliance capability for South Asia in scientific research and development was essential, given a global context in which barriers to the free flow of technology still remained in place. The Heads of State or Government appreciated the efforts to foster under the SAARC umbrella, collective co-operation in this field.

The Heads of State or Government welcomed the offer by the Government of India to hold a Special Meeting of SAARC Science and Technology Ministers to consider a SAARC Technology Initiative to Identify and implement specific regional projects in rural areas which would have the direct impact in improving the day-to-day life of people there. Such an initiative could include rural telecommunications, drinking water and sanitation and improvement of life standards.

The Heads of State or Government reiterated their earlier call for the effective and rapid institutionalization of SAARC co-operation in the field of bio-technology. They pointed out that South Asia with its vast reservoir of bio-diversity and tropical climate, has substantial potential for bio-industry development on a sustainable basis. Many of the food and nutritional needs of the SAARC region could be met by the application of bio-technology. Contemporary developments in intellectual property and patent law, moreover, heightened the need for vigilance against encroachment on the regional bio-diversity heritage by external entities.

The Heads of State or Government accordingly requested the Standing Committee, with assistance of the SAARC Secretariat, to report to the forthcoming Twenty-First Session of the Council of Ministers on practical and cost effective measures towards rapidly operationalising SAARC cooperation in bio-technology.

Environment

The Heads of State or Government expressed their deep satisfaction at the positive outcome of the Environment Ministers' Conference held in Malé in October 1997, and called for the effective and early implementation of the SAARC Environment Action Plan. In this context, they welcomed the offer of Maldives to prepare a feasibility study on the establishment of a Coastal Zone Management Centre. The Heads of State or Government also committed their governments to prepare National Environment Action Plans and State of the Environment Reports before the end of 1998.

The Heads of State or Government expressed their satisfaction over the adoption of a common position by Member States prior to the Third Session of the Conference of the Parties to the United Nations Framework Convention on Climate Change, held in Kyoto, Japan and welcomed the adoption of the Kyoto Protocol to the United Nations Framework Convention on Climate Change in December 1997, and underscored the importance of the Protocol for the protection of the climate system. They urged all industrial countries to ratify the Protocol and to undertake urgent and effective steps to implement the commitments undertaken by them to reduce their emissions of green-house gases.

The Heads of State or Government also emphasized the need for complementary action by organizations and institutions in the region in their efforts to protect the environment and achieve sustainable development in the region.

The Heads of State or Government noted that the SAARC Environment Ministers would be meeting in Sri Lanka in late 1998. They urged that the Ministers should at this forthcoming meeting also mandate any specific measures required for SAARC to further strengthen cooperation on environment issues, with other international or regional organizations engaged in the same field.

Youth

The Heads of State or Government affirmed the importance they attached to providing adequate opportunities to youth in South Asia to participate productively in national development and underscored the need for developing programmes in this regard at the national and regional levels.

Children

Recalling targets and objectives set out in the Rawalpindi Declaration of 1996, the Heads of State or Government noted that the 1997 Review of the Situation of Children in South Asia had revealed progress in the reduction of infant mortality and increased coverage of immunization programmes. They stressed, however, that continued efforts required to be sustained in these areas. Serious efforts were also required in respect of education for all children and the reduction of gender disparities. In addition to national programmes, the Heads of State or Government called for the identification of practical regional programmes which could benefit from cooperation with relevant regional and international organizations with which SAARC has cooperative arrangements for the promotion of the welfare of children.

The Heads of State or Government condemned the exploitation of children by terrorist groups in hostilities and called for special measures for the psychological, physical and social rehabilitation of child victims. In this respect, the Heads of State or Government noted the initiative taken by Maldives in pursuance of their directive at the Ninth SAARC Summit in drafting the Convention on Regional Arrangements for the Promotion of Child Welfare in South Asia. They welcomed the offer of Maldives to hold an Expert Group Meeting to finalize the draft Convention for its adoption at the Eleventh SAARC Summit.

Situation of Women and the Girl Child

The Heads of State or Government noted that many groups of women and girl children in South Asia continue to be in disadvantaged positions and lack equal opportunities for economic and social development. They were of the view that sustained efforts and practical affirmative action was required to offset the effects of discriminatory, social and psychological perceptions and to empower women through affirmative action, including where necessary, legislative measures. The Heads of State or Government condemned in particular violence against women and acts of discrimination and humiliation which tend to depress the status of women. They also expressed concern over the plight of women and girl children in situations of conflict. Equal opportunities in education, health facilities and nutrition were vital for the integration of women in the mainstream of national development. They agreed to work in close association, where possible, with professional and other women's groups in the region to ameliorate their conditions.

The Heads of State or Government recalled that the Ninth SAARC Summit expressed concern at the trafficking of women and children within and between countries and pledged to coordinate efforts of Member States to take effective measures to address this problem. In this context, they welcomed the finalization of the draft text on the Regional Convention on Combating the Crime of Trafficking in Women and Children for Prostitution and noted that this would be a vital instrument in dealing with this problem. They approved that the Convention be signed at the Eleventh SAARC Summit.

The Heads of State or Government also recommended that the feasibility of establishing a Regional Fund for Rehabilitation of Victims of Trafficking in Women and Children for Prostitution on a voluntary basis may be explored.

The Heads of State or Government were also of the view that the scope of the Convention should be broadened to cover purposes other than prostitution.

The Heads of State or Government noted that a gender disaggregated database on the basis of data provided by Member States would be a valuable means of assisting the formulation of national and regional policies and programmes in respect of women and the girl child.

Health

The Heads of State or Government noted the rich heritage of traditional systems of medicine (TSM) in the region. They observed that regional cooperation in this area would be worthwhile and relevant for meeting basic health needs. They welcomed the offer of India to host the First Health Ministers Conference to evolve proposals for cooperation in this field.

The Heads of State or Government urged that the regional pharmaceutical industries should strengthen cooperation. They were further of the view that the Member States could establish Action Committees in terms of Article VII of the SAARC Charter for such cooperation, if required.

Disabled Persons

The Heads of State or Government recalled the Islamabad Resolution on Disabled Persons and underscored the importance of having a very definite humanistic approach to ensuring the welfare of the 100 million disabled persons of this region. In this respect, the Heads of State or Government accepted the proposal of the Prime Minister of Bangladesh for the establishment of a SAARC Voluntary Fund for Disabled Persons.

Information

The Heads of State or Government welcomed the recommendations of the First Meeting of SAARC Information Ministers held in Dhaka in April, 1998 and the offer of Pakistan to host the Second Meeting of Information Ministers of SAARC Countries.

The Heads of State or Government called for concerted endeavors for the promotion of practical programmes among South

Asian countries, including through professional organizations, in the field of information and media exchanges benefitting from technological advances. Such action would help promote deeper understanding of issues common to the region, as well as to project a more balanced view of developments in the region. They welcomed the offer of India to host the First Meeting of SAARC Editors and Journalists.

Terrorism and Drug Trafficking

The Heads of State or Government recognized that the Member States and peoples of South Asia continue to face the serious threat of terrorism in all its forms and manifestations and drug trafficking. They reiterated their firm commitment to combat these activities in the region. They emphasized the urgent need to complete enabling legislation in order to implement the SAARC Regional Conventions on Suppression of Terrorism and on Narcotic Drugs and Psychotropic Substances.

The Heads of State or Government urged all Member States to enhance cooperation against terrorism, wherever, by whomever, against whoever it occurs and to fully observe and implement the SAARC Regional Convention on Terrorism.

The Heads of State or Government affirmed that criminal acts intended to provoke a state of terror in the general public, a group of persons or particular persons, for whatever purposes, are unjustifiable in any circumstances.

The Heads of State or Government recalled the adoption of the 1996 UN Declaration on Measures to Eliminate International Terrorism and urged all Member States to work towards its implementation. They called for international action to prevent the abuse of Refugee Conventions and to halt activities which help terrorist groups to collect funds for their activities in South Asia.

The Heads of State or Government noted that two SAARC Conferences on Cooperation in Police Matters had been held since 1996. They called for the continued sharing of expertise with regard to the different areas of police investigation, and investigation of organized crime and drug related crimes.

Universal Declaration of Human Rights

The Heads of State or Government taking note of the 50th Anniversary of the Universal Declaration of Human Rights, reaffirmed their commitment to the further promotion of human rights and fundamental freedoms by strengthening the respective national institutions in South Asia in this field. The Leaders agreed that tolerance and mutual accommodation, combined with the strengthening of participatory governance, constituted the foundation for the sustainable economic and social development of the SAARC region.

International Political Developments

The Heads of State or Government consulted informally on a range of international issues, particularly those which have a bearing on South Asia. They re-affirmed their strong commitment to the purposes and principles of the UN Charter and agreed that their delegations would work closely in the ongoing negotiations for the reform and strengthening of the UN system, so that the Organisation could be more democratic, efficient and financially viable and responsive to the interests of its membership, especially developing countries.

The Heads of State or Government also underscored the importance of the role of the Non-Aligned Movement in promoting a just and equitable global order and called for the further enhancing of the efforts of the Movement to influence positively contemporary international relations. In this context, they expressed full confidence that the Twelfth Summit of the Movement scheduled to take place in South Africa would contribute towards augmenting the Movement's effectiveness.

The Heads of State or Government were of the view that stability, peace and security in South Asia could not be considered in isolation of the global security environment. Although great power rivalry which the NAM had consistently opposed, no longer posed a serious threat and the danger of a global nuclear conflagration had abated, yet some States had sought to maintain huge arsenals of nuclear weapons. The NPT and the CTBT, to which some SAARC members were signatories, had not led to any progress towards nuclear disarmament nor prevented proliferation. They underscored their commitment to the complete elimination of nuclear weapons and the need for promoting nuclear disarmament on a universal basis, under effective international control. They recognized that global non-proliferation goals cannot be achieved in the absence of progress towards nuclear disarmament and in this context called upon all nuclear weapon states, whether party or non-party to the NPT to engage constructively through a transparent and credible process of negotiations at the Conference on Disarmament.

The Heads of State or Government therefore urged the Conference on Disarmament to commence negotiations on a comprehensive, universal and non-discriminatory international instrument prohibiting the use or the threat of nuclear weapons as well as eliminating such weapons in existing arsenals.

The Heads of State or Government noted the outcome of the recent UN Diplomatic Conference on the establishment of an International Criminal Court and the fact that the Conference had not addressed such issues as the crime of drug trafficking and the crime of terrorism with its use of indiscriminate violence aimed at innocent civilians and use of weapons of mass destruction. They emphasized the need to ensure that the proposed Court should respect the sovereignty of States consistent with the principle of complementarity with national jurisdiction on which the Statute of the Court is based.

The Heads of State or Government welcomed the enhanced status accorded to Palestine at UN fora. They however expressed growing concern at numerous setbacks affecting the peace process in the Middle East, including illegal attempts to change the jurisdiction and borders of Jerusalem. They re-affirmed their support for the achievement of a just, lasting and comprehensive peace based on Security Council Resolution 242 (1967) and Resolution 338 (1973) to restore the inalienable national rights of the Palestinian people.

The Heads of State or Government called for intensification of efforts for promoting peace and stability at the global and regional levels for realizing universal progress and prosperity.

Dates and Venue of the Eleventh Meeting of the Heads of State or Government

The Heads of State or Government accepted with deep appreciation the offer of His Majesty's Government of Nepal to host the Eleventh SAARC Summit in the second half of 1999.

The Heads of State or Government of Bangladesh, Bhutan, India, the Maldives, Nepal and Pakistan expressed their appreciation for the skilful manner in which the President of the Democratic Socialist Republic of Sri Lanka had conducted the meeting and guided its deliberations, in her capacity as Chairperson. They also expressed their deep gratitude for the warm and generous hospitality extended to them by the Government and the people of Sri Lanka and the excellent arrangements made for the Summit and the meetings preceding it.

At Colombo, Sri Lanka, 29th -31st July, 1998.

Issues: People to people contact, Copyright, Patents.

Decisions: Second and Third Trade fair in Sri Lanka and Pakistan Respectively.

11th Summit

The Prime Minister of the People's Republic of Bangladesh, Her Excellency Begum Khaleda Zia; the Prime Minister of the Royal Government of Bhutan, His Excellency Lyonpo Khandu Wangchuk; the Prime Minister of the Republic of India, His Excellency Mr. Atal Behari Vajpayee; the President of the Republic of Maldives, His Excellency Mr. Maumoon Abdul Gayoom; the Prime Minister of the Kingdom of Nepal, Right Honourable Mr. Sher Bahadur Deuba; the President of the Islamic Republic of Pakistan, His Excellency General Pervez Musharraf; and the President of the Democratic Socialist Republic of Sri Lanka, Her Excellency Mrs. Chandrika Bandaranaike Kumaratunga met at the Eleventh Summit meeting of the South Asian Association for Regional Cooperation (SAARC) in Kathmandu, Nepal from 4 to 6 January 2002.

Regional Cooperation

The Heads of State or Government reaffirmed their commitment to regional cooperation through SAARC and underscored the importance of annual Summit meetings in charting common strategies for the realization of the objectives and principles set out in the Charter of the Association. Meeting for the first time at the dawn of the new millennium, they solemnly renewed their pledge to strengthen the Association and make it more cohesive, result oriented, and forward looking, by adopting clearly defined programs and effective implementation strategies in line with popular expectations. To give effect to the shared aspirations for a more prosperous South Asia, the Leaders agreed to the vision of a phased and planned process eventually leading to a South Asian Economic Union.

The Heads of State or Government stressed that equitable sharing of the benefits of regional cooperation is essential to achieve and maintain a minimum acceptable level of economic and social development in each Member State. To this end, they expressed their commitment to a speedier process of harmonizing their policies and practices and imbibing regional goals and strategies in their national development programs.

The Heads of State or Government expressed their firm determination to fully benefit from the wealth of traditional wisdom, creativity and enterprise in the region. They also pledged to enhance transparency and accountability in governance and to encourage effective participation of the peoples and civil societies in the formulation as well as implementation of the programs of cooperation.

Reiterating their resolve to promote South Asian regional identity and to strengthen cooperation at the international level, the Heads of State or Government also reemphasized the need to evolve common positions on issues of shared interest at the international fora.

Cooperation in the Economic Sector

The Heads of State or Government agreed to accelerate cooperation in the core areas of trade, finance and investment to realize the goal of an integrated South Asian economy in a step-by-step manner. They expressed their determination to make full use of regional synergy to maximize the benefits of globalization and liberalization and to minimize their negative impacts on the region. While recognizing that trade and economic expansion is closely inter-linked, the Leaders made a commitment to widen and deepen the scope of regional networks of activities in trade and financial matters.

The Heads of State or Government noted with satisfaction the outcomes of the successive meetings of the SAARC Commerce Ministers aimed at enlarging the scope of cooperation in the core areas. They recognised the importance of achieving a free trade area and reaffirmed that the treaty regime for creating a free trade area must incorporate, inter alia, binding timeframes for freeing trade, measures to facilitate trade and provisions to ensure an equitable distribution of benefits of trade to all states, especially for small and least developed countries, including mechanisms for compensation of revenue loss.

Recognizing the need to move quickly towards a South Asian Free Trade Area, the Heads of State or Government directed the Council of Ministers to finalize the text of the Draft Treaty Framework by the end of 2002. They also directed that in moving towards the goal of SAFTA, the Member States expedite action to remove tariff and non-tariff barriers and structural impediments to free trade. They also instructed to conclude the meeting of the Inter Governmental Group on Trade Liberalization for the Fourth Round of Trade Negotiations under SAPTA as early as possible as per the decision of the Tenth SAARC Summit in Colombo.

The Heads of State or Government renewed their commitment to encourage the participation of the private sector and assured their full support for their socially responsible economic initiatives. While welcoming the practice of holding trade fairs in cooperation with the private sector at the regional level, they appreciated the efforts of the SAARC Chamber of Commerce and Industry to promote regional economic cooperation in the spirit of public and private sector partnership.

The Heads of State or Government also decided to instruct the Secretary-General to facilitate the early finalization of a regionally agreed investment framework to meet investment needs of the SAARC Member States.

The Heads of State or Government recognized the immense tourism potential of South Asia and underlined the need to take measures to promote South Asia as a common tourist destination through joint efforts in areas such as upgrading of infrastructure, air linkages, simplification and harmonization of administrative procedures and training and joint marketing.

Poverty Alleviation

The Heads of State or Government acknowledged that investment in poverty alleviation programs contributes to social stability, economic progress and overall prosperity. They were of the view that widespread and debilitating poverty continued to be the most formidable developmental challenge for the region. Conscious of the magnitude of poverty in the region, and recalling also the decision of the UN Millennium Summit 2000 to reduce world poverty in half by 2015, and also recalling the commitments made at the five year review of the World Summit for Social Development to reduce poverty through enhanced social mobilization, the Heads of State or Government made a review of the SAARC activities aimed at poverty alleviation and decided to reinvigorate them in the context of the regional and global commitments to poverty reduction.

The Heads of State or Government expressed their firm resolve to combat the problem of poverty with a new sense of urgency by actively promoting the synergetic partnership among national governments, international agencies, the private sector, and the civil society. They reaffirmed their pledge to undertake effective and sustained poverty alleviation programs through pro-poor growth strategies and social as well as other policy interventions with specific sectoral targets. The Leaders also agreed to take immediate steps for the effective implementation of the programs for social mobilization and decentralization, and for strengthening institution building and support mechanisms to ensure participation of the poor, both as stake-holder and beneficiary, in governance and the development process.

The Heads of State or Government decided to undertake sustained measures to extend rural micro-credit programs with focus on women and the disadvantaged sections of society. They also stressed the need for widening the opportunities for gainful employment. While highlighting the importance of promoting agriculture, indigenous skills and small scale and cottage industries to address the incidence of rural poverty, they decided to enhance cooperation in agricultural research, extension and adoption. They specifically instructed that the Technical Committees should identify programmes and activities that impact on poverty alleviation. They urged the need to create gainful employment and promote cooperation in vocational training.

The Heads of State or Government emphasized the need to promote sharing of the best practices and experiences among the Member States and to this end, instructed the Secretary-General to disseminate such information to the Member States on a regular basis. They directed the Council of Ministers to review, on a continuous basis, the regional poverty profile to be prepared by the Secretary-General with the assistance of the related UN agencies, nodal agencies and independent research institutions specialized in the field.

In order to ensure social stability and to protect the vulnerable sections of population from the adverse impacts of globalization and liberalization, the Heads of State or Government stressed the need to enhance cooperation to create and maintain appropriate safety nets.

The Heads of State or Government agreed that a Special Session on poverty alleviation at the Ministerial level should undertake a comprehensive review and evaluation of the status of implementation of poverty eradication policies and programs carried out so far, and to recommend further concrete measures to enhance effective cooperation at the regional level to the Twelfth SAARC Summit. They also directed the Council of Ministers to take necessary steps to fully activate the existing three-tier mechanism for poverty alleviation.

The Leaders directed the Council of Ministers to coordinate efforts to integrate poverty alleviation programs into the development strategies of Member States. In this context, they agreed to reconstitute the Independent South Asian Commission on Poverty Alleviation, with Nepal as its Convener and Bangladesh as Co-convenor, for reviewing the progress made in cooperation on poverty alleviation and for suggesting appropriate and effective measures. They instructed the Chairman of the Council of Ministers to seek two nominations from each Member State by end of January 2002 to enable the convening of its first meeting before the proposed Ministerial Meeting on Poverty Alleviation in Pakistan in April 2002.

Expressing concern at the region's special vulnerability in the slowdown in world economy and its negative impact on the poor and the marginalized, the Heads of State or Government called for a supportive international environment and an enhanced level of assistance by the international community for poverty alleviation programs in South Asia.

Cooperation in the Social and Cultural Sector

The Heads of State or Government reiterated the need for an early finalization of the SAARC Social Charter and instructed the Inter Governmental Expert Group to expedite their work on the basis of the draft to be submitted by the Secretary-General, as a working paper for its consideration and to complete the draft framework of the Charter as early as possible for consideration at the next meeting of the Council of Ministers. In drawing up the Charter, they also directed the Council of Ministers to include the important areas of poverty eradication, population stabilization, the empowerment of women, youth mobilization, human resources development, the promotion of health and nutrition and the protection of children as decided at the Tenth Summit.

The Leaders recognized the debilitating and widespread impact of the HIV/ AIDS, TB and other deadly communicable diseases on the population of South Asia and stressed the need for evolving a regional strategy to combat these diseases. The strategy should include, inter alia, culturally appropriate preventive measures, an affordable treatment regime and should specially target the vulnerable groups. In this regard, they felt that SAARC should collaborate with the international organizations and civil society. They also emphasized that the SAARC Tuberculosis Centre in Kathmandu should play a coordinating role in the related areas.

In accordance with the Colombo Declaration, the Heads of State or Government decided to mandate the Meeting of Ministers of Cultural Affairs in Sri Lanka to finalise the details relating to the establishment of the SAARC Cultural Centre including its financing and to submit its report to the next session of the Council of Ministers.

Women and Children

The Heads of State or Government welcomed the signing of the SAARC Convention on Preventing and Combating the Trafficking in Women and Children for Prostitution and expressed their collective resolve to treat the trafficking in women and children for commercial sexual exploitation as a criminal offence of a serious nature. They also welcomed the signing of the SAARC Convention on Regional Arrangements for the Promotion of Child Welfare in South Asia and observed that the Convention reflected their commitment to place the child first in the national and regional programs of the Member States. They instructed the Secretary-General, in consultation with Member States and other specialised agencies, to present a report on measures for the effective implementation of the Conventions to the next meeting of the Council of Ministers.

The Heads of State or Government agreed to establish, on the basis of recommendations of the Regional Task Force responsible for the implementation of the provisions of the SAARC Convention on Preventing and Combating Trafficking in Women and Children for Prostitution, a voluntary fund with contributions from Member States, individuals, and donor countries and agencies for the rehabilitation and reintegration of the victims of trafficking.

The Leaders recognized the need to form an autonomous advocacy group of prominent women personalities from the Member States with a view to making recommendations to the SAARC bodies on a broad spectrum of gender related issues. They directed the Council of Ministers to take necessary steps to prepare and present, for consideration at their next meeting, the Terms of Reference for the purpose.

The Heads of State or Government recognized the need to actively pursue and promote social development through empowerment of women and to achieve their full participation in decision making at all levels. They reaffirmed their commitment to uplift the social status of the people, women and children in particular, in the region and expressed their common resolve to accord the highest priority to promoting social development through specific and targeted programs. The Leaders directed the Council of Ministers to take necessary measures to ensure the enjoyment by women and girl children of their inherent potential. They also directed the Council of Ministers to constitute a Task Force to review the status of implementation of past decisions related to the social sector and to suggest guidelines for their effective implementation in the future.

The Leaders directed the Council of Ministers to take concrete steps to give priority to investing in children as an effective means for poverty reduction in the long run. Reaffirming their commitment to the Colombo Plan of Action and the Rawalpindi Declaration and recalling the declaration of 2001 to 2010 as the SAARC Decade of the Rights of the Child, the Heads of State or Government noted with appreciation the South Asia High-level Meeting on Children held in Kathmandu in May 2001. They reaffirmed their conviction that the children in South Asia deserve urgent and focused attention to enhance the long-term and overall progress of the countries of the region.

The Heads of State or Government agreed to mobilize the necessary resources and intensify broad based actions to achieve a set of priority goals related to improving the status of children, such as polio eradication by 2005, protection of children from mother-to-child transmission of HIV/AIDS, and quality basic education to the children within a time-bound period.

Education

The Heads of State or Government instructed the concerned Ministries of Governments to devise appropriate strategies for raising the quality of education through the exchange of information among the universities in the region. While emphasizing the importance of mutual recognition of the educational institutions, they agreed to give the necessary impetus to realize the goal of a common regional educational standard through uniform methods of instruction and teaching aids. They were unanimous in recognizing the benefit of introducing SAARC in the national curricula at appropriate levels of study in order to enhance the awareness about Association's goals and objectives.

The Heads of State or Government recognized that access to quality education was an important element for the empowerment of all segments of society, and undertook to develop or strengthen national strategies and action plans to ensure that all children particularly the girl child have access to quality primary education by 2015; and to improve levels of adult literacy by fifty percent by eliminating gender disparities in access to education as envisaged in the Dakar Framework for Action on Education for All adopted by the World Education Forum held at Dakar in April 2000.

International Political and Economic Environment

The Heads of State or Government reiterated their firm support for the principles and purposes of the United Nations in order to create a just, balanced and equitable world order. They reaffirmed their commitment to continue working with the NAM and other like-minded countries for the reform and democratization of the United Nations System with a view to making it an effective and more democratic institution for international peace, security, progress and cooperation.

The Heads of State or Government were of the view that stability, peace and security in South Asia should be promoted together with efforts to improve the global security environment. They underscored their commitment to general and complete disarmament including nuclear disarmament on a universal basis, under effective international control. They agreed that global non-proliferation goals could not be achieved in the absence of progress towards nuclear disarmament and in this context called upon all nuclear weapon states, whether party or non-party to the NPT, to engage constructively through a transparent and credible process of negotiations at the Conference on Disarmament. The Leaders also recognized the linkage between disarmament and development.

The Leaders emphasized the need to take appropriate measures to make international financial institutions and the global trading regime more responsive to the needs and concerns of the developing countries. They reiterated the call for genuine partnership among the developed and developing countries in international trade and finance and for the reform of the global financial architecture with an enhanced level of resources.

The Leaders also called upon the developed countries to facilitate and ensure an unimpeded and enhanced level of market access to products from the developing, the least developed and the land-locked countries.

Recognizing the important role that trade can play in advancing the overall development of a country, thus contributing to an equitable and sustainable world order, the Heads of State or Government also called for an early realization of a rule-based and non-discriminatory world trade regime. In this context, they appreciated the positive elements of the Fourth WTO Ministerial Conference held in Doha and called upon the developed countries to fulfill their commitments to address the particular concerns and needs of the developing and the least developed countries. The Leaders also instructed the forthcoming meeting of the Committee on Economic Cooperation to devote at least half a day for discussions on the evaluation of the decisions of the recently concluded Doha conference in order to evolve better positions among the Member States on all WTO issues. They further stressed the need to intensify coordination among the SAARC missions in Geneva and begin the necessary preparation to advance the common interest of the region in the Fifth WTO Ministerial conference.

The Heads of State or Government noted with serious concern the adverse impact of the shrinking Official Development Assistance (ODA) and other concessional financial flows on developing countries in general, and the least developed among them in particular. They further noted with concern the current trend of the global economic slowdown and its adverse effects on these economies. Taking into account the interdependent nature of the global economy, the Leaders urged the developed countries to enhance the level of ODA flows to meet the internationally agreed targets.

Recalling the recommendations of the Third United Nations Conference on the Least Developed Countries held in Brussels in May 2001 and the decisions of the Zanzibar Declaration of July 2001, the Leaders urged the developed countries to adopt more liberal trade and aid policies responsive to the particular needs of the least developed countries. Referring to the forthcoming International Conference on Financing for Development to be held in Mexico in March 2002, the Leaders urged the international community to strengthen cooperation for development by addressing international and systemic issues related to financing for development in the developing and the least developed countries in a holistic manner.

The Heads of State or Government welcomed the initiative of the donor countries to relieve the external debt burden of the Highly Indebted Poor Countries. They urged the international donor community and financial institutions to widen the scope and extent of debt relief initiatives to cover all those developing and the least developed countries, which are facing developmental difficulties particularly due to the current global recession. In the context of growing global interdependence, they underlined the importance of forging cooperative partnership between the developed and the developing countries to ensure equitable benefits to all.

The Heads of State or Government expressed concern over the continued violence and bloodshed in the Middle East, and the set backs suffered by the peace process. They reaffirmed their support for the achievement of a just, lasting and comprehensive peace based on Security Council Resolution 242 (1967) and Resolution 338 (1973) and the establishment of a sovereign Palestine State under the leadership of PLO, which could coexist with its neighbors in peace, security and harmony.

Security of Small States

The Heads of State or Government recognized that due to their particular vulnerability, small states require special measures for support from the international community for the safeguarding of their sovereign independence and territorial integrity. They reiterated that the real protection of small states should be firmly rooted in the scrupulous adherence to the UN Charter, the rule of law and the strict adherence to universally accepted principles and norms related to sovereign rights and territorial integrity of all states, irrespective of size. This, they stressed, should be ensured by all the countries, either severally or collectively through the pursuit of appropriate action.

Terrorism

The Heads of State or Government were convinced that terrorism, in all its forms and manifestations, is a challenge to all states and to all of humanity, and cannot be justified on ideological, political, religious or on any other ground. The Leaders agreed that terrorism violates the fundamental values of the United Nations and the SAARC Charter and constitutes one of the most serious threats to international peace and security in the Twenty-first century.

The Heads of State or Government emphasized the need for the urgent conclusion of a Comprehensive Convention on Combating International Terrorism. They also emphasized that international co-operation to combat terrorism should be conducted in conformity with the UN Charter, international law and relevant international conventions.

The Heads of State or Government reiterated their support to the United Nations Security Council Resolution 1373 of September 28, 2001 and affirmed their determination to redouble efforts, collectively as well as individually, to prevent and suppress terrorism in all its forms and manifestations, including by increased cooperation and full implementation of the relevant international

Conventions relating to terrorism to which they are parties. In this context, they called on all states to prevent and suppress the financing of terrorist acts by criminalizing the collection of funds for such acts and refraining from organizing, instigating, assisting or participating in terrorist acts in states or acquiescing in organized activities within its territory directed towards the commission of such acts. The Leaders reaffirmed that the fight against terrorism in all its forms and manifestations has to be comprehensive and sustained.

The Heads of State or Government were unanimous in recognizing the distinct ominous link between terrorism, drug-trafficking, money laundering and other trans-national crimes and emphasized the need to coordinate efforts at the national and regional levels to strengthen the global response to this serious challenge and threat to international security. They called upon the international community to assist Member States of SAARC to deal effectively with the adverse economic effects of terrorism in general and to meet the rising insurance and security related costs in particular.

The Heads of State or Government reaffirmed their commitment to SAARC Regional Convention on Suppression of Terrorism, which, among others, recognizes the seriousness of the problem of terrorism as it affects the security, stability, and development of the region. They also reiterated their firm resolve to accelerate the enactment of enabling legislation within a definite time-frame for the full implementation of the Convention, together with strengthening of SAARC Terrorist Offences Monitoring Desk and the SAARC Drug Offences Monitoring Desk in an effective manner.

Report of the Group of Eminent Persons

The Leaders noted with appreciation that the Report of the Group of Eminent Persons (GEP) was an important contribution in the on-going process of introspection into the functioning of the Association as well as in setting out a perspective plan of action for that purpose. They endorsed the report of the Council of Ministers on the implementation of the recommendations of the GEP Report, and directed the Council of Ministers to undertake a review of progress in this regard.

Enhancing Political Cooperation

The Heads of State or Government reaffirmed their commitment to the promotion of mutual trust and understanding and, recognizing that the aims of promoting peace, stability and amity and accelerated socio-economic cooperation may best be achieved by fostering good neighbourly relations, relieving tensions and building confidence, agreed that a process of informal consultations would prove useful in this regard. The Leaders further recognized that this process would contribute to the appreciation of each other's problems and perceptions as well as for decisive action in agreed areas of regional cooperation. They underlined the importance of informal political consultations in promoting mutual understanding and reinforcing the confidence building process among the Member States.

Sub-regional Cooperation

The Heads of State or Government reaffirmed the validity of the idea of encouraging the development of specific projects relevant to the individual needs of three or more Member States under the provisions of Articles VII and X of the SAARC Charter.

South Asian Development Fund (SADF)

The Heads of State or Government underlined the urgent need to make the South Asian Development Fund operational by making utilization of the existing funds. They also instructed the Secretary-General to submit a proposal for seeking possible assistance from regional and international sources for the implementation of specific regional poverty alleviation priority projects.

Environment

The Heads of State or Government noted with satisfaction the growing public awareness on the need for protecting the environment within the framework of regional cooperation. They reiterated their call for the early and effective implementation of the SAARC Environment Plan of Action as endorsed by the SAARC Environment Ministers. They directed their Environment Ministers to take this into account and come up with an agreed position in their forthcoming meeting.

The Heads of State or Government also felt a strong need to devise a mechanism for cooperation in the field of the early warning on as well as preparedness and management of natural disasters, along with programs to promote conservation of land and water resources.

The Heads of State or Government also stressed the need to develop a cooperative mechanism for the protection, enrichment and utilization of bio-diversity as provided for in the UN Convention on Biological Diversity and to establish a regional bio-diversity database with a view to providing equitable benefits to all Member States. They also underscored the importance of protecting associated knowledge and other indigenous intellectual manifestations for the advancement of the region. They also directed the Council of Ministers to explore the possibility of establishing a SAARC Seed Security Reserve to strengthen cooperation in the field of agriculture and to protect IPRs of the seeds of the Reserve.

People-to-People Contact

The Heads of State or Government were unanimous in recognizing the need for further promoting a sense of regional identity amongst the peoples of the region. The Leaders lauded the roles played by intellectuals, professionals and eminent persons in promoting people-to-people contacts within the region and agreed to encourage such endeavors as a healthy sign of regional cohesion and fraternity. In this context, they took note of the activities of the SAARCLAW including other recognized bodies. They also took note of the First Meeting of the Chief Election Commissioners of SAARC Countries held in Kathmandu in February 1999 and appreciated the initiative on free and fair election. The Leaders instructed the Secretary-General to collect on a regular basis study reports and other relevant documents and information from the civil society on matters relating to regional cooperation for dissemination to Member States.

Rationalization and Institutional Issues

The Heads of State or Government were in agreement that the Summit and all other meetings of SAARC needed to be made more business-like and result-oriented with focus on programs and activities supported by informed regional inputs from the cross-sections of the society. They directed the Chairman of the Council of Ministers to undertake a review of the functioning and operation of SAARC Secretariat, and to make recommendations to advance the process of rationalisation and to make SAARC more functional and business-like, to the next meeting of the Council of Ministers.

SAARC Award

The Heads of State or Government noted with appreciation the proposal made by Nepal to institute a SAARC Award to honour the outstanding work of individuals and organizations within the region in the fields of peace, development, poverty alleviation and regional cooperation, and requested His Majesty's Government of Nepal to submit a concept paper for consideration by the next session of the Council of Ministers.

Date and Venue of the Twelfth Summit

The Heads of State or Government welcomed with appreciation the offer of the Government of the Islamic Republic of Pakistan to host the Twelfth Summit Meeting of the Heads of State or Government of the South Asian Association for the Regional Cooperation (SAARC) in Pakistan in early 2003.

The Heads of State or Government of Bangladesh, Bhutan, India, Maldives, Pakistan and Sri Lanka expressed their deep appreciation for the exemplary manner in which the Right Honourable Prime Minister of Nepal conducted the proceedings of the Eleventh SAARC Summit in his capacity as Chairperson. They also expressed their deep gratitude for the generous hospitality extended to them by His Majesty's Government and people of Nepal, and for the excellent arrangements made for the Summit.

12th Summit

We, the Prime Minister of the People's Republic of Bangladesh, Begum Khaleda Zia, the Prime Minister of the Kingdom of Bhutan, Lyonpo Jigmi Yoezer Thinley, the Prime Minister of the Republic of India, Atal Behari Vajpayee, the President of the Republic of Maldives, Maumoon Abdul Gayoom, the Prime Minister of the Kingdom of Nepal, Surya Bahadur Thapa, the Prime Minister of the Islamic Republic of Pakistan, Mir Zafarullah Khan Jamali and the

President of the Democratic Socialist Republic of Sri Lanka, Chandrika Bandaranaike Kumaratunga:

Having met at the Twelfth Summit meeting of the South Asian Association for Regional Cooperation (SAARC) in Islamabad, Pakistan on 4-6 January 2004;

Guided by the vision of a peaceful and prosperous South Asia and proud of its rich culture and traditions;

Deeply conscious of the growing interdependence within and amongst nations and regions in an increasingly globalizing world;

Desirous of promoting peace, stability, amity and progress in the region through strict adherence to the principles of the United Nations Charter and Non-Alignment, particularly respect for the principles of sovereign equality, territorial integrity, national independence, non-use of force and non-interference in the internal affairs of the states and peaceful settlement of all disputes;

Reaffirming the centrality of SAARC for promoting regional cooperation and emphasizing the need to enhance its efficacy;

Strongly reaffirming our commitment to the objectives, principles and provisions of the Charter of the South Asian Association for Regional Cooperation (SAARC);

Declare that:

Regional Cooperation

Economic

We renew our commitment to the objectives and principles of SAARC and pledge to reinvigorate cooperation to realize peace, amity, progress and prosperity of all peoples of South Asia.

We affirm our determination to create an inclusive, just and equitable partnership for peace, development and prosperity. Satisfactory progress has been made in the SAARC Preferential Trading Arrangement (SAPTA). The signing of the Framework Agreement on the South Asian Free Trade Area (SAFTA) is a major milestone. It is important to maintain this momentum and move towards further broadening of economic cooperation and to ensure equitable distribution of benefits of trade and cater to the special needs of the small and LDC Member States by providing them special and deferential treatment.

We reiterate our commitment made at the 11th SAARC Summit at Kathmandu in January 2002 for the creation of a South Asian Economic Union. In this context, we underline that creation of a suitable political and economic environment would be conducive to the realization of this objective.

A study on creating a South Asian Energy Cooperation including the concept of an Energy Ring should be undertaken by the Working Group on Energy.

For accelerated and balanced economic growth it is essential to strengthen transportation, transit and communication links across the region.

Public and private sector cooperation, particularly joint ventures, holds great promise. It is important to move towards project cooperation under SAARC. Prospects for setting up of a South Asian Development Bank should be examined by the SAARCFINANCE and report through the Council of Ministers.

Priority attention should also be given to the need for harmonization of standards, simplification of custom procedures, as well as cooperation among the central banks.

Development of tourism within South Asia could bring economic, social and cultural dividends. There is a need for increasing cooperation to jointly promote tourism within South Asia as well as to promote South Asia as a tourism destination, inter alia, by improved air links. To achieve this and to commemorate the twentieth year of the establishment of SAARC, the year 2005 is designated as "South Asia Tourism Year", for the success of which, each member would individually and jointly organize special events.

SAARC members should continue to safeguard their collective interests in multilateral forums by discussing, coordinating and exchanging information with a view to adopting common positions, where appropriate, on various issues.

Poverty Alleviation

We recognize poverty alleviation as the greatest challenge facing the peoples of South Asia and declare poverty alleviation as the overarching goal of all SAARC activities. It is imperative to relate regional cooperation to the actual needs of the people.

Provision of basic needs, promotion of literacy, and better health care are regional priorities. It is important to undertake effective and sustained poverty reduction programmes through pro-poor growth strategies and other policy interventions with specific sectoral targets.

The Plan of Action on Poverty Alleviation, prepared by the meeting of Finance and Planning Ministers in Islamabad in 2002, is hereby approved.

The reconstituted Independent South Asian Commission for Poverty Alleviation (ISACPA) has done commendable work. An effective strategy should be devised to implement suggestions made in its Report "Our Future Our Responsibility". In this context, ISACPA should continue in an advocacy role. It should prepare and submit to the next SAARC summit a comprehensive and realistic blue-print setting out SAARC Development Goals for the next five years in the areas of poverty alleviation, education, health and environment giving due regard, among others, to the suggestions made in the ISACPA report.

The SAARC Secretariat should periodically update and submit Regional Poverty Profiles.

SAARC should continue to collaborate with international organizations and UN agencies in the field of poverty alleviation. Arrangements for SAARC Food Security Reserve should be made more effective. We also recommend the establishment of a Regional Food Bank for which a concept paper should be prepared.

Investment in human resources is critical for future development of South Asia. It is, therefore, essential to establish a network of centres of higher learning and training, and Skill Development Institutes (SDIs) across South Asia. In this context, the role of the SAARC Human Resource Development Centre (SHRDC) is important.

Science and Technology

Strengthening of scientific and technological co-operation across the region is fundamental to accelerating the pace of economic and social development. Sharing of scientific and technological expertise, joint research and development and industrial application of higher technology should be encouraged and facilitated.

Social Issues

We hail the signing of the SAARC Social Charter as a historic development, which would have a far-reaching impact on the lives of millions of South Asians. Issues covered under the Charter, such as poverty alleviation, population stabilization, empowerment of women, youth mobilization, human resource development, promotion of health and nutrition, and protection of children are keys to the welfare and well being of all South Asians.

Progress has been made in the constitution of SAARC Autonomous Advocacy Group of Prominent Women Personalities (SAWAG). To enable women to contribute to the socio-economic development, there is a need for SAARC to encourage women entrepreneurs in the region.

Member States should move towards an early ratification of the two Conventions on Child Welfare and Trafficking in Women and Children for Prostitution.

Easy and affordable health care, and prevention and treatment of HIV/AIDS, Tuberculosis and other serious communicable diseases are priorities. The year 2004 is declared as the "SAARC Awareness Year for TB and HIV/AIDS". The SAARC Secretariat should effectively implement the proposed programmes on the observance of the SAARC Awareness Year and develop a regional strategy through a consultative process and collaborate closely with the Joint UN Programme on HIV/AIDS (UNAIDS) and other international organizations and civil society.

The important initiative taken by the Maldives in hosting the Emergency Meeting of the SAARC Health Ministers on SARS Epidemic in Male' on 29 April 2003, was a welcome development.

As agreed by the SAARC Health Ministers' Conference held recently in New Delhi, a SAARC Health Surveillance Centre and a Rapid Deployment Health Response System should be set up to deal with the emerging and re-emerging diseases as well as to establish a network between various institutions dealing with malaria and other vector borne diseases in the Member States. Also, documentation of traditional knowledge to safeguard Intellectual Property Rights (IPRs) in medicine needs attention.

The importance of cooperation in medical expertise and pharmaceuticals as well as in the field of traditional medicine requires elaboration of a SAARC Plan of Action that should be developed in the shortest possible time.

Culture

We take pride in the rich cultural mosaic of the peoples of South Asia and underline the need for preservation of traditional skills and crafts, and promotion of cultural exchanges between nations.

We welcome the establishment of a SAARC Cultural Centre in Kandy, which will serve as a symbol of South Asian shared cultural heritage.

Environment

It is important to undertake and reinforce regional cooperation in the conservation of our water resources and environment, pollution prevention and control as well as our preparedness to deal with natural calamities. We welcome the early establishment of the Coastal Zone Management Centre in the Maldives.

The early and effective implementation of the SAARC Environment Plan of Action is important. We further stress the early submission of country state of the environment reports to expedite the preparation of a SAARC state of environment report and the commissioning of the work on drafting a Regional Environment Treaty.

Combating Terrorism

We condemn terrorist violence in all its forms and manifestations and note that people of South Asia continue to face a serious threat from terrorism.

We are convinced that terrorism, in all its forms and manifestations, is a challenge to all states and to all of humanity, and cannot be justified on any ground, whatsoever. Terrorism violates the fundamental values of the United Nations and the SAARC Charter and constitutes one of the most serious threats to international peace and security. We agree to fully implement the relevant international conventions to which we are parties.

We reaffirm our commitment to the SAARC Regional Convention on Suppression of Terrorism, which, among others, recognizes the seriousness of the problem of terrorism as it affects the security, stability, and development of the region.

The signing of the Additional Protocol to the SAARC Regional Convention on Suppression of Terrorism to deal effectively with financing of terrorism is a further manifestation of our determination to eliminate all forms and manifestations of terrorism from South Asia.

SAARC Award

We welcome the institution of the SAARC Award on the basis of a concept paper drawn up by His Majesty's Government of Nepal and decide to present the award during the Summits in future. The Award will honour and encourage outstanding individuals and organizations within the region in the fields of peace, development, poverty alleviation, and in other areas of regional cooperation.

Information and Communication

We recognize the vital role that information and media can play in the promotion of peace, progress and harmony in South Asia. In this context, the initiatives for introducing regular 'SAARC Roundup' and 'SAARC News' programmes for telecast and broadcast on National TV and Radio Channels respectively in Member Countries is a welcome development. We agree to the establishment of a SAARC Information Centre in Kathmandu.

SAARC should endeavour to bring the benefits of information and communications technology to all peoples of the region, bridging the digital divide and assist in the development of knowledge based societies.

SAARC Integrated Programme of Action (SIPA)

We note with satisfaction the progress achieved in regional cooperation through SIPA. The commitment to SIPA must be matched by a corresponding allocation of resources for it.

Strengthening of the SAARC Secretariat

We agree to strengthen the capacity of the SAARC Secretariat. In this regard a Committee comprising of a Member from each Member State should meet soon and submit its recommendations within three months for consideration of the next session of the Council of Ministers. The Secretary General would coordinate the work of the Inter-Governmental Committee. Pending implementation of the recommendations of the proposed Committee a Poverty Alleviation Cell at the Secretariat should start functioning with a view to following up the Summit decisions on poverty alleviation.

Sub-Regional Cooperation

We encourage the development of specific projects relevant to the individual needs of three or more Member States under the provisions of Articles VII and X of the SAARC Charter.

Inter-Regional Cooperation

We express our determination to develop mutually beneficial links between SAARC and other regional and international organizations, bodies and entities and agree to establish dialogue partnership with other regional bodies and with states outside the region, interested in SAARC activities.

Enhancing Political Cooperation

We envision South Asia to be a peaceful and stable region where each nation is at peace with itself and its neighbors and where conflicts, differences and disputes are addressed through peaceful means and dialogue.

We reaffirm our pledge to promote good neighbourly relations on the basis of the principles of sovereign equality, territorial integrity and national independence, non-use of force, non-intervention and non-interference and peaceful settlement of disputes and recognize the importance of informal political consultations in promoting mutual understanding and reinforcing confidence building process among Member States.

Security of Small States

We are particularly mindful of the security concerns of small states that arise, inter alia, from their particular vulnerabilities, which should be firmly addressed by scrupulous adherence to the UN Charter, rules of international law and strict adherence to the universally accepted principles and norms related to sovereign rights and territorial integrity of all states. This should be ensured by all, both severally and collectively, through appropriate actions.

We endorse the recommendations made by the Council of Ministers at its Twenty-third and Twenty-fourth Sessions.

Thirteenth SAARC Summit

We appreciate the offer of the People's Republic of Bangladesh to host the Thirteenth SAARC Summit in January 2005.

13th summit

The Prime Minister of the People's Republic of Bangladesh, Her Excellency Begum Khaleda Zia; the Prime Minister of the Kingdom of Bhutan, His Excellency Lyonpo Sangay Ngedup; the Prime Minister of the Republic of India, His Excellency Dr. Manmohan Singh; the President of the Republic of Maldives, His Excellency Mr. Maumoon Abdul Gayoom; the King of Nepal, His Majesty Gyanendra Bir Bikram Shah Dev; the Prime Minister of the Islamic Republic of Pakistan, His Excellency Mr. Shaukat Aziz; and, the President of the Democratic Socialist Republic of Sri Lanka, Her Excellency Mrs. Chandrika Bandaranaike Kumaratunga met at the Thirteenth Summit meeting of the South Asian Association for Regional Cooperation (SAARC) in Dhaka, Bangladesh on 12 - 13 November 2005.

Regional Cooperation

The Heads of State or Government noted that the Thirteenth Summit was taking place at an important moment in the evolution of South Asia when SAARC stood at the threshold of a new decade of its existence. They agreed that the Summit provided a unique opportunity to consolidate the gains made in regional cooperation during its first two decades and to chart a forward-looking strategy to promote effective cooperation at all levels to realize the objectives and principles set out in the Charter of the Association.

The Heads of State or Government noted that cooperation and partnership within the framework of SAARC is based on the sound foundation of shared values, beliefs and aspirations. The objectives and goals of SAARC, they affirmed, were of continuing relevance and importance to all Member States. The dynamics of recent political and economic changes in South Asia and the world highlighted the importance of, and the compelling logic for, a more vibrant and effective process of constructive regional cooperation. They emphasized their commitment to making such cooperation an enduring feature and thus contribute to the region's peace, progress and stability.

The Heads of State or Government noted that SAARC has evolved in a positive direction during the first two decades of its existence and that its agenda encompassed concerns and areas vital for the fulfillment of the Charter objectives of promoting the welfare of the peoples of South Asia, accelerating economic growth, social progress, cultural development and strengthening collective self-reliance among the countries of South Asia. They stressed that realization of these objectives not only called for continued and serious result-oriented efforts but also for consistent endeavours to translate pledges and commitments into concrete actions, regional initiatives and projects. They reiterated their commitment to making SAARC an effective instrument for cooperation, which will visibly improve the quality of life of millions in South Asia.

The Heads of State or Government emphasized that efforts must continue to free South Asia from poverty, hunger and other forms of deprivation and social injustice which present a daunting challenge. Member States expressed determination to work towards significantly accelerating regional cooperation in economic areas. The main emphasis will be to secure a wider economic space, so that benefits and opportunities offered therein can be shared by all, and that the true economic potential of South Asia can be fully realized. Efforts will be made to create dynamic complementarities in the development of human resources and capacity of Member States to address their common challenges. They underlined the need to accelerate regional cooperation through all possible means and mechanisms, including exchange of best practices in various fields in the Member States.

The Heads of State or Government reiterated that the peoples of South Asia are the real source of strength and driving force for SAARC and resolved to make regional cooperation more responsive to their hopes and aspirations. They agreed that the Association should broaden its engagement with the civil society organizations, professional groups, and entrepreneurs. Member States should also strive to promote and assert their South Asian identity, encourage greater people-to-people contact and draw strength from their shared cultural heritage.

The Heads of State or Government emphasized the importance of initiating project cooperation under the SAARC auspices. They encouraged Member States to undertake projects, as per existing provisions of the Charter. These projects may pertain to economic and social sectors, including Human Resource Development and Poverty Alleviation. These may be undertaken, where required, with financial or technical assistance, from International Financial Institutions (IFIs) or, UN Funds and Programmes or, any extra-regional State, as appropriate.

Poverty Alleviation

The Heads of State or Government decided to declare the decade of 2006-2015 as the SAARC Decade of Poverty Alleviation. During the Decade, endeavours – both at the national and regional level - will continue to be made with a sense of commitment and urgency to free South Asia from poverty.

The Heads of State or Government appreciated the valuable work of the Independent South Asian Commission on Poverty Alleviation (ISACPA). They also endorsed the SAARC Development Goals (SDGs), as recommended by the Commission, and called for follow-up and implementation of the Plan of Action on Poverty Alleviation, adopted by the 12th SAARC Summit. They entrusted the ISACPA to continue its advisory and advocacy role in this regard. They endorsed the priorities for action identified in the Report of ISACPA adopted by the Twelfth SAARC Summit. They agreed that these priorities would be duly taken into account while working out the elements for regional initiatives in this vital area. They decided to focus on formulation and implementation of concrete regional programmes and projects as well as forging partnerships among all stakeholders.

Underlining the need for an exclusive forum for focused and comprehensive examination of poverty related issues, the Heads of State / Government decided to replace the three-tier mechanism on poverty alleviation by a two-tier one, comprising the Ministers and the Secretaries dealing with Poverty Alleviation at the national level.

Funding Mechanisms

The Heads of State or Government decided to establish a SAARC Poverty Alleviation Fund (SPAF) with contributions both voluntary and/or, assessed, as may be agreed. They called upon the Finance Ministers to formulate recommendations on the operational modalities of the Fund, taking into consideration the outcome of the Meeting of the Financial Experts. In this regard, they welcomed the offer of Pakistan to host the next meeting of the Finance Ministers. The operational modalities of the SPAF shall be decided by the Finance/Planning Ministers. They agreed that the SPAF shall function within the SADF to be reconstituted, as SAARC Development Fund (SDF), to serve as the umbrella financial institution for all SAARC projects and programmes and comprise three Windows namely Social Window, Infrastructure Window and Economic Window with a Permanent Secretariat.

The Heads of State or Government decided that Finance Ministers should meet within the first quarter after every Summit and also on the sidelines of the World Bank and ADB annual meetings, to take stock of macro-economic developments and outlook for South Asia, achievement of SAARC Development Goals as co-related to Millennium Development Goals (MDGs) and to assess the investment climate, foreign capital inflows, financial sector reforms and other areas of cooperation.

Advancing Economic Cooperation

The Heads of State or Government stressed that accelerating cooperation in the core economic areas was of vital importance for the realization of Charter objectives and also for making South Asia truly vibrant, dynamic and secure in its robust progress. They reaffirmed their commitment to accelerate cooperation in the economic and commercial fields, especially in the energy sector. They noted the progress in the negotiations on outstanding issues and directed early finalization of all the Annexes ensuring entry into force of the SAFTA Agreement as agreed, with effect from 1 January 2006.

The Heads of State or Government stressed the importance of the entry into force of the SAFTA Agreement on the scheduled date i.e. 1 January 2006. The launching of SAFTA would mark an important milestone on the road to a South Asian Economic Union.

They directed that the negotiations on the outstanding issues under the Agreement should be completed by end November 2005. They further directed that the necessary national procedures should be completed in time to facilitate the operationalisation of the Agreement.

They reiterated the need to strengthen transportation and communication links across the region for accelerated and balanced economic growth. They directed further measures aimed at trade liberalisation, as provided for in the SAFTA Agreement. They noted with satisfaction the ongoing SAARC Regional Multimodal Transport Study to enhance transport connectivity among the Member States. The Heads of State or Government agreed to undertake trade facilitation measures, including transit among SAARC countries, on the basis of understanding among concerned countries, for enhancing intra-regional trade and other economic activities. They noted the Indian proposal in this regard. They agreed to study the proposal by India for daily air service facility by designated airlines, on a reciprocal basis and without prejudice to existing rights, to all the SAARC Member States and also the proposal to extend fifth freedom rights to designated airlines from the Member States, both intermediate and beyond, within the SAARC region on a reciprocal basis.

The Heads of State or Government recognized the need to take the process of regional economic integration further by expanding the scope of SAFTA to include trade in services, enhanced investment and harmonized standards.

The Heads of State or Government welcomed the signing of the following Agreements during the thirteenth SAARC Summit:

The Agreement on Mutual Administrative Assistance in Customs Matters

The Agreement on the Establishment of SAARC Arbitration Council

The Limited Agreement on Avoidance of Double Taxation and Mutual Administrative Assistance in Tax Matters

They emphasized the need for parallel initiatives for dismantling of non-tariff and para-tariff barriers. In this context, they called for expeditious action on conclusion of agreements on mutual recognition of standards, testing and measurements with a view to facilitating intra-regional trade. They recognized the potential of trade in services which have expanded rapidly at the informal level. They called for a study to see how services could be integrated into the SAFTA process.

The Heads of State or Government decided to encourage, where appropriate, trade-creating investment in the Member States. They stressed the need for closer regional cooperation in the field of Information and Communication Technologies (ICT), including Telecommunications.

The Heads of State or Government welcomed the Joint Statement of the First SAARC Energy Ministers meeting in October 2005 in Islamabad. They agreed to the recommendation to establish the SAARC Energy Centre in Islamabad; to promote development of energy resources, including hydropower; and energy trade in the region; to develop renewable and alternative energy resources; and promote energy efficiency and conservation in the region. They underlined the need to constitute a South Asian Energy Dialogue process, involving officials, experts, academics, environmentalists and NGOs, to recommend measures to tap potentials of cooperation in energy sector to provide inputs to the Working Group on Energy.

The Heads of State or Government noted the proposal for the establishment of a Regional Food Bank proposed by India and agreed to examine the proposal.

With regard to paragraph 15 of the Council of Ministers Report, the Heads of State or Government noted the offer of Nepal to host the Regional Support Unit.

South Asia's Social Challenges

The Heads of State or Government reiterated their commitment to take initiatives at national as well as regional levels for achieving the specific objectives contained in the SAARC Social Charter. They recognized that realization of these objectives is crucial to enable SAARC to meet the hopes and aspirations of the common peoples of South Asia and visibly improve the quality of their lives. They emphasized that in outlining future actions in this regard national implementation efforts should be complemented by regional programmes and projects in areas requiring collective regional response. They appreciated the establishment of National

Coordination Committees (NCCs) in all Member States, decided on annual meetings of the Heads of NCCs and directed convening of their first meeting at the earliest for follow-up and implementation of the Social Charter. In this regard, they noted the proposal from the Maldives to convene an experts' group meeting on establishing a Civil Society Resource Centre.

The Heads of State or Government called upon the Member States to expeditiously complete the process of preparing their national strategy and plan of action. They also emphasized that national implementation efforts should be complemented by regional projects and programmes. In this context, they directed that regional projects, particularly in health and poverty alleviation, should be initiated.

The Heads of State or Government reiterated their pledge to continue to work in the next decade and beyond to address the formidable challenges faced by women and children, especially the girl child. They noted that sustained efforts were needed on the part of the Member States not only to free them from all types of deprivation but also to make them full partners and beneficiaries of South Asian progress and development. In this context, they decided that a mid-term review of the progress in realizing the objectives of SAARC Decade on the Rights of the Child (2001 – 2010) should be undertaken in 2006.

The Heads of State or Government affirmed their strong resolve to continue to work together to address the problem posed by trafficking in women and children. They expressed satisfaction at the ratification of the SAARC Conventions relating to Trafficking in Women and Children and Promotion of Child Welfare by all Member States and called for effective measures for their early implementation. They noted that the civil society organizations and the media have an important role to play in raising awareness of the degrading and inhuman treatment faced by the victims of trafficking. They encouraged them to continue their constructive role in this regard. They stressed that law enforcement agencies in the Member States should also coordinate and strengthen their efforts to address this problem effectively.

The Heads of State or Government noted the achievements of the Member States during recent years in the area of primary education through sustained efforts and adoption of country specific innovative approaches. They recognized that regional initiatives in this particular area might focus on sharing of experiences and best practices. They also called for optimal utilization of resources and identification of strategic interventions in the area of training, management and performance evaluation of these programmes so as to ensure sustainability, coverage and quality of education imparted and services provided. They stressed that freeing South Asia from the scourge of illiteracy is a major objective of SAARC in the third decade of its activities. They called for effective measures to realize the SDGs, in particular universal primary education in the context of pursuing the Millennium Development Goals.

The Heads of State or Government stressed that to meet the challenges of the twenty-first century Member States must make important strides in the areas of science, technology and higher education. They decided to give priority attention to encourage regional cooperation in these areas to derive benefits from the synergy of collective, well-planned and focused initiatives undertaken by Member States. They directed that a SAARC Plan of Action for Science, ICT and Technology be elaborated for consideration during a Meeting of SAARC Science, ICT and Technology Ministers to be convened as soon as possible. They noted the offer of India to establish a South Asian University and agreed to examine this matter further.

The Heads of State or Government recognized the need to collaborate on preparedness for addressing health emergencies, including prevention and control of pandemics like avian influenza, as these pose a major global threat with impact on health, trade and tourism involving human mobility. They emphasized on the need to develop a regional strategy for such emergencies as soon as possible; and identify and strengthen collaboration within and beyond the region and establish links with other regional organizations. They called for early establishment of a SAARC Health Surveillance Centre and a Rapid Deployment Health Response System, to deal with emerging and re-emerging diseases.

The Heads of State or Government welcomed the preparation of a strategy for collective SAARC response to prevent the spread of HIV/AIDS. They noted that regional response in this regard should be further enhanced to eliminate this dreadful disease from South Asia. In this regard, they emphasized the importance of early implementation of the Regional Strategy of HIV/AIDS. At the same time, they underscored the need for increasing cooperation to develop regional strategies for the prevention and treatment of Dengue, Malaria and other infectious or communicable diseases constituting major public health concerns.

The Heads of State or Government agreed to launch a regional initiative with regard to basic healthcare services and sanitation in the rural areas and encouraged exchange of experience and best practices within the region. They called for expediting elaboration of a SAARC Plan of Action for cooperation in medical expertise and pharmaceuticals, as well as traditional medicine, and availing affordable pharmaceuticals produced in the region, harmonization of standards and certification procedures and production of affordable medicines. They also agreed that steps should be taken to promote traditional medicine and to protect the intellectual property rights related to them as a matter of regional priority.

South Asia's Environmental Challenges and Natural Disasters

They further decided to consider the modalities for having a Regional Environment Treaty in furthering environmental cooperation among the SAARC Member States. They expressed deep concern at the continuing degradation of environment and reaffirmed the importance of concerted action in the protection and preservation of environment. While expressing satisfaction at the progress in implementation of the SAARC Environment Action Plan, the Leaders welcomed the decision of the Council of Ministers to establish a SAARC Forestry Centre in Bhutan. They emphasized on the need for the Centre to have a coordinating role in the field of Forestry for exchange of information, expertise, training and formulation of regional projects with emphasis on social forestry.

The Heads of State or Government welcomed the Declaration of the Special Session of the SAARC Environment Ministers in Male in June 2005 convened in the wake of the tsunami catastrophe. They endorsed the recommendation for elaboration of regional programmes and projects for early warning, preparedness and management of tsunami and other natural disasters. They called for elaboration of a Comprehensive Framework on Early Warning and Disaster Management.

They endorsed the decision of the Special Session of the SAARC Environment Ministers to further enhance the capacity of the existing SAARC Institutions namely, SAARC Meteorological Research Centre and SAARC Coastal Zone Management Centre, to carry out their mandated tasks.

In view of the extensive loss of life and colossal damage to property as a result of earthquake and tsunami and other natural disasters in South Asia, the Heads of State or Government underscored the urgency to put in place a permanent regional response mechanism dedicated to disaster preparedness, emergency relief and rehabilitation to ensure immediate response. They directed the concerned national authorities to coordinate their activities in such areas of disaster management as early warning, exchange of information, training and sharing of experiences and best practices in emergency relief efforts.

The Heads of State or Government underlined the need for collaborative action in the area of environment, including water conservation, to promote sustainable development. They decided to proclaim the Year 2007 as the "Year of Green South Asia" devoted to a region-wide aforestation campaign. They also agreed to address the problem of arsenic contamination of groundwater and assistance to affected peoples.

Combating Terrorism

The Heads of State or Government agreed that terrorism violates the fundamental values of the SAARC Charter and the United Nations, and constitutes one of the most critical threats to international peace and security. The Heads of State or Government expressed their satisfaction at the ratification of the Additional Protocol to the SAARC Convention on Suppression of Terrorism by all Member States and called for putting in place effective mechanisms for its implementation. They strongly condemned terrorist violence in all its forms and manifestations, agreed that terrorism is a challenge to all States and a threat to all of humanity, and cannot be justified on any grounds. They underlined that there should be no double standards in the fight against terrorism. In view of the continuing and recent terrorist attacks in the region and their impact on security, economic stability and social development, they expressed their determination to unite in their efforts in preventing and combating terrorism. They also noted the United Nations Security Council resolution 1373 (2001) in this regard.

They called for early and effective implementation of the Additional Protocol to the SAARC Convention on Suppression of Terrorism. They underscored the need for an early conclusion of a Comprehensive Convention on International Terrorism. They also agreed that Member States would strengthen their cooperation in such important areas as exchange of information, coordination and cooperation among their relevant agencies.

They decided that SAARC Interior/Home Ministers would meet annually preceded by a meeting of the Interior/Home Secretaries.

The Heads of State or Government directed that concrete measures be taken to enforce the provisions of the Regional Convention on Narcotic Drugs and Psychotropic Substances through an appropriate regional mechanism.

Security of small states

The Heads of State or Government noted that due to their specific vulnerabilities, small states require special measures for support from all concerned for safeguarding their sovereignty, independence and territorial integrity. In this context, they stressed that protection of small states should be firmly rooted in scrupulous adherence to the UN Charter, rule of law and the strict adherence to universally accepted principles and norms related to sovereign rights and territorial integrity of all States, irrespective of their size. They committed themselves to give concrete expression to protect the interest and security of all small states through the pursuit of appropriate policies and actions.

People-to-people contact and cultural cooperation

The Heads of State or Government noted that the spirit of SAARC needed to be sustained by efforts to promote people-to-people contact and by a vibrant civil society throughout South Asia actively engaged in forging links across national boundaries. They felt that the Association of SAARC Speakers and Parliamentarians should meet at an early date to establish a mechanism for periodic contacts among the Parliamentarians of South Asia. They stressed that continued efforts would be made by the Member States at all levels to promote people-to-people contact by facilitating travel among SAARC countries, promotion of youth exchanges in culture and sports, promotion of intra-SAARC tourism, establishment of linkages among professional bodies and through adoption of other concrete measures. They decided to launch 2006 as "South Asia Tourism Year." They directed their Ministers for Tourism to meet at an early date and elaborate a plan of activities to be undertaken during the year 2006. They also stated that Member States would encourage initiatives by private sector entities in promoting understanding and harmony in the region.

The Heads of State or Government recognized the crucial role of culture in bringing the peoples of South Asia closer. They also stressed that cooperation in the area of culture was vital for reinforcing and projecting the distinct identity of South Asia. In this context, they expressed satisfaction on the progress made in establishing the SAARC Cultural Centre in Kandy and underlined the importance of making it operational at the earliest. They also directed the SAARC Ministers of Culture to meet as soon as possible to elaborate a SAARC Agenda for Culture. They noted the offer of India to establish a SAARC Museum of Textiles and Handicrafts inter alia to preserve designs in various crafts and related traditions, train artisans and crafts persons, foster design skills, hold promotional events, undertake research.

International political and economic environment

The Heads of State or Government reviewed international political and economic developments since their last Summit in Islamabad. They underscored the imperative need to ensure universal adherence to the principles and objectives enshrined in the UN Charter. They called upon the international community to redouble efforts to meet the commitments of the Millennium Summit and the Monterrey consensus. They noted the outcome of the UN World Summit 2005 and underlined the need for meaningful reforms of the United Nations system in consonance with its role as the central organ for the cooperative management of the global problems and for the promotion of peace, security, development, justice and human rights. They also reiterated their full support for a comprehensive approach, which would facilitate implementation of the Millennium Declaration and the Millennium Development Goals (MDGs) in a time bound manner.

The Heads of State or Government stressed that promotion of global peace and security inter alia called for removing the existing asymmetries in security and in ensuring undiminished security for all, at the regional and global levels. They also emphasized the importance of pursuing effectively the global objectives of universal disarmament and preventing the proliferation of weapons of mass destruction.

The Heads of State or Government reaffirmed their commitment to further strengthen the multilateral trade regime of WTO. They called upon all WTO members to demonstrate necessary understanding and accommodation for a breakthrough at the Hong Kong Ministerial meeting in December 2005 to pave the way for the successful conclusion of the Doha Development Round. They underscored that the development dimension should continue to be at the heart of the on-going negotiations so that the legitimate concerns of the developing countries are adequately reflected in the outcome of the current round of trade negotiations. They agreed that the SAARC Member States would work closely together to coordinate their positions in the on-going negotiations on trade and other key economic issues. The Heads of State or Government directed the Commerce Ministers to hold consultations on the sidelines of the 6th WTO Ministerial Conference to be held in Hong Kong in December 2005, to evolve a common SAARC Position on issues of common concern.

The Heads of State or Government addressed the question of electing the Secretary-General of the United Nations in the year 2006, being aware of the unanimous view that the well-established principle of geographical rotation should be observed and that an Asian should be appointed as the next Secretary-General of the United Nations. In this regard, they noted that Sri Lanka has offered a candidate.

Enhancing Political Cooperation

The Heads of State or Government welcomed the growing importance being placed by all Member States to promote cooperation in an environment of enduring peace and stability in South Asia. They reiterated their commitment to the principles of sovereign equality, territorial integrity and national independence, non-use of force, non-intervention, and non-interference in the internal affairs of other Member States. Recognizing the increasing interdependence and the imperative of pursuing the objectives of peace, freedom, social justice and economic prosperity, they re-affirmed their resolve to foster mutual understanding, good neighborly relations and a more meaningful cooperation through sustained constructive engagement among Member States.

External Profile and Linkages of SAARC

The Heads of State or Government welcomed the observer status granted to SAARC by the United Nations General Assembly at its Fifty-ninth Session; and expressed the hope that this would not only enhance the profile of SAARC in the world body but would also enable Member States to project common positions of SAARC in various multilateral forums. They also acknowledged the renewed interest of other regional and international organizations, bodies and entities to cooperate with SAARC in various collaborative endeavors in accordance with the objectives and priorities of SAARC. The Heads of State or Government welcomed the request by the Islamic Republic of Afghanistan for membership and invited Afghanistan as a member, subject to the completion of formalities. They also welcomed and agreed in principle with the desire of the People's Republic of China and Japan to be associated as observers. The Council of Ministers will decide the modalities in this regard at their twenty-seventh meeting in July 2006.

Strengthening Institutional Mechanisms of SAARC

The Heads of State or Government agreed that with the incremental broadening of the SAARC agenda and increased emphasis being placed on implementation of plans and programmes, there was a need for a commensurate strengthening of institutional capabilities of SAARC. Recognizing the importance of thematic Ministerial meetings, they emphasized that these meetings should focus on regional challenges and priorities and contribute to the realization of the objectives of SAARC. They agreed that on completion of twenty years of SAARC's existence, it was essential that a comprehensive review and reform of all SAARC institutions and mechanisms, including the Secretariat and the Regional Centers should be undertaken. In this context, they called on the Council of Ministers to convene a Meeting of Experts, to be nominated by each

Member State, to undertake a detailed Study and present a report to the next Council of Ministers. They empowered the current Chairman of the Council of Ministers to prepare within the next fifteen days a draft Terms of Reference for the Study to be approved, if necessary, by tele-conferencing of all SAARC Foreign Ministers.

SAARC Vision: An Agenda for Third Decade of SAARC

The Heads of State or Government reiterated their commitment to the realization of the vision of South Asian Economic Union in a phased and planned manner. They agreed that as SAARC completed its twenty years of its existence, it was an opportune occasion to draw a roadmap for regional cooperation in South Asia for the next decade. In view of the new challenges facing the region, pledges and commitments made in the last two decades should be translated into concrete actions in the form of regional projects and programmes and innovative initiatives.

They directed all SAARC institutions and mechanisms to work collectively towards a decade dedicated to implementation so that a visible and discernible impact can be felt across South Asia. They emphasized that while this would enable SAARC to realize its basic objectives of improving the quality of life of all South Asian peoples, it would at the same time create an enabling environment towards the establishment of a South Asian Economic Union. They directed the Standing Committee to formulate its recommendations, at its next Special Session, on a Vision for SAARC's Third Decade and the course of action for its realization, to be elaborated by a high-level Committee of Senior Officials.

Date and Venue of the Fourteenth SAARC Summit

The Heads of State or Government welcomed the offer of the Government of India to host the Fourteenth SAARC Summit in 2007.

14th Summit

DECLARATION OF THE FOURTEENTH SAARC SUMMIT

The President of the Islamic Republic of Afghanistan, His Excellency Mr. Hamid Karzai; the Chief Adviser of the Government of the People's Republic of Bangladesh, His Excellency Dr. Fakhruddin Ahmed; the Prime Minister of the Kingdom of Bhutan, His Excellency Lyonpo Khandu Wangchuk; the Prime Minister of the Republic of India, His Excellency Dr. Manmohan Singh; the President of the Republic of Maldives, His Excellency Mr. Maumoon Abdul Gayoom; the Prime Minister of Nepal, Rt. Hon'ble Mr. Girija Prasad Koirala; the Prime Minister of the Islamic Republic of Pakistan, His Excellency Mr. Shaukat Aziz; and the President of the Democratic Socialist Republic of Sri Lanka, His Excellency Mr. Mahinda Rajapaksa, met at the Fourteenth Summit meeting of the South Asian Association for Regional Cooperation (SAARC) held in New Delhi, India on April 3-4, 2007.

The Heads of State or Government welcomed the entry of the Islamic Republic of Afghanistan into SAARC. This was a historic moment as Afghanistan assumed its rightful place as a valued member of the SAARC fraternity.

The Heads of State or Government reiterated their commitment to the principles and objectives enshrined in the SAARC Charter. With the welfare of the peoples of South Asia uppermost in their mind, they agreed to build a Partnership for Prosperity and work towards shared economic cooperation, regional prosperity, a better life for the people of South Asia, and equitable distribution of benefits and opportunities of integration among the peoples and the nations.

The Heads of State or Government recognized the importance of connectivity in fulfilling these objectives. It was vital to first have better connectivity within South Asia and then with the rest of the world. They agreed to improve intra-regional connectivity, particularly physical, economic and people-to-people connectivity. They agreed to the vision of a South Asian community, where there was smooth flow of goods, services, peoples, technologies, knowledge, capital, culture and ideas in the region. The SAARC Car Rally, in the run-up to the Fourteenth SAARC Summit, had vividly symbolized this connectivity.

The Heads of State or Government recognized that the remarkable growth of the economies of SAARC countries has opened new opportunities to pursue the fight against poverty with firm resolve. They called for deepening of pro-poor orientation of growth process, including through enhancing investment in human capital and infrastructure, increasing budgetary allocations for relevant sectors and improved delivery of services. They reiterated their commitment towards project-based cooperation to strengthen collective efforts in the region.

The Heads of State or Government acknowledged that there is a wide range of homegrown best practices and innovative solutions for transforming the lives of peoples in South Asia. They decided to earmark one rural community as SAARC Village in each Member State to showcase these innovative models of development in order to further replicate these across the region.

The Heads of State or Government recognized that the implementation of the Social Charter needs focused attention and directed the National Coordination Committees (NCCs) to formulate concrete programmes and projects to complement national implementation efforts. They underscored that civil society organizations have a vital role to play in driving forward the implementation of the Social Charter and directed the NCCs to mobilize civil society organizations to achieve this end.

The Heads of State or Government appreciated the Independent South Asian Commission on Poverty Alleviation (ISACPA) for its elaboration of the SAARC Development Goals (SDGs), which reflect the regional determination to make faster progress towards attaining the Millennium Development Goals (MDGs). They agreed that the national plans for poverty alleviation should appropriately mirror the regional consensus reached in the form of the SDGs and the Plan of Action on Poverty Alleviation. Deciding that resource mobilization for achieving the SDGs would remain a high priority in the Decade of Poverty Alleviation, the Leaders directed translation of the highest regional level political commitment into action for creating opportunities for productive employment and greater access to resources for the poor that are essential for them to enhance their livelihood and realize their potentials. They entrusted the Two-tier Mechanism on Poverty Alleviation to monitor the progress and fine-tune the approaches towards pro-poor growth process.

The Heads of State or Government recognized the full benefits of an integrated multimodal transport system in the region. They emphasized that this would not be realized unless physical infrastructure and matters relating to customs clearance and other facilitation measures, including multimodal transport operations, were addressed comprehensively. They called for an extension of the SAARC Regional Multimodal Transport Study (SRMTS) to include Afghanistan as well. They also called for early implementation of the recommendations contained in the Study in a phased manner. In this context, the Heads of State or Government directed the Inter-Governmental Group on Transport to identify and develop sub-regional and regional projects based on the prioritised recommendations of the SAARC Regional Multimodal Transport Study (SRMTS) and to develop appropriate regional agreements. They noted the offer of India to hold the Meeting of SAARC Ministers of Transport in New Delhi in 2007. They also directed that pilot projects for improving connectivity be identified and implemented through mutual consultations among the Member States.

The Heads of State or Government emphasized that in its third decade of existence, there was an urgent need to move SAARC from declaratory to implementation phase. They directed that the focus of SAARC should be on implementing collaborative projects that are concrete and effective. The SAARC Development Fund (SDF) is an important pillar that would bring concrete benefits to the people of the region. They directed that the SDF be made operational at the earliest. They agreed that the resources for SDF would be mobilized both from within and outside the region. They stressed the importance of decision making and working of the SDF being consistent with the SAARC Charter. They called for early identification and implementation of regional and sub-regional projects under the SDF.

The Heads of States or Governments recognized the region's rapidly increasing energy demands for meeting the developmental needs of SAARC countries. They also acknowledged the need of expediting development of conventional sources of energy in a sustainable manner and for strengthening renewable energy development such as in hydropower, bio-fuel, solar and wind. They welcomed the organizing of the first ever South Asia Energy Dialogue in March 2007 in Delhi. They called for early implementation of the recommendations of the Second SAARC Energy Ministers' Meeting to enhance regional cooperation.

The Heads of State or Government reiterated their deep concern at the continued degradation of environment and reaffirmed the need to further strengthen cooperation towards protection and conservation of the environment as a priority area. In this regard, while noting the progress in the implementation of the SAARC Plan of Action on Environment, they called for concerted efforts to implement various initiatives under the Plan in a timely manner.

The Heads of State or Government expressed satisfaction at the launching of 2007 as the 'Year of Green South Asia'. They reiterated that collaboration in addressing the problem of arsenic contamination of groundwater, desertification and melting of glaciers and assistance to affected peoples should be deepened. They expressed deep concern over global climate change and the consequent rise in sea level and its impact on the lives and livelihoods in the region. They emphasised the need for assessing and managing its risks and impacts. They called for adaptation of initiatives and programmes; cooperation in early forecasting, warning and monitoring; and sharing of knowledge on consequences of climate change for pursuing a climate resilient development in South Asia. They agreed to commission a team of regional experts to identify collective actions in this regard.

The Heads of State or Government stressed the need for closer regional cooperation in the field of information and communication technology. They noted with appreciation the establishment of a collaborative health care project involving a regional telemedicine-network. They directed that steps be taken to extend it to other ICT enabled fields such as education. They agreed to take steps to facilitate rationalization of telecom tariff on a reciprocal basis. They also agreed that national and regional telecom infrastructure should be upgraded to boost people-to-people connectivity in the region.

The Heads of State or Government noted with satisfaction timely ratification of SAFTA Agreement by all member countries. They stressed the need for ensuring effective market access through smooth implementation of trade liberalization programme and directed the SAFTA bodies to review the progress on a regular basis. They emphasized that SAFTA should be implemented in letter and spirit. Successful implementation of SAFTA will catalyze other areas of regional economic cooperation. They stressed that to realize its full potential, SAFTA should integrate trade in services. They called for a finalization of an Agreement in the services sector at the earliest.

They also directed that the Agreement on Investment Promotion and Protection be finalized.

The Heads of State or Government underlined the importance of implementing trade facilitation measures, especially standardization of basic customs nomenclature, documentation and clearing procedures. They directed that a comprehensive agreement on harmonizing customs procedures be finalized. They also noted that harmonization of technical and phyto-sanitary standards and their implementation in a trade-friendly manner is important in boosting intra-regional trade. They appreciated the establishment of the SAARC Standards Coordination Board that would function as a precursor to the SAARC Regional Standards Body.

The Heads of State or Government complimented the SAARC Finance Ministers for finalizing the framework of cooperation on financial issues in the region. They expressed satisfaction at the work of the Inter-Governmental Expert Group on Financial Issues.

The Heads of State or Government emphasized the need to develop, at an early date, a roadmap for a South Asian Customs Union and a South Asian Economic Union in a planned and phased manner.

The Heads of State or Government noted the cultural and social ties among the SAARC countries, based on common history and geography, and reiterated that the future of peoples of South Asia is interlinked. They stressed the importance of people-to-people contact as a key constituent in regional connectivity. They acknowledged the importance of intra-regional tourism and increased exchanges, particularly among the youth, civil society, and parliamentarians. They launched the SAARC Agenda for Culture and directed that annual SAARC Festivals for cultural exchange be institutionalized. They agreed to take measures to charge nationals of SAARC Member States fees for entry into archeological and heritage sites as applicable to their own nationals. They also directed that an enlarged SAARC Scholarship Scheme in ICT and related areas be instituted. They welcomed the offer of Bangladesh to host the First SAARC Youth Camp in 2007.

The Heads of State or Government decided to establish the South Asian University in India. They welcomed the signing of the Intergovernmental Agreement establishing the University. They further directed that the Intergovernmental Steering Committee be set up at the earliest to complete its tasks relating to the Charter, bye laws, rules and regulations, curriculum development, business plans and other issues. They also decided to strengthen cooperation and dialogue on educational matters through development of exchanges between academics, experts, policymakers, students and teachers. They called for inter-institutional cooperation, partnerships, and other regional initiatives in the field of education.

The Heads of State or Government acknowledged that women's full participation in all spheres of society, including participation in the decision-making process are fundamental for the achievement of equality and development. They noted that many sections of women and children continue to be in disadvantaged positions and lack equal opportunities for economic and social development. They emphasized that women's empowerment should be a major objective of regional cooperation. Regional projects should focus on addressing issues relating to women and children.

The Heads of State or Government stressed the need to collectively overcome the challenges of poverty, disease, natural disasters and terrorism. They confirmed that countries of South Asia must work together to deal with these challenges in order to secure the region's collective prosperity.

The Heads of State or Government acknowledged that countries of South Asia face challenges of food insecurity and malnutrition. In order to manage emergencies caused by natural and manmade calamities and food shortages, they welcomed the signing of the Intergovernmental Agreement establishing the SAARC Food Bank with the participation of all the SAARC countries. The Food Bank will supplement national efforts to provide food security to the people of the region.

The Heads of State or Government noted the challenges confronted by the countries of South Asia in ensuring food and nutritional security as well as in maintaining vibrant rural economy for agricultural development. They underscored the need for enhancing productivity and real wage in rural sectors, and for creating adequate non-farm employment to sustain the progress made in reducing poverty. Noting the constant decline in land availability and biodiversity, depleting soil and natural resources, lowering ground water levels, shrinking farm holdings as well as low and stagnating productivity, they recognized the imperative of reducing the wide gap between yields at the research and the farm level. They stressed, in particular, that South Asian agriculture must benefit from collaborative efforts within and among SAARC countries in developing an effective agriculture research, extension and farmers' linkages, and exchange of farm technology.

The Heads of State or Government underlined that terrorism is a threat to peace and security in the region. They condemned the targeted killing of civilians and terrorist violence, in all its forms and manifestations, wherever and against whomsoever committed. The Heads of States or Government affirmed that terrorism violates the principles of the Charters of the United Nations and SAARC and is a clear and present threat to international peace and security. They reaffirmed their commitment to implement all international conventions relating to combating terrorism, to which SAARC Member States were respectively parties, as well as the SAARC Regional Convention on Suppression of Terrorism and the Additional Protocol to the SAARC Regional Convention dealing with the prevention and suppression of financing of terrorism. While urging continued efforts to combat terrorism, the Heads of State or Government also called for urgent conclusion of a Comprehensive Convention on International Terrorism.

The Heads of State or Government agreed to work on the modalities to implement the provisions of the existing SAARC Conventions to combat terrorism, narcotics and psychotropic substances, trafficking in women and children and other trans-national crimes. They expressed their commitment to take every possible measure to prevent and suppress, in particular, financing of terrorist acts by criminalizing the provision, acquisition and collection of funds for such acts, including through front organizations and also to counter illicit trafficking of narcotic drugs, trafficking in persons and illicit arms. They reiterated the need for law enforcement authorities of Member States to enhance cooperation in the prevention, suppression and prosecution of offences under these Instruments. They noted the initiative of India to prepare a draft of SAARC Convention on Mutual Assistance in Criminal Matters and welcomed the offer of Sri Lanka to hold a meeting of Legal Advisers to examine the idea of a draft convention, before the Second Meeting of SAARC Interior/Home Ministers scheduled to be held in October 2007 in India. They also directed them to ensure regular follow-up and implementation of the decisions taken.

The Heads of State or Government recognized that corruption was an issue of serious concern and agreed to exchange information on national experience in combating corruption to effectively address this problem.

The Heads of State or Government reaffirmed their commitment to a rule-based multilateral trading system. They recalled that the Doha Round was premised on the centrality of development. They directed the Commerce Ministers to work closely to co-ordinate their positions to ensure that the centrality of the development dimension in all areas of negotiations for creating new opportunities and economic growth for developing countries was fully realized. They called upon all members of WTO to show commitment for a successful conclusion of the Doha Round.

The Heads of State or Government welcomed the People's Republic of China, Japan, European Union, Republic of Korea and the United States of America, to be associated as Observers to SAARC. The region would benefit from these external linkages and help its economic integration with the international community. The Heads of State or Government also welcomed the Islamic Republic of Iran to be associated as Observer to SAARC.

The Heads of State or Government welcomed with appreciation the offer of the Maldives to host the 15th Summit Meeting of the Heads of States or Governments of the South Asian Association for the Regional Cooperation (SAARC).

15th Summit

THE COLOMBO DECLARATION

INTRODUCTION

The President of the Islamic Republic of Afghanistan, His Excellency Mr. Hamid Karzai; the Chief Adviser of the Government of the People's Republic of Bangladesh, His Excellency Dr. Fakhruddin Ahmed; the Prime Minister of the Kingdom of Bhutan, His Excellency Lyonchhen Jigmi Y. Thinley; the Prime Minister of the Republic of India, His Excellency Dr. Manmohan Singh; the President of the Republic of Maldives, His Excellency Mr. Maumoon Abdul Gayoom; the Prime Minister of the Federal Democratic Republic of Nepal, the Rt. Hon'ble Girija Prasad Koirala; the Prime Minister of the Islamic Republic of Pakistan, His Excellency Syed Yousuf Raza Gilani; and the President of the Democratic Socialist Republic of Sri Lanka, His Excellency Mr. Mahinda Rajapaksa, met at the Fifteenth Summit meeting of the South Asian Association for Regional Cooperation (SAARC) held in Colombo, Sri Lanka on August 2-3, 2008.

Regional Cooperation

The Heads of State or Government reaffirmed their commitment to the principles and objectives enshrined in the SAARC Charter. They renewed their resolve for collective regional efforts to accelerate economic growth, social progress and cultural development which would promote the welfare of the peoples of South Asia and improve their quality of life, thereby contributing to peace, stability, amity and progress in the region.

The Heads of State or Government recognized that SAARC has been making steady and incremental progress over the years, in particular since the last Summit held in New Delhi in April 2007, towards realizing the objectives of the Charter. They accordingly emphasized the importance of maintaining the momentum, through clear links of continuity between the work already underway and future activities. The Heads of State or Government recognized the need for SAARC to further strengthen its focus on developing and implementing regional and sub-regional projects in the agreed areas on a priority basis. Each Member State may consider taking up at least one regional/ sub-regional SAARC project as the lead country.

The Leaders noted with satisfaction the considerable progress made in various domains of partnership among SAARC Member States and emphasized the need to consolidate and ensure effective implementation of all SAARC programs and mechanisms by rationalization and performance evaluation on a regular basis.

A Partnership for Growth for the Peoples of South Asia

The Heads of State or Government were convinced that the process of regional cooperation must be truly people-centered, so that

SAARC continues to strengthen in keeping with expectations as a robust partnership for growth for the peoples of South Asia. They accordingly directed all SAARC mechanisms to abide by the Charter objective of promoting the welfare of the people and improving their quality of life. In this regard they directed the Council of Ministers to ensure that SAARC mechanisms identify further areas of cooperation where people-centric partnership projects could be initiated.

The Heads of State or Government observed that an effective and economical regional tele-communication regime is an essential factor of connectivity, encouraging the growth of people-centric partnerships. They stressed the need for the Member States to endeavour to move towards a uniformly applicable low tariff, for international direct dial calls within the region.

Connectivity

The Heads of State or Government recognized the importance of connectivity for realizing the objectives of SAARC. They accordingly directed the SAARC mechanisms to continue to embody in their programs and projects a strong focus on better connectivity not only within South Asia, but also between the region and the rest of the world. They further stressed the necessity of fast-tracking projects for improving intra-regional connectivity and facilitating economic, social and people-to-people contacts.

Energy

The Heads of State or Government noted that increased access to energy is critical for fulfilling the legitimate expectations of growth and development in South Asia. They observed in this regard that the escalation of oil prices threatens both the energy security of the region, as well as the economic growth witnessed in South Asia. In this context, they recognized the need to expeditiously develop and conserve the conventional sources of energy and to build up renewable alternative energy resources including indigenous hydro power, solar, wind and bio, while introducing energy reforms, energy efficiency and the trade and sharing of technology and expertise. They also noted that there is tremendous potential for developing regional and sub-regional energy resources in an integrated manner and noted the efforts being made to strengthen regional cooperation in capacity development, technology transfer and the trade in energy. While expressing satisfaction at the progress over the recent years to strengthen energy cooperation, the Leaders directed that the recommendations of the Energy Dialogue be implemented through an appropriate work plan.

The Heads of State or Government stressed the urgent need to develop the regional hydro potential, grid connectivity and gas pipelines. They noted that the possibility of evolving an appropriate regional inter-governmental framework may be explored to facilitate such an endeavour. They welcomed Sri Lanka's offer to host the Third Meeting of SAARC Energy Ministers in Colombo in 2009.

Environment

Being increasingly aware of global warming, climate change and environmental challenges facing the region, which mainly include sea-level rise, deforestation, soil erosion, siltation, droughts, storms, cyclones, floods, glacier melt and resultant glacial lake outburst floods and urban pollution, the Heads of State or Government reiterated the need to intensify cooperation within an expanded regional environmental protection framework, to deal in particular with climate change issues. They were of the view that SAARC should contribute to restoring harmony with nature, drawing on the ancient South Asian cultural values and traditions of environmental responsibility and sustainability.

The Leaders expressed satisfaction at the adoption of SAARC Action Plan and Dhaka Declaration on Climate Change by the SAARC Environment Ministers at the SAARC Ministerial Meeting on Climate Change held at Dhaka on 3 July 2008. In this context they stressed the need for close cooperation for capacity building, development of CDM projects and promotion of programs for advocacy and mass awareness raising on climate change. They also expressed satisfaction at the adoption of a SAARC Declaration on Climate Change for the United Nations Framework Convention on Climate Change (UNFCCC) by the Twenty-ninth Session of the Council of Ministers.

The Heads of State or Government expressed deep concern over global climate change and its impact on the lives and livelihoods in the region. They also noted the urgency of the immediate need for dealing with the onslaught of climate change including sea level rise, on meeting food, water and energy needs, and taking measures to ensure the livelihood security of the peoples in the SAARC region. They resolved to work together to prevent and address the threats to the livelihoods of the peoples and to provide access to remedies when these rights are violated and also to find an equitable distribution of responsibilities and rights among the Member States. They also emphasised the need for assessing and managing its risks and impacts. In this regard, they called for an in-depth study on "Climate Justice: The Human Dimension of Climate Change," to come up with a rights-based approach that would highlight the human impact when responding to the impacts of climate change.

The Heads of State or Government affirmed that every citizen of this planet must have an equal share of the planetary atmospheric space. In this context, they endorsed the convergence of per capita emissions of developing and developed countries on an equitable basis for tackling climate change. They were of the view that any effort at addressing climate change should take into account historical responsibility, per capita emissions and respective country capabilities.

The Heads of State or Government expressed concern at the human loss suffered through natural disasters in the region and stressed the need for the timely provision of relief in humanitarian emergencies. In this regard they directed that a Natural Disaster Rapid Response Mechanism be created to adopt a coordinated and planned approach to meet such emergencies under the aegis of the SAARC Disaster Management Centre.

Water Resources

The Heads of State or Government expressing their deep concern at the looming global water crisis, recognized that South Asia must be at the forefront of bringing a new focus to the conservation of water resources. For this purpose they directed initiation of processes of capacity building and the encouragement of research, combining conservation practices such as rain water harvesting and river basin management, in order to ensure sustainability of water resources in South Asia.

Poverty Alleviation

The Heads of State or Government while acknowledging the

significant steps taken to alleviate poverty in the region, resolved to continue to combat poverty through all available means, including especially through people's empowerment. They committed themselves to continuing to share each other's experiences and success stories of pro-poor poverty reduction strategies such as micro-credit systems, community-driven initiatives and the raising of the consciousness of the poor on their right to resources and development.

In this respect, they emphasized on undertaking sustained efforts, including developing and implementing regional and sub-regional projects towards the attainment of SAARC Development Goals (SDGs). They noted the decision by the Ministers on Poverty Alleviation to obtain an inter-governmental mid-term review of the attainment of the SDGs to be completed by 2009.

The Leaders welcomed the offer of Nepal to host next Ministerial Meeting on Poverty Alleviation.

SAARC Development Fund (SDF)

The Heads of State or Government expressed satisfaction at the signing of the Charter of the SAARC Development Fund (SDF), and finalization of its Bye-laws, and called for an early ratification of the SDF Charter. They also welcomed early operationalization of the Fund from the available funds. They expressed satisfaction at the launching and identification of the projects on women empowerment, maternal and child health and teachers' training under the social window of the SDF, as directed by the Finance Ministers. They reiterated their commitment to expedite their financial contributions to the Fund. In this regard, the Heads of State or Government accepted with appreciation the offer of the Kingdom of Bhutan to host the SAARC Development Fund Secretariat in Thimphu.

Transport

The Heads of State or Government expressed satisfaction at the progress through the Meetings of the Ministers of Transport. They reiterated the critical importance of an efficient multi-modal transport system in the region for integration and for sustaining the region's economic growth and competitiveness. They urged early implementation in a gradual and phased manner of the proposals of the SAARC Regional Multimodal Transport Study (SRMTS).

They noted the progress made in the consideration of the draft Motor Vehicle Agreement (MVA) by Member States. They also noted that technical inputs related to Regional Transport and Transit Agreement and Regional Multilateral Railway Agreement were being examined by the Member States. In this context, they directed the next Transport Ministers Meeting to expedite work in this regard. They appreciated the offer of Sri Lanka to hold the Second Meeting of SAARC Ministers of Transport in Colombo in 2008.

Information and Communications Technology (ICT) Development

The Heads of State or Government urged the need for even more expeditious and close regional cooperation in information and communication technology. They welcomed the enhanced digital connectivity among the Member States and the ongoing work to upgrade the regional telecommunication infrastructure. They directed that the arrangements needed to implement the proposed collaborative tele-projects such as those for health care and education, be expedited.

Science and Technology

The Heads of State or Government acknowledged the ongoing contribution of Science and Technology including cutting edge technology in information and bio-technology in improving the quality of life of the peoples of South Asia. They noted the offer of India to host the Ministerial Meeting on Science and Technology on September 15-16, 2008 for development of a roadmap on identifying implementable focused regional and sub-regional projects in SAARC.

Tourism

The Heads of State or Government underscored the vital contribution that tourism could afford to the economic development of the SAARC region. They agreed to make every effort to implement the comprehensive action plan adopted by the Second Ministerial Meeting held at Cox's Bazaar, Bangladesh. These efforts would include facilitating the movement of people through improved travel infrastructure and air, sea and land connectivity among the SAARC countries, collaboration in human resource development and the promotion of SAARC as a common destination through public-private partnerships and joint campaigns.

Culture

The Heads of State or Government emphasized the role of cultural connectivity in bringing the peoples of South Asia closer, while reinforcing and projecting a distinct South Asian identity. They directed that the Agenda for Culture be implemented in full.

SAFTA and Trade Facilitation

The Heads of State or Government emphasized their commitment to implement SAFTA in letter and in spirit, thereby enabling SAARC to contribute as well to the dynamic process of Asia's emergence as the power house of the world. Recognizing the need to continue to address the major barriers hindering effective trade liberalization in the region, which include sensitive lists of items and Non-Trade Barriers (NTBs), they directed that the decision to revise the sensitive lists by the SAFTA Ministerial Council (SMC) be implemented early. They also recommended that while revising the Sensitive Lists, special consideration be given to the LDCs. The Leaders directed that SAFTA Committee of Experts (SCoE) to expeditiously resolve the issue of Non Tariff Measures (NTMs) and Para Tariff Measures (PTMs) in order to facilitate and enhance the trade under SAFTA.

The Heads of State or Government underlined the need for taking concrete measures to improve trade facilitation in terms of the mutual recognition of standards, the adoption of common tariff nomenclatures, the harmonization of customs procedures. They directed the relevant SAARC bodies to expedite their work in these areas. They also recognized the importance of development of communication system and transport infrastructure and transit facilities specially for the landlocked countries to promote intra-SAARC trade.

The Heads of State or Government observed that the SAARC legal instruments on trade liberalization and the measures and initiatives for trade facilitation are increasingly affording significant openings for mutually beneficial trade, investments and economic co-operation within South Asia. These openings are complemented by the uniformly sound levels of national economic growth being attained by the Member States of SAARC. The Leaders accordingly noted the growing and urgent need for enhancing capacity within SAARC dedicated to encouraging national and regional strategies that would further maximize the positive trade, investments and economic cooperation climate in South Asia. In this regard they welcomed the offer of Sri Lanka to prepare a Concept Paper and a Working Paper on the subject and directed that the Paper be discussed at a Session of the Standing Committee specially convened for this purpose, to enable the adoption of appropriate follow-up measures.

The Heads of State or Government welcomed the signing of the text of the Agreement on the Establishment of the South Asian Regional Standards Organization. The Heads of State or Government welcomed the signing of the Protocol on Afghanistan for Accession to SAFTA.

Trade in Services

The Heads of State or Government expressed satisfaction at the conclusion of the Study on Trade in Services and welcomed the decision of SAFTA Ministerial Council to commence negotiation on the Framework Agreement on Trade in Services. Towards achieving further economic integration, they directed that the Draft Agreement on Investment Promotion and Protection be finalized early and the SAARC Arbitration Council be operationalized.

SAARC Social Charter

The Heads of State or Government underscored the imperative to make steady progress in the implementation of the SAARC Social Charter and directed the Member States to complete the National Plans of Action with a perspective of seeking to transform current challenges into opportunities. They further directed the National Coordination Committees (NCCs) to recommend activities in conformity with the Social Charter and to introduce an efficient and effective monitoring and evaluation mechanism for reviewing the progress in the implementation of the Social Charter. The Leaders emphasized the need to implement the selected regional and sub regional programs and projects to complement national implementation efforts. They urged that such activities be suitably accommodated in the SAARC Calendar. They called for people's participation in strategy initiatives, planning and implementation to ensure people's responsibility and ownership. The Leaders directed to develop a policy on the protection of rights of the senior citizens for their geriatric care taking into account existing national policies of the Member States.

Women and Children

The Heads of State or Government noted with satisfaction the increased cooperation in the region towards achieving the all important goal of bringing women fully into the mainstream of development, on the basis of gender equality. They called for focused attention on women's economic empowerment and skills development, while addressing key health issues and violence against women. The Leaders directed to work for a regional cooperation for the elimination of all forms of discrimination and abuse against women in general and widows in particular and guarantee their rights to live in the society in a dignified manner.

Education

The Heads of State or Government welcomed the substantial progress made in the establishment of the South Asian University in New Delhi and directed that the University should begin its Session from 2010. They also directed that increased interaction between students should be encouraged through institutionalization of students, academics, teachers and youth exchange programs. They further directed early institutionalization of an elaborate SAARC Scholarship Scheme in ICT and related areas.

Combating Terrorism

The Heads of State or Government strongly condemned all forms of terrorist violence and expressed deep concern over the serious threat posed by terrorism to the peace, stability and security of the region.

They further recognized the growing linkages between the phenomenon of terrorism, illegal trafficking in narcotic and psychotropic substances, illegal trafficking of persons and firearms and underscored the need to address the problem in a comprehensive manner. They reiterated their commitment to strengthen the legal regime against terrorism, including by undertaking to implement all international conventions relating to combating terrorism to which Member States are parties, as well as the SAARC Regional Convention on Suppression of Terrorism and the Additional Protocol to the SAARC Regional Convention on the Suppression of Terrorism. The Head of States or Government while recalling United Nations Security Council Resolution 1373 (2001) emphasized the importance of criminalizing any act for the provision, collection and acquisition of funds for the purpose of committing terrorist acts.

The Heads of State or Government recognized in this regard the value of the proposed UN Comprehensive Convention on International Terrorism. They noted the progress made during recent rounds of negotiations and called for an early conclusion of the Convention.

They emphasized the need for strongest possible cooperation in the fight against terrorism and transnational organized crime amongst the relevant agencies of the Member States especially in the area of information exchange. The Heads of State or Government further emphasized the importance of completing all legislative and other relevant measures to implement within Member States, the provisions of the Regional Convention on Narcotic Drugs and Psychotropic Substances. The Leaders noted the considerable work done to promote cooperation in Police matters. They appreciated the offer of Pakistan to host the Third Meeting of SAARC Ministers of Interior/Home in Islamabad during 2008.

The Heads of State or Government expressed satisfaction on the finalization of the text of the SAARC Convention on Mutual Legal Assistance in Criminal Matters at the Fifteenth Summit and its signing. They expressed appreciation at the accommodating manner in which the negotiations were conducted by the Member States to provide each other the widest measures of mutual assistance in criminal matters to ensure a greater sense of security within the region, the Heads of State or Government urged for early ratification and implementation of the Convention.

Joint Positions

The Heads of State or Government resolved to encourage consultations among delegations of SAARC Member States at the appropriate international forums and agreed to cooperate accordingly.

Observers

The Heads of State or Government welcomed the Observers

namely the People's Republic of China, the Islamic Republic of Iran, Japan, the Republic of Korea, Mauritius, the United States of America and the European Union and appreciated their participation in the Summit. They also welcomed Australia and Myanmar to be associated as Observers to SAARC. They approved the guidelines for cooperation with Observers and looked forward to working with them in the common pursuit of the partnership for growth for our people.

16th Summit

The Heads of State or Government welcomed with appreciation the offer of the Maldives to host the Sixteenth Summit Meeting of the Heads of State or Government of the South Asian Association for Regional Cooperation (SAARC).

DESIGNATED SAARC YEARS

SAARC Year of Combating Drug Abuse and Drug Trafficking

SAARC Year of Girl Child

SAARC Year of Shelter

SAARC Year of Environment

SAARC Year of Disabled Persons

SAARC Year of the Youth

SAARC Year of Poverty Eradication

SAARC Year of Literacy

SAARC Year of Participatory Governance

SAARC Year of Biodiversity

SAARC Year of Contribution of Youth to Environment

SAARC Awareness Year for TB and HIV/AIDS

South Asia Tourism Year

SAARC DECADES

1991-2000 SAARC Decade of the Girl Child

2001-2010 SAARC Decade of the Rights of the Child

5

SAARC'S SOCIAL CHARTER

Recognizing Social, Economic and Cultural Demands of the Region

Regionalism in South Asia is celebrated through the South Asian Association for Regional Cooperation (SAARC). But, in practice regionalism rarely functions through the activities of SAARC. Regionalism in South Asia is viewed as a tool to manage the structural dynamics of the region and not as a mechanism to address regional concerns. The purpose of a regional dialogue is to discuss common problems and evolve remedial measures to which all parties can contribute and reap comparable benefits. But, in practice regional dialogue in South Asia is an exercise in one-upmanship where the regional blame-game is exhibited at its worst[1].

Deacon in his writing says that the social dimension of regionalism can provide an alternative to the current pattern of globalization[2].

Regionalism refers to intensifying political, economic or strategic processes of cooperation among states. Such intensification and coordination of activities is not visible in the SAARC. There has been multiplication of institutional structures and proliferation of regional meetings, but few successes in terms of specific action-based programmes. Regional dialogue is dominated by the negative agenda of thrusting the responsibility for the regional challenges on specific national policies, rather than evolving a mutual approach to address the concerns[3].

---

1 Madhavi Bhasin, SAARC: Moving from Programmes of Cooperation to a Cooperative Programme available at. http.//www.ipcs.org/article-details.php?.article No = 2465.

2 Deacon, Bob, Ortiz, Isabel and Zelenev, Sergei, Regional Social Policy (June 2007). UN DESA Working Paper No. 37. Available at SSRN: http://ssrn.com.

3 Ibid.

Another scholar shares similar apprehensions regarding SAARC and says that, the concept of 'regionalism' has not yet emerged in South Asia despite the existence of SAARC, mainly due to the missing degree of complimentarity. Although South Asian states have a common history (in terms of state formation), not all SAARC countries share common values that are rooted in culture, language and religion. And it is absolutely important to have common values for a successful regional bloc, say scholars on regionalism.

The success of the European Union, ASEAN and NAFTA rest on these basic common values, and they are hardly available in South Asia. All regional states and observers have their own reasons for joining SAARC, which were driven more from the point of national interest than by regional interests. The level of mistrust that runs through South Asia, the inability of SAARC to assist in resolving internal conflicts in the region, which has created a space for extra regional forces, makes it almost impossible to have any sort of collective Endeavour in the region[4].

SAARC Initiatives on Social Issues

The draft of SAARC Social Charter mentions the need for enhancing coherent social priorities, policies and programs and the qualities of living conditions of South Asian peoples. All the SAARC Summit declarations have consistently focused on the social dimensions of national and regional development. They provide a substantial base for defining the main elements of a Social Charter.

From the 1991 Colombo Summit onwards, the social issues are more clearly identified and addressed under separate headings. The Dhaka declaration (1993) has added women in development and youth; the Delhi declaration (1995) has included the problems disability and illiteracy, the need for people-to-people contact. Implicit in all these commitments is the recognition that the different elements of social development are closely interlinked, so the strategies to deal with them must necessarily be integrated, with each strategy supporting the others in a virtuous cycle. In the 1987 Summit (Pakistan), the leaders articulated the basic elements for sustainable human development in terms of "eradication of poverty,

[4] Bhatta, C.D., SAARC: Where Does it Stand? Available at : http.//www gorkhpatra.org.np/detail.php?article_id=4606&cat_id=7.

hunger, disease, illiteracy, unemployment and environmental degradation".

Ministerial meetings and regional initiatives have followed these declarations. For many of the social goals, countries have set targets and resolved to achieve them within a clearly defined time frame. The most specific of these resolutions was that of the Ministerial Conference on Children in Rawalpindi in 1996 which agreed on two set of targets covering mortality, fertility, education, nutrition, health, water, sanitation and gender quality - one set of targets to be achieved by 2000, and the other set by 2010. The focus on children and the girl child in particular is perhaps the strongest and most positive feature of SAARC's concern for social development. The priority given to children's development and welfare evokes the deepest motivations for sustainable human development. We see children as the human bridge between what the community actually is and what it aspires to be. This suggests that the challenge is to link public policy precisely with family and community behavior in support of children.

SAARC'S Social Charter

The Group of Eminent Persons constituted by the Ninth Summit (Male, 1997) had formulated the broad objectives and social agenda for mutual cooperation between the SAARC nations, and also developed a detailed action plan in specific areas. This event may be said to have articulated the idea of formulating a Social Charter for the SAARC region. The Tenth Summit (Colombo, 1999) had reiterated similar idea in terms of defining regional dimensions in the social sector that go well beyond the national plan of action. The Eleventh Summit (Kathmandu, 2002) finally declared that a SAARC Social Charter be formulated at the earliest. The Council of Ministers was entrusted with the responsibility of working out the framework of the proposed Social Charter. Evidently, the genes of the SAARC Social Charter were present in the several resolutions passed by the SAARC leaders from time to time.

It was time to consolidate the multifarious resolutions of the SAARC Summits into a single document on social sector development, which would help determine social priorities and formulate policies and programs in coherent and complimentary ways. The plans of action developed on basis of so formulated Social

Charter would lead to improved efficiency in the utilization of resources (national, regional and external), to sustainability of development programs -- all with the ultimate goal of improving the quality of living conditions of the targeted beneficiaries, the poor people of South Asia. The preliminary text of a working draft on Social Charter prepared in 2002 underlines to seek equitable growth through the promotion of the status of women, promotion of the interests and well-being of children, population stabilization, poverty alleviation, and drug de-addiction, rehabilitation and reintegration.

The SAARC leaders agreed to incorporate in the proposed Social Charter the following major goals:

- to recognize social development of the people as a prime national responsibility;
- to integrate economic, cultural and social policies in direction that they reinforce each other, and, to that end, recognize the interdependence of the public and private sectors of development activities;
- to promote participatory governance, human dignity, social justice and solidarity at the national, regional and international levels and ensure tolerance, non-violence, pluralism and non-discrimination in full respect of the diversities within and among societies;
- to promote respect for and observance and protection of human rights and fundamental freedoms for all;
- to promote equality and equity between men and women and the welfare and interest of children and youth;
- to promote social integration and strengthen the civil society;
- to empower people, particularly women, for building up their capacities;
- to promote full participation of concerned beneficiaries at all stages of development schemes; and
- to harness new information technologies and productivity raising technologies for improving the living conditions of the poor people.

Importance of the Social Charter

The manifold development directives articulated in the proposed Social Charter clearly reflect the SAARC leaders' deep concern to give the development initiatives a human touch with unprecedented stress on improving the living conditions of the teeming millions of the South Asian poor. Reflected in the Charter are five ingredient principles of human well-being: (a) enlightenment (access to education), (b) enablement (capacity building), (c) enfranchisement (embracing all sectors of the society, (d) empowerment (promotion of participation opportunities to people to make decisions that affect them), and (e) entitlement (observance and protection of human rights and all fundamental freedoms). These ingredients of human development go to make the Social Charter as great as a Human Charter, to and make it correspond with the Millennium goals of the UN, and to with the goals formulated in other international conventions. If the spirit of humanness so well reflected in the proposed Social Charter is translated into designing and implementing programs and actions of development in literal sense, the battle against poverty and miseries in the South Asian regions will and can be won.

The Nation-States under the umbrella of the SAARC have so far been launching development programs each in its own ways and assessing also its performance in its own way. The Social Charter goals now impinge on each nation to move toward the regional goals and make assessment of their performance also against the regional standards. As can be conceived, the external assistance may help improve the development content and implementation modality, ushering in the South Asian region newer paradigms of planning, implementations and evaluation.

With the roles and rights of different stakeholders of development clearly defined, the Social Charter would assume the form of a social contract between the State and its citizens. With the strengthening of civil society and with the empowerment of the people so long deprived of playing their legitimate potential roles, the whole of society will serve as custodians of the Charter, not merely the State.

Some Imperatives

The SAARC Social Charter represents the culmination of declarations made by the Heads of State and Government of the SAARC region. Declarations as such represent only pious intentions, they ought to be translated into concrete action plans to be pursued by each member state either in coalition or within the national context. In giving the Social Charter a final shape and substance that can guide the development of such plans of action, attention needs to be given to the following considerations:

1. The South Asian Charter needs to comply with the realities of the South Asian context and to the possibilities of attaining certain goal by a certain time.

2. The Charter needs to be of standard quality comparable with the standard of the declarations made in major international summits or conferences taken place during the 1990s, namely the World Summit on Children's Rights (New York, 2000), the Beijing Conference on Women (1996), the World Social Summit (Copenhagen, 1995), and the World Food Summit (Rome, 1996).

3. As there are differences on many aspects across the South Asian nations, particularly with respect to economy, stage of development, availability of resources and institutional capability, it is also an imperative that each SAARC nations identifies its own issues and problems of development, draws up the action plans to address the structural, cultural and institutional barriers to poverty alleviation, and takes effective collective action.

4. As such, the time frame for attaining the different development goals agreed upon collectively by the SAARC nations must be scheduled in consideration of the status, capability and resources of individual SAARC nation. The important issue is not the attainment of certain goal by a common deadline, but the sustenance of strategic actions toward achieving significant progress in all directions to capture the development synergy.

5. In the zeal of going collectively, one should never ignore the awful disparities within each SAARC Nation-State. As such, macro-level yardsticks to compare the progress made in the social development sector in the SAARC nations may fail to capture the substantive progress made in reducing the intra-nation disparities. Macro-level comparisons are necessary to some extent and on only selected aspects but never to the extent of ignoring the realities of intra-level disparities. Therefore, the major criterion of measuring/assessing the progress made should be to look into the extent of reduction of the disparities within each member State. For example, what has happened to the core group of the disadvantaged

and the deprived sections of the population as a result of interventions founded on the SAARC initiatives, should govern the assessment exercise.

6. Considering the scale and intensity of the poverty problem in the South Asian region, it is unlikely that certain poverty alleviation programs declared by the Rawalpindi Summit (1996) targeted to be achieved by 2010 or even by 2020 may look ambitious. As a matter of principle, a Social Charter must necessarily be inspired by long-term vision, say 40 or even 50 years, and go by strategic phases of 10 years' interval.

7. When all said about the desirable imperative steps that ought to go into the blueprint and the modus operandi of the Social Charter, it must be emphasized that the human values and aspirations so well reflected in the summit declaration should not be by-passed in the spirit of going into "regional" ways - rigid "regionalism" is as bad as blind "nationalism" both as a political principle and a culture of practice.

Form and Structure of the Social Charter

The envisaged Social Charter for the SAARC region has to incorporate some important elements: set of directive principles, strategic objective and targets, major policies and programs. These elements may be used as a frame of reference in formulating plans of action encompassing the reform measures the SAARC nations have already been implementing in their respective nation in response to international mandates which they have ratified. These include several conventions such as: Drug Abuse, and Trafficking of Children and Women, Human Resource Development, Food Security, Poverty Monitoring, Girl Child, SADF, Disabled, etc.

Regarding the process of finalizing the SAARC Social Charter, attention should be given to three considerations:

1. The formulation of the national Charter of the SAARC Social Charter must be based on the broadest participation of all concerned - national planners, political parties, members of civil society, administrators and managers of the concerned sectors of political economy. Such participatory process is necessary to meet two ends: (a) to ensure national willingness to participate in the regional

endeavor, and (b) to provide legitimacy to the national chapter founded on popular will. Such a participatory process can even curb the likehood of treating joint venture undertakings simply as "closed" bureaucratic exercises at the inter-governmental level. In one of the SAARC Summit in the future, reports of the national as well as the regional synthesis of these reports need to be presented for consideration and adoption by the SAARC leaders.

2. A few suggestions are presented on matters related to the framework for regional cooperation. The framework needs to be made clear about:

    I. What regional support will be made available to the member states on matter of institution building?

    II. How much resource will be made available to member states to carry out the regional plans of actions, especially to those states that have inadequate resources at their disposal?

    III. Who will be charged with the task of carrying out R&D activities -- a committee of experts outside SAARC or a committee of experts pooled together form the member states?

    IV. Likewise, who will do the task of monitoring the scale and impact of the implementation of the regional schemes of social development?

3. In the same vein, it can be suggested that similar considerations need to be given to matters of building up national institutions of development, mobilization of resources for implementation of the plans and programs under the Nation-States, R&D activities, and monitoring of the process of implementation of plans and programs regarding poverty alleviation, employment generation, social integration and, consequently, realization of the rights, entitlements and social opportunities for people of diverse origins.

Conclusions

Sustainable economic and political cooperation requires strong social foundation and societal legitimacy. The development of the

cooperate mechanism in South Asia through the SAARC enables the regional states to utilize efficiently the scarce regional resources for their long-term benefit. This is because such development is based on rational cost-benefit calculation where the cost of non-cooperation is far greater than that of cooperation. Benefits of cooperation tend to minimize the political consideration of resource allocation -- thus establishing the role of government and non-government actors as facilitator in infrastructure-creation and maintenance as well as sustainability of development. It is only in cooperative institutions that people offer labor, resources and other services and nurture economic and social integration. This means that legislative power of the regional people needs to be enhanced for purposes of evolving institution management rules, monitoring compliance, and enforcing sanctions, thus making the whole development process sustainable. Only through sustainable social development, people can control regional markets, not just by regulating price but basically addressing issues of quality, innovation and management of goods and services. Such measures give ample space for civil society to organize and work for collective action. There are several social areas where the primary interests of South Asian people converge.

The growing interdependence within South Asian states and the rest of the world is a matter of stark necessity rather than a matter of choice. SAARC embodies a common framework of development goals for member nations and implementation of common policies directed at poverty alleviation, improvement of quality of life, and social justice. The increasing realization of common commitment to non-offensive defense and conflict-resolution at the national and regional levels is expected to generate energy for addressing the common challenges of poverty, disempowerment, and disenfranchisement. Clearly, cooperative development cannot move in the absence of participatory regional processes where regional governments at the apex and people at the bottom marshal their resources and maintain their confidence in the SAARC's Charter. Fellowship can be derived from intimacy in cooperative behavior, rather that in obsolete hegemonies, in sharing of common wealth of the region for collective self-reliance, so necessary to attain sustain development and sustain it in a world seeking Continental identity and existence.

When all said about SAARC, a final observation could be that the proposed SAARC Social Charter can be treated as an epic document to be formulated by the Asian people for the well-being of the Asian people, provided that three things go with the Charter. First the finalization of the Charter must reflect the common aspirations of the Asian people. Second, concrete programs of development need to be blueprinted best suited to the stage of development of each member country. Third, the member nations must be held accountable to both their respective people in particular and sensitive to the South Asian community. Doing things regionally naturally differs from doing things nationally. The SAARC leaders must necessarily define the terms and conditions of disciplining themselves to attempt doing as committed to the sense of brotherhood of nations. If these things are not attended, the Charter, will for sure, be treated as "utopian" dreams so recurrently visiting in the great documents of mankind.

As an institution, SAARC has remained an intergovernmental mechanism, which has had little relevance for the people of South Asia.[5] However, the social charter was a step towards the people of south asia.

The modern South Asian culture was shaped by historical circumstances, by the economic, political and cultural impacts of British colonialism. The colonial masters tried to undermine the faith of these people in their culture in their age-old concepts, beliefs, values and institutions which had given meaning and direction to their lives thought their existence. Since imperialism employed the weapon of culture very effectively for the domination of the South Asian people, it became a historic necessity that the battle for independence should be fought in the realm of culture.

So culture became the fountainhead of political awakening, and politics stimulated creative activity, leading to an unprecedented flowering of national art and culture. In this struggle for independence, poets, novelists, musicians, artists and writers played a vital role in the spiritual awakening of the South Asian people and in building their national cultural identity. In this heroic age of

---

5 Mohammed Mohsin, *"The Twelfth SAARC Summit: Quest for Durable South Asian Cooperation"*, South Asian Survey, Vol. 12, No. 1, 2005, pp. 35-46.

independence movements, politics was transformed into a cultural force, and culture into a political force[6].

The Social Charter of South Asia represents the awareness and recognition of the regional aspirations of the states as well as the peoples' demand for the social, economic and cultural rights. It would not be wrong to say that by the adoption of this charter SAARC has proven that its vision and approach towards regionalism is quite similar to that of the European Union. The European Union adopted its Social Charter in 1961, thereby recognizing Social, economic and Cultural rights of the people of the region.

---

[6] S.K. Chaturvedi, S.K. Sharma and Madhurendra Kumar, "*Encyclopedia of SAARC: Economic Cooperation*", Vol. 4, Pragun Publications, New Delhi, 2006, pp.235-236.

6

SAARC
Challenges and Progress

Ever since the establishment of the South Asian Association of Regional Cooperation in 1985, an attempt is being made to improve the well-being of the people through regionalism. SAARC by focusing on economic and other non-political issues is instrumental in creating a climate to promote regionalism. The formation of SAARC parliamentarians has led to new ways of cooperation and friendship among South Asian countries. On the economic front, the expansion of regional trade has resulted in South Asian Preferential Trade Agreement (SAPTA) to become operational. South Asia Free Trade Asia (SAFTA) is also being mooted to have more transparent rules and regulations and free flow of capital in the region. As the scope of SAARC widens, it is increasingly realized that this forum could serve as a vehicle of regional integration. Further, the countries of the region could gain immensely provided they after into contact and interaction with other member countries of NAFTA, GCC, ASEAN and EEC to benefit from their experience.

The existing, international economic order has been operating against the basic interests of the poor countries due to the growing protectionist tendencies in the rich countries. In the World market, the products of the poor countries are facing tough competition with the products of the rich countries. As a result, the share of the poor countries has been decreasing in the world market with the passage of time. On the other hand, the share of the rich countries has been increasing in the world market. The poor countries are left with only one option i.e. to promote mutual economic relations in order to solve their economic problems and to achieve collective self-reliance. Thus, it is required that the South should explore seriously the ways of mutual cooperation reduce its dependence on the North. Such cooperation is also beneficial to the poor countries in order to improve their prospects of cooperation with the rich countries in future. The idea of regional cooperation has already gained support at many international forums. The United Nations Conference on Trade and Development-III (UNCTAD-III) emphasized various aspects of regional cooperation. The non-aligned summit held in Algeria in September 1973 also emphasized that the poor countries should try to maximize trade and economic cooperation among themselves. The South Asian Association for Regional Cooperation (SAARC) is an indication of regional cooperation among the countries of the region. The scope of SAARC regional cooperation is very vast and all the countries of this region can extend their mutual regional cooperation and collective self-reliance. The countries of this region can achieve their objective of economic development more easily and more speedily, if they begin to form themselves into a regional economic group.[1]

It may be noted that by the turn of the last decade the global scenario underwent considerable change. The cold war politics between two super powers and a mad spree of winning over the third world countries by extending enormous economic aid and assistance became more and more bleak since a thaw came into their relations. As such, South-South cooperation became an intense need of the day and therefore, the South Asian Countries also started to think in this direction. It also became clear to them that by mutual cooperation they can fight out the problems of intense poverty and can achieve the goal of socio-economic development. In this context it became apparent that by joint efforts the limited natural resources can be exploited, industrial growth achieved and increased economic efficiency through the expansion of market can be realized. Jointly, they can make their voice heard in the international institution. The cooperation amongst actors can make joint venture programmes a success and utilize their technological know-how for common benefit and may contribute to the release of regional tensions in the subcontinent and channelising ever rising defense expenditure towards development process. With these environmental compulsions, the smaller actors of South Asia though towards formulating a regional cooperation and after great persuasion, debate and discussions the same could materialize in December 1985. It declared that the fundamental goal of SAARC is to

---

[1] S.D. Muni and Anuradha Muni; *Regional Cooperation in South Asia*, New Delhi, 1984, pp. 1-4.

accelerate the process of economic and social development in the region through the optimum utilization of the human and material resources. So as to promote the welfare and prosperity of the peoples and to improve the quality of life since the regional is facing the problems of poverty, low-levels of production, unemployment, underdevelopment, and pressure of population. An intense cooperation is a logical response to these problems. By making use of the potentialities of the huge market, substantial human and natural resources and the complementarities of their economics, the South Asian actors may benefit their people. In this context, at the very outset these countries recognized eleven core areas for cooperation such as, tourism, shipping, agriculture, telecommunication, joint venture, transport, market promotion, science and technology, education and cultural cooperation etc.[2] These countries also created a buffer stock of grain and a development fund, a secretariat at Kathmandu and a common market with the name of SAPTA.[3]

As far as the working of the SAARC or its relations with other regional and sub regional groups are concerned, it seems that there would be a fine tuning or cordial relationship among them in the present century. The twenty-first century will see a multiplicity of active regional and sub-regional groups. SAARC has already made some progress in establishing contacts with like-minded organizations, the most prominent being the European Union with which SAARC has a Memorandum of Understanding. The effort that SAARC has made to establish a relationship with ASEAN, which is our geographically closest regional grouping, has not met with the same success. This is despite the fact that individually all the SAARC countries enjoy close bilateral relations with each ASEAN member. Moreover, India has already graduated to the status of being a full dialogue partner with ASEAN in a cooperative relationship.

In the context of increasing economic global interdependence, prudence dictates that countries and regional groups should maximize their spread of connections in order to guard against the risks of over dependency.

---

[2] Mohammad Shamsul Haq; *International Politics*, New Delhi, Sterling Publishers, p. 49.

[3] Times of India, New Delhi, 11 November, 1986, p. 1.

Other regional and sub-regional groups have been formed in our vicinity with which SAARC will surely interact. The Indian Ocean Rim Association for Regional Cooperation (IOR-ARC), group of 14 African, Asian and Gulf countries including the SAARC States - India and Sri Lanka, and three ASEAN States - Indonesia, Malaysia and Singapore - in an economic block built on a unique tripartite structure. Each State will participate in the activities of IOR-ARC through its government, its private sector and its academic community. A new sub regional grouping known as BIMSTEC brings together for economic cooperation to Bangladesh, India, Myanmar, Sri Lanka and Thailand.

It will be noted that both IOR-ARC and BIMSTEC have SAARC and ASEAN States in associations for economic cooperation. This may be a sign of future developments in SAARC-ASEAN cooperation.[4]

The formation of the South Asian Association of Regional Cooperation (SAARC) in 1985 was to accelerate the process of socio-economic development in the region through a cooperative endeavour of the member States on the agreed areas. The main aim was to cooperate positively for regional betterment and not to get bogged down by bilateral contentious issues affecting the countries which did not need regional discussion.

The seven member countries accorded primacy to IPA which could help in promoting regional interdependence while cooperating in the agreed areas of the programme. This would help in evolving regional economic complementarily rather than competitiveness with each other. The agreed areas were agriculture, communication, education, culture and sports, environment and meteorology, health and population activities, prevention of drug trafficking and drug abuse, rural development, science and technology, tourism, transport and women in development. There were twelve technical committees for the above mentioned areas to implement, coordinate and monitor the respective programmes. Representatives from all the member States constituted the technical committees for the agreed areas of cooperation.

South Asia is united by its poverty. It contributes the largest

---

[4] Ross Masood Husain, *The Dynamic of South Asia: Regional Cooperation and SAARC*, New Delhi, Sage Publication, 1992, pp. 21-22.

share of the world's poor, illiterate, hungry and medically deprived, though Sri Lanka, and Maldives contribute little to these numbers. Any move to integrate South Asia cannot therefore, bypass this defining social reality. It was therefore, appropriate that the Colombo Summit of 1991 set up the independent South Asian Commission on Poverty Alleviation (ISACPA). A quite creative document on how to alleviate South Asia's poverty was prepared by ISACPA and placed before the SAARC Summit in Dhaka in 1993. The Summit indeed set 2001 as the date by which poverty would not just be alleviated but eliminated from South Asia. However, between 1993 and 2001 not much was done at the national level to honor this commitment, nor was any attempt made at successive SAARC Summits to take account of the lack of progress in this area. The emerging global impact in the wake of the Millennium Summit of 2000 has focused attention on poverty reduction and has led to the formulation of the Millennium Development Goals (MDG) which is expected to be realized in each country by 2015. This global emphasis on poverty as also the awareness that poverty was endemic in South Asia even, after 2001, seems to have excited the Kathmandu summit of 2002 revisit poverty. However, poverty reduction is not just an exercise in development budgeting but is integral to the political economy of the concerned society. Given the salience of political and social variables it is less clear how for ISACPA can discharge its roll as a watchdog of the progress in poverty alleviation in South Asia without major back up from South Asian Civil society. South Asia contains a strong civil society that has been at the vanguard of research on poverty and hosts NGO's that have became global role models in developing, implementing and advocating programmes which help to alleviate poverty.[5]

In keeping with the spirit of the SAARC charter to promote mutual trust, understanding and appreciation of one another's problems, the member countries also emphasized the promotion of people to people contact. The role of media was recognized as a medium for fostering cultural consciousness and greater understanding among the people of the region. In 1986, the SAARC Audio-Visual Exchange (SAVE) programme was launched which

---

[5] For further details see : Rehman Sobhan; *South Asian Survey, Charting a Road Map for South Asian Cooperation*, Sage Publications, New Delhi, 2005.

decided to telecast regular television and radio programmes concerning the social and cultural heritage of the member countries.

The SAARC Visa Exemption scheme was introduced in 1992 to encourage people to travel within the region. In 1991, the SAARC fund for regional projects was established to make finances available for the identification and development of regional projects.[6]

The SAARC countries have not only moved ahead in identifying the core areas of cooperation but have also taken initiatives to set up regional institutions such as the SAARC Agricultural Information Centre set up in 1988, which compiles and makes available information on agricultural research and development to the national information centre of the member States. In 1992, the SAARC tuberculosis centre was set up in Kathmandu to coordinate the activities of the national tuberculosis control programmes of the member States. The SAARC meteorological research centre set up in 1995 at Dhaka deals with research on weather forecasting. SAARC regional convention on suppression of terrorism was signed in November 1987 and was ratified on 22 August 1988 under which the member States agreed to prevent the entry of terrorists and their activities on their soil and to extradite or prosecute them on receiving information, to combat terrorism regionally. Hence, the SAARC Regional convention on Narcotic Drugs and Psychotropic substances was signed in November 1990 at Male. Other schemes included: SAARC scheme for promotion of organized tourism (SSPOT) for providing inter-alia concessionary air fare to the tourist traveling under the scheme; SAARC documentation centre (SDC), New Delhi for providing ready access to reliable and up to date information on technical, scientific and development matters; SAARC chairs, Fellowship and Scholarship scheme (SCFSS) for providing greater interaction among students, scholars and academics in the SAARC region.

In 1988, SAARC leaders agreed to Observe 1989 as "SAARC year for combating Drug Abuse and Drug Trafficking and 1990 as the "Year of SAARC Girl Child". Thus, the scope of SAARC was extended and the greater prospects of regional cooperation emerged.

The other greatest achievements or progress of SAARC, that, all

---

[6] S.D. Muni and Anuradha Muni; *Regional Cooperation in South Asia*, National Publications House, 1984, Delhi pp. 31-33.

the seven members decided to sign an agreement with the 15 members European Union (EU) for the Cooperation in various spheres.[7] It was also decided to explore the possibility of SAARC-ASEAN (Association of South East Asian Nations) Cooperation. A proposal was endorsed to take measures for the establishment of a South Asian Free Trade Area (SAFTA). It was felt necessary because SAPTA was a loose arrangement, and flexible trade regime was the need of the hour.

The scope of SAARC cooperation in economic field is tremendous. The export realization of tea and raw jute for Bangladesh would be higher if it is sold in the region. Sri Lanka will get better prices by selling coconut oil and natural rubber in the region. Buying wheat from Pakistan and rubber from Sri Lanka would be cheaper for India. Manufactured consumer products bought from India would be cheaper from Bangladesh, Pakistan, Nepal, Bhutan, Sri Lanka and Maldives. Electricity from Nepal and Bhutan would be cheaper for India and Bangladesh.[8] Another achievement of the regional cooperation is that these SAARC Nations can sell primary products and manufactured goods to India and other member countries. For example, Bhutan is currently providing India with electricity from Chukha Hydel Project, a major source of export revenue. Bilateralism is strengthened to improve and normalize political relations. The SAARC charter makes room for other members to join the association; it will be no doubt a helpful exercise if efforts are made and particularly through Indian Initiatives to make Burma, Thailand, Afghanistan and Iran to join this forum. Iran, Burma have already expressed their willingness to become members of SAARC grouping.[9] On February 2005, the Foreign Minister of Iran, Kamal Kharrazi, indicated Iran's Interest in joining SAARC, saying that his country could provide the region with "East West Connectivity". On November 13, 2005, the Dhaka Summit issued a declaration to admit the Islamic Republic of Afghanistan as a member and to accord observer status to China and Japan. The

---

[7] Chandrakant Yatanoor; "Small States invade SAARC", *Third Concept*, August, Vol. 17, No. 198, 2003 p. 14.

[8] V.K. Panchamuki, *Economic Cooperation in the SAARC Region: Potential Constraints and Policies*, New Delhi, Interest Publications, 1990, p. 8.

[9] Vijay Shukla, "New Frontiers of SAARC", *India Quarterly*, Vol. 52, ICSSR North-West Regional Centre, Chandigarh 1996, p. 94.

nations also agreed to organized, development funds under a single financial institution with a permanent secretariat that would cover all SAARC programmes ranging from social, to infrastructure to economic ones.[10]

SAARC has established trade cooperation with international and regional organizations. In April 1993, a memorandum of understanding (MOU) on the Trade Analysis and Information systems (TRAINS) between SAARC and UNCTAD (United Nations Conference on Trade and Development) was signed. This will facilitate global exports. The SAARC secretariat in turn would provide data on trade control measures prevailing in the SAARC countries. A framework agreement or cooperation on trade promotion was also signed between SAARC and ESCAP (Economic Commission for Asia and the Pacific).[11] The possibilities are also being explored for trade cooperation with EU (European Union) and ASEAN, SAARC has emphasized the need for greater participation of the Non-government Organizations (NGOs) in the process of trade cooperation. During eleventh session of the SAARC Council of Ministers in Colombo in July 1992, certain guidelines and procedures for granting recognition by SAARC to regional apex bodies were approved. Thus SAARC Chamber of Commerce and Industry (SCCI) was been established in February, 1994 with its headquarters in Karachi. The SCCI set its goals to raise the level of awareness about the policy initiatives of the SAARC and to provide a strong thrust to the movement of SAARC by providing necessary information and services to the business community. It launched an on-line computerized information network called SAARC-Net in January 1996. The Net with its headquarters based in the office of Federation of Indian Chambers of Commerce and Industry (FICCI), New Delhi, has computer linkages in all seven SAARC countries. It provides information on policy update about SAARC countries, business profiles, business offers and opportunities, calendar of national and international trade fairs, conferences and important business events.[12]

India's high growth rates in recent years has enabled it to draw

---

10 Available at : www.south-asia.com/saarc.

11 Ibid.

12 D.K. Maddan; *SAARC Origin, Development and Programmes,* Deep and Deep Publications, New Delhi, 1997, pp.38, 39.

towards the ASEAN region, the message clearly being that ASEAN agreed to have a more meaningful trade partnership with India only when it could perceive gains from such a pact. The SAARC summits provide an ideal opportunity for the two countries to exchange trade concessions under SAPTA-India and Pakistan to enter into special arrangements with respect to trade between them. It is now in Pakistan's interest, and perhaps the only option left to play a pro-active role in improving trade relations with India. Such a step would not only benefit the two countries but would also benefit the South Asian region as a whole.

There is a good chance that Indo-Pakistan trade relations may improve substantially in the coming months. This time, improved trade relations may well be on a more sustainable basis.[13]

The geographical cohesiveness of the region has also led the member countries to share the anxieties of environmental hazards. The continuing degradation caused by ecological hazards led to the commissioning of two studies by the SAARC Secretariat, one on the 'causes and consequences of natural disasters and protection and preservation of the environment' and another on the 'Greenhouse Effect on the Region' in 1988. Both the studies have been completed and a technical committee on environment within the IPA has been set up.[14]

The economies of South Asian countries are gradually becoming competitive in view of the new mantras of post-Cold War age-globalization and economic liberalization is catching up. Efforts are on, to make them complimentary.[15] India and Bangladesh for example, have identified some products for trade which are to be conducted through free convertible currencies.[16] Between India and Nepal custom regulation has been relaxed to facilitate the volume of

---

[13] Jitendra, J. Ahirrao; *Third Concept,* April, Vol. 18, No. 205, 2004, p. 14.

[14] Iftikhar Uzzaman; *Institutional Sources of Conflict and Opportunities for Cooperation under the Aegies of SAARC* in D.D. Khanna; *Sustainable Development: Environment Security in South Asia,* Macmillan India Ltd., 1997, Delhi p. 120.

[15] For further details see : Rizvi, Gowher; *South Asia in Changing International Order,* Sage Publication, New Delhi, 1995.

[16] For further details see : Hussian, Akmal; *Bangladesh Search for South Asian Regionalism in Bangladesh: Global Politics,* Vol. 3.

trade and there are joint ventures between India and Nepal.[17] Similarly both India and Sri Lanka are coming closer through joint collaboration.[18]

Even though, the volume of trade remains very low, India and Pakistan are also realizing the potential of economic cooperation. But, unfortunately due to the border tension, cross border terrorism, they have not been able to register an impressive growth in the recent years. The era of economic liberalization has ushered in a new beginning in the area of region, but at the moment there is only 3.5% of the total export within the SAARC countries.[19]

SAARC has identified many areas for cooperation, particularly in the field of trade. A regional study on trade, manufactures and services completed in 1991 clearly spelt out the need for promoting regional cooperation in core economic areas, at the Male Summit in July 1991. In December 1991, the heads of governments meeting in Colombo decided to set up an Inter-Governmental Group to provide specific measures for trade liberalization among SAARC countries. On 11 April 1993, the Agreement on South Asian Preferential Trade Agreement (SAPTA) was signed by the Council of Ministers. SAPTA, aims to promote mutual trade through exchanging concessions relating to tariffs, para-tariffs, non tariff measures and direct trade measures. The SAPTA process remains in place with the member States exchanging their offer list of tariff concessions covering over 2000 items during the Colombo Summit in 1998.[20]

Another positive contribution to the development of SAARC that some steps, some SAARC members have already taken, and others intend to take in the near future. The establishment of National Human Rights Commissions by India and Pakistan, Sri Lanka Commission had its members appointed earlier this year. Both Bangladesh and Nepal, are taking measures to establish their own national commissions. There had already been some contact between the Human Rights Commissions of South Asia at meetings of the

---

[17] Narayan, Khadka; "Challenges to Developing the Economy of Nepal," *Contemporary South Asia*, Vol. 7, No. 2, July 1998, p. 147.

[18] The Economic Intelligence Unit. Country Report, Sri Lanka, 2001.

[19] The Economic Intelligence Unit, Country Report, Sri Lanka, Nepal, Bangladesh, Pakistan, Maldives and Bhutan, 2001. Available at : http://www.economist.com/countries/Sri Lanka.

[20] Economic Times, New Delhi, 29 November, 1996. Available at : http://www.economist.com/countries/Sri Lanka.

Human Rights Commissions of the Asia-Pacific region under the sponsorship of the United Nations. As the Human Rights Commissions of our own region become operational and their numbers increase, as they are bound to do in the near future, we should have our own grouping of South Asian Human Rights Commissions. As SAARC has moved into the 21st century, it must establish its own regional institution and cooperative framework for promotion and protection of human rights, with the respective national commissions taking the lead. While doing so, SAARC would also make it clear that these measures are not being taken on the dictation of the outside world, but rather in response to a profound commitment from within the region to the furtherance of human rights.

Another question is how will SAARC handle the environmental issues that will assume increasing importance in the coming years? Environment lobbies will continue to grow in influence. Governments will need to be responsive to their concerns, not only in order to safeguard the environment within their own borders, but also to protect their trade and economic prospects. Environmental issues compel the South Asian countries to co-operate more closely. It is only through their collective strength that the South Asian countries will be able to negotiate their global environmental obligations, without compromising their targets for national development.

At recent Kyoto meeting on global warming, the European Union advocated the concept of the bubble. At Kyoto, the developing countries were not compelled to undertake obligations to cut back on their own commissions of such gases. It is that the regional cohesion on environmental issues would become imperative, so that for instance South Asia too could have its own bubble proposal, like the EU at Kyoto. Alternatively, we could contemplate environmental trade – off's, whereby in return for action taken by one SAARC country with advanced environmental technology to protect the eco-diversity in another country of the region, the first country would get credits to offset insufficient cuts in its own emission levels.

SAARC has included environment-related issues in its programme of activity since 1990. SAARC countries had a tradition of adopting a common SAARC position in global fora on the environment. The manifest peril of global warming causing the rise of the seabed can have devastating effect on the territory, and large sections of the population of our South Asian Region.[21]

Yet another question that SAARC would need to respond to is explosion of information technology. The last decades of the twentieth century have been spectacular developments in the field of information technology. It is correct that in the past there have been discussions within SAARC on proposals such as a SAARC satellite for education. At that time the attendant costs and other problems appeared too difficult to overcome. The advances of information technology will make the global economy of the 21st century essentially knowledge driven.[22] A regional economic group will not be able to function successfully without the capacity to utilize the latest technologies to transmit and exchange information freely. SAARC must soon seriously confront the issue of how to make the best collective use of the advances in information technology.

The benefits of information technology can be used to craft common education programmes, especially in the scientific and technological field, to the distinct needs of South Asian youth. SAARC is fortunate that it has among its ranks India, which is one of the world leaders in information technology. India may play the lead role in bringing to and spreading throughout, our region the benefits of advanced information technology.[23]

In the 21st century, it is often is of the view or question arises that, will the political and security environment be in South Asia in the 21st century? The South Asian region is certainly not unique in having to grapple with contentious issues. Other regions also have their problems. The difference in South Asia, however, is that the contentious issues are taking a relatively long time to resolve. Two factors have contributed to this situation. One is the asymmetry in the region, where India not only completely over-shadows the other countries, but is also the only State which has common borders with

21 Lakshman Kadirgamar, *South Asian Cooperation in the Twenty-first Century: Opportunities and Challenges,* South Asian Survey, Vol. 5, No. 1, Jan-June, 1998, pp. 32-34.

22 Rahul Tripathi, Bringing SAARC closer to South Asia, World Focus, Vol. 341. May, 2008. Also See : Dipanker Bannerjee. SAARC in the 20th Year : Meeting the challenges of a New Era, available at http;//www.ila.org.np

23 P.J. Lauakare, *Technology Missions for South Asia: Cooperation in the High-Tech-Domain*, Delhi, Omega Publication, 1996, p. 141.

four of the other six States. The second factor has been less geographical and more historical, namely, the involvement in the affairs of the region of other parties outside the region which has in turn complicated the resolution of problems between the two largest States in the region. At the height of cold war, both the United States and Russia, the successor State to the USSR. The dominance of the sole surviving super-power, the United States, is likely to continue well into the 21st century. Hence, with the disappearance of this second factor, the political and security environment in South Asia must surely begin to improve. The complications once caused by great power rivalry will fade into a memory.

South Asian Cooperation faces the problem of terrorism. There was a time when South Asia was engaged in trying to extricate itself from defining terrorism. Fortunately, for those countries like Sri Lanka, who are in the forefront of combating terrorism, the international consensus against terrorism based on the recognition of reality has matured over the years. The process of globalization is erasing national boundaries; terrorism is openly contemptuous of national boundaries. No single country, however isolated it may be in a geographical sense, can insulate itself totally against terrorism, without the cooperation of the international community.[24]

In the context of SAARC, all the fruits of prosperity that we hope to gather in the next century, all our hopes for securing an enhanced quality of life for our people could be brutally denied if we in South Asia turn a blind eye to the menace of terrorism.

In this regard, the signing and ratification of the SAARC Conventions on Suppression of Terrorism and on Narcotics and Drugs are important steps in the right direction. We now need countries to practice what they agreed to.

No doubt a number of problems faced by the SAARC countries, but increasing pressures for faster progress on growth and poverty reduction have led to an era of reform. South Asian countries are dismantling restrictions on domestic and foreign private investment, removing trade restrictions and reducing tariffs. International financial markets have reacted favourably to these reforms. This new found access to international capital markets a major change in the South Asian economic environment but inflows, particularly of

---

[24] Lakshman Kadirgamar, (1998) pp. 37-38.

foreign direct investment (FDI), continue to be bureaucratic regulation and low labour market flexibility.

Creating adequate political will among the SAARC leadership and public is required to improve free trade, industrial and economic cooperation in an era of globalization and liberalization. Removal of discriminatory trade practices among member countries should be the first step. Secondly, macro economic reforms aimed at higher growth and greater economic resilience must be extended and deepened. Thirdly, collective negotiating mechanism in dealing with multinational institution is called for. For instances, some trade is routed through non SAARC countries to by-pass restrictions. It should be removed, and the coverage of intra SAARC trade should be prompted by encouraging multinationals and by establishing joint ventures in the SAARC countries. India may take initiatives in this regard, establishing joint ventures in Nepal, Sri Lanka, Bangladesh, Pakistan, Bhutan and Maldives.

Similarly, these SAARC nations can sell primary products and manufactured goods to India and other member countries. For example, Bhutan is providing India with electricity from Chukha Hydel Project, a major source of export revenue bilateralism should be strengthened to improve and normalize political relations. Fourthly, natural resources must be managed so that the region's development path is environmentally sustainable. Fifthly, bilateralism should be strengthened to improve and normalize political relations since the SAARC charter makes room for other members to join the association, it will be no doubt a helpful exercise if efforts are made and particularly through Indian initiatives to make Burma, Thailand, Afghanistan and Iraq to join this forum. Iran and Burma have already expressed their willingness to become members of SAARC grouping. It is hoped that with the passage of time SAARC nations will be able to harmonize their views on economic issues, so that they can exert greater influence in relevant international form as a group.[25]

PROGRESS REPORT OF THE SAARC

Much has been achieved since the formation of SAARC, even though much more remains to be done. Lack of information on

---

[25] Vijay Shukla, *New Frontiers of SAARC,* India Quarterly, Vol. 52, ICSSR, North-West Regional Centre, 1996, pp. 93-94.

SAARC and associated regional matters is a major problem. When even the embassies of member countries lack the address of the SAARC Secretariat, there is little hope for members of the public, and many opportunities for regional cooperation are missed.

Integrated Program of Action (IPA)

The IPA is the key component of the SAARC's functions. It now includes 11 areas of cooperation, each covered by a Technical Committee:

- Agriculture
- Communications
- Education, Culture and Sports
- Prevention of Drug Trafficking and Drug Abuse
- Rural Development
- Science and Technology
- Tourism
- Transport
- Women in Development

Trade and Economic Cooperation

Agreement on **SAPTA** (South Asian Preferential Trading Arrangement) signed during the Seventh SAARC Summit in Dhaka. SAPTA entered into force on 7 December 1995 when all Member States met the necessary conditions. Under this agreement, the gradual reduction and eventual elimination of tariffs within SAARC is envisaged.

SAPTA is considered to be a step on the road to creating **SAFTA** (South Asian Free Trade Area), which is still at the discussion stage.

Initiatives taken towards promoting trade cooperation within SAARC include:

- Cooperation in the fields of Handicrafts and Cottage Industries.
- Study on Transport Infrastructure and Transit Facilities.

Member countries have also implemented bilateral and multilateral initiatives to promote economic cooperation.

Poverty Eradication

1991: Sixth SAARC Summit (Colombo) decided to establish an Independent South Asian Commission on Poverty Alleviation (ISACPA).

1993: Seventh SAARC Summit (Dhaka) adopted consensus on poverty eradication.

Poverty remains a defining feature of the SAARC region. However the establishment of SAARC has at least helped to get governments talking on plans to alleviate and eradicate poverty.

Promoting People-to-People Contact

1986: Second SAARC Summit (Bangalore) laid special emphasis on promoting people-to-people contact in the region and approved the following five initiatives:

- SAARC Audio-Visual Exchange (SAVE) Program.
- SAARC Documentation Center (SDC).
- SAARC Scheme for Promotion of Organizing Tourism.
- SAARC Chairs, Fellowships and Scholarships Scheme.
- SAARC Youth Volunteers Program (SYVOP).

Other initiatives include:

- SAARC Visa Exemption Scheme (initiated in 1988)
- South Asian Festivals (9-24 October 1992, India)
- Non-Governmental Organizations (NGOs)
- Association of SAARC Speakers and Parliamentarians
- SAARC Chamber of Commerce and Industries (SCCI)
- SAARCLAW

The easing of travel and business restrictions within the SAARC region is a visible and enduring achievement of SAARC. This has directly and indirectly resulted in increased economic and social benefits to people in all member countries.

SAARC: Regional Institutions

- SAARC Agricultural Information Center (SAIC), Dhaka/Bangladesh
- SAARC Tuberculosis Center (STC), Baktapur/Nepal

- SAARC Meteorological Research Center (SMRC); Dhaka/Bangladesh
- SAARC Documentation Center (SDC), New Delhi/India

Regional Conventions/Agreements

- Agreement on Establishing the SAARC Food Security Reserve (SFSR) - Third SAARC Summit (Kaṭhmandu, 1987).
- SAARC Regional Convention on Suppression of Terrorism - Third SAARC Summit (Kathmandu, 1987).
- SAARC Convention on Narcotic Drugs and Psychotropic Substances - Fifth SAARC Summit (Male', 1990).
- Agreement on SAARC Preferential Trading Summit (Dhaka, 1993) has been ratified by all Member States.

SAARC Funds

- SAARC Fund for Regional Projects (SFRP) – established in 1991.
- SAARC – Japan Special Fund – established on 27 September 1993, Kathmandu.
- South Asian Development Fund (SADF) – approved by the Fifteenth Session of the Council of Ministers (New Delhi, 1995).

Harnessing the Potential of South Asia

The SAARC brings together countries which, in combination, offer a wide range of opportunities for devclopment.

The region is already the powerhouse for manpower to the Middle East and to the burgeoning economies of South-East Asia. It would be fair to say that labour inputs from SAARC nations provided the boost these economies needed in order to reduce manpower costs and to remain competitive.

The SAARC region is already a significant provider of:

- agricultural produce from tea to exotic fruits to coconut oil,
- manufactured goods from garments to gloves to industrial machinery,

- services from tourism to construction to software development.

However, much of the potential in all these areas remains untapped.

The SAARC region represents an untapped market of over a billion people, the majority of whose incomes have now started to rise. An integrated approach towards development, which SAARC hopes to promote with the establishment of SAPTA and SAFTA, will provide access to a common market of South Asia.

The institutional structure built by SAARC has provided a useful platform for conceptualization, if not full implementation of programmes of regional significance and for an exchange of views of experiences at various levels on issues of common concern to the member States.

The SIPA which has formed the core programme for regional cooperation under SAARC has a general, succeeded in fostering personal contacts, through seminars, workshops and training programmes between experts of the region and facilitated exchange of data and in information in the identified sectors.

The SIPA gradually extended its activities to cover as many as eleven areas. However, noting the overlapping jurisdictions of these activities and also be enhance clarity in terms of goals and objectives. SIPA was reconstituted in 1999 on the recommendations of an Independent Group of Experts to cover seven areas, namely, (*i*) Agriculture and Rural Development, (*ii*) Communications and Transport, (*iii*) Social Development, (*iv*) Environment, Meteorology and Forestry, (*v*) Science and Technology, (*vi*) Human Resource Development and (vii) Energy.

Further, the compilation of regional directives and bringing out State of art reports on areas of common interest has contributed to knowledge sharing for mutual benefit.

The involvement of SAARC with the problem of poverty alleviation in the region is another SAARC initiative. The establishment of SAARC three-tier mechanism States with useful institutional mechanism to constantly monitor the poverty profiles of the member States and in this process exchange the varied experiences of effective strategic interventions needed in this key area.

The social agenda of SAARC has also been addressed to important concerns relating to women, children and other deprived Groups in the region. SAARC has played a particularly important role n building a region-wise consensus on protecting the rights of children, creating awareness on the problems of girl child and women.

SAARC has identified environment as an important area of regional concern. Two important studies relating to protection of the environment and on the impact of greenhouse effect on the region has been completed. Over the years, SAARC has set up a number of regional institutes to supplement the work of technical committees to share information and coordinate activities in priority areas identified by the member States. Five such institutions are: the SAARC Agricultural Information Centre (SAIC), the SAARC Documentation Centre (SDC), the SAARC Meteorological Research Centre (SMRC), the SAARC Tuberculosis Centre (STC), and SAARC Human Resource Development Centre (SHRDC). In addition three new Regional Centres are being established under SAARC umbrella. These are: SAARC Cultural Centre (Sri Lanka), SAARC Coastal Zone Management Centre (Maldives) and SAARC Information Centre (Nepal).

Another notable achievement has been an effort to tackle several regional threats through regional agreements/conventions. To date, three such conventions have been concluded, namely, the SAARC Regional Convention on Suppression of Terrorism (1998) and the SAARC Convention on Narcotic Drugs and Psychotropic Substances (1990) and SAARC Convention on Preventing and Combating Trafficking in Women and Children for Prostitution (1997). A SAARC Food Security Reserve has also been established to provide for a reserve of food-grains in case of emergency food shortages in the member States.

An important achievement of SAARC has been its success in putting in place schemes designed for; include the SAARC Audio-Visual Exchange Programme, the SAARC Chairs, Fellowships and Scholarships Scheme, the SAARC Volunteer Exchange Programme and the SAARC Visa Exemption Scheme.

Another notable step forward has been the decision of the Association to grant recognition or affiliation to professional bodies established to promote regional cooperation in their respective specialized fields. Three SAARC apex Bodies, the SAARC Chamber of Commerce and Industry (SCCI), the SAARC Law, and South Asian Federation of Accountants (SAPA) have received such recognition.

The signing of the Framework Agreement on the South Asian Free Trade Area (SAFTA) is a major milestone. Another notable development has been the signing of the SAARC Social Charter. Issues covered under the Charter, such as poverty alleviation, population stabilization, empowerment of women, youth mobilization; human resource development, promotion of health and nutrition, and protection of children are key elements in the promotion of welfare and well being of all South Asian.

THE GROUND REALITY OF THE PROGRESSES OF SAARC AND G.E.P. ASSESSMENT

The SAARC, in its ninth summit constituted a Group of Eminent Persons (GEP). This group has made a retrospective appraisal of SAARC's achievements. It was felt by this group that the SAARC has passed through two distinct phases, the first was the preparatory phase in which gradual imitation of regional cooperation started. This phase was mostly non-controversial. During the second phase, SAARC moved into expansionary stage wherein it expended both in social and core economic sectors such as preferential trading and poverty alleviation. However, the group also found out lack in sufficiency of political bill and adequate the sources for carrying out commitment and plans. 'A disjunction developed between the decisions taken by the associations and their implementation' observed the group.

The GEP is of the view that SAARC is still very far from maturing as a regional economic grouping. It took several years for SAARC to move to hardcore economic areas. The first scheme of cooperation in the economic area was launched in 1993 in the form of the SAARC Preferential Trading Arrangement (SAPTA) and was implemented from end 1995.

The progress under SAPTA has been extremely slow and protracted. Even though as many as around 5500 products have been conceded tariff concession, the actual and potential trade coverage has been modest. Many products offered concessions are not even imported by the member States. The depth of tariff concessions have generally ranged from 10-20 per cent, except for India which has offered concessions ranging from 50-100 per cent for least developed countries (LDC). The problems of non-tariff barriers were largely ignored. Among the non LDCs the main problems have been of Pakistan not agreeing to offer MFN status in its trade relations with India. This has prevented the full potential of regional trade liberalization being realized particularly among non-LDCs. The protected nature of negotiations following frequent postponements of meetings has induced India to come to a free trade agreement with Sri Lanka which became operational w.e.f. March 2000. India and Bangladesh are also currently negotiating a free trade agreement among them. Given the fact that historically India had free trade agreements with both Nepal and Bhutan since the fifties, the relevance of SAFTA in promoting regional trade expansion is questionable.

The facilities provided under SAARC Food Security Reserve have never been utilized notwithstanding the need for urgent food imports by member States. Again, the conventions on Suppression of Terrorism and on Narcotic Drugs and Psychotropic Substance have had no impact on controlling terrorism or drug trafficking through regional cooperation in South Asia. Some of the countries have still not even enacted enabling national legislations to give effect to these conventions.

The schemes of people-to-people contact have been stagnating and as yet vast number of people in the region have problems moving from one country to another.

In the field of environment, SAARC has made no tangible progress beyond producing the two studies referred to earlier. These studies call for urgent follow up action.

Many of the objectives of SAARC remained far from any meaningful follow up actions for many years. For instance, the crucial objectives like "cooperation with international and regional organizations with similar aims and purposes" remained unattended for almost a decade. Only in the very recent past SAARC has signed Memorandum of Understanding with a number of organizations including United Nations Conference on Trade and Development UNCTAD (1993), UNICEF (1993), APT (1994), UNDP (1995), UNDCP (1995), European Commission (1996), International Telecommunication Union (1997), and Canadian International Development Agency (CIDA, 1997). However, except one or two organizations, the activities have not really been effective.

CONCLUSION

While analyzing the performance of SAARC some of the critics hold the view that in the history of South Asia, the countries had no experience of working together for common regional purposes. The sense of nationalism was still very strong which critics said was not very conducive to regional approach to solve problem. Most of SAARC countries in recent times, had their relations marked by suspicion, misunderstanding and even by conflict. As a result, cooperation has been shrinking in recent years for political reasons. Thus SAARC had not been able to tangibly solve and major problems, like economic problems, trade problems etc.

But on the other hand, while reviewing the progress of the activities of SAARC, Mr. Abdul Ahsan said that SAARC has achieved "quite good progress" SAARC had atleast created a framework to bring people together, so that they càn know each other, understand each other and see what their problems and possibilities are and thereby narrowing the information which had separated them from each other. He also said that SAARC was not a forum where one could expect anything dramatic. But there is the possibility for economic and social cooperation among SAARC countries in the coming years.

Inspite of all problems that appear to be retarding the growth of South Asian regionalism there are also certain positive elements (aspects). For example, till very recently South Asia was one of the least militarized regions. With 20% of the world's population it contributed to only one percent of the world's military expenditure. Compared to this, other developing regions (excluding China) with the same percentage of population, accounted for about 15% of the global military expenditure. The developed world, which is proud to announce that there has not been war on its soil ever since the end of the World War II accounted for 80% of global military R & D expenditure and 97% of world's arms trade. Although there have been three intra-regional wars, they have been short and affected the civilian population little.

Even as the demographic and ethnic problems cause disharmony among the regional consciousness and cooperation. One may recall in this connection the reaction of Pakistani Prime Minister Liaquat Ali Khan. When his military adviser suggested that the time was opportune to take military action against India. Brushing aside the suggestion, Liaquat said: When you have in mind only military strategic considerations, I have to think of the whole of subcontinent. Have you ever realized what would happen to the Muslims on the other side in case of an all out war? We trust that the same considerations will be kept in mind by the ruling elites in all the respective national capitals in South Asia.

Beside the steps that have been taken in the fields of technical and economic cooperation among the South Asian States, there are three achievements which deserve special mention - the SAARC audio-visual cooperation which makes possible the exchange of TV and radio programmes among the regional States: the SAARC food security scheme which provides for food relief in times of crisis and the convention against terrorism. Though both India and Pakistan continue to abuse each other of aiding and assisting the respective ethnic and minority groups that threaten the integrity of both the nations, the fact that they have signed the convention along with each other members of SAARC speaks of the commonality of the stimuli.

SAARC AND OTHER REGIONAL ORGANIZATIONS

In trying to examine the inadequacies of SAARC, it would be useful to first briefly look at the origins and objectives of some of the other regional organizations that had come up around the globe to meet similar aspirations and to also review their performance. In doing so, it is indeed an interesting revelation that the Arab League which comprises 22 member countries today is the earliest regional organization set up in 1945 with the objective of forming a closer union among Arab states and fostering political and economic cooperation. An agreement for collective defense among the members was signed in 1950.

The Map of the Members of the Arableague

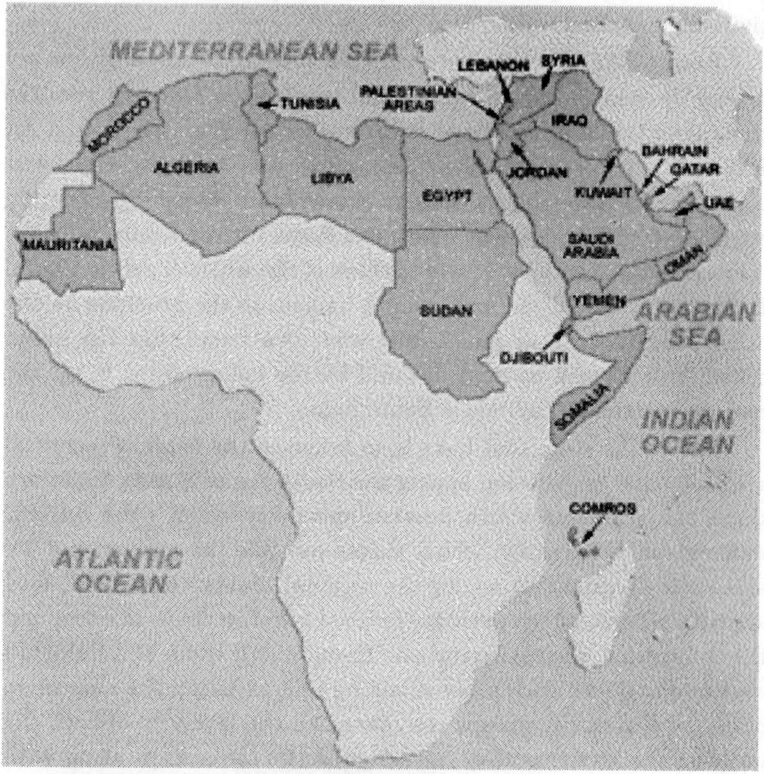

The Flag of the Arab League

The Organisation of American States (OAS) with 35 states in the Americas was set up in 1948 with the objective of strengthening peace and security in the Western Hemisphere. While both organizations still exist and meet regularly, it is a matter of opinion whether they have fully served their original purpose.

The map of the members of OAS

The Flag of OAS:

The North Atlantic Treaty Organization (NATO), though not a regional organization in the strict sense of the term, being a military alliance, was set up in 1949 and now has 19 members plus France. This alliance has generally served its purpose, in the sense that it can rightfully claim to have prevented war in Western Europe by its very existence and capability built up over the years.

It has also successfully (from its point of view) intervened in the conflicts in the Balkans, and continues to retain a significant presence there in the maintenance of peace and security. It is a matter for some detailed consideration whether or not this alliance has provided the impetus for closer political and economic ties and arrangements between the countries of Western Europe. Of particular recent importance is the involving of Article 5 of the treaty that commits member states to "respond to an armed attack on any party", when terrorists attacked the World Trade Centre in New York and the Pentagon in Washington on 11 September 2001. The Western European Union (WEU) was set up in 1954, but has now transferred most functions to the European Union (EU) which was created in 1992. The Warsaw Treaty Organization or Warsaw Pact was formed in 1955 by the Communist countries of Eastern Europe and the USSR as a counter to NATO. It was dissolved in 1991. The Organization for Security and Cooperation in Europe (OSCE) was initiated as the Conference on Security and Cooperation in Europe (CSCE) in 1975, with a mandate that included implementation of human rights, pluralistic democracy (election monitoring), and economic and environmental security. In 1995, it was renamed the OSCE and transformed into an organization that world serve as an instrument for early warning, conflict prevention and crisis management. It comprises several institutions dealing with a variety of subjects. It has a membership today of 55 countries and can boast of deploying its resources to manage conflicts, though largely on the strength of NATO deployment in the Balkans.

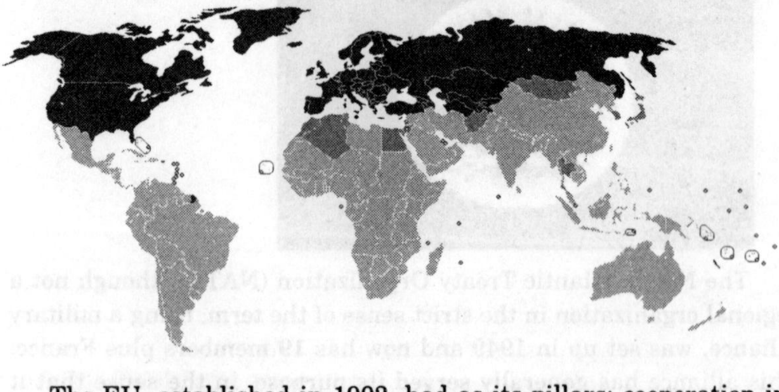

The EU, established in 1992, had as its pillars: cooperation in economic and monetary affairs; the Common Foreign and Security

Policy (CFSP); and cooperation in justice and home affairs. The concept of European Security and Defence Policy (ESDP) initiated in 1999 envisages the setting up of an EU rapid reaction force by 2003, of up to 60,000 troops to be deployed within 60 days and for a period of a year; NATO assets may be used in accordance with an agreement to be reached between NATO and the EU; a long way yet. The Partnership for Peace (PfP) launched in 1994 is a programme for political and military cooperation between NATO and some member states of the OSCE and provides the stage for interaction between NATO, countries of Eastern Europe and some of the former Soviet republics.

The Organisation of African Unity (OAU) and renamed African Union in 2002, has 54 members today and was set up in 1963 to promote African international cooperation and harmonization of defence policies. It has mediated in a number of conflicts and prepared peace and arms control agreements. It has had mixed results, but is nevertheless a vibrant institution. The Economic Community of West African States (ECOWAS), comprising 16 states, was established in 1975 with the aim of promoting trade and cooperation and contributing to development in West Africa. The ECOWAS Cease-fire Monitoring Group (ECOMOG) was established in 1990 and has produced mixed results insofar as maintenance of peace and security in the region is concerned. It, however, remains an effective tool for this purpose with some support from other international players for funds, equipment and training. The South African Development Community (SADC), today comprise 14 member countries of the region and was established in 1992 to promote regional economic development and fundamental principles of sovereignty, peace and security, human rights, and democracy. Its record has been rather mixed, but it certainly has a great deal of potential. The Arab Maghreb Union set up by five African states in 1989 to ensure regional stability, enhance policy coordination and promote common defence appears to have been a largely symbolic exercise.

The Association of South-East Asian Nations (ASEAN), now comprising 10 countries, was established in 1967 to promote economic, social and cultural development as well as regional peace and security in South-East Asia. The ASEAN Regional Forum (ARF) was formed in 1993 to address security issues; its membership includes all ASEAN countries, together with 21 other partners. This has been a vibrant organization that has generally avoided dealing with security issues in any significant manner. The Commonwealth of Independent States (CIS) was formed in 1991 for multilateral cooperation between 12 former Soviet republics. It continues to serve as a useful forum for that purpose. The Council for Security Cooperation in the Asia Pacific (CSCAO), comprising 18 member states, was set up in 1993 for regional confidence building and security cooperation through dialogue and consultation. It is quite active, but being an informal, non-governmental process, cannot influence policy decisions in any meaningful way. Even so, it does provide a useful forum for free and forthright exchange of views. The Shanghai Forum comprising China, Russia, Kazakhstan, Kyrigistan, and Tajikistan was set up in 1996 to resolve issues along the CIS-China border. The member states cooperate on confidence building measures and regional security and in the economic sphere.

The Organisation of Islamic Conference (OIC) was established in 1971 and has 55 members and four observer countries. It was set up to promote cooperation among members and to support peace, security and the struggle of the people of Palestine and all Muslim people. Whether it has been able to achieve its objectives is a matter of opinion. The Gulf Cooperation Council (GCC) was set up in 1981 by six Arab states to assure security and stability of the region through economic, political and security cooperation. It continues to provide a useful forum for exchange of views and consultation on wider issues in the region.

Lessons from the Experience of Other Regions

The brief survey undertaken above provides us with some useful indicators and parameters that could form the basis for an objectives scrutiny of the arrangements that have been set up for South Asia so as to access their appropriateness or otherwise. In many (if not all) cases, the organization appear to have evolved on the basis of common understandings that emerged in the shadow of years of disagreement, distrust, and, in some cases, conflict. Hence, there is no reason for immediate despair. However, one feature that stands out distinctly - except in the case of military alliances like NATO - is that the motivating element was the economic well-being of the peoples of the regions, the motivating factor being that regional cooperation would enable the people of member states to attain living standards that they deserved. In some cases, the achievements have been remarkable, in other somewhat less so but a considerable improvement on what it was earlier, and in many others less than satisfactory because of lack of commitment to the objectives of the regional organizations.

The South Asian Dimension

It would be appropriate to dwell briefly on some of the factors that limit the application of lessons or observations from the experience of other regions to the South Asian framework. The colonial legacy is certainly one of the factors that contributed to distrust and even animosity, but it would be an indication of immaturity and incompetence to dwell on that aspect at any great length. India's predominant size and status is probably the most debilitating factors inasmuch as it is resented by almost all the other countries of the region to varying extents. This is often used as a convenient tool even in domestic politics. The other major element is the fact that all the countries share common borders with India but not with each other. Equally, trans-border ethnic affiliations that are often the source of tensions also relate only to India and each of the other countries. As such, all the differences or problems that arise in the organization are generally between the other countries and India, but not with each other. Another major aspect on which comments are offered from a personal perspective, pertain to how India has dealt with some of the situations on the subcontinent. Some of these have been characterized by expediency, inadequacy and occasionally insensitivity. These instances have obviously caused avoidable misunderstandings with our some of our neighbours, even to the extent of causing them to be deeply distrustful of our attitudes and actions. Cases in point are the suspension of free movement of goods to Nepal a couple of decades ago, the patronizing attitudes displayed towards the newly emerged regime in Bangladesh soon after the 1971 war of liberation, and the initial support accorded to the cadres of the Liberation Tigers of Tamil Eelam (LTTE) in the mid- 1980s. External manipulation is another factor that has often been the source of soured relations between the countries of the region, and needs to be taken into account while evaluating the interstate dynamics of the region. Finally, the demographic movements within the region need to be factored into all the calculations because the social pressures so generated are often exploited for political purposes both internally and in the external dialogue.

If the above aspects are consciously factored into the deliberations for the evolution of a cooperative framework for the region, and a realistic perspective formulated, the negative connotations could well be transformed into positive mechanisms that lead to greater mutual confidence and understanding. For this to be achieved, the foremost requirement is recognition that use of force cannot be the means of changing these realities and that any interference in the internal affairs of other states is not only against international norms, but also counterproductive. Among such realities is India's overwhelming size, and resources. It cannot be wished away. If anything, it needs to be used by the other countries to supplement their needs. Another is the fact of the partition of the subcontinent and the later further division of what was Pakistan. A third reality is that ethnic affiliations will impact on the moods and reactions of people to events in neighbouring states. A major reality that the region must immediately come to terms with is that the perennial adverse bilateral relationship between India and Pakistan has stymied forward movement on every single issue that SAARC has tried to address in recent years.

The Way Ahead

In looking ahead, it may be useful to record the spirit in which SAARC was established. It is an association based on the consciousness that in an increasingly interdependent world, the objectives of peace, freedom, social justice and economic prosperity are best achieved in the South Asian region by fostering mutual understanding, good-neighbourly relations and meaningful cooperation among the member states, which are bound by ties of history and culture. The idea of regional cooperation in South Asia was first mooted around November 1980. After consultations, the foreign secretaries of the seven countries met for the first time in Colombo in April 1981. This was followed, a few months later by a meeting of the Committee of the Whole, which identified five broad areas for regional cooperation. The foreign minister of South Asia, at their first meeting in New Delhi in August 1983, adopted the Declaration on South Asian Regional Cooperation (SARC) and formally launched the Integrated Programme of Action (IPA), initially in five agreed areas of cooperation, namely, Agriculture; Rural Development; Telecommunications; Meteorology, and Health and Population Activities. The heads of state or government, at their First SAARC Summit held in Dhaka on 7-8 December 1985, adopted the charter formally establishing the South Asian Association for Regional Cooperation (SAARC).

Notwithstanding all the above visionary ideals, the ground reality is that, as things stand, SAARC does not appear to have a future, unless India and Pakistan are able to refrain from raising their bilateral differences in this forum.

South Asian regional cooperation is beneficial and hence is desirable for South Asian countries. It helps both in bilateral and multilateral transfer of knowledge and skills. All the member countries of SAARC desire growth and development. They also realize that this can be possible by regional cooperation. They plan to eradicate poverty and unemployment etc. in order to create favourable development and technological self reliance naturally, the experiments carried out by one member of SAARC have value for others. Each member can learn a lot from the success and failure of others. The SAARC can be meaningful only if each nation of South Asian region is to go along with all thus to solve basic problems more effectively and with greater speed.

As regard its progress during 20 years, SAARC confine itself to cementing ties in such peripheral areas as telecommunications, transport, sport, art and cultural, rural development and population control.

After going through the challenges and progress of SAARC and their progress could come closer to realize that there are certain problems faced by the SAARC, which are hampering its potential performance. An attempt to bring out those problems has been made in the next chapter.

7

CONCLUSIONS AND SUGGESTIONS

In the beginning the study of 'SAARC: Its Problems and Prospects' the very concept of regional cooperation was explained and analyzed. While doing so, Regionalism was understood as a dynamic concept which is the need of the hour as far as international polities is concerned. Regional cooperation or regionalism is materialized through the formation of regional organizations. No doubt the motives and purposes of these regional organizations are limited to the region they belong to, but the interpretation of a region is again confusion if not a problem. In fact the answer to "what constitutes a region and why?" has become relative. Because now-a-days a region is not merely an area embracing the territory of some States rather it is where a States interests can be better served secured and promoted. Therefore, a number of different institutions of regional basis are seen in modern times. Multiplicity of concern and interest of the States has definitely increased the importance of tools of global governance. These tools sometimes present a combination of thesis, antithesis and synthesis e.g. inter (governmental) organizations; non-governmental organizations have so much effected each other that there is a new genes of international organization which combines the features of both making the scope, Statues and relevance of international organizations much wider, higher and deeper. This synthesized form of intentional organizations (of global or regional scope) indicates a great merit of being dynamic and flexible. And it is this feature particularly why this study is so relevant.

Along with this it was tried to identify certain functions which an international (governmental) organization (global or regional) must perform. It was a very important measurement for this study because the performance and functioning of SAARC could be measured using this. Some light was also thrown on some theoretical aspect of regionalism, so that the study could be related to all the theories. Infact, every international organization automatically relates to these theories either completely or in parts and so was true in case of SAARC. This specific study tried to identify certain peculiar features of Asian Regionalism which have a visible of effect on SAARC: its problems and prospects. These were later picked up while discussing the problems of SAARC.

Before highlighting the problems of SAARC, in this study it was felt better to mention the progress and plans of SAARC. As a young organization SAARC has been quite active and had taken several steps in different directions to become effective. While discussing these plans and policies it came up that these plans were either badly implemented or could not get implemented at all due to the challenges and problems of SAARC. Having reached this turn of the study it became more apt to discuss problems of SAARC.

SAARC is facing a variety of problems. Some of them are related to the commonality of the member States, some are due to certain independent reasons, some are caused by the faulty *modus oprendi* of the organization itself, some are due to estranged relationship of India and Pakistan – the biggest members in case of area as well as economies, and some problems are caused by globalization. These were the five categories into which the problems of SAARC were discussed. Having made an attempt to analyze the problems of SAARC is definitely not the ultimate motive of any study. A research work contributes through the suggestions it makes to remove obstacles or to solve the problems of the study subject.

In this chapter an attempt has been made to bring out certain conclusions on the basis of this study and to propose certain suggestions for better working of SAARC. As mentioned earlier, the problems of SAARC were discussed in five dimensions. Therefore, the suggestions made would also be different for each dimension of problems of SAARC.

In the post Second World War period, regionalism is one of the most interesting developments in international relations. This trend towards regionalism seems to indicate that the Nation State system, which has been the dominant pattern of international relations for some centuries, has been evolving a system in which regional groupings of State will be more important than the independent sovereign units. Regional core areas can be determined and various boundaries delineated by analysis of mutual transactions and other inter-dependencies, but which of a large number of potential regions become relevant for Organization depend upon political decisions.[1]

A region is invariably an area embracing the territories of some States which may or may not be geographically contiguous but are bound together by ties of common interests. The dynamics of the evolutionary process of regionalism are constituted by the needs and aspirations of the region.[2]

In international relations, there are basically three approaches to the study of regional integration. The federalist approach conceives of integration in legal and institutional terms. For federalist scholars, integration is an end product rather than a process. It stands for a political union among previously sovereign and independent territories. Functionalists tend to emphasize cooperative aspects of international behavior and sidestep conflictive aspects. They hope that with the accumulation of a large variety of functional Organizations linking people and their interests across national boundaries, a transformation in both national attitudes and institutions will take place. The third approach is neo-functionalism. They view integration as both a process and an outcome, but they prefer to emphasize cooperative decision-making processes and elite attitudes in order to assess the progress towards integration.

Regional cooperation has been a conspicuous trend in world politics since the end of the Second World War. It has been considered a useful strategy for accelerating security concerns comprising seven countries of the region namely Bangladesh, Nepal, Bhutan, India, Pakistan, Sri-Lanka, Maldives, South Asia possess a great deal of potential for mutual cooperation and benefits. The concept of regional cooperation had its inception in 1981 and in 1985 it developed into a full fledged forum called the South Asian Association for Regional Cooperation (SAARC).[3]

SAARC (South Asian Association for Regional Cooperation), consists of seven countries: India, Bangladesh, Pakistan, Bhutan and Nepal in Indian Subcontinent, and Sri-Lanka and Maldives in

---

1 Emanual Nahar; *SAARC Problems and Prospects,* New Delhi, Sehgal Publication, 1991, p. 1.

2 P.A. Joy; *SAARC Challenges before New Millennium,* New Delhi, Deep and Deep Publications, 1995, p. 2.

3 Emanual Nahar (1991) at pp. 3.5.

Indian Ocean. It was established on 8th December 1985 after about four and a half years of its preparation. The basic aim of the association is to accelerate the process of economic and social development in member countries through joint action in the agreed areas of cooperation. The region of SAARC lies in the South of Himalayas surrounded by Hindu Kush Mountains.

SAARC is a unique example of regional cooperation. It is not shaped on any existing model of regional or sub-regional cooperation and is different from the Association of South East Asian Nations (ASEAN), Latin America Free Trade Association (LAFTA), European Economic Community (EEC) and European Free Trade Association (EFTA). The model of SAARC is in accordance with the realities and compulsions of the region. It has evolved modalities which do not allow bilateral stresses and strains to hinder regional cooperation.[4]

NEED OF REGIONAL COOPERATION (SAARC)

In fact, the existing international economic order has been operating against the basic interest of the poor countries due to growing protectionist tendencies among the rich countries. In the world market, the products of the poor countries are facing tough competition with the products of the rich countries. As a result, the share of the poor countries has been decreasing in the world market, with the passage of time. On the other hand, the share of the rich countries has been increasing in the world market. The poor countries are left with only option, i.e., to promote mutual cooperation in order to solve their socio-economic and politico-ethnic problems and to achieve collective self-reliance.

Thus, it is required that the South should explore seriously the ways of mutual cooperation and reduce its dependence on the North. Such cooperation is also beneficial to the poor countries in order to improve their prospects of cooperation with the rich countries in future.

The idea of regional cooperation has taken shape somewhat slowly in South Asia and is of relatively recent origin. This is largely because of the trauma of partition and the decisive legacy of the cold war in our region. With the launching of the South Asia Association

---

[4] Shashi Upadhyay, *Pakistan SAARC*, Kalinga Publications, Delhi, 2000.

for Regional Cooperation in December 1985, however a new vista was opened up for building a durable framework of cooperation in our region.[5]

Now that SAARC has completed twenty years of its existence, we need to assess the achievements, set out new goals for the future and devise policies and strategies for achieving these goals.

Since its inception in December 1985, SAARC has developed and consolidated its institutional framework and the scope and volume of its activities has expanded, with the setting up of 11 technical committees. It also has some notable achievements to its credit, including the setting up of a Food Security Reserve and SAARC regional conventions on suppression of terrorism and trafficking in narcotics. These gains, though significant, are relatively modest and problems remain with regard to the implementation of these agreements.

SOUTH ASIA: A REGION OF REGIONS

South Asia has been more or less by passed by the processes of globalization. There is, thus, no real alternative to regional cooperation if the limits by the inward-looking models of growth adopted.

The stakes of South Asian People(s) in regional cooperation are too vast and vital to allow the luxury of endless waiting so that evolutionary process could gradually unfold itself. We may thus be well justified in asking more proactive intervention on the part of those who can possibly accelerate the pace of cooperation.

It should be elementary to any student of social sciences that the State has no substantial self, no mind, volition of its own. States are run by human agents and these agents have their ideologies as well vested interests. Inter-State relations are nothing but interaction among these agents who occupy positions of power and decision making in different States.

South Asia is, in one sense, among the most natural but, in another, functionally among the most difficult to harmonize and full together. Objectively, there is no denying the fact that there are

[5] For further details see : South Asian Survey, Vol. 6, No. 1, New Delhi/ Thousand Oaks/London.

commonalties and continuities of history, geography and culture. More important, however, are the ways in which these are subjectively perceived by the managers of South Asia States. Regions are only as natural as they are constructed. Large States appear hegemonic only when they are made to appear so. Nothing illustrates this point better than the contrast between what has come to called 'Gujral Doctrine'. The Gujral Doctrine as vehicle of regional integration is that it is conceived firmly within the State-centric paradigm.

The promotion of the SAARC and the SAPTA, the assumption has been that South Asia is a region of seven Nation-States, and the internal political structure of these Nation-States has no direct bearing on how they develop strategies, channels and institutions of regional cooperation. SAARC is a regional cooperation among South Asians countries to overcome or to solve the economic as well as other problems.

If we look at the global experience of regional cooperation, the most notables is in the field of economic cooperation and building a larger regional economic space. This has led to foster economic growth and greater prosperity for the people of the region. It is in this area that SAARC has the greatest potential for cooperation. The SAARC countries need to evolve and implement specific bilateral, regional and sub-regional arrangements to facilitate continuous and speedy movement of goods. It would also be essential to identify, develop, upgrade and maintain East-West and North-South transport corridors to handle the anticipated expansion of trade in the region and also connect to the trans-Asian Road and rail networks.

THE NEED FOR A SUB-REGIONAL APPROACH

The focus of South Asian States was more on the conventional form of security which emanated from the actual realities of the region which was bedeviled with political dissent and armed conflicts. The region has not only witnessed three armed conflicts between India and Pakistan but is also embroiled in political, economic, socio-cultural, ethnic and linguistic tensions. India is the only country in the region which shares its borders with all the other regional States and is the hub of all regional activities.

The idea of regional cooperation was first spelled out by Bangladesh in May 1980. On 7-8 December 1985, the charter was adopted by the regional actors formally establishing the South Asian Association of Regional Cooperation (SAARC). The objective set out the need for promoting welfare of the South Asians by providing them an opportunity to live in dignity and realize their full potential which would help in accelerating the social progress, economic growth and cultural development of the region.[6]

The Government in South Asia has begun to realize the basic thrust in the changing global environment where they have to achieve economic stability by developing inter-regional and intra-regional trade with each other based on trust and confidence.

It is very important for the South Asian countries to ensure that the trend of cooperation continues and adequate momentum of regional cooperation gets generated.

SUGGESTIONS MADE THROUGH THIS STUDY

First Dimension of the problem of SAARC mentioned in chapter V of this study was based on commonality among the members. For this category of obstacles and problems, the SAARC members must come forward with open and neutral approach.

- Rather than showing mistrust and suspicion the members must recognize, respect and support the capabilities of each other so that they all can benefit from each other's potential.
- Continuous contacts, whether on diplomatic, ministerial or citizen level, must help in bringing transparency among the members, this will also weaken the clutches of cross border terrorism which are choking the development of these countries.
- Common patrolling and free communication at different levels can also help in checking unfavorable activities in these countries. This will also help to identify the role of any third country (other than SAARC members) which tries to create doubt among the SAARC members.

---

[6] Mahendra P. Lama, "SAARC: Integrated Programme of Action towards More Effective Cooperation," *South Asian Survey*, Vol. 5, No. 1, 1998, p. 39.

- **All the SAARC members must promote such a political culture which is free from the shadow of colonial period. SAARC members must target present and plan for future rather than carrying forward rotten past.**
- **Population control is a big problem which carries several other problems in its womb. SAARC countries have to deal with it strategically because unwanted and uncontrolled growth of population is like a blood sucking parasite. SAARC members must work devotedly to educate people, to spread awareness regarding family planning. More importantly these States must ensure that at least one member of the family gets job so that people do not have more and more children to earn labor. In executing this program, help of youth and retired persons or of different NGOs can be taken to save extra burden on the administration. Backward segments of population must be inspired towards gender equality because in these countries families keep on having children to have a male child or to have another male child.**
- To bring SAARC members together the concept of cross border nations can be used. Cultural links between these members may be invoked to bring them together.

Second Dimension of SAARC problems which is due to independent reasons. Some very important steps need to be taken in this regard.

- To bring harmony between unequal economies of SAARC members there can be a three way plan –
  (*a*) Pooling of resources
  (*b*) Dividing the industries
  (*c*) Creating separate market of this region

(*a*) Pooling of resources should be applicable to those resources for which each nation can not compete with the global market but by bringing together of the resources it can be done. Joint ventures to process these resources may also be taken up.

(*b*) Those industries, for which the conditions are suitable only in one or two of the member countries, must be allocated to those member States only. However, monetary help can be given by the member States or any other State.

(*c*) A separate market may be created using pooled resources, joint ventures and independent industries. This should involve minimum barriers on cross border trade, relaxation is visa policies, opening up of a common banks for these members.

- Also, this economic structure should target export of finished goods to other regions rather than raw materials. Secondly, they should welcome foreign investments (from non-SAARC members) but should not allow them to exploit the local markets. Much similar to what China did to develop its economy.[7]
- We must remember that Europe's history has not been complicated than Asia even then the concept of common market, common currency is working there. It should be more applicable to the developing members of SAARC who have nothing to loose but all to gain. Such an approach of recognizing and taking neutral benefit from each other will diminish the image of India as a threat to SAARC members. Rather, using status of India world over. SAARC members should make India a representative of SAARC in international arena. India should be entrusted to bring finance for SAARC plans and to divert attention of the world towards SAARC's development.
- Research fellowships should be awarded regularly by the SAARC for those who want of know more of SAARC and to suggest ways to improve its working. It will serve a twofold purpose, firstly, SAARC will gain from the research and its suggestions, and secondly, SAARC will be taken more seriously by the contemporary intellectuals, world over.

Third Dimension of the problems of SAARC was observed in its own modus oprendi. It can also be improved by taking certain steps:

- The most effective and active post of the SAARC is its Secretary General. This office faces a lot of problem while

---

[7] For further details see : Dr. Shrikant Paranjpe in *India Quarterly: A Journal of International Affairs,* Vol. LII, July-September 1996, No. 3

understanding, analyzing and planning for different problems of SAARC. This is due to complex nature of SAARC's geopolitical, economical and historical environment. To do so much just two years of tenure is definitely not enough. By the time the general secretary gets closer to the solution of the trouble his tenure is over. Hence the term of this office should be increased adequately.

- Secondly the office of general secretary of the highest esteem and responsibility as for as SAARC is concerned. Therefore, rotational system of this office is quite inadequate arrangement. No doubt all the countries should have a chance to take control of the secretariat through this office, but along with this the Secretary General must be an eminent and exceptionally talented and experienced person who could pull the status of SAARC up. Also, an office of assistant secretaries or counselors to the secretary general can be created. And the number of this office can be made six. So that every member does feel involved.
- The funds collected or received by the SAARC must be used strategically. As for all the members multiple use of funds can be a big turning point. The funds of SAARC should remain neither unused nor misused.
- The postponement of summits has become as if a trait of SAARC. Any unfavorable incident should not be allowed to postpone or the summit. Also if these summits are held even in tense atmosphere it might help to melt the ice between the troubled members and if the problem is due to an outsider members State then the members can offer a hand of help and can boost the image of the concerned State by supporting it.
- Article X of the charter of SAARC which probable discussion of bilateral issues on the platform of SAARC, becomes a hurdle in mutual cooperation among members because almost all the members share boundaries and have bilateral issues regarding river waters, territories, terrorism etc. and in the frozen status of these issues mistrust and hindrance in cooperation is inevitable. To solve this there can be a forum constituted under SAARC for the bilateral issues of its members similar to ARF formed by ASEAN. This forum

should investigate, discuss the core bilateral problems and suggest solution to the members which should be binding at some minimum level.[8]

- SAARC members should be bound by some code of conduct and some rules, which help in creating a sense of self restraint and respect for the Organization.[9]
- To implement the socio-cultural plans of the SAARC several youth forums can be formed under SAARC in all the member States. It will serve a number of purposes. Firstly, it will channelize young energy towards better direction and purposes. Secondly it will reduce the financial burden on the SAARC and will save time as well. Thirdly, it will prepare young seedlings by training youth of the members which could be transplanted in the mainstream works of the SAARC. The initiative and zeal of youth if bunds with training and experience can prove an asset as well as an investment for SAARC.[10]

Fourth Dimension of SAARC problem is rather a sensitive one as it is due to estranged relations between its biggest members India and Pakistan. Due to the involvement of biggest members of SAARC, and complex nature of the problems, one has to be most cautious while suggesting any solutions. No doubt, these are sovereign States and to start afresh they must let go certain issues which are hindering their progress.

- The major issue between India and Pakistan is that of Kashmir. India claims the whole territory of Kashmir (including Pakistan occupied Kashmir) to be Indian Territory. However, it was Indian leadership who decided not to order their forces to move further to get whole of Kashmir back. It is that line from which Indian forces retreated which is now considered line of control. One faulty decision on part of India, and one wrong intension. On part of Pakistan has

[8] For further details see : Raju G.C. Thomas, Afghanistan, Kashmir, China and the Territorial Questions in South Asia, Mediterranean Quarterly, Vol. 13, No. 3, Summer, 2002, pp. 109-118.

[9] M.S. Naidu, *Economic Integration for Peace and Stability: A Case Study of European Community,* (Unpublished Ph.D. Thesis, Pune).

[10] For further details see : Pramod K. Mishra; *South-South Co-operation and SAARC,* IDSA, Vol. XII, No V, August, 1989.

been responsible for killing people of Kashmir, destroying its art and craft and tourism, providing a shelter to terrorism in the valley and putting unnecessary financial burden on the both governments. Now, behaving like grown, matured States, both countries should admit the LoC as the permanent boundary.

- India and Pakistan have so much to gain from each other. If the trade between these two countries flourishes it will make both the countries economic giants of Asia. And Pakistan would not have to please its western patrons. Due to indirect trade will cost minimum. The healthy trade will lead to healthy economy by which not only all of SAARC members but whole of the region can be helped.[11]
- The nature of political regimes in Pakistan needs to be made democratic in true sense. The democratic values of Pakistan have been swallowed by army control over the government. Pakistan's society must react against the rule of government. President of a democracy and General of army can not be synonymous. This gap in political set up plays a negative role in the relationship of India and Pakistan.
- In case of cross border terrorism in India, India's stand should be stronger than it is. Here allegations and detailing the proofs against Pakistan is not enough. India must leave the image of a soft State. Statesman of India must realize that they are facing army (regime) personnel as Head. Hence, he needs to be answered in army style. This does not mean a war against Pakistan but to answer them in their language along with maintaining diplomatic measures like negotiation and gaining world support.[12]

Fifth Dimension of SAARC's problems in due to the obstacles and it faces posed by globalization. This problem needs a united effort. This problem can be answered by the region of SAARC members and not the States individually.

- To this problem are also discussed in the second dimensions of SAARC's problems when it was proposed that the SAARC

---

[11] The Tribune; Regional SAARCasm, Jan. 4, 2002, p. 9.

[12] J.N. Dixit; "Prospect of South Asian Cooperation in the Transformed World." *South Asian Survey*, New Delhi, Vol. 10, No. 1, Jan-June 2003, pp. 1.

countries must come forward with a three step economic formula:

(*a*) pooling of resources (*b*) allocating industries (*c*) creating a separate market for members wherein (*i*) finished products and not raw material will be exported (*ii*) foreign investment will be exported (iii) foreign investment will be welcomed but no local market will be provided.

- **Research centres and committees should be constituted to find out new prospects of economic growth, trade and multipurpose industries and its work must be taken seriously.**
- **SAARC members should claim patents of their important resources ayurvedic medicines, medicinal plants, tea, sea-food and natural cosmetics and spices etc. There is considerable scope and potential for undertaking joint ventures for exploiting the resources of seabed as well.[13]**
- **International seminars must be conducted to spread awareness regarding the growing industries, handicrafts, tourism offered by the SAARC members.**
- **Youth forums should be assigned the respect of making new generation aware of threat of globalization to our economics and it was towards developed part of the world. These youth forums may inspire young generation to give priority to indigenous products. After having conducted a detailed study on SAARC its problems and prospects, certain conclusions can be drawn.**

WHAT ELSE SAARC MUST DO ?

SAARC must not shy away from its responsibility towards developing a human rights culture in South Asia. Problems related to Terrorism, Refugees, Mutual distrust etc. can be addressed through human rights initiatives taken in the region. Asian Centre of Human Rights (ACHR) has also supported the same view, in its August 2008 report.

By working towards human rights in the region, SAARC will

---

[13] For further details see : B.C. Upreti; *SAARC, Dynamics of Regional Cooperation in South Asia,* and S.D. Muni; *Regional Cooperation in South Asia,* South Asia, South Asia in 21st Century.

benefit in general as the member States will become more responsible and answerable if their human rights record is on the agenda of SAARC, and SAARC would be a global symbol of their goodwill and credibility which is very essential in this era of globalization.

And in particular, human rights agenda of SAARC will bring it closer to the more successful international organizations of the world which are dealing with regional human rights, like Council of Europe (COE), Organization of American States (OAS), Organization of African Union (OAU), and The Arab League.

Moreover, SAARC is already on the way of developing human rights culture in the region by adopting several conventions which deal with some aspect of human rights.

As Neera Chandhoke in her article in Himal magazine entitled A South Asian Charter of Human Rights South Asia is the only declared region of the world not to have adopted such a Charter, despite multiple initiatives.

In 1997 the Declaration of the Ninth Summit of the SAARC countries was adopted and it recognizes the importance of gender equality and empowerment of women, raising education and literacy rates, and the reduction of population rates, among others. The Declaration expressed concern at the trafficking of women and children within and between countries. They decided upon the feasibility of establishing a Regional Convention on Combating the Crime of Trafficking in Women and Children for Prostitution and Convention on Regional Arrangement on the Promotion of Child Welfare in South Asia.

In 1993, the Declaration of the Seventh SAARC Summit was adopted. The Declaration states that governments commit unequivocally to eradication of poverty in South Asia, the provision of universal primary education, primary health care, shelter for the poor and protection of children.

In 1995, the Delhi Declaration was adopted, which reaffirms the realization of the rights of all, in particular those of the poor, to food, work, shelter, health, and education. Considering that the exploitation of the Girl Child is a direct reflection of the status of women in society, the Leaders reaffirmed their resolve to take necessary measures to eliminate all forms of discrimination against women and female-children.

SAARC also has adopted the Convention on Terrorism and the Regional Convention Against Drug Abuse and Drug-Trafficking, SAARC decided to observe the years 1991-2000 as the "SAARC Decade of the Girl Child" and the years 2001-2010 as the "SAARC Decade of the Rights of the Child".

The Declaration states that governments commit unequivocally to eradication of poverty in South Asia, the provision of universal primary education, primary health care, shelter for the poor and protection of children.

In 1995, the Delhi Declaration was adopted, which reaffirms the realization of the rights of all, in particular those of the poor, to food, work, shelter, health, and education. Considering that the exploitation of the Girl Child is a direct reflection of the status of women in society, the Leaders reaffirmed their resolve to take necessary measures to eliminate all forms of discrimination against women and female-children.

SAARC has also adopted the Convention on Terrorism and the Regional Convention Against Drug Abuse and Drug-Trafficking, SAARC decided to observe the years 1991-2010 as the "SAARC Decade of the Girl Child" and the years 2001-2010 as the "SAARC Decade of the Rights of the Child". The problem with SAARC is India's hegemonic role in the region. India is considered gross violator of human rights and SAARC cannot achieve anything without the blessing of India.

Dias has been quoted in Hidetoshi Hashimoto's The prospects for a Regional Human Rights Mechanisms in East Asia, "SAARC countries agreed to take an issue-oriented approach, for example, to focus on child labor, migrant workers, refugees, poverty problems and the education of the girl-child. This is a beginning. From there they can move forward. They are moving forward in the direction of establishing a human rights institution".

What is lacking is the political will of the members of SAARC. However, I see this aspect of SAARC emerging very soon on the international and regional platform.

ANALYSIS OF THE OBJECTIVES

An analysis of the objectives, with which this study began, shows that all the objectives have been achieved and also the hypothesis has come out to be valid. It was observed that SAARC members are a victim of mistrust due to several political, economical and historical conflicts. Hence, it is humbly stated that this study has been a successful one from the researcher's point of view.

CONCLUDING OBSERVATIONS

The economic considerations, developmental compulsions, information and communication revolution and cultural factors are knitting the region together in view of internationalism and globalization. On the other, certain factors and issues like terrorism, drug trafficking, ethnicity, migration, smuggling of small arms, organized crime, sub-nationalism and religious revivalism are a real challenge to the countries of South Asia. At the moment, the forces of division have gained an upper hand and those of cooperation remain in subordination.

The national security of South Asian countries mostly hinges on equitable socio-economic development. The sooner they accept primacy of the economic imperatives, the better would they guarantee their security. It is high time that the countries of the region understand that economic growth is the key to prosperity and security. Self-respect and honor in the emerging world order will be difficult unless they take note of the unifying factors in the region and cooperate.

The twenty first century holds a lot of promise for South Asian countries and its people. But however on the road to development and prosperity lie a host of challenges (internal and external), which they have to take up seriously to catch up with the rest of the world.

The five wars off globalization-the illegal trade in drugs, arms, intellectual properties, people and money are booming in South Asia. Like the war on terrorism, the fight to control there markets pits governments against agile, Stateless and resourceful network empowered by globalization. But the governments will continue to lose these wars unless they adopt new strategies to deal with a trend that now shapes the world.

Lastly, the future of South Asia will be based on the political, goodwill of all the participating nations and more so between India and Pakistan. The countries of this region have to definitely set in motion a gigantic plan for their socio-economic development and technological advancement for overcoming their problems and challenges through increased bilateral and regional cooperation as could be seen in the recent SAARC meetings.

The countries of this region have started looking at regional economic integration as a means of strengthening their international competitiveness and as an engine of economic growth in recent years. South Asian Free Trade Association (SAFTA) would lead to expansion of Intra-regional trade.[14] Thus, the regional economic integration in South Asia could generate billions of dollars of new income, employment, trade could help the region in its fight against poverty.

For the last few years, South Asia has seen an unmistakable interplay of the politics of conflict and of cooperation. At present the politics of conflict is dominant but the mere fact that the politics of cooperation has made a beginning in the strife and suspicious ridden environment of South Asia gives grounds for optimism.

Regionalism, as against only formally organized associations like SAARC, can be a reality only when the member States reach a stage where they can think and act as a group on the basis of a commonly inculcated culture of cooperation and understanding of issues and events facing them. Nation States as independent units acting individually rather than collectively can not promote the spirit of regionalism. Realization came slowly to the SAARC countries, that the best way to respond to the emerging economic system is to act together to safeguard and promote their regional interests.

Being two decades old is only a toddler's age for an International Organization. And SAARC is justified in having its teething problems. Every International Organization must be given to exceptionally and extremely complicated environment in which SAARC has been working, and as seen in its progress report SAARC has taken vital steps in all important areas. SAARC has definitely given a binding force to its members and its importance cannot by underestimated. An attempt has been through this study that SAARC has a long way to go and has endless prospects. It represents the region of South Asia which may be have remained subdued and exploited but is certainly not any lesser in potential. SAARC is still

---

14 Gustavo Conoero; *Preferential Trade Arrangement,* Partial Equilibrium, Estimates for South Asian Countries, The World Bank Publication, 1994.

growing and as it grows will find many more way to elevate its position. Till then SAARC and its members must work selflessly and relentlessly.

SAARC's Future Membership

The People's Republic of China has shown its interest in joining SAARC. While Pakistan and Bangladesh support China's candidature, India is more reluctant about the prospect of Chinese membership, while Bhutan does not even have diplomatic relations with China. However, during the 2005 Dhaka summit, India agreed on granting observer status to the PRC along with Japan. During the 14th summit, Nepal along with Pakistan and Bangladesh, announced their support for the membership of China. China seeks greater involvement in SAARC, however, finds it too early to apply for full membership.

The Islamic Republic of Iran, a state with borders to two SAARC members, has traditionally enjoyed strong cultural, economic and political relationships with Afghanistan, Pakistan, India and Bangladesh and has expressed its desire to become a member of the South Asian organization. On 22 February 2005, the Foreign Minister of Iran, Kamal Kharrazi, indicated Iran's interest in joining SAARC by saying that his country could provide the region with "East-West connectivity". On 3 March 2007, Iran asked to join the SAARC as an observer. SAARC Secretary-General Lyonpo Chenkyab Dorji responded by saying that Iran's request for observer status would be taken up during a meeting of ministers of foreign affairs of SAARC member countries in the 3 April summit in New Delhi.

The Russian Federation intends to become an observer as well, and is supported by India.

Union of Myanmar has expressed an interest in joining as a full member. If done so, Myanmar will become the ninth member in the group. India is currently backing Myanmar.

The Republic of South Africa has participated in meetings.

Much popular words of Robert Frost are so true for SAARC:

Woods are ugly dark and deep,
But I have promises to keep,
And miles to go before I sleep,
And miles to go before I sleep...

ANNEXURES

ANNEXURE I

BALI DECLARATION ON REGIONAL AND SUBREGIONAL ECONOMIC COOPERATION OF THE DEVELOPING COUNTRIES

1. Pursuant to the provisions of the Caracas Programme of Action, adopted in 1981, and of the San Jose Declaration adopted by the Group of 77 Conference on Trade, Investment and Finance held in San Jose, Costa Rica, from 13-15 January 1997, and endorsed by the 22nd Ministerial Meeting of Foreign Affairs held in New York on 25 September 1998, a High Level Conference on Regional and Subregional Economic Cooperation of the Developing Countries was held in Bali, Indonesia, from 2-5 December 1998.

2. The Conference was attended by high level participants from member countries of the Group of 77, the United Nations organs and bodies and regional and subregional economic groupings/communities. The Conference focused on identifying innovative strategies for the promotion cooperation between and among regional and subregional economic groupings/communities, and arrangements of the developing countries. The outcome of this Conference should also serve as a useful input for the South Summit to be held in Havana in the year 2000 which should provide a forum at the highest political level for reviewing progress made and identifying constraints so as to strengthen South South Cooperation.

3. The Conference took place at a time when the twin forces of globalization and liberalization of trade and capital flows are profoundly changing global economic processes and relations. It recognized that globalization and liberalization present challenges and opportunities as well as risks.

4. The Conference noted with deep concern that notwithstanding the promise of a new dawn of prosperity through the phenomenon of globalization and liberalization, the world economy is on the brink of recession and is characterized by with uncertainty and instability. Economic growth has slowed down for developed and developing countries alike. Growth in world trade has also suffered an acute setback. Developing countries, particularly the least developed among them, have been adversely affected by declining of Official Development Assistance (ODA), excruciating debt burdens and falling commodity prices. Foreign Direct Investment flows have concentrated in few countries and sectors and although FDI is no substitute for ODA, the Conference noted the potential that FDI offers for development. In this context, the Conference called for a more broad-based and enhanced flows of FDI so that all developing countries may benefit from it.
5. The financial crisis, which began in Asia, seriously undermining the development efforts of the developing countries, was a matter of concern to the Conference. The Conference was convinced that in addition to direct contagion and spillover effects from one economy to another, a generalized loss of confidence has exacerbated the crisis. As a result, many developing countries have suffered colossal losses of financial resources which affected production, export and economic growth. Unemployment has soared and the number of people living below the poverty line has tremendously increased. Food is in short supply while education and health services have been severely affected. The devastating social and economic costs wrought by the crisis, including slowdowns, outright economic collapse and the threat of a deep global recession are cause for serious alarm.
6. The Conference recalled the Ministerial Declaration of the Group of 77 and China of 25 September 1998 and noted in particular paragraphs 11, 12, 13, 62 and 63 of the Declaration and the adverse impact of the issues raised in this paragraph on regional and subregional economic cooperation.

7. The Conference noted that the economic and social setbacks have highlighted the need and urgency of strengthening South-South cooperation. The political and strategic importance of South-South cooperation lies in its ability to provide developing countries with appropriate stimuli to intensify and widen the scope of economic relations and tap the vast potential of intra-South cooperation, as well as ensuring an equitable North-South partnership in managing globalization. It stressed the critical need to promote truly meaningful and concrete forms of South-South cooperation to further enhance our collective self-reliance endeavors.

8. South-South cooperation is poised to play a more dynamic and critical role in the global economy and geopolitics of the 21st century. This cooperation over the years has progressed on its own; its successes and shortcomings have been amply identified and assessed. There are critical areas which require further strengthening of South-South cooperation, and there are cooperative endeavors which have been slow and sporadic in nature. In fact, there are possibilities and potentials that remain dormant and untapped.

9. The Conference underlined the important role of regional and subregional economic cooperation among developing countries in promoting South-South cooperation. For these cooperative endeavors to concretely bolster South-South cooperation, they must evolve into long-term sustainable undertakings, keep pace with global developments, and provide prospects for economic, social and institutional linkages among the countries of the South.

10. The Conference stressed the significant role of regional and subregional economic and technical cooperation in improving the welfare and standard of living of peoples in the developing countries and thus contribute to the effort of international community in eradicating poverty.

11. Regional and subregional economic cooperation through, inter alia, custom unions, free trade areas, common markets and other preferential arrangements which provide the raison d'etre of many subregional groupings/communities, should be seen as complementary and an important tool for global economic integration. They should constitute building

blocks rather than stumbling blocks to multilateralism. At the same time, the international economic environment should be supportive of the full development of regional and subregional economic groupings/communities.

12. The Conference emphasized the relevance of Economic and Technical Cooperation among Developing Countries (ECDC/TCDC) in the context of globalization and interdependence. ECDC/TCDC can be a tool to maximize benefits that can be derived from economies of scale and complementarities which will enable countries of the South to participate more effectively in the global market. Various regional and subregional cooperation groupings/ communities among the countries of the South are, by their very nature, ECDC/TCDC in its broadest sense.

13. In order to strengthen cooperation among regional and subregional groupings/communities of developing countries, the Member of Countries of the Group of 77 will undertake the following priority actions:

- Provide strong linkages between or among these groupings/communities as a means to revitalize and strengthen ECDC/TCDC;
- Establish or strengthen regular mechanisms for consultation, communication and the sharing of information, experience and expertise as well as the identification and execution of joint projects and activities;
- Develop supportive network, institutions and human resources;
- Strengthen cooperation in the areas of transport and communications;
- Revitalize cooperation in such areas as trade, industry and finance, in order to enhance intra-regional trade and investment;
- Promote the participation of the private sector and civil society in strengthening South-South cooperation in regional and subregional economic cooperation;
- Promote the involvement and support of the international community, the United Nations system,

funding institution and other international organizations in strengthening South-South cooperation through regional and subregional economic cooperation.

14. The Conference agreed on the need for a closer coordination between the Group of 77 and China and the Non-Aligned Movement through the Joint Coordination Committee in New York, including for the advancement and the implementation of the Bali Plan of Action on the Regional and Subregional Economic Cooperation of the Developing Countries and stressed the importance of this plan of action for the development of the economic agenda for the South.
15. The Conference underscored the importance of the Perez-Guerrero Trust Fund in enhancing concrete cooperation schemes among countries in the South, and in this regard, it encouraged contributions to the Perez-Guerrero Trust Fund to enable it to support more cooperative projects among developing countries.
16. The Conference therefore reaffirmed its commitments to promote and strengthen regional and subregional economic cooperation among developing countries and adopt the Bali Plan of Action for implementation, with a set of specific measures identified to strengthen and deepen the work ahead as well as to knit closer ties and cooperation among us, to provide further political, financial and institutional impetus to regional and subregional cooperation as we approach the new millennium.
17. The Conference also declared its collective appreciation of its very warm hospitality, excellent facilities and leadership provided for the meeting by the Government and people of the Republic of Indonesia.

ANNEXURE II

KUALA LUMPUR DECLARATION ON THE EAST ASIA SUMMIT KUALA LUMPUR, 14 DECEMBER 2005

WE, the Heads of State/Government of the Member Countries of the Association of Southeast Asian Nations (ASEAN), Australia, People's Republic of China, Republic of India, Japan, Republic of

Korea and New Zealand, on the occasion of the historic First East Asia Summit on 14 December 2005 in Kuala Lumpur, Malaysia;

RECALLING the decision of the 10th ASEAN Summit and supported by the 8th ASEAN Plus Three Summit held on 29 November 2004 in Vientiane, Lao PDR, to convene the First East Asia Summit in Malaysia in 2005;

REITERATING our commitment to the purposes and principles of the Charter of the United Nations, the Treaty of Amity and Cooperation in Southeast Asia and other recognised principles of international law;

ACKNOWLEDGING that in a rapidly changing international environment, our economies and societies have become increasingly interlinked and interdependent;

REALISING the increasing range of challenges facing the world and the need for concerted regional and global efforts to respond to these challenges;

RECOGNISING our shared interests in achieving peace, security and prosperity in East Asia and the world at large;

DESIROUS of creating a peaceful environment by further enhancing cooperation and strengthening the existing bonds of friendship among our countries in keeping with the principles of equality, partnership, consultation and consensus thereby contributing to peace, security and economic prosperity in the region and the world at large;

CONVINCED of the importance of strengthening bilateral and multilateral interactions and cooperation among the participating countries of the East Asia Summit and the world at large on issues of common interest and concern in order to enhance peace and economic prosperity;

REITERATING the conviction that the effective functioning of multilateral systems will continue to be indispensable for advancing economic development;

RECOGNISING that this region is today a source of dynamism for the world economy;

SHARING the view that the East Asia Summit could play a significant role in community building in this region;

FURTHER RECOGNISING the need to support efforts to build a strong ASEAN Community which will serve as a solid foundation for our common peace and prosperity;

DO HEREBY DECLARE:

FIRST, that we have established the East Asia Summit as a forum for dialogue on broad strategic, political and economic issues of common interest and concern with the aim of promoting peace, stability and economic prosperity in East Asia.

SECOND, that the efforts of the East Asia Summit to promote community building in this region will be consistent with and reinforce the realisation of the ASEAN Community, and will form an integral part of the evolving regional architecture.

THIRD, that the East Asia Summit will be an open, inclusive, transparent and outward-looking forum in which we strive to strengthen global norms and universally recognised values with ASEAN as the driving force working in partnership with the other participants of the East Asia Summit.

FOURTH, we will focus, among others, on the following:

- Fostering strategic dialogue and promoting cooperation in political and security issues to ensure that our countries can live at peace with one another and with the world at large in a just, democratic and harmonious environment;
- Promoting development, financial stability, energy security, economic integration and growth, eradicating poverty and narrowing the development gap in East Asia, through technology transfer and infrastructure development, capacity building, good governance and humanitarian assistance and promoting financial links, trade and investment expansion and liberalisation; and
- Promoting deeper cultural understanding, people-to-people contact and enhanced cooperation in uplifting the lives and well-being of our peoples in order to foster mutual trust and solidarity as well as promoting fields such as environmental protection, prevention of infectious diseases and natural disaster mitigation.

FIFTH, that:

- Participation in the East Asia Summit will be based on the criteria for participation established by ASEAN;

- The East Asia Summit will be convened regularly;
- The East Asia Summit will be hosted and chaired by an ASEAN Member Country that assumes the ASEAN Chairmanship and held back-to-back with the annual ASEAN Summit; and
- The modalities of the East Asia Summit will be reviewed by ASEAN and all other participating countries of the East Asia Summit.

SIGNED at Kuala Lumpur, Malaysia, on the Fourteenth Day of December in the Year Two Thousand and Five.

ANNEXURE III

DECLARATION OF THE ASSEMBLY OF EUROPEAN REGIONS ON REGIONALISM IN EUROPE

PREAMBLE

The Assembly of European Regions (AER) meeting in Basel on 4th December 1996:

1. *Considering* that the AER represents almost 300 European regions of varying sizes and different administrative and political structures with a total population of nearly 400 million;
2. *Considering* that the Regions have different statuses, which vary according to their history, their culture and their constitutional principles and characterize the territorial organisation of each State. Whilst respecting this diversity, this common declaration expresses the Regions' aspirations to further regionalism within the institutional framework of their own country, which have a federal, decentralised or autonomous structure. This text cannot be interpreted as binding the regions to any of these structures.
3. *Considering* that the regions are an essential and irreplaceable element of European development and integration;

4 *Conscious* that the regions have different origins and functions, with some historically based on distinct communities, ethnic groups or even nations, and others

created as administrative districts, exercising powers delegated to them by the State;

5. *Considering* the importance in Europe of the process of integration and regionalisation;
6. *Noting* that people through historical, linguistic, cultural, social, economic and geographical ties, increasingly identify themselves with their region, the variety of which, constitutes an inexhaustible richness;
7. *Considering* that States with strong regional political structures, ie. with legislative powers and their own finances can optimally resolve their economic and social problems;
8. *Considering* also that the regional reality justifies the participation of the regions in State bodies and actions at an international level;
9. *Being aware* that the regions, within the national legal order, are an indispensable element of democracy, decentralisation and self-determination, by allowing people to identify with their community and by increasing the opportunities for their participation in public life;
10. *Conscious* that the regions and their peoples have endless possibilities to carry out and further develop mutually advantageous political, economic and cultural cooperation between themselves;
11. *Noting* the vast potential for political, social, economic and cultural cooperation between European regions and the significance of such cooperation at national, transfrontier and international level for the development of a united and cohesive Europe and for improved knowledge and understanding of its actions among the general public;
12. *Considering* that regional participation in the decision-making process of the European institutions, in accordance with the principle of subsidiarity, contributes to improving transparency of European Union actions for citizens;
13. *Considering* the relevance of the Council of Europe's draft European Charter of Regional Self-government (1996) and the European Parliament's "Community Charter for Regionalisation" (1988);

14. *Convinced* of the significance of this declaration, which reflects a political will and aspirations that the regions wish to promote in Europe, while respecting the diversity of their situations which call for a variety of solutions; have adopted the following Declaration:

ARTICLE 1. THE REGION: DEFINITION AND CONCEPT

1. The region is the territorial body of public law established at the level immediately below that of the State and endowed with political self-government.
2. The region shall be recognised in the national constitution or in legislation which guarantees its autonomy, identity, powers and organisational structures.
3. The region shall have its own constitution, statute of autonomy or other law which shall form part of the legal order of the State at the highest level establishing at least its organisation and powers. The status of a region can be altered only in cooperation with the region concerned. Regions within the same State may have a different status, in keeping with their historical, political, social or cultural characteristics.
4. The region is the expression of a distinct political identity, which may take very different political forms, reflecting the democratic will of each region to adopt the form of political organisation it deems preferable. The region shall resource and staff its own administration and adopt insignia for its representation.

ARTICLE 2. INSTITUTIONAL ORGANISATION

1. The region shall have full legal status.
2. The region's basic structure shall comprise a representative assembly and an executive body. Its organisation shall be a matter for the region alone.
3. The members of the representative assembly shall be directly elected by free and secret ballot on the basis of equal and universal suffrage. The assembly may be granted legislative powers, subject to the limits laid down in the domestic legal order.

4. The executive body shall be politically answerable to the representative assembly, subject to the conditions and procedures prescribed in domestic legislation.
5. Members of both the representative assembly and the executive body shall not be subjected to supervision by the central authority which would prejudice the free exercise of their functions.

ARTICLE 3. POWERS

1. The apportionment of powers between the State and the regions shall be determined in the national constitution or in legislation in accordance with the principles of political decentralisation and subsidiarity. Under these principles, functions should be exercised at the level as close to the citizen as possible.
2. The implementation of national law, either directly or by delegation, should, as a general rule, be the responsibility of the region.
3. The region should have responsibility for all functions with a predominantly regional dimension.
4. Where the State has decentralised administration at regional level, it shall transfer the corresponding staff and financial resources to the regional bodies in order to avoid duplication.
5. The regions shall exercise the powers assigned to them on an individual basis. The regions within a single State shall agree to harmonise, where appropriate, the action taken within their specific spheres of competence. To that end, they shall decide on the required procedures.
6. State decisions and measures which affect regional powers or interests - in particular measures which have implications for their financial situation or that of the local authorities, and decisions which affect the scope of any legislative powers the regions may have - may not be adopted without the prior assent of the regions involved.

ARTICLE 4. FINANCING

1. The region shall enjoy financial autonomy and have sufficient own resources to develop its powers fully. It shall

be governed in particular by the principles of economy, efficiency, effective use of resources, service to the citizen, and transparency in its budgetary decisions.

2. **The fundamental principles governing the public finances and apportionment of revenue as well as State guidelines for regional budget management shall be laid down in the national constitution or in legislation. The regions shall also play a decisive role in the shaping of financial legislation at national level.**

ARTICLE 5. FINANCIAL RESOURCES OF THE REGION

1. **The financial resources of the region shall consist basically of taxes partly or wholly transferred by the State, and of its own taxes.**
2. **The region shall receive the income necessary for the performance of its functions. It shall be entitled to an appropriate share of national tax revenue for this purpose. Its income shall be sufficient and concentrated uniformly on a small number of major sources of tax revenue in order to ensure stable regional budget management and allow the implementation of an economic policy directed towards sustainable development.**
3. **Under national legislation, the region shall be entitled to levy its own taxes and determine sources of tax revenue. For this purpose, it shall set the criteria for determining its taxes, duties and dues. Where the law permits, it may decide to charge supplements on State taxes.**
4. **Where a number of authorities share a source of tax revenue, the scale and procedure for the distribution of such revenue shall be prescribed by legislation. State financial allocations of a general nature shall take precedence over special allocations, which shall be governed only by statutorily prescribed criteria.**
5. **Where the region is not empowered to collect taxes, it shall be involved in determining the organisation of the relevant bodies and tax procedures. It shall likewise be involved in determining the composition and procedure of the competent courts.**

6. Within the limits prescribed by law, the region may seek credits to finance investments. Credit limits and arrangements for monitoring their legality shall be laid down by law.

ARTICLE 6. INTER-REGIONAL FINANCIAL EQUALISATION

1. The principle of solidarity entails the existence of national systems of financial equalisation. The aims and procedure of financial equalisation shall be prescribed in the national constitution or legislation. Account shall be taken of the uneven distribution of the financial burdens borne by the regions, on the basis of objective criteria. However, financial equalisation shall not dissuade those regions required to make equalisation payments from making appropriate use of the sources of tax revenue available to them. The needs of municipal authorities shall also be taken into account in the calculation of equalisation payments. Equalisation shall take the form of transfers from the State to the regions, and between regions.
2. The principle of solidarity shall also be expressed in the EU for reducing the interregional inequalities in order to achieve the aim of social and economic cohesion in Europe. The Structural Funds of the European Union shall be one instrument for the achievement of this aim.

ARTICLE 7. INVOLVEMENT AT THE CENTRAL LEVEL OF THE STATE

1. The regions shall play an appropriate part in the legislative bodies of the State.
2. The State, within the scope of its own powers, shall make arrangements to coordinate the participation of the regional institutions in the State's decision-making processes, where such decisions affect the region's powers.
3. The regions shall be involved in appointing the judicial bodies responsible for the settlement of disputes over the division of powers between the State and the regions. Disputes between the regions and the State shall be settled by court proceedings or arbitration.

ARTICLE 8. THE STATE AND THE REGIONS

1. Relations between the State and its regions and among the regions themselves shall comply with the principles of mutual respect, cooperation and solidarity. The regions and the State shall promote mutual cooperation and refrain from adopting measures which could prejudice or limit the exercise of powers at other levels.
2. Where it exists, State control over the regions shall be regulated by the national constitution, or failing that, by appropriate legislation.
3. Regions should be permitted to sign treaties or agreements with other regions within the same State.
4. As a general principle, administrative powers should be exercised by the regions and only in exceptional circumstances by the State.

ARTICLE 9. THE REGIONS AND LOCAL AUTHORITIES

1. In exercising the powers assigned to them, regions and local authorities shall cooperate in a spirit of mutual trust and in accordance with the principle of subsidiarity. Regions and local authorities shall take all necessary measures to promote mutual cooperation, bearing in mind the control which regions may exercise over local authorities.
2. Local authorities shall be consulted on all regional measures which affect their sphere of competence or individual interests. In practice, these measures shall include any which have a bearing on the financial powers of the local authorities.

ARTICLE 10. THE REGIONS AND INTERNATIONAL RELATIONS

1. Regions shall have the capability to act at an international level. They may conclude treaties, agreements or protocols which are international in scope, subject to approval by the central Government where this is required by national legislation.
2. The regions shall promote bilateral and multilateral domestic and transfrontier cooperation among themselves for the purpose of carrying out joint projects.

3. Regions shall have the right to set up their own representations, either individually or in conjunction with other regions, in other States and in appropriate international organisations.
4. Subject to the provisions of paragraph 1 of this Article, the regions shall participate in the international activities of their State, in accordance with the relevant domestic legislation, whenever their own powers or essential interests are concerned.
5. Prior to the conclusion of an international treaty which affects their essential interests, the regions shall be consulted by the State. Should the State intend to sign an international treaty which affects the powers of the regions, the regions shall participate in the drafting and conclusion of the treaty. The exact manner of their participation shall be governed by the domestic procedures in force between the State and its regions. Treaties shall be executed in accordance with the apportionment of powers between the State and its regions.

ARTICLE 11. THE REGIONS AND TRANSFRONTIER COOPERATION

1. Regions with common frontiers shall, in compliance with relevant domestic legislation and international law, promote transfrontier cooperation.
2. Regions, taking due account of domestic legislation and international agreements between States, shall be entitled to conclude transfrontier agreements in order to develop their cooperation within the limits of their powers.
3. Regions shall have the right, within the legal framework of each State concerned, to establish joint deliberative or executive bodies.
4. The actions of these bodies shall be subject to the procedures of the competent courts in the same manner as actions of regional bodies.

ARTICLE 12. THE REGIONS AND EUROPEAN UNION

1. The European Union shall recognise the regions of its Member States and associations of a regional nature as

active participants in its policies. It shall have a body of regional composition which shall participate in decision-making on issues having a regional dimension. Its members shall be proposed by the regions.

2. The regions may make representations to the institutions of the European Union. Such representations may be established jointly by several regions. The European Union and the Member States where they are located shall recognise their proper status.
3. The regions, within the scope of their powers, or where their interests may be affected, should participate in the determination of the positions taken by their States in the Community institutions.
4. Where an issue is the exclusive responsibility of the region or has a particular bearing on its interests, the State shall not be able to deviate from the position adopted by the region, save where domestic legislation requires this in the interests of unity. The State shall be required to justify any deviation from the region's position. On such issues, the region shall also be entitled to take part in the decision-making process of European institutions and shall in particular have the right to have its representation within the national delegation.
5. The regions shall implement Community legislation within their sphere of competence.
6. The regions shall manage assistance from the Community Funds for matters within their powers. For this purpose, the regions shall liaise with the European Union without the intermediation of the State.
7. The regions may enter into agreements designed to improve the implementation of Community policies. The courts shall supervise the implementation of Community legislation by the regions. The State and the regions shall keep one another informed of the measures they adopt in the implementation of Community legislation and programmes.
8. The regions shall have the right to bring proceedings before the European Court of Justice where measures taken by the Community institutions affect their powers or interests.

9. The legislation on elections to the European Parliament shall refer to regional constituencies in States which have decentralised political or administrative structures.
10. Arrangements must be made for contact between the European Parliament and regional parliaments in their capacity as institutions which directly represent the will of the citizen.

ARTICLE 13. FINAL CONSIDERATIONS

1. The Assembly of European Regions (AER), in adopting the present Declaration, which is inherently political in character, aims to promote and strengthen regionalism in Europe. In view of the wide variety of regional situations and aspirations, this document, which is not legally binding, is intended to serve for some regions as a guide containing basic standards or goals for regionalisation.
2. The AER and its members shall make such approaches to national governments, European Union institutions and other European bodies as are necessary to achieve the objectives of this document.
3. The Declaration also illustrates the fact that the region is the best form of organisation for resolving regional problems in an appropriate and independent manner. The States of Europe shall undertake to pursue as far as possible the devolution of powers to the regions and to transfer the financial resources necessary for their exercise, amending international legislation as necessary.
4. AER and its members shall also promote European interregional cooperation at all levels and shall offer assistance in their regionalisation where necessary by proposing amendments to the constitution or constitutional law to allow for the creation of the most appropriate forms of regional structure.
5. Transfrontier cooperation strengthens and consolidates regionalism. The development of a regional identity based on transfrontier cooperation promotes political and social stability.
6. The establishment of the Committee of the Regions within the European Union and the Congress of Local and Regional

Authorities of Europe within the Council of Europe is a great step forward for regionalism in Europe. A longer-term goal shall be to establish a Europe of the regions as a third level of government; this would entail the Committee of the Regions attaining the status of a genuine regional chamber.

7. The AER and its members shall lend support to associations of local authorities. Its central aim, however, shall remain the development of a genuine regional identity.
8. The AER shall monitor the progress made in the individual European States towards achieving the goals set forth in this Declaration.

APPENDIX TO ARTICLE 3, PARAGRAPH 1

Examples of the existing regions' powers:

- regional economic policy,
- regional planning, building and housing policy,
- telecommunications and transport infrastructures,
- energy and environment,
- agriculture and fisheries,
- education at all levels, universities and research,
- culture and media,
- public health,
- tourism, leisure and sport,
- police and public order.

ANNEXURE IV

BANGKOK DECLARATION

Bangkok, 8 August 1967

The Presidium Minister for Political Affairs/ Minister for Foreign Affairs of Indonesia, the Deputy Prime Minister of Malaysia, the Secretary of Foreign Affairs of the Philippines, the Minister for Foreign Affairs of Singapore and the Minister of Foreign Affairs of Thailand:

MINDFUL of the existence of mutual interests and common problems among countries of South-East Asia and convinced of the

need to strengthen further the existing bonds of regional solidarity and cooperation;

DESIRING to establish a firm foundation for common action to promote regional cooperation in South-East Asia in the spirit of equality and partnership and thereby contribute towards peace, progress and prosperity in the region;

CONSCIOUS that in an increasingly interdependent world, the cherished ideals of peace, freedom, social justice and economic well-being are best attained by fostering good understanding, good neighbourliness and meaningful cooperation among the countries of the region already bound together by ties of history and culture;

CONSIDERING that the countries of SouthEast Asia share a primary responsibility for strengthening the economic and social stability of the region and ensuring their peacefull and progressive national development, and that they are determined to ensure their stability and security from external interference in any form or manifestation in order to preserve their national identities in accordance with the ideals and aspirations of their peoples;

AFFIRMING that all foreign bases are temporary and remain only with the expressed concurrence of the countries concerned and are not intended to be used directly or indirectly to subvert the national independence and freedom of States in the area or prejudice the orderly processes of their national development;

DO HEREBY DECLARE:

FIRST, the establishment of an Association for Regional Cooperation among the countries of South-East Asia to be known as the Association of South-East Asian Nations (ASEAN).

SECOND that the aims and purposes of the Association shall be:

1. To accelerate the economic growth, social progress and cultural development in the region through joint endeavours in the spirit of equality and partnership in order to strengthen the foundation for a prosperous and peaceful community of South-East Asian Nations;
2. To promote regional peace and stability through abiding respect for justice and the rule of law in the relationship

among countries of the region and adherence to the principles of the United Nations Charter;

3. To promote active collaboration and mutual assistance on matters of common interest in the economic, social, cultural, technical, scientific and administrative fields;

4. To provide assistance to each other in the form of training and research facilities in the educational, professional, technical and administrative spheres;

5. To collaborate more effectively for the greater utilization of their agriculture and industries, the expansion of their trade, including the study of the problems of international commodity trade, the improvement of their transportation and communications facilities and the raising of the living standards of their peoples;

6. To promote South-East Asian studies;

7. To maintain close and beneficial cooperation with existing international and regional organizations with similar aims and purposes, and explore all avenues for even closer cooperation among themselves.

THIRD, that to carry out these aims and purposes, the following machinery shall be established:

(*a*) Annual Meeting of Foreign Ministers, which shall be by rotation and referred to as ASEAN Ministerial Meeting. Special Meetings of Foreign Ministers may be convened as required.

(*b*) A Standing committee, under the chairmanship of the Foreign Minister of the host country or his representative and having as its members the accredited Ambassadors of the other member countries, to carry on the work of the Association in between Meetings of Foreign Ministers.

(*c*) Ad-Hoc Committees and Permanent Committees of specialists and officials on specific subjects.

(*d*) A National Secretariat in each member country to carry out the work of the Association on behalf of that country and to service the Annual or Special Meetings of Foreign Ministers, the Standing Committee and such other committees as may hereafter be established.

FOURTH, that the Association is open for participation to all States in the South-East Asian Region subscribing to the aforementioned aims, principles and purposes.

FIFTH, that the Association represents the collective will of the nations of South-East Asia to bind themselves together in friendship and cooperation and, through joint efforts and sacrifices, secure for their peoples and for posterity the blessings of peace, freedom and prosperity.

DONE in Bangkok on the Eighth Day of August in the Year One Thousand Nine Hundred and Sixty-Seven.

ANNEXURE V

KUALA LUMPUR CONCORD ON REGIONALISM

History does not travel in a straight line. But over the last few decades, the history of the Pacific has been travelling - with twists and turns - towards a single direction: the emergence of a Pacific community and the primacy of the Pacific as the centre of economic gravity of the world.

In 1889, one of the earliest Pacificians said: "The Mediterranean is the ocean of the past, the Atlantic the ocean of the present, and the pacific, the ocean of the future." It is clear that the future has arrived. The Pacific shift has been more rapid than most could have imagined. The Pacific Age has indeed begun.

The PECC was formed when the glimmerings of a Pacific Age could just be seen by those blessed by a clear vision. The dream of our founding fathers was of a diverse and rich Pacific that was whole and at one, imbued with a growing sense of community; not only co-existing in but also working actively and together for a common peace and harmony: not only developing vigorously but also working actively and together for a common and mutually shared prosperity.

PECC has already played a role in moving the Pacific super-region towards a Pacific partnership for cooperative peace and prosperity. We must remain true to the vision of our founding fathers. We must continue to play a role in the strengthening, enriching and maturing of such a Pacific partnership in the years to come. The future has, of course, to be created from today.

The danger to a Pacific community, to the Pacific Age, to our common future, can come from many directions. The end of the Cold War has clearly contributed to the making of a wider Pacific community. However, excessive domestic pre-occupation can put a brake on the Pacific movement. A diversion of commitment to narrow regional interests and pursuits can be a serious detour from a path to which some might never return.

Obviously all the issues cannot and should not be addressed by a single instrument or approach. The Pacific Age that we wish to see flourish must continue to be made each day by millions of hands in business, government and academic and other institutions.

We in PECC commit ourselves to becoming, quickly and effectively, a forceful movement for open regionalism. Such a commitment would constitute, in large part, a return to our roots: When the PECC movement was launched in Canberra in 1980, the concept of an "open region" was not only an inspiration but also a cornerstone of the movement itself. Prime Minister Masayoshi Ohira of Japan said:

"For the first time in history, the vast and broad Pacific Basin region has come to meet the pre-requisites for making possible the creation of a regional community."

We must establish, he said, "open regional cooperation befitting the age of the global community".

That Commitment was unequivocally reaffirmed in PECC's San Francisco Declaration on Open Regionalism. This Declaration states:

"The Council has agreed ... that its work in support of multilateralism will now be strengthened by a collective commitment to a dynamic vision of open regionalism, and declares that its future efforts will be directed towards supporting those public and private practises which help regional economies to:

- become increasingly open to flows of goods, investment, services, information and technology;
- comply with the disciplines, principles and practices developed by the world community through the General Agreement on Tariff and Trade;
- benefit from trade creation flowing from sub-regional arrangements that are consistent with GATT principles as a

means of maintaining and promoting the overall benefits of the region's increasingly open character;

- develop commerce with economies outside the region and in the global economic system."

PECC does have the largest geographical spread and is the largest and most inclusive Pacific grouping involving no fewer than 21 economies from the north, south, east and west Pacific. And, because of its independent and tripartite nature, involving officials, business and academia, PECC Ministers' pledge to solicit the advice of the business/private sector on issues relevant to APEC's work, especially PECC.

A commitment to open regionalism is also necessary and appropriate because there is clear and present danger and because this clear and present danger -- from the many points of the compass -- will not go away.

PECC's commitment to open regionalism must of course start from the premise that this will contribute to the region of greater prosperity for all. We therefore wholeheartedly welcome the conclusion of the Uruguay Round and urge all governments to speedily implement the commitments made which will reduce obstacle and distortions impeding global trade and further extend the range of GATT's rules, disciplines and dispute settlement procedures.

Reaffirming the importance of global multilateralism, we believe that a world trade organisation must also work on the basis of inclusiveness and in this regard we urge the future inclusion of all PECC economies in the GATT process. Similarly, PECC expresses concern about the tendencies of some member economies to condition trade and investment on achievement of political or ideological objectives.

In order to meet the challenges of open regionalism, PECC will:

First, review its priorities in allocating resources to the mission of championing open regionalism in the pursuit of regional economic cooperation.

Second, fully develop the doctrine and legitimacy of open regionalism, two of whose central tenets must be the desire to open and liberalise a region and the actual achievement of regional liberalisation and opening.

Third, establish processes and instrumentalities for studying and monitoring the development of protectionism and liberalisation in the Pacific and elsewhere. In keeping with the historic San Francisco Declaration, PECC supports the right of all regions to organise in non-discriminatory groupings -- whether this be in the northern, southern, eastern or western Pacific. PECC will attempt to ensure that any sub-regional grouping contributes to open regionalism and to lowering the barriers to non-member economies.

Fourth, join hands and work together with processes, institutions and movements which are similarly committed to open regionalism and global liberalisation, and to take measures to ensure greater involvement of the business sector.

BIBLIOGRAPHY

Arjun et al. (eds.) *Human Rights: A Source Book*, NCERT, New Delhi, 1996.

"SAARC Summit Charter (8 December 1985), Indian Journal of International Law, vol. 26, (1986), pp. 323-326.

"SAARC Summit Declaration (8 December 1985)", Indian Journal of International Law, vol. 26, (1986), pp. 321-322.

"SAARC: Bangalore Declaration, 1986", Indian Journal of International Law, vol. 26 (1986), pp. 619-62.

A Paper on the Proposal for Regional Cooperation in South Asia, November, 1980 in From SAARC to SAARC: Milestones in the Evolution of Regional Cooperation in South Asia (1980-88), SAARC Secretariat, Kathmandu, Vol. I, 1988.

Abbas, A.T., B.M., *The Gangas Water Dispute,* Dhaka, University Press, 1982.

Abbas, A.T., B.M., *The Gangas Water Dispute,* Dhaka, University Press, 1982.

Abeyrantne, S., 'Policy and Political Issues in Economic Growth of Sri Lanka' in S.T. Hettige and M. Mayer (eds.), *Sri Lanka at Crossroads: Dilemmas and Prospects after 50 Years of Independence,* Macmillan, New Delhi, 2000.

Abeyrantne, S., 'Policy and Political Issues in Economic Growth of Sri Lanka' in S.T. Hettige and M. Mayer (eds.), *Sri Lanka at Crossroads: Dilemmas and Prospects after 50 Years of Independence,* Macmillan, New Delhi, 2000.

Aditya Annand; *SAARC The Call for Cooperation and Concept of a South Asian Regime,* South Asia Forum (7), 1984.

Agarwal, Govind R., *South-South Economic Cooperation Problems and Prospects,* New Delhi, Radiant Publishers, 1987.

Agarwal, H.O., "International Law", Allahabad Law Agency, Allahabad, 1992.

Aggarwal M.R., *Regional Economic Cooperation in South Asia,* New Delhi, S. Chand & Co. 1979.

Aggarwal, M.R., *Regional Economic Cooperation Among SAARC Countries*, New Delhi, Allied Publishers Ltd., 1995.

Agwani, M.S. South Asia: Stability and Regional Cooperation, CRRID, Chandigarh, 1987.

Ahasn, Abul, *SAARC: A Perspective*, University Press, Dhaka, 1992.

Ahirro Jitendra, J., *Third Concept*, Vol. 18, No. 205, April 2004.

Ahmad, Imtiyaz: India and Lankan Tamils War of Liberation, Regional Studies, New York, 1992.

Ahmed Ishiaq; *State, Nation and Ethnicity in Contemporary South Asia*, London Printer, 1996.

Ahmed Lamina; *SAARC : At the Cross Roads*, in Nassem Ayaz (ed) International Relations, A New Perspective, Lahore, Progressive Publishers, 1989.

Ahmed Sabina; *SAARC Regional Studies 1 (3) Summ 1983: 84-10*, South Asia *World Today*, 34 (10) Oct. 1978, 390-400.

Ahmed, Moudud, *Democracy and the Challenge of Development: A Study of Politics and Military Intervention In Bangladesh*, Dhaka, University Press, 1995.

Akbar, M.K., *Pakistan Today*, New Delhi, Mittal Publications, 1998.

Akehurst, Micheal, "A Modern Introduction to International Law", 1970.

Alailima, P.J., 'The Human Development Perspective' in W.D. Lakshman and C.A. Tisdell (eds.), *Sri Lanka's Development since Independence: Socio-Economic Perspectives and Analyses*, Nova Science Publishers, Inc., New York, 2000.

Alam, Shah, Charter of the South Asian Association for Regional Cooperation: A Critique", Indian Journal of International Law, vol. 26 (1986), pp. 452-463.

Alexander, Larventyev: USA and Asia, Sterling Publishers, New Delhi, 1982.

Ali, Akhtar: South Asia: Nuclear Stalemate or Conflagration, Research on Armament and Poverty, Karachi, 1987.

Ali, M. Ramjan; *Regional Studies*, Vol. XXII, No. 1, Winter, Islamabad Institute of Regional Studies, 2003-2004.

Anand, R.P., "Studies in International Adjudication", New York, 1969.

Anand, R.P.: South Asia: In Search of Regional Identity, Banyan Publishers, New Delhi, 1991.

Andrassy, Juraj, "Uniting for Peace", AJIL, Vol. 50 (1956).

Appadorai, A.: India, Studies in Social and Political Development, Asia Publishing House, Mumbai, 1961.

Ardy, Stont: Economic Integration among Developing Countries, IBRD, Washiogton, 1974.

Armonk, N.Y.: SAARC: Asian Countries, Oxford, New York, 1995.

Athukorala, P. and S. Rajapatirana, *Liberalization and Industrial Transformation: Sri Lanka in International Perspective*, Oxford University Press, New Delhi, 2000.

Athukorala, P. and S. Rajapatirana, *Liberalization and Industrial Transformation: Sri Lanka in International Perspective*, Oxford University Press, New Delhi, 2000.

Bahadur Kalim; *The Politics of SAARC*, World Focus, Vol. 25, No. 6, June 2004.

Bahadur, Kalim; *South Asia in Transition*, Conflicts and Tensions, New Delhi, Patroit Publishers, 1986.

Balwant, Bheneja: The Polities of Triangles: The Alignment Patterns in South Asia Relations, Asia Pub., New Delhi, 1973.

Bandyopadhaya, J.: The Making of India's Foreign Policy: Determinant, Institutions Processes and Personalities, Allied Publishers, New Delhi, 1970.

Banskota, N.P.; *South Asian Trade Cooperation : Global Perspective*, Kathmandu, Ratha Pustak Bhandar (2052) 1995.

Baxter, Craig, "Democracy and Authoritarianism in South Asia", *Journal of International Affairs*, vol. 38, no. 2, Winter 1985, pp. 307-319.

Bezbaruah, Manoranjan: US Strategy in the Indian Ocean: The International Response, Praeger Publishers, New York, 1977.

Bhargav Kant Kishore, Bongartz Meinz, Sobhan Farooq (eds.), *Shaking South Asia's Future Role of Regional Cooperation*, 1995.

Bhargava, K.K., *South Asia : Towards Dynamism and Cooperation*, New Delhi, Popular Prakashan Pvt. Ltd., 1994.

Bhatia, Kanta, *Reference Sources on South Asia*, Popular Prakashan, Bombay, 1999.

Bhatt, Maqbool Ahmad; *The Future of SAARC,* Regional Studies, Vol. 10, No. 1, Winter 1991-92.

Bhutani, D.H., *The Future of Pakistan*, Promula & Co., New Delhi, 1984.

Bilgrami, S.J.R., "International Organisation-A View from Within", (Vikas Publishing House Pvt. Ltd., New Delhi), 1977.

Bindra S.S., *India and Her Neighbours : A Study of Political, Economic and Cultural Relations and Interactions*, New Delhi, Deep and Deep Publications, 1984.

Biswas, S.: The Bangkok Agreement - An evaluation of Preferential Agreement in Escap Region, RIS, New Delhi, 1987.

Black, Robin, *Explosion in a Subcontinent: India, Pakistan, Bangladesh and Ceylon,* Penguin, London, 1975.

Blackburn Robert and James J. Busuttil (eds.), *Human Rights for the 21st Century*, Printer, London, 1997.

Blunder, S.S., *India .and Her Neighbours: A Study of Political, Economic and Cultural Relations,* Deep and Deep Publishers, New Delhi, 1984.

Bowett, D.W., "The Law of International Institutions", Fourth Edition (Second Indian Reprint, Delhi) 1995.

Brar Bhupinder; *A Region of States or a Region of Regions* in South Asian Survey, Vol. 6, No. 1 (1999) New Delhi, Sage Publications.

Braun, Dieter, *The Indian Ocean: Region of Conflict or Zone of Peace*, Oxford University Press, New York, 1983.

Brownlie, Ian, "Principles of International Law", (Clarendon Press, Oxford), 1973.

Bruton, H.J., *The Political Economy of Poverty, Equity and Growth: Sri Lanka and Malaysia,* Oxford University Press, New York, 1992.

Bruton, H.J., *The Political Economy of Poverty, Equity and Growth: Sri Lanka and Malaysia,* Oxford University Press, New York, 1992.

Buergenthal, Thomas, *Human Rights International Law and the Helsinki Accord*, Allied Publishers Pvt. Ltd., Bombay, 1979.

Burton, J.W., *Non-Alignment*, Andre Deutsch Ltd., London, 1965.

Chakarvarthy Nikhil; *South Asia as a Concept,* World Focus 4 (11-12) Nov.-Dec., 1983-3-6, Fourth Annual Number, South Asia Today.

Chakervartty, Nikhil, "South Asia: Looking Beyond SAARC", *World Focus*, Concept, New Delhi, 1991.

Chakrabarty Nitya, "SAARC : Bumpy Road Ahead", New Delhi, Hindustan Times, August 1998.

Chavan, Y.B., *India's Foreign Policy*, Samiaya Publishers, New Delhi, 1979.

Cheever, Daniel S., and Haviland, H. Field, "Organising for Peace-International Organisation in World Affairs", (Boston, Houghton Miffins Co.), 1954.

Chodhry, G.W., *India, Pakistan, Bangladesh and the Major Powers: Politics of a Divided Subcontinent*, Free Press, New York, 1975.

Chopra Pran; *Future of South Asia*, New Delhi, Macmillian India Ltd., 1986.

Chopra, Mahajan K., *India and the Indian Ocean: New Horizons*, Sterling Publishers, New Delhi, 1982.

Chopra, Pran, *Future of South Asia*, MacMillan India Ltd., New Delhi, 1986.

Chopra, Pran; *Regional Cooperation*, World Focus 4(11-12) Nov.-Dec. 1983, 35-8/Search for South Asia Perspective (8) March 1978, 9-13/3, March 1982, 3-8 Why South Asia and How-World Focus/Commerce (147) 3768 Aug 20, 1983, 2177.

Clark, Ian and Bowman, L., *The Indian Ocean in Global Politics*, Westview Press, USA, 1981.

Das, Dependra K., *SAARC Regional Cooperation and Development*, New Delhi, Deep and Deep Publications, 1999.

De Silva, K.M., *A History of Sri Lanka*, Oxford University Press, New Delhi, 1981.

Deo, A.R., *Politics of SAARC*, World Focus, Vol. 17, No. 7, July 1996.

Deo, A.R.; *SAARC: Making its Mark*, World Focus, Vol. 22, No. 27, July 2001.

Dharamdasani, M.D.: Political Participation and Change in South Asia, in the Context of Nepal, Shalimar Publishing House, Varanasi, India, 1984.

Dharmedasani, M.D., *South Asian Regional Cooperation*, Varanasi, Shalimar Publishing House, 1985.

Dixit Aabha, "SAARC Towards Greater Cooperation", *Strategic Analysis*, New Delhi, Vol. XX, No. 4, July 1997.

Dixit J.N., "South Asian Regional Cooperation : Problems and Prospects", *South Asian Survey*, Vol. 1, No. 2, July-December 1994.

Dixit, J.N., "Prospects of South Asian Cooperation in the Transformed World", *South Asian Survey*, Vol. 10, No. 1, June-2003, New Delhi, Sage Publication.

Dutt, Ashok K.: Atlas of South Asia, Concept, New Delhi, 1999. Dutt, Devi: The Himalayan Subcontinent: Emerging Pattern, Rachna Prakashan, New Delhi, 1972.

Eagleton, Clyde, "International Government", (Ronald Press Co., New York), 1957.

Edrisinha, R. and N. Selvakkumaran, 'The Constitutional Evolution of Ceylon/Sri Lanka 1948-98' in W.D. Lakshman and C.A. Tisdell (eds.), *Sri Lanka's Development since Independence: Socio-Economic Perspectives and Analyses,* Nova Science Publishers, Inc., New York, 2000.

Emajuddin Ahmed; *SAARC : Seeds of Harmony*, Dhaka, the University Press, 1985.

Farmer, S.H., *Introduction to South Asia*, Methuen, London, 1983.

Fawcett, J.E.S., "The International Law and the Outer-space", (London), 1963.

Fawcett, J.E.S., The Application of the European Convention on Human Rights, Clarendon Press, Oxford 1969.

Fenwick, Charles G., "International Law", (Vakil, Feffer and Simmon Pvt. Ltd., Bombay), Second Indian Edition, 1967.

Fernando, L., 'Three Phases of Political Development after Independence' in W.D. Lakshman and C.A. Tisdell (eds.), *Sri Lanka's Development since Independence: Socio-Economic Perspectives and Analyses,* Nova Science Publishers, Inc., New York, 2000.

Fernando, L., 'Three Phases of Political Development after Independence' in W.D. Lakshman and C.A. Tisdell (eds.), *Sri Lanka's Development since Independence: Socio-Economic*

Perspectives and Analyses, Nova Science Publishers, Inc., New York, 2000.

From SAARC to SAARC : Milestones in the Evolution of Regional Cooperation in South Asia (1980-1988), Secretariat of the South Asian Association for Regional Cooperation, Kathmandu, Vol. 1, December 1988, pp. 135.

Ghosh, Partha S., "Terrorism and SAARC", India Quarterly, vol. XLII, no. 2 (1987), pp. 121-137.

Ghosh, Partha S., *Cooperation and Conflict in South Asia*, New Delhi, Manohar Publishers, 1995.

Ghosh, Sambhu Chandra, *Commentary on Human Rights Law Research Institute,* Calcutta, 2002.

Ghuman, R.S., *Indo-Pakistan Trade Relations*, New Delhi, Deep and Deep Publication, 1986.

Goodrich, L.M., "The United Nations", (Boston, World Peace Foundation), 1949.

Goodspeed, Stephen S., "The Nature and the Functions of International Organisation", (Oxford University Press, New York), 1967.

Gopal Krishan Narain Virendra, Upreti B.C., (eds); *Sri Lanka and SAARC in SAARC : A Study of Perceptions and Policies*, New Delhi, Asian Publishers, 1991

Guha-Khasnobis, B. and E Bari, *Sources of Growth in South Asian Countries* (mimeo), Global Research Project of the World Bank, South Asia Network of Economic Research Institutes (SANEI), New Delhi, 2000.

Guha-Khasnobis, B. and E Bari, *Sources of Growth in South Asian Countries* (mimeo), Global Research Project of the World Bank, South Asia Network of Economic Research Institutes (SANEI), New Delhi, 2000.

Gulati Mukesh; *Regional Trading Blocs : Lessons for SAARC*, South Asian Studies, Vol. 30, No. 1, January-June, 1995.

Gupta Bhabanisen; *Regional Cooperation and Development in South Asia*, New Delhi, South Asian Publishers 1988.

Gupta Bhabanisen; *SAARC - ASEAN: Prospects and Problems of Inter-Regional Cooperation*, New Delhi, South Asian Publishers, 1988.

Gupta Sen: SAARC-ASEAN: Prospects and Problems of Inter-regional Cooperation, South Asian Publishers, New Delhi, 1989.

Gupta, Bhabani Sen: Regional Cooperation and Development in South Asia, Vikas Publishing House, New Delhi, 1987.

Gupta, R.C.: US Policy towards India and Pakistan, B.R. Publishing House, New Delhi, 1977.

Gupta, Sisir: India and Regional Integration in Asia, Asia Publishing House, Mumbai, 1964.

Gupta, Subenduda Das; *The Limits of SAARC,* Journal of International Relations, Vol. 5, No. 1-2, July-June 1997-98.

Gupta, U.N., "Developments on the Frontiers of International Law", (Allahabad Law Agency, Allahabad), 1981.

Gupta, Vijay K., *Perspectives on Human Rights,* Vikas Publishing House Private Limited, New Delhi, 1996.

Gupta; Bhabanisen, *Problems of Governance in South Asia*, New Delhi, Konark, 1996.

Gutteridge, J.A.C., "United Nations in the World", 1969.

Haass, Richard N.: US and South Asia, Oxford, New York, 1990.

Hammond, Grant T.: Counter Trade: Offsets and Barter in International Political Economy, Printer Publishers, London, 1990.

Haq, Muhamad Shamsul; *International Politics*, New Delhi, Sterling Publishers.

Harris, D.J., Mo'Boyle and Oloarbrick, *Law of the Euro Convention of Human Rights*, Butterworths, London, 1995.

Hassan Abdul; *Third SAARC Summit*, SAARC Perspective, Vol. 2, No. 3, May 1988.

Hellman, Donald C.: South Asia: The Politics of Poverty and Peace, Lexington Book, Massachusetts, USA, 1976.

Henkin, Pugh, Schachter and Smith, "International Law-Cases and Materials", 2nd Edition.

Hill, Norman, "International Organisation", (New York, Harper & Brothers), 1952.

Hussain Abid; *Prospects for South Asian Regional Cooperation, Strategic Studies Journal*, Vol. 1, No. 2, July 1988.

Hussain Akmal; *Bangladesh Search for South Asian Regionalism* in S.K. Chakravarty and Virendra Narain (ed); *Bangladesh Global Policies*, South Asian Publishers, 1988.

Hussain Golam; *Bangladesh and SAARC* in Virendra Narain and B.C. Upreti (ed); *SAARC : A Study of Perceptions and Policy*, New Delhi, South Asian Publishers, 1991.

Hussain Syed Anwar; *Prospects of Peace in South Asia : Politico-strategic Perspective*, South Asia Survey, Vol. 1, No. 2, July-December 1994.

Hussain, M.M., *Prospects and Problems in Cooperation Among Small Nations in South Asia*, Colombo, Margo Institute, 1980.

Hussain, M.M.: Prospects and Problems in Cooperation among Small Nations in South Asia, Marge Institute, Colombo, 1980.

Iftekharuzzaman; *South Asian Trade Cooperation with SAARC and ASEAN: Potential, Prospects, Realities Biss Journal*, Vol. 10, No. 1, January 1989.

Islam, Nurul: Pakistan in Asian Economic Development, Baylis and Son Ltd., London, 1990.

Jain, B.M., *South Asian Security : Problems and Prospects*, New Delhi, Radiant Publishers, 1985.

Jain, B.M.: South Asian Security: Problems and Prospects, Radiant Publishers, New Delhi, 1985.

Jain, P.K.: International Marketing, Printwell Publishers, Jaipur, 1988.

Jain, R.K.: US-South Asian Relation, 1974-1982, Radiant Publishers, New Delhi, 1983.

Jalal, Ayesha, *Democracy and Authoritarianism in South Asia: A Comparative and Historical Perspecitves*, New York, Cambridge: Cambridge University Press, 1995.

Jalal, Ayesha, *The State of Martial Rule: The Origins of Pakistan's Political Economy of Defense*, Cambridge: Cambridge University Press, 1991.

James, J.K.: The Third World: South Asia, Dushkin Publishing Group, Guillurd, USA, 1980.

Jenks, "International Immunities", First Edition.

Jenks, C.W., "Social Justice in the Law of Nations", (Published in International Labour Code, 1951).

Jetly Nancy; *Emergence of SAARC* in Bimal Prasad (ed.), *Regional Cooperation in South Asia : Problems and Prospects*, New Delhi, Vikas Publishing House, 1989.

Jetly, Nancy; *India and SAARC* in Lall K.B. Chopra H.S. and Meyer Thomas, (eds); *European Community and SAARC*, New Delhi, Radiant, 1993.

John, M.S., *South Asian Association for Regional Cooperation : A Theoretical Perspective, Unpublished Ph.d. Thesis Submitted to the School of International Relations*, Mahatma Gandhi University, Kottayam, 1993.

Johnson, "The Constitution of an Arbitral Tribunal", (1953) 30 RY. RLL.

Johnson, B.L.C.: South Asia: Elective Studies of the Essential Geography of India, Pakistan, Ceylon, Heinemann Educational Books Ltd., London, 1969.

Johnson, Harry G.: New Trade Strategy for the World Economy, George Allen & Urwin Ltd., London, 1988.

Joy P.A., *SAARC Trade and Development*, New Delhi: Deep and Deep Publications 1995.

K. Satyamurti; *South Asian Regional Cooperation, Institute of Asian Studies*, Hyderabad, 1982.

Kaneslingam, V.: Political Dimensions of South Asian Cooperation, MacMillan India' Ltd., New Delhi, 1991.

Kappor, S.K., "International Law and Human Rights", (Central Law Agency, Allahabad), 2002.

Kappor, S.K., "International Law", (Central Law Agency, Allahabad), 1994.

Kapur Pratap; *SAARC : Whither Regional Cooperation*, Democratic World, New Delhi, Vol. XII, No. 35, 28 August 1983.

Karns and Mingst, *International Organizations: The Politics and Processes of Global Governance,* New Delhi, Viva Books Pvt. Ltd., 2005.

Katyal G. Bhushan, K., *SAARC Challenges Bejore*, New Millennium, Delhi, A.P.H., 2002.

Katyal, K.K., "India and SAARC Summit", World Focus, vol. 22, no. 7 (July 2001), pp. 6.

Katyal, K.K., *India and SAARC Summit*, World Focus, Vol. 22. No. 7, July 2001.

Kaur Tejinder; *India and South Asian Cooperation : The Study of Problems and Prospects* (Ph.D. Thesis), Panjab University, Chandigarh, 1994.

Kemal, A.R. and Kanesahingam, V.: Trade Liberalisation in South Asia: Liberalisation and Mechanisms, MacMillan India Ltd., New Delhi, 1990.

Kezilbash, Hamid H., *SAARC : Security Concerns and Regional Cooperation, in Khan Zillur* R. (ed); *SAARC and Super Powers*, Dhaka, University Press Limited, 1991.

Khanal, Y.N., *South Asian Association for Regional Cooperation: An Overview*, Kathmandu, April 30, 1991.

Khatri, Sridhar K., *A Decade of South Asian Regionalism: Retrospect and Prospect*, Contemporary South Asia, Vol. 1, No. 1, 1992.

Khatri, Sridhar K.; *South Asian Regional Cooperation: Its Implications for Nepal*, Asian Survey, April 1985.

Kingsbury, Robert C.: South Asia in Maps, Denoyer-Geppert, Chicago, 1974.

Kodikara, Shelton U.: Strategic Factors in Inter-State Relations in South Asia, Heritage Publishers, New Delhi, 1983.

Kodirgamar Lakshman; *South Asian Survey*, Vol. 5, No. 1, New Delhi, Sage Publication 1998.

Kohli, Atul, *Democracy and Discontent India's Growing Crisis of Governability*, Cambridge, Cambridge University Press, 1990.

Korey, William, *NGO's and the Universal Declaration of Human Rights*, McMıllan Press Ltd., London, 1998.

Kukreja, Veena, "Parliamentary Democracy in South Asian Regional Comparative Perspective", India Quarterly, vol. XLI, no. 2 (1986), pp. 166-175.

Kumar Rupesinghe & Khanwar Mumtaz (eds.), *Internal Conflicts in South Asia*, London, 1996.

Kumar, Rupesinghe, Khawar Mumtaz (eds); *Internal Conflicts in South Asia*, New Delhi, Sage Publications, 1996.

Kunj, Josef. L., "Recent Trend & Development of International Law and Organisation", 1969 Edition.

Lama, Mohindra P., *SAARC Report: Poverty, Migration and Conflict in South Asia*, World Focus, Vol. 25, No. 6, June 2004.

Lauterpatch, H., "The Development of International Law by the International Court", (London, 1958).

Levi, Werner, "Fundamentals of World Organisation", 1950.

Lloyd I. Rudolph and Susanne Hoeber Rudolph, the Modernity of Tradition, Part I, University of Chicago Press, Chicago, 1967.

Madaan, Davinder Kumar; *SAARC : Origin, Development and Programmes*, New Delhi, Deep and Deep Publications, 1997.

Madan, B.K.: Towards Monetary Cooperation in South Asia, Concept Publishing Co., New Delhi, 1988.

Madan, T.N.: Muslim Countries of South Asia: Culture and Society, Vikas Publishing House, New Delhi, 1976.

Mahapatra Chintamani; *SAARC has to Adopt New Approach,* The Tribune, August 6, 1988.

Mahapatra, P.C., *South Asian Economic Cooperation : Problems and Prospects*, in Das Debendra Kumar (ed); *SAARC : Regional Cooperation and Development*, New Delhi : Deep and Deep Publications, 1996.

Malhotra, Kumar Vinay; *Clinton Administration and South Asia*, 1993-97, New Delhi, South Asian Publishers.

Malik, Ross, *Development, Ethnicity and Human Rights in South Asia*, Sage Publications, New Delhi, 1998.

Man Singh Surjit; *Regional Cooperation in South Asia*, Delhi 1984, Foreign Policy of Nepal, 1973.

Mangone, Gerard J., "A Short History of International Organisation", Mc Graw-Hills Book Co., New York, 1954.

McMillan, Donald Huge: Asian Perspective on International Security, The MacMillan Press Ltd., London, 1984.

Mehrotra, L.L., Chopra H.S. Kueck Gert W. (ed.), *SAARC 2000 And Beyond*, New Delhi, Omega Scientific Publishers, 1996.

Mehta, D.S., "A Mere Talking Shop?", World Focus, vol. 14, (July 1993), pp. 6-7.

Mehta, Rajesh, Bhattacharya Swapank; *SAPTA-I/II, SAPTA and SAFTA: Implications for SAARC*, South Asian Survey, Vol. 2, July-December 1997.

Melkote, Rama S. (ed.), *Regional Organisations : A Third World Perspective*, New Delhi, Sterling Publishers, 1990.

Melkotie, Rama S.: Regional Organizations: A Third World Perspective, Sterling Publishers, New Delhi, 1990.

Mendis, V.L.B.: SAARC: Origins, Organization and Prospects, Indian Ocean Centre for Peace Studies, Western Australia, 1991.

Menon, M.P.M., "Evolution of South Asian Regional Cooperation", Indian Foreign Review, vol. 23, no. 5 (1985), pp. 4-6.

Mishra, K.P. & Others: Southern Asia-Pacific Perceptions and Strategies, Continental Publishing House, New Delhi, 1983, Moore, B.J.: Tradition and Politics in South Asia, Vikas Publishing House, New Delhi, 1979.

Mishra, Pramod Kumar; *Dhaka to New Delhi : One Decade of SAARC*, India Quarterly, Vol. LII, nos 1-2, January-June 1996.

Mishra, Pramod Kumar; Regional Cooperation in South Asia *Nepalese Journal of Political* Science and SAARC, UDM Publishers, 1984.

Mishra, R.C., *Security in South Asia* : *Cross Border Analysis*, Delhi, Authors Press, 2000.

Mohla Vandana; *SAARC and Super Powers*, New Delhi, Deep & Deep Publication, 1998.

Mukherji, I.N., "Economic Advantages of SAARC", World Focus, vol. 22 (September 2001), pp. 20.

Mukherji, I.N., "Economic Advantages of SAARC", World Focus, vol. 22, no. 7 (July 2001), pp. 10-13.

Mukherji, I.N.: South Asia: Problems and Prospects, Vikas Publishing House, New 'Delhi, 1988.

Mukherji, Indra Nath, "SAARC: It Economic Achievements", World Focus, vol. 14 (July 1993), pp. 8-9.

Mukherji, Indra Nath: Trade Liberalisation in South Asia, School of International Studies, JNU, New Delhi, 1985.

Muni, S.D. and Muni Anuradha; *Regional Cooperation in South Asia*, New Delhi, 1984.

Muni, S.D., *Regional Conflicts in South Asia and the Role of SAARC in their Management*, New Delhi, Radiant, 1993.

Muni, S.D., *SAARC at Crossroads*, Himal South Asia, Vol. 10, No. 3, May/June 1997.

Muni, S.D.; *Strategic Aspects of SAARC*, Strategic Analysis, Vol. IX, No. 1, April 1994.

Murthy Padmaja; *Relevance of SAARC, Strategic Analysis*, Vol. XXIII, No. 10, January 2000.

Murthy, B.S., "International Relations and Organisation", Eastern Book Co., Lucknow, 1993.

Myers, Ramon H.: US Foreign Policy for Asia: the 1980s and Beyond, Stanford University Press, London, 1982.

Myron Weiner and Mary Fainsod Katzenstein, India's Preferential Policies: Migrants, the Middle Classes, and Ethnic Equality, University of Chicago Press, Chicago, 1981.

Nahar Emanual; *SAARC: Problems and Prospects*, Delhi, Sehgal Publishers Service, 1991.

Nahar Emanul; *Problems Before SAARC*, Mainstream, Vol. XXVII, No. 5, November 25, 1989.

Nahar, Emanuel: SAARC: Problems and Prospects, Sehgal Publisher's Service, New Delhi, 1991.

Naik, J.A., "A Text-Book of International Relations", Macmillan Co. of India Ltd., Delhi, 1978.

Naqash, Nasir A., *SAARC: Challenges and Opportunities*, New Delhi, Ashish Publishing House, 1994.

Naqvi, Syed Nawab Hyder: SAARC Link: An Economic Approach, Oxford & IBH Publishing Co., New Delhi, 1991.

Nayar Kuldip; *Male Summit, Gujral-Sharif Talks and SAARC*, Mainstream, Vol. XXXV, No. 24, May 24, 1997.

Nelson, David N.: Bibliography of South Asia, MacMillan, London, 2000.

Neqvi, M.B.: Security Perspectives on SAARC, MacMillan, London, 1989.

Niaz A-Naik; *South Asian Survey*, Vol. 6, No. 2, New Delhi, Sage Publications, 1999.

Noorani, A.G., *Repression in Kashmir*, Economic and Political Weekly, July 22, 1989.

Noorani, A.G.: Repression in Kashmir, MacMillan, London, 1989.

Norman, W. Brown: United States, India, Pakistan and Bangladesh, Harvard University Press, Cambridge, Massachusetts, 1972.

Osmani, S.R., 'The Impact of Economic Liberalization on the Small-Scale and Rural Industries of Sri Lanka' in L. Islam (ed.), *Rural Industrialization and Employment in Asia*, International Labour Organization, New Delhi, 1987.

Osmani, S.R., 'The Impact of Economic Liberalization on the Small-Scale and Rural Industries of Sri Lanka' in L. Islam (ed.), *Rural Industrialization and Employment in Asia*, International Labour Organization, New Delhi, 1987.

Padmaja Murth; *Role of Smaller Members in SAARC Forum, Strategic Analysis*, XXII (8), November, 1998.

Palmer, Norman D. and Perkins, Howard C. Potter, P.B., "International Relations", Calcutta Scientific Book Agency, 1976. "Introduction to the Study of International Organisation", Appleton Century, New York, 1948.

Panchamukhi, V.R. and Others: Economic Cooperation in the SAARC Region: Potential, Constraints and Policies, Interest Publications, New Delhi, 1990.

Panchmukhi V.R., *Economic Cooperation in the SAARC Region : Potential Constraints and Policies, Research and Information System*, New Delhi, 1990.

Panda, Snehalata, "Revamping Policy to Rejuvenate SAARC", India Quarterly, vol. Lxi, no. 3 (2005), pp. 66-100.

Pandey, B.N.: Leadership in South Asia, Vikas Publishing House, New Delhi, 1977.

Paranjpe Shrikant; *From State Centricism to Translationalism SAARC, SAPTA and SAFTA*, India Quarterly, Vol. LII, No. 18/2, January-June 1996.

Parsad Bimal; *Regional Cooperation in South Asia*, New Delhi, Vikas Publishing House (P) Ltd., 1989.

Pattanaik, Smruti S; *Indo-Pak Relations and the SAARC Summits*, Strategic Analysis, July-September, 2004.

Patterson, Maureen L. P.: South Asian Civilizations: A Bibliographic Synthesis, MacMillan, London, 1998.

Payer, Cheryl: Commodity Trade of Third World, MacMillan Press Ltd., London, 1986.

Phadhis, Urmila and Ganguly Rajat; *Ethnicity and Nation Building in South Asia*, New Delhi, 2001.

Phadnis Shunker; *Progress for Some Visible Gains*, World Focus, Vol. 3, No. 3, March 1983.

Phadnis, Urmila: Domestic Conflicts in South Asia: Political Dimensions, South Asian Publishers, New Delhi, 1986.

Phandis Urmila; *Ethnic Tensions in South Asia : Implications for Regional Cooperation*, New Delhi, South Asian Publishers, Vol. II, 1986.

Pradhan Bishma; *SAARC and Its Future*, Delhi, Vikash Publishing House Pvt. Ltd., 1989.

Prasad Bimal; *Regional Cooperation in South Asia-Problems and Prospects*, New Delhi, Vikas Publishing House (P) Ltd., 1989.

Prasad, Simal: Regional Economic Co-operation in South Asia, Vikas Publishing House, New Delhi, 1989.

Qureshi, M.L.: Survey' of Economic Resources and Prospects of South Asia, Marga Institute, Colombo, 1981.

Raghavan, S.N., *Regional Economic Cooperation Among SAARC Countries*, New Delhi, Allied Publishers Ltd., 1995.

Raghavan, S.N.: Macro Economic Performance and Policy Framework in the SAARC Countries, Interest Publications, New Delhi, 1991.

Rahman Atiur; *Political Economy of SAARC*, New Delhi, Sterling Publication, 1986.

Rai, Lajipathi and Reddi, Subbi T.: India's Foreign Trade: Retrospectives and Prospectives, Uppal Publishing House, New Delhi, 1990.

Rais, Rasul B., *Politics of Regional Cooperation in South Asia*, Asian Survey, Vol. 30, No. 8, August 1990.

Raj, Baral Lok: Regional and Extra-regional Link and South Asian Cooperation, Tribhuvan University, Kathmandu, 1999.

Raja Ram Kalpana, *International Organizations, Conferences and Treaties*, New Delhi, Spectrum Books Pvt. Ltd., 2001.

Rajni B., *India and South Asianism*, Third Concept Vol. 4, No. 58, December, 1991.

Raju, P.V.: Economic Development of Asian Countries, Deep & Deep Publications, New Delhi, 1990.

Ramana, Raja: Security: Deterrence and the Future, Alice Pub., New Delhi, 1992.

Rana A.P.; *New Directions in the Study of SAARC : Evaluating the Basis of Regional Cooperation in South Asia*, South Asian Survey 10:1 (2003) Delhi, Sage Publications.

Rana, A.P.; *Regionalism as an Approach to International Order, International Studies*, Vol. 21, JNU, New Delhi, 1979.

Rao, P. V. Narsimha: SAARC: Learning from Experience, Indian Dominion, New Delhi, 1993.

Rao, V.L., *South Asian Regional Cooperation: Problems and Prospect*, New Delhi, Radiant Publishers, 1987.

Reddy, B. Murlidhar; *SAARC Nations Sign Social Charter*, The Hindu, New Delhi, January 6, 2004.

Reddy, B. Murlidhar; *Sense of Betrayal*, Frontline, Vol. 21, No. 2, January 30, 2004.

Rizvi Hasan Askar; *Problems and Prospects of South Asian Regional Cooperation*, Regional Studies, Vol. 2, 1983.

Rizvi, Hasan Askari, *The Military and Politics in Pakistan,* 3rd ed., Lahore, Progressive Publishers, 1986.

SAARC Official Documents

SAARC Vision Beyond the Year 2000 *South Asian Association for Regional Cooperation*, New Delhi, Shipra, 1999.

Sahaha Rishikesh; *Imperatives for Regional Cooperation in South Asia*, South Asia Forum, Vol. I, No. 1,Winter 1982.

Sahai, Paramjit S; *Cultural Diplomacy, Mass Media and SAARC : A Case Study of the 12th SAARC Summit*, India Quarterly, Vol. LK, No. 3, New Delhi, July-September, 2004.

Sattar Abdus; *Changing Global Scenario* Implications for South Asia, Regional Studies (Islamabad), Vol. VII, No. 1, Winter 1989-90.

Schleicher, Charles, P., "International Relations, Co-operation & Conflict", Prentice Hall of India Pvt. Ltd., New Delhi, 1963.

Schuman, L. Frederick, "International, Politics" Mc-Graw-Hills, Tokyo, 1958.

Schwarzenberger, George, "Manual of International Law", Stevens &. Sons Ltd., London, 1967.

Serenson, Max, "Manual of Public International Law", Macmillan, St. Martins Press, New York, 1968.

Sharma, Gokulesh, *Constitutional of SAARC Nations,* Deep and Deep Publications Pvt. Ltd., New Delhi, 2008.

Shelton, V. Kodikara (eds); "External Compulsions of South Asian Politics", New Delhi, Sage Publications, 1993.

Shrestha, B.P., *Prospects of Economic Cooperation in South Asia*, The Economic Journal of Nepal (Kathmandu), Vol. II, No. 1, January-March 1988.

Shukla Vijay; *New Frontiers of SAARC*, India Quarterly, Vol LII, No. 18, 2, January-June 1996.

Singh Jagjit; *Transport Linkages in South Asia,* in India Quarterly, Vol. XI, No. 324, July-December 1984.

Singh Tarlok; *Special Issue on South Asian Cooperation, Prospects and Potentials*, World Focus, March, 1982.

Singh, Hari Govind; *South Asian Cooperation : Problems and Prospect*, New Delhi, Mainstream, Vol. XXVII, No. 14, December 31, 1988.

Sinha, Manoj Kumar, *Implementation of Basic Human Rights,* Manak Publications, Pvt. Ltd., Delhi, 2002.

Snodgrass, D.R., 'The Economic Development of Sri Lanka: A Tale of Missed Opportunities' in R.I. Rotberg (ed.), *Creating Peace in Sri Lanka: Civil War and Reconciliation*, Brookings Institution Press, Washington D.C., 1999.

Snodgrass, D.R., "The Economic Development of Sri Lanka: A Tale of Missed Opportunities", in R.I. Rotberg (ed.), *Creating Peace in Sri Lanka: Civil War and Reconciliation*, Brookings Institution Press, Washington D.C., 1999.

Sobhan Rehman; *Regional Cooperation in South Asia : A Quest for Identity*, South Asian Survey, Vol. 5, No. 1, January-June 1998.

Sorokin, P.A., "The Reconstruction of Humanity", 1st Edition.

Starke, J.G., "Introduction to International Law", Butterworth International Edition, London, Tenth Edition, 1989.

Steiner, Henery J. and Philip Alston, *International Human Rights in Context: Law Politics, Morals*, Clarendon Press, Oxford, 1996.

Sudhakar E., *SAARC - Origin, Growth And Future*, New Delhi, Gyan Publishing House, 1994.

Syed M.H.; *Encyclopaedia of SAARC Nations*, Delhi, Kalpaz Publications, Vol. 1, 2002.

Syed, M.H.; *Encyclopaedia of SAARC*, Delhi, Kalpaz Publications, Vol. II, III, 2002.

Syed, M.H.; *SAARC: Challenges Ahead*, New Delhi, Kilsaso Books, 2003.

Symonides, Janusz and Vladimir Volodin (eds.), *A Guide to Human Rights: Institutions Standards Procedures*, UNESCO publishing, Span, 2003.

Taneja Nisha; Trade Relations : Opportunities For Growth *Economic and Political Weekly*, Vol. no. XXXIX, No. 4, January 24, 2004.

Tang, James, T.H. (ed.), *Human Rights and International Relations in Asia-Pacific,* Printer, London, 1994.

Thomas, Philip: Potential of Financial Cooperation in the SAARC Region, R.I.S., New Delhi, 1990.

Trivedi Sonu, *International Organizations,* New Delhi, Atlantic Publishers and Distributors, 2005.

Udaykumar, S.P., *Regional Cooperation in South Asia : The People Factor*, SAARC Perspective, Vol. 3, No. 5, June 1989.

Umar, Ghulam: SAARC: Analytical Survey, Renaissance Publishing House, New Delhi, 1992.

Upadhyay Shashi; *Bhutan and SAARC,* in Ramakant and R.C. Misra (eds); *Bhutan: Society and Policy*, New Delhi: Indus Publishing Company; 1996.

Upadhyay, Shashi; *Pakistan SAARC: A Study of Perception, Attitude and Role*, Delhi, Kalinga Publications, 2000.

Upadhyaya Shashi; *Pakistan's Perception of India's Role in SAARC*, South Asian Studies, Vol. 31, Nos. 1 and 2, January-December 1996.

Upreti B.C., *SAARC: Dynamics of Regional Cooperation in South Asia*, New Delhi, Kalinga Publications, 2000, Vol. I and II.

Varshney, R.L.: Economic Cooperation in South Asia, Foreign Affairs, Indian Council of World Affairs, New Delhi, 1988.

Verma, S.P. and Misra, K.P.: Foreign Policies in South Asia, South Asian Studies Centre, University of Jaipur, Jaipur, 1969.

Verma, S.P.: South Asia a Region: Problems and prospects, Charanjit Channa, New Delhi, 1989

Vignaraja, Poona & Hussain, Akmal: The Challenge in South Asia, Sage Publications, New Delhi, 1989.

Vohra, Dewan C.: India's Trade Diplomacy in the Third World, Vikas Publishing House, New Delhi, 1987.

Wadhwa, Charan, D.: Regional Economic Cooperation in South Asia, Allied Publishers, New Delhi, 1988.

Wag if, Arif: South Asian Cooperation in Industry Energy and Technology, Sage Publications, New Delhi, 1990.

Walnut, Creek C.A.: SAARC, Alta Mira Press, Sri Lanka, 1997. Zafar, Imam: World Power in South Asia and South East Asia, Indian Council of World Affairs, New Delhi, 1972.

Weeramantry C.G., *Justice Without Frontiers: Furthering Human Rights*, Vol. I, Kluwer Law International, The Hague, 1977.

Wilcox, Francis O., "Regionalism and the United Nations, International Organisation", Summer, 1965.

Woodiwiss Anthony, *Human Rights,* Routledge, London, 2005.

Wright, Quincy, "The Study of International Relations", Scientific Book Agency, Calcutta, 1st Indian Edition.

Yatanoor Chandarkant; *Small State in EU,* Third Concept, August, 2000.

Yogi, Parveen, *Human Rights and Equal Opportunities*, Isha Books, Delhi, 2006.

Zimmern, Alfred, "The League of Nations and the Rule of Law", Macmillan, London, 1945.

Zudyr, B., A Historical Atlas of South Asia, Oxford University Press, New York, 1992.

SAARC LAW

Chhiber, Bharti, "Environmental Dimension of Regional Security: A Comparative study of Asian and SAARC", *World Affairs* Vol. 10, no. 2 (2006), pp. 110-125.

"The Kathmandu Declaration of the SAARC, 2002", Asian Yearbook of International Law, vol. 11 (2004), pp. 361-372.

NEWSPAPERS

1. Indian Express
2. The Hindustan Times
3. The Statesman
4. The Hindu
5. Times of India
6. Frontline
7. The Indian Express
8. The Tribune
9. Economic Times
10. The Pioneer

DECLARATIONS

1. Dhaka Declaration, 8 December, 1985, SAARC Document, Dhaka, 1985.
2. SAARC in Brief, SAARC Secretariat, Kathmandu.
3. Charter of SAARC, SAARC Secretariat, Kathmandu.
4. Mohammed Humayan Kabir; "Sub-regional Cooperation in ASEAN: Lessons for South Asia", Paper Presented at a Seminar on "Subregional Cooperation in South Asia: Learning from the ASEAN" Organised by the BIISS Dhaka, on May 31, 1998.
5. Abdur Rob Khan; "Sub-regional Cooperation in South Asia: Problems and Prospects", Paper Presented at a Seminar on Sub-regional Cooperation in South Asia : Learning from the ASEAN Organised by the BIISS Dhaka, on May 31, 1998.
6. M. Anwarul Maq; "Dhaka Preparing Concept Paper on Sub-regional Grouping", The Daily Star, 6 February 1997.
7. SAARC Council of Ministers, Sixteenth Session, New Delhi, December 18, 1995.
8. World Develop Report, 1996.
9. SAARC-A Publication, Lok Sabha Secretariat, New Delhi 1998.
10. SAARC Secretariat, Meeting the Challenge, Report of the Independent South Asian Commission on Poverty Alleviation, November 1992, p. 13.

11. Asian Recorder (New Delhi), Vol. VIII, No. 1, November 12-18-1964.
12. SAARC Newsletter, Vol. VI, No. 586, January-June 1993.
13. SAARC Newsletter, Vol. VI, No. 2, April-June 1995.
14. SAARC Newsletter, Vol. VIII, No. 5, May 1997.
15. Statement by Mohammad Khan Juneja; "Prime Minister of Pakistan at the Second SAARC Summit", Bangalore, 16 November, 1986.
16. Extracts of Prime Minister Juneja's Statement during the Third SAARC Summit, Kathmandu, 1987.
17. Dhaka Declaration, 8 December, 1985, SAARC Document, Dhaka, 1985.
18. Twelfth SAARC Summit Declaration, Islamabad, 6th January, 2004.

WEBSITES

1. http://hdr.undp.org/statistics/data/cty/cty.BGD.html
2. http://hdr.undp.org/statistics/data/cty/cty.MDV.html
3. http://hdr.undp.org/statistics/data/cty/cty.IND.html
4. http://hdr.undp.org/statistics/data/cty/cty.BTN.html
5. http://hdr.undp.org/statistics/data/cty/cty.NPL.html
6. http://hdr.undp.org/statistics/data/cty/cty.PAK.html
7. http://hdr.undp.org/statistics/data/cty/cty.LKA.html
8. www.worldbank.org/data/wdi2004/section4-intro pdf.
9. newsbbc.co.uk/hi/english/world/southasia/nensid.